THE
TROUBLED
LAND

THE TROUBLED LAND

SOCIAL PROBLEMS IN MODERN AMERICA

SECOND EDITION

ELBERT W. STEWART

Chairman,
Department of Sociology and Anthropology
Bakersfield College

McGRAW-HILL
BOOK
COMPANY

New York
St. Louis
San Francisco
Auckland
Düsseldorf
Johannesburg
Kuala Lumpur
London
Mexico
Montreal
New Delhi
Panama
Paris
São Paulo
Singapore
Sydney
Tokyo
Toronto

**THE
TROUBLED
LAND**
SOCIAL
PROBLEMS
IN
MODERN
AMERICA

1 2 3 4 5 6 7 8 9 0 K P K P 7 9 8 7 6 5

This book was set in Helvetica by Black Dot, Inc.
The editors were Lyle Linder, Helen Greenberg, and Susan Gamer;
the designer was Nicholas Krenitsky;
the production supervisor was Leroy A. Young.
Kingsport Press, Inc., was printer and binder.

Soft cover photo courtesy of Charles Moore/Black Star.

Library of Congress Cataloging in Publication Data

Stewart, Elbert W
  The troubled land: social problems in modern America.

  Bibliography: p.
  Includes index.
  1. United States—Social conditions—1960-
—Addresses, essays, lectures. I. Title.
HN65.S73 1976   309.1′73   75-25660
ISBN 0-07-061417-2
ISBN 0-07-061418-0 pbk.

TO
MY WIFE,
LILLIAN

CONTENTS

A very few years ago, *The Troubled Land* was selected as the title for the first edition of this book. It was then a title that brought to mind the war in Vietnam and the student riots and disorders that resulted largely from that war, as well as the disorders accompanying the civil rights movement. Now Vietnam is no longer our central issue, but not because the struggle resulted in any type of victory or even a peace that denotes the healing of wounds. Instead there is the bitter feeling that, all to no avail, our country spent too much of its strength, wasted too much of its wealth, and shed too much of its blood. Just as tragically, another resource has been seriously depleted, a resource that can be called the "fund of devotion" of the citizens to their state. A citizenry can easily rise to heroic heights in pursuit of a great cause, but when sacrifice becomes futile, the call to service results only in division and disillusionment.

Against the background of battle for a dubious cause, the United States has been shaken by the corruption of power in the highest places, followed by the forced resignation of a president. Along with the disclosure of affairs collectively referred to as "Watergate" came increasing rumors, and later confirmations, of a government engaged in illegal spying on its citizens, and of a government hiding its affairs from public scrutiny. While reeling from these blows, we have also faced our first great energy crisis and another of our periods of high unemployment, increased poverty, economic stagnation, and decline in production. This land, already perturbed by a seeming inability to live up to its ideals, has suffered a loss of confidence as a result of these many setbacks.

Yet, to succumb to despair would be as great a folly as the earlier philosophy of the inevitability of progress. What has happened is that

America has reached a watershed in its national development. Before our time in history, the gigantic expansion of industry and technology seemed adequate to confirm our buoyant optimism that America would forever soar to new heights and lead the world into a utopia of affluence and social justice. Now the time has come to realize that there are limits to what can be achieved by industrial technology, and that there are even limits to the earth. Shaping the future must depend upon using the earth and its physical and human resources wisely and embarking on policies guided by social research and social policy. Technology and science alone do not reshape cities, reduce crime, diminish interracial strife, or ensure justice. Progress in the industrial sector of society is futile without progress in the human sector.

Although social science and social research are greatly needed, the assault on our social problems cannot be monopolized by trained experts or national leaders. It was neither national leaders nor bureaucratic experts who mounted the attacks on racism in American society; it was the black people themselves, mainly poor, and without recognized political influence. While the national leadership was finding more and more reasons for staying at war in Southeast Asia, it was the students in our colleges who most clearly saw and persuaded us of the futility of the war. Progress in environmental issues and in consumer rights has been pushed mainly from the grass roots by groups of organized, concerned citizens, not from Washington. The disadvantaged position of women was barely perceived except by an educated and aroused segment of the women themselves. Even the issue of abuse of power by President Nixon might eventually have been whitewashed had it not been for the increasingly obvious anger of the people over such a situation. In this case, it must be acknowledged that much of the leadership was taken by a free press, which refused to allow the issue to die; but the people, finally informed of the facts, were determined to see the return of constitutionalism.

It is only this ability of the people to make things happen that gives us continued reason for hope in our troubled land. Whatever the failings of our society, it yet has the resilience to meet its problems, to eliminate some, and to ameliorate others. Such progress depends upon interest in a wide range of social problems and involvement in those problems by a very large public. The aim of a book about social problems should be to help create that awareness, particularly among young people, who have shown themselves so capable of sympathy and involvement. In this second edition, as in the first, every attempt has been made to give clear explanations, meaningful examples, and suggestions for improving the social problems discussed. Suggestions are usually controversial, as they must necessarily be in the field of social problems, since solutions always depend on the weighing of alternatives and the appraisal of conflicting values. Questions at the ends of chapters are intended to provoke exchanges of opinions, as are many of the suggestions for activities scattered throughout the book. At the end of each chapter are recommended readings by authors who are deeply concerned with the issues of the day and whose views are varied and challenging.

A book of this type is never exclusively the product of its author but always incorporates ideas suggested by others. My colleague Mita

Dhariwal has provided a number of helpful ideas, especially in the fields of race, poverty, and the position of women in society. Thomas E. Drabek, of the University of Colorado, and William Goldmann, of Pasadena City College, California, have read the manuscript carefully and suggested many new ideas and research sources. Otto Larsen of the University of Washington, and now Chairman of the American Sociological Association, was good enough to read the newly added materials, and it was he who recommended the new chapter I have entitled "Is Big Brother Watching You?" Ronald Kissack, who edited the first edition, was able to provide several helpful ideas before his untimely death. Since then the editor has been the very capable Helen Greenberg, whose suggestions have also helped to keep the book timely and student-oriented—one of our major aims throughout. May our cooperative effort prove challenging to college students, for it is their interest and concern that can make the America of the future a less troubled land.

Elbert W. Stewart

Twentieth-century America presents a strange paradox of scientific and technological achievement accompanied by mounting concern over social troubles. Sometimes the promises of a scientific age are obscured from sight by concern over increasingly deadly war potential, deterioration of the natural environment, urban dislocation, racial and intergenerational conflict, and the uneasy feeling that an age of certainty and optimism is at an end. Today's threats and uncertainties bring an unquestioned relevance to the study of social problems. The troubles of society must be faced and studied if they are ever to be ameliorated.

THE UNIQUE NATURE OF THE TROUBLED LAND

Trouble and strife have accompanied the human race through much of its history, but there is a difference between the problems of the present and those of the past. The differences are reassuring in some ways and threatening in others. When historians relate the record of earlier crises in human affairs, they are often speaking of problems that are no longer major worries. Wars and threats of wars remain, of course, and are even more menacing than in the past, but many of the problems have changed. Our fear of devastating plagues has nearly disappeared, and to a great degree so has our fear of flood and drought, of famine, of declining populations, and of the physical inability to supply the needs of the people. Gone are the high infant-mortality rates that made parents compulsive about having large families. No longer is poverty made inevitable by economic scarcity, and no longer need certain races and classes be submerged into peonage in order to support a leisure class.

Successive scientific triumphs of the last century or more have virtually freed us from such types of worry, but they have opened new problems. These problems have produced such strains and maladjustments in social systems that we can hardly keep abreast of technological change. Greater productivity and scientific knowledge have outmoded many old customs, folkways, and mores and have brought a demand for new values. The need to adjust to new conditions has complicated the problems of deviance and crime by adding new types of value conflict and new means of evading the law. The great industries that have promised an abundant life have also poured their poisons into the waters and the air. Finally, modern science has made the ancient custom of fighting wars so deadly that it could well bring the human race to an untimely end.

Everyone but the totally unobservant is concerned with the types of problems developing in the new society, and nearly everyone is looking for explanations of their causes and possibilities for their solution. The politician, the minister, the reformer, the campus militant, the businessman, the farmer, the laborer—all have their points of view and their social concerns, depending on their training, interests, and conceptualizations of social reality.

Sociologists also have their special orientation to the field of social problems. They attempt to give careful attention to facts and trends, to develop explanations and concepts for analysis, and to avoid being swayed by vested interests. They conceptualize social systems in a way that shows their strains and suggests possible means of ameliorating problems. Sociology, along with other sciences, seeks method and system in its approach. Obviously the first step in a systematic approach to the study of social problems is that of defining the field.

DEFINITION: THE CRITERIA OF SOCIAL PROBLEMS

Although all the social concerns of the day are generally regarded as social problems, some are more important than others. Some problems belong only to a limited locality or period of time or only to a few individuals. Are they also social problems? Very often situations that are now regarded as social problems have existed for many years but were once considered so much the natural order of things as to be largely ignored. What, then, converts a particular situation or development into a social problem?

Three commonly used criteria Three commonly used criteria for defining social problems are: numbers of people involved, conflict with societal norms, and amenability to improvement. All are valid points but, as we shall see, are not quite sufficient. A problem is not considered social unless it affects a fairly large segment of society. One man's loss of a job is simply his own personal problem; mass unemployment is a social problem. Or, if a mere handful of women encounter unequal employment rights, their cases will probably be dismissed as exceptional; if large numbers encounter inequalities such that complaints and protests are common, then female inequality becomes a social problem. The only difficulty with this type of definition is that it omits certain cases involving rather few people, but cases that the knowledgeable public, nevertheless, regards as highly undesirable, such as the inhumane treatment formerly accorded the mentally ill or the inhumane treatment of many juvenile cases, uncovered by a Senate committee headed by Senator Bayh. Such cases do not involve large segments of the population or the possibility of mass protests, but can we refuse to call them social problems? Little-noticed cruelties reveal a social blindness that can lead to much greater cruelties and neglects. The idea was once expressed by Blake in "A dog starved at his master's gate/Foretells the ruin of the state."

The second common criterion—a situation violating social norms—is definitely involved in both the examples just given. In other cases, though, we have to ask "whose norms?" Low wages are a social problem for labor unionists, but for some employers they might be desirable. And at the same time many people are complaining about the harshness of our laws against marijuana, others are saying that the laws are not harsh enough. So rather than say that social problems arise from situations conflicting with the social norms of the entire society, we must widen our category to say they conflict with the norms of large segments of the population. Not only is there disagreement about societal norms, but the normative definition of social problems is complicated in another way: sometimes the norms themselves have to change. In Chapter 10, the dictum of "multiply and replenish the earth" will be spoken of as an outmoded norm. The problems of ecology discussed in Chapter 2 will be seen partly as the result of a mastery-of-nature norm that has become a threat to the survival of the human race and many other species. Many modern-minded people consider the eye-for-an-eye definition of justice an idea that should have been discarded long ago. New conditions, new cultural habits, and additions to knowledge often change the norms. Our normative definition of a social problem should be stated as "a condition of normative violation, normative conflict, or a need for normative change."

The third common criterion—amenability to improvement through social effort—is clear in one respect but not in another. If astronomers predict the eventual death of the earth by the sun's turning into an exploding star, we can hardly apply the words "social problem," because there are no conceivable social solutions. There are marginal cases, however, where we might debate whether there are social solutions. At one time poverty was regarded as an inevitability that could be relieved slightly by charity but not really ended. Now there is repeated talk of ending poverty, and there are economic possibilities for doing so. A problem still remains, though, regarding improvement. Not all elements of society will always agree on what constitutes improvement. Problems, therefore, are matters for lengthy debate until some kind of consensus is reached. Agreement to take action sometimes depends upon whether or not the problem looks threatening to the society.

Social problems as social threats   Many militant followers of various causes feel that social concern is often awakened only when social situations pose a threat to the system. Even the late Dr. Martin Luther King, Jr., noted for his nonviolent philosophy, wrote in his famous "Letter from a Birmingham Jail" of the need for creating a "situation that cannot be ignored." Frances F. Piven and Richard A. Cloward[1] make a strong case historically for saying poverty has generally been dealt with in an ameliorative manner only when it begins to pose a threat to the social order. The philosophy behind early English poor laws of the Tudor period and French poor laws of about the same era was to make almshouses capable of allaying violence but miserable enough to drive people to work if there were available jobs. A much more contemporary example is that of racial and ethnic inequality. For the vast majority of whites, gross inequality of treatment of the black race and Spanish-speaking minorities was barely noticed until organized protest began to threaten business, urban areas, political alignments, and the nation's reputation abroad.

It can be argued that the matter of threat is not part of the social problem itself but rather an indication of whether anything will be done about it. The reason for calling it an actual part of the problem is that the criterion of normative strain is not met until there is a strong awareness of normative strain. Situations are not necessarily definable as problems until they are brought to public consciousness. The sociologist, however, should be more aware of potentially threatening developments than is the layman and also of the possible consequences of trying to solve

[1]Frances F. Piven and Richard A. Cloward, "The Relief of Welfare," *Transaction*, vol. 8, pp. 31–39, May 1971.

problems. In trying to perform a role in this respect, he or she will often think in terms of "latent functions."

Latent function and problem definition   Occasionally a social problem exists partly because it is a natural consequence of something the society strongly desires. This idea was originally developed by Robert K. Merton[2] and is termed "latent function." Various customs and institutions of society have their "manifest" or intended consequences, as well as certain unexpected, and ofted undesired, consequences known as "latent" functions. The institutions of courtship and romantic love in our society, for example, have the manifest function of ensuring that most people get married, even though marriages are not arranged as in some cultures. Romantic love is glorified, and the freedom of people to choose their own partners is considered a natural, inalienable right. Implied in the right of choice, however, is the right to individual happiness, which may or may not be attained in the marriage. If the individuals are not happy, then they will probably get a divorce. Thus the loudly acclaimed belief in individual freedom has the latent function of a high divorce rate, which the society regards as a social problem.

Some types of crime are analyzed by Merton as the latent cnsequence of the generally approved American requirement that everyone be judged on the basis of how well he or she succeeds. Since people do not all have equal access to success goals (for such reasons as deprived background or discrimination), some find success possible only through illegal means. Hence, the "good norm" of success striving can lead to an unusually high incidence of larceny, graft, and embezzlement. This problem will be discussed more fully in Part Three.

Merton's idea can be used for visualizing the possible consequences of solutions to problems. The problem of crime could probably be greatly reduced by giving police and other investigative authorities vastly greater powers than they now have, but such a policy would have the latent function of eliminating many of our civil liberties. In the long run, it could perhaps have the latent consequence of public outrage against law enforcement and an increasing number of acts of defiance.

Social problems and the future   Finally, a definition and delineation of social problems should attempt to take the future into consideration. Often the problems of public concern are essentially problems about the future—e.g., population growth, pollution, education, and automation. Sometimes the future results of the problems are less obvious. A childhood of malnourishment might cause cerebral damage throughout life; if it exists in all the poorest parts of a country it could seriously impede any later attempts at self-improvement. Chemical contaminants and atomic radiation might cause genetic damage to future generations. The likelihood may be slight, but any possibility must be viewed as a social problem.

Most problems discussed in this book have their implications for the future and are thus of particular concern. Much of the younger generation is idealistic enough to be concerned not only with their own survival, but also with the problems of racial and ethnic equality, humane

[2]Robert K. Merton, *Social Theory and Social Structure*, The Free Press, New York, 1968, pp. 71–81.

treatment of the poor and sick and deviant, and the quality of justice. They are worried about pollution, the future availability of jobs, and the quality of education and its relevance to the future. They are particularly concerned about the horrendous possibility of nuclear destruction and the need for a better type of international order. Most problems of this type meet all the criteria suggested above: societal concern, normative strain, and amenability to improvement. If not handled correctly, these problems are a threat to the total society and in some cases to the entire human race. In many cases the problems themselves are the latent consequences of what was once seen as desirable change. For this and other reasons, problems do not appear suddenly and in isolation, but are of an interlocking nature.

THE INTERLOCKING NATURE OF SOCIAL PROBLEMS

In thinking of the modern problems that concern us most, it is helpful to visualize them as arising in various ways. Some are most clearly understood as the consequences of invention and social change; others are best understood as a consequence of normative strain, a gap between the ideal and reality. A third type of social problem arises out of the inability or unwillingness of people to conform to the roles expected of them by society—a type encompassing health and mental health problems as well as crime and delinquency. Finally, there are problems that arise out of the nature of societies and their interaction with others—aggression and war. These types of problems are all interrelated, however. One cannot think of war without thinking of normative breakdown, terrifying inventions, and social change. Problems can hardly be seen in isolation.

There are many examples of the interlocking nature of social problems. In the case of modern urban problems, for example, good automobiles and roads (technical change) have led to the feeling of a need to move about easily and at will (normative change) and have contributed to a pattern of suburban growth. Suburban populations have made the location of industry in the suburbs profitable (technical change), and this change has dried up employment opportunities in the central slum areas (normative strain). Idleness and unemployment have led in turn to resentment, higher crime rates (deviant behavior), and to quarrels over police treatment (normative conflict). All these problems have led to demands for urban renewal (technical and social change) and for public transportation systems (technical change) that will bring benefits especially to the urban poor (redress of normative strain). As another example, family problems involve an interplay of the type of social change that separates parents from their children during work and school hours, changing norms about the roles of women and children, and even deviance in cases where the family is unable to perform its role of properly socializing the young. And social problems are interrelated in that often the solution of one creates another. Ending the problem of premature death has led to the problem of population explosion. Solving the problem of population increase leads to normative conflict over contraception and abortion and may even downgrade the traditional role of woman as housewife and mother.

The social change perspective   The first set of problems discussed in this text refers to technological change and the resulting strains in the social system. The industrial-urban revolution of the last centuries has brought new types of urban and environmental problems, problems of industrial labor, distribution of wealth, economic cycles, the shrinkage of agricultural employment and rural life, greater interdependence, and greater potentials for both the enrichment of life and the destruction of life. Industrial change has its ramifications in all the other types of problems we shall discuss. As one billiard ball strikes another, and that one in turn strikes a third, technological change sets off a chain reaction, first changing the means of livelihood and then affecting the normative system, possibly leading to new types and degrees of deviant behavior. As progressive change is brought about in the world's potential for destruction in warfare, the problems of human organization and of survival also become more acute.

William Fielding Ogburn[3] used the concept of "cultural lag" to explain how scientific and technical change begin to exert influence on all elements of a culture. Since a culture includes both material traits (cars, factories, airplanes) and nonmaterial traits (values, ideals, regulations), the various parts of a culture can develop inconsistencies. Ogburn's idea was that some elements of a culture become antiquated relative to the rest of it, are no longer appropriate, and constitute strains or disjunctures. He termed these out-of-date elements and the time required for them to catch up with societal needs as cultural lags. One of his examples was that of the size of counties made small so they could be traversed by horse and buggy in one day. Such boundary lines are cultural lags in an age of rapid transportation. Other examples include a wasteful, exploitative attitude toward natural resources, outdated as resources are depleted (although it might have served fairly well when rapid development was the primary aim), and the continued use of forms of city government that were intended for small towns and do not fit modern organizational needs. In these cases, norms are involved, but the strain is described primarily as a need for adjustment to technological and other forms of change.

Normative strain and incongruity   All societies are based upon normative systems, rules of right and wrong, enforced by custom and tradition and sometimes by law. Changing technologies, living habits, and educational requirements often interfere with long-established behavioral rules of this type. Consequently, although social change may be involved in the genesis of social problems, many problems can be seen primarily in the light of normative strain—an inconsistency between the dominant beliefs of the society and actual practice. All societies have their incongruities between social practice and stated belief, but they often find means for rationalizing them away, or they manage to keep them out of their consciousness.

In an age of considerable education and sophistication, however, incongruities are often laid bare. Why should racial or ethnic inequality exist in a society whose norms speak of a dedication to the proposition that all men are created equal? Why should there be a strong reproductive norm in a world worried about overpopulation? Why must some segments of the population be relegated to poverty? Why cannot a merciful society take care of the people who are afflicted with serious

[3]William Fielding Ogburn, *Social Change*, The Viking Press, Inc., New York, 1964, pp. 200–220.

illness without frequently forcing them into financial ruin? What are we
to do about a series of moral dilemmas developing in our society,
brought on by changes in our ability to search the mind and emotions,
to ferret out information, and to control behavior in new ways? Will the
acquisition of new information conform to our belief that the truth will
set us free, or will new knowledge be used for invasion of privacy,
manipulation, and limitation of freedom?

Role failure and deviance   In all societies there are problems of failure
of conformity to the norms and to proper role behavior. The failures are
sometimes the results of inability to perform required roles, as in the
case of the physically or mentally handicapped. More frequently the
problem is one of unwillingness to abide by the rules and to perform as
expected. Occasionally people deviate from the rules as a matter of
principle, as in the case of peace demonstrators or the civil rights
leaders who deliberately challenged Jim Crow laws. More common
types of crime will be given considerable attention—white- and
blue-collar crimes, crimes for money, crimes of revenge and violence,
crimes with victims, and crimes without victims—certain types of sex
"crimes," for example, and the use of various drugs.

Drugs of all types, including legal alcohol, are included in the section
on role failure and deviance. In a search for excitation or relief from
boredom, people often find outlets that lead to excess. Sometimes
social traditions are able to prescribe limits on the use of alcohol or
drugs so that they are little or no problem. When it becomes possible
to use various forms of alcohol, marijuana, drugs, and tranquilizers in
excessive amounts, however, many problems are created for society.
They interfere seriously, even tragically, with the performance of
socially prescribed roles, and they lead the society to ask if its drug
problem is symptomatic of some chronic illness.

The treatment of those who deviate from the law is as much a social
problem as deviance itself. It constitutes a normative problem for a
society that believes in due process and equality of treatment and in
the possibility of rehabilitation. What is possible in the name of justice,
and what happens to those behind bars?

THE SEARCH FOR SURVIVAL

After examining a host of problems, many of which seem to threaten
the very existence of human life, we must turn to the question of
prospects for the future. Despite many lamentations over past and
present failures, we cling to the belief that the human mind is capable
of solving problems—even the extremely complex problems of our
period of history. Such problems will not yield to complacency, but
despair is even more of a danger. Both complacency and despair are
psychological mechanisms for the avoidance of responsibility and
action. The third alternative calls for thought, for weighing alternatives,
making decisions, and becoming involved individually and collectively.
We must examine the prospects for war or peace, food or famine,
freedom or suppression, clean air or contamination, and resource
protection or resource exhaustion. Upon the choices made between
these alternatives rests the future of the world in its search for
survival.

In the discussion of Merton's analysis of latent function, we were examining one well-known concept in the field of sociology. A concept is an idea about a class of events or phenomena. For example, in Merton's concept of latent function the idea applies to latent or unintended results of romance, individual choice of marriage partners, and of striving for success. The idea of latent function is applicable to a class of phenomena (unanticipated results) whether we are talking about marriage, deviant behavior, religion, education, or any other social institutions or traits.

Sociology deals in concepts of this type and helps to explain the social order with them. We have already looked at a second example—Ogburn's idea of cultural lag. Cultural lag can refer to the failure of highways to keep up with the production of automobiles, the failure of contraception customs to keep up with the problem of population explosion, or any of the other consequences of the gap between technical possibilities and social realities. There has already been a reference to role expectations. Actually, all society can be analyzed as a system of positions and roles, and most of its problems can be seen as failures in the definition or performance of social roles.

Such concepts are helpful in organizing our thoughts about society and about social problems. The concepts mentioned are discussed in the introductions to various sections of this book. In the part dealing with incongruities, the idea of normative strain and value conflict will be discussed further. In the section on deviant behavior the very important concept of anomie is explained, as well as the concept of learned patterns of deviance. In the final section, the concept of culture—the greatly varying patterns of living devised by the various peoples of the world—is inquired into as a possible explanation for patterns of war or peace. Subcultural differences within a society are prominent in the investigation into the nature of racial and ethnic problems in Chapter 7. All such concepts are important tools of analysis for sociological inquiry. Equally important is the model of society perceived by the sociologist.

Societal model　A model is a simplified pattern with which a difficult system can be compared. A very common sociological model of society is sometimes referred to as "organismic," meaning that society is seen almost as a great living organism, with each member resembling a cell, making a contribution to the whole. There are two troubles with such a model. First, it makes society seem even more prescriptive than it is and turns the human being into a creature without individual will. Second, all organisms die, and an organismic analogy can make it seem that all societies are doomed to eventual extinction. Sociology likes to think of systems as undergoing change but not going through birth, maturity, and death.

A much more common sociological perspective is to view society as an ongoing system of interaction between individuals and the total culture, always subject to change and minor dislocations, but with a tendency to restore a balance between its parts. Such a model has the advantage of avoiding the tragically dramatic view of social systems as entities that inevitably die. People with individual lives and wills are still discernible through the theory. The only trouble with the equilibrium view is that it goes too far in playing down the conflicts within society.

A conflict view represents society as being in a state of open or potential conflict between opposing forces. To the Marxists, the opposing forces are social classes. To most political scientists, they are large numbers of competing interests—business, agriculture, labor, geographical regions, and racial and ethnic groups. Both views, equilibrium and conflict, will be apparent in the chapters to follow. Consistent with the conflict view, we will not assume that all problems are always and inevitably solved or that periods of strain and crisis are necessarily of short duration; and we will grant, too, that a social system might have to be changed drastically, not merely in minor details. In this respect, the view is somewhere between an easy reassurance that all will be well and a gloomy prediction of doom.

Struggles will occur and adjustments will be made. Whether the adjustments will improve the quality of tomorrow's society and make it less troubled than today's depends upon public awareness, study, and action. An involved generation can make the difference.

I
RESPONSE TO CHANGE

The following six chapters will examine city, environmental, consumer, educational, occupational, and family problems. These topics are all united by a common thread. All contain many elements of cultural lag, being unable to keep pace with the challenges presented by modern science and technology. Normative change is involved too, of course, and sometimes even deviant behavior, but social change is the theme that links the topics together most clearly. All these areas of study have drawn attention before, but in the rapidly changing modern world they present new complications, and some, especially urban and environmental problems, are reaching the stage of crisis.

WHAT IS NEW

In each of the areas under consideration in this section, long-existent problems appear in new forms. City problems are new in their vastness, their heterogeneity, and their governmental and social chaos. Modern transportation, productivity, disease control, and displacement of rural workers have caused urbanization and suburbanization on a scale never before achieved. The environmental pollution problem results partly from the very growth of the city, but even more from modern industry and transportation. Environmental pollution is not entirely new, but its scale is such as to dwarf all previous contamination problems.

Consumers have been bilked before and have some legal protections today that they did not have in the past, but the techniques of deception have grown. It is now possible to use the findings of chemical science in a manner inimical to the public welfare and to use all the techniques of modern psychology and sociology to develop ways of trapping the consumer. Education and its costs and failures have always been problems of public concern, but now the educational system has to take on a greater burden than ever before. It has to train and retrain and relegate people to the innumerable and changing occupational roles required by society. The nature of work has changed drastically as hours decline, automation renders many skills obsolete, and doubts arise about what jobs still have a future. Finally, the family becomes an embattled institution, unable to perform many of its older educational, protective, and integrative functions as other institutions expand at its expense.

MEETING THE SOCIAL PROBLEMS CRITERIA

The topics of Part One are social problems in that they meet the criteria discussed in the Introduction. They involve large—tremendously large—numbers of people; there are always strains between what society perceives as desirable and what is actually accomplished. All the problems included are amenable to improvement—of being brought closer to societal ideals. On the other hand, if not improved they are all threats to the social order and to future generations. Reform attempts, however, must be studied with care. Many proposed solutions could result in unforesesn (latent) consequences of an undesirable type. Already we have witnessed the development of certain detergents and fuels that solve one problem only by creating an even more serious one.

INTERRELATIONSHIPS

The problems of the city, it will be pointed out, are a combination of many other social problems. The urban industrial changes and the general technological inventiveness of the society have solved many of the problems of want and created many of the problems of abundance: crowding, disposal of wastes, and air and water pollution. Inventions, however, are adopted readily by societies whose customs and needs have prepared them for more and more inventions. Inventions change the way of life of a people, but the people in turn develop the habits of thought and action that call for even more inventions. Transportation can never be fast and efficient enough to suit the people, and products cannot be sufficiently packaged, loaded with preservatives and "cosmetic" effects, and made sufficiently disposable and convenient. There is a two-way interaction between invention and demand for invention.

Similarly, there is a two-way relationship between inventive change and social norms. What was once the luxury of a college education is perceived as a necessity and a right as the technical society finds room only for the educated. Education, in turn, accelerates inventiveness and social change. High productivity makes poverty much more of a normative strain than in the past, and education is looked upon as one means of alleviating poverty.

The rapid pace of social change also has its effects upon role problems and deviance. The residents of slum areas are left in the backwash of social change; their self-image suffers and they become alienated. Deprived conditions in a relatively affluent society create the resentments that are one of the correlates of high delinquency rates. Finally, technological change results in a potential for more destructive wars, and modern economic needs concentrate populations into highly vulnerable, congested urban areas. The problems are all interrelated.

THE SOCIAL CHANGE PERSPECTIVE

The social change perspective emphasized in this section is largely an elaboration of the ideas of Ogburn. Important inventions lead to a need for shifts in all segments of social systems. The development of efficient agriculture not only replaces farm workers but also demands their urbanization. Once in the city they can become welfare cases unless new opportunities are developed for them. The internal combustion engine not only has led to new means of transportation but has resulted in new problems of air pollution and a demand for new laws for safety in auto design. It concentrates industry and jobs. It leads to greater mobility of families, new dating customs, and drive-in theaters, banks, and even churches. The need to keep pace with industrial change and to regulate industries in the public interest increases the power of government; but as will become clear in the discussion of the food industry, regulated businesses try to thwart too much regulation.

Families are wrenched by the economic changes that have ended most farms and other small family enterprises and have employed the father and often the mother away from home, making the status and duties of men and women more similar. Educational systems find a gap between their institutional ways and the demands for training personnel for the industrial-scientific society. Technological changes occur so rapidly that the importance of a man's work is lessened, and sometimes his job is made obsolete. For young people, the problem of occupational choice becomes difficult not because the new type of society lacks a variety of jobs but because many of the jobs are not rewarding and others face possible obsolescence. These and many others of the problems of city, environment, family, education, and labor can be seen, then, as the direct or indirect consequences of technological change. The following chapters will examine these problems in more detail.

As a result of their size and rapid growth, American cities could be listed among our most spectacular successes. Why, then, do we speak of urban crisis and dislocation? Does the very technical change that has made modern cities so gigantic also threaten to undermine them; if so, can science and technology reverse the process? Why, after a century of campaigns to clean up the slums, do slums remain an integral part of all large American cities? Why is urban renewal often looked upon as an enemy by the poor and by racial and ethnic minorities? And why do ghetto developments and housing segregation continue unabated in a society that speaks so loudly of racial equality?

The problems of urban growth and of vulnerability of the city to economic and political forces will be discussed in this chapter, and also the problems of slums and social segregation. We shall look, too, at the contention that there is something about city life, or at least parts of city life, that has a strong effect on one's mental and emotional development. Finally, we shall look at the governmental and ecological problems of urban sprawl and ask what better suggestions can be made. Despite the problems of the great city, it is a place of interest and growth, economically necessary. Are there ways of managing city and suburbs in a pattern of harmony? What have other countries done? What can we do?

Societies are often compared with living organisms, and although the analogy can be overdrawn, it is a useful model for viewing some types of social problems. A weakness in one part of the organism affects all other parts, and it is hard to find one specific center for a general malaise. Similarly, the problems of modern society interconnect, but for many of them the city becomes a common meeting ground. A study of the city is a study of racial problems and poverty, air pollution and environment, population growth and distribution, the problems of government and justice, and the psychological and emotional adjustment of people to a new style of life. City and suburb seem to symbolize today's society and the observable trends into the future, rich in possibilities but with problems requiring public concern and action.

A population of more than 200 million in a country the size of the United States is not terribly crowded by global standards, and yet the majority of the 200 million crowd themselves into standard metropolitan areas, drawn in by economic opportunities or pushed in by shrinking needs for farming and other rural occupations. The trend is typical of industrial countries throughout the world. It is in the standard metropolitan areas (areas dominated by a city of 50,000 or more) that many problems are shown in sharpest silhouette, including poverty against a background of affluence, and rats, filth, and squalor in little alleys overshadowed by the great structures of modern engineering. Just as starkly, the city develops its personality types, sharp and tense, geared to noise and congestion, and ill at ease in the natural world that was the physical and spiritual home of the ancestors of modern humanity. If, as seems likely, the trend of human habitation is to continue to be toward city and suburb, can we develop all the potential benefits of urban living without leaving an undesirable backwash of crime, hypertension, divisiveness, and riot?

The city also brings out in sharp focus the major emphasis of the first section of this book—the consequences of technical change. Although cities have been part of the human scene for 5,000 years, today's standard metropolitan areas are something different from the cities of the past—a result of technological change. The new type of city is a consequence of improved engineering skills, a very large agricultural surplus that frees the majority of people for urban life, improved sanitation and means of coping with disease in crowded areas; most of all, and most recently, it is a consequence of transportation, especially automobiles and freeways. These changes have caused the modern city to dwarf all those of the past and to have made a majority of the people of industrialized lands urbanites or suburbanites.

The modern city is a region of strain, the strain of noise and congestion, of construction, demolition, and repair, of high rates of crime, and of thousands of anonymous faces. It is also a place of normative strain—a strain involving the norms of equal opportunity and the reality of grossly unequal opportunity, sometimes resulting in explosions of violence. Some of these strains are inevitable parts of city life. The city's size, pace, and heterogeneity make it an exciting place for commerce, science, and the arts and entertainment, but it is nevertheless a place of strain.

THE VULNERABLE GIANT

The contrast in size between modern cities and those of antiquity is striking and reflects the new scientific-industrial possibilities for supporting huge, congested

Ancient cities*		Modern cities†	
Ur	20,000	Shanghai	10,800,000
Babylon	85,000	Tokyo	9,012,000
Syracuse	150,000	New York	7,771,000
Athens	150,000	London	7,763,000
Thebes	225,000	Moscow	6,942,000
Rome	1,000,000	São Paulo	5,685,000

*Adapted from Frank M. McGraw and Dean L. Phelps, *The Rise of the City,* Field Educational Publications, Inc., San Francisco, 1971, pp. 205–227.
†Source: *Information Please Almanac,* Simon & Schuster, New York, 1972, except for Shanghai, first reported in *U. N. Demographic Yearbook,* Office of Public Information, United Nations, New York, 1973, as world's largest city. The United Nations also calls New York City and suburbs the world's largest urban conglomerate, with 11,572,000.

populations. Statistics on the size of ancient cities are only approximate, but even rough estimates show the contrast.

The ancient cities of the Near East were sometimes seen as fields of greenery in an arid land and compared with the spreading branches of a mammoth tree, protecting human beings with its merciful shade. Today the metaphor no longer applies. Concerned social critics and ecologists are more likely to compare the city and its suburbs with malignant cancer cells, spreading voraciously, devouring the fertile land, and threatening the host on which they feed. Both pictures—the picture of protection and that of threat—are but exaggerations of observable realities. Today's city, as in earlier times, offers its comforts and its beauty but also has its disturbing problems—so many, in fact, that such terms as "urban crisis" and "sick cities" are often used to describe the situation.

The contrasts within A panoramic view of the great cities of today is a study in contrasts. Seen from a distance, particularly at night, the city is a sea of brilliance. The long chains of light denoting highways and freeways speak of a level of commerce and affluence undreamed of in earlier times. The lights cluster around many centers, marking new suburbs, until the main nucleus is hard to discern. The lights from a thousand palaces of commerce and entertainment seem to tell us that "thine alabaster cities gleam undimmed by human tears." The very physical size of the city is staggering, sprawling up hills, across rivers, through what were once agricultural valleys—an uncontrolled giant of as many as eight or ten million people. Its lights are lost in the distance, drowned in a haze of low visibility.

A closer look in the clearer light of day shows that only part of the lights denote affluence. Some are from the world's most expensive hotels, nightclubs, and theaters; others are the lights of cheap hotels, impoverished tenement districts, skid rows, and brawling taverns. Even many of the new skyscrapers, whose lights give an impression of great beauty, turn out to be rather ugly, resembling, as Frank Lloyd Wright once observed, gigantic steel and concrete filing cases, featureless monotones.

Urban costs In the morning the traffic begins to increase along all the highways that are engineering miracles in themselves but never adequate for the rush hours.

The
contrasts
within the
city:
wealth
and
poverty

It seems that whoever lives at one end of the city works on the other side, and each driver, alone in his car, contributes to the dangerous rush and level of noise and congestion that fray the nerves of even the most hearty. If a visitor to the city should decide to take public transportation, in most cases he will find it grossly inadequate, poorly maintained, and given little financial support or attention. City residents would not even know how to direct him. Public transportation is generally not adequate, although in recent years city mayors have become increasingly concerned about the matter and have appealed for federal funds for transportation systems.

Near the core of the city are the old tenement buildings, some being torn out for the sake of urban renewal, others still standing, decadent, but the only places with rent low enough for poor families. Children grow up here, learning the ways of the street, outwitting the police and the school, surviving in their gangs, defending their turf, both loving and hating the city, scarred and toughened by it, and often embittered by it. Some may later set fire to it.

Meanwhile the well-to-do escape farther and farther from the urban centers, spilling over old villages, building new suburbs, and agitating for better freeways and transportation to travel back to the city. The city finds its tax base shrinking as the rich exit and the poor enter. Crime rates are high in the slums and the costs of police and fire protection mount, as do the costs of garbage disposal, sanitation, transportation, parks and recreation, welfare, and education. On a national average, per capita taxes are nearly $25 higher in the city than in the surrounding areas, and the cities receive less per capita in governmental aid for education and other purposes than do the surrounding suburbs.[1] In a sixteen-year period, local government revenues increased by $29.8 billion, but expenses increased by $43.7 billion and debts by $58.7 billion.[2] Some people would question calling the cities sick; few would question calling them financially starved.

URBAN VULNERABILITY

Often the prosperity of cities and towns is dependent mainly on outside forces, such as the general state of the economy, domestic and foreign markets, federal financing for urban improvements, or government contracts to supply the demands of the voracious defense industry. The latter source of prosperity has the effect of giving sections of the country a vested interest in defense spending, and their representatives in Congress are alert to this reality.

Small towns have been known to die as a consequence of the very industrial change that has created the big cities. The people of the little town of Bay St. Louis, Mississippi, experienced the ordeal of industrial life and death. After encouraging its development as a testing center for NASA, the government changed policies, making deep cuts in the NASA budget and ending the town's boom. The government announced that the space center would be closed at the end of 1970. Meantime local residents had bonded themselves for millions of dollars for water, power, schools, airport, and other facilities, looking forward to growth and prosperity, with solid promises from well-known leaders of the space program. Then the government ax fell, leaving the town to atrophy or to find some new ways for the government to restore it to life. Homes that were built for rental are now tenantless, and the villagers who had invested their savings are now thousands of dollars deeper in debt.[3]

Even the big city is not immune to recession by governmental decision. Seattle depends overwhelmingly on the aircraft industry, and Los Angeles finds the same industry to be a vital part of its economic diet. A major shift to public transportation and a corresponding decline in private automobiles could be a blow to Detroit. Many seaports would find a large portion of their spending money cut were it not for generous government subsidies to ship lines. For example, from 1958 to 1973, $7.5 billion was spent on containerized ships, of which $2.3 billion was federal subsidy.[4]

---

[1]Alan K. Campbell and Philip Meranto, "The Metropolitan Education Dilemma: Matching Resources to Needs," *Urban Affairs Quarterly*, vol. II, p. 57, September 1966.
[2]The President's Commission on Civil Disorders, *Report of the National Advisory Committee on Civil Disorders* (The Kerner Report), Bantam Books, Inc., New York, 1968, p. 392.
[3]"Boom Town Deeply Hurt by Space Cuts," *Los Angeles Times*, April 22, 1970, part I, pp. 1, 15.
[4]*New York Times*, February 19, 1973, p. 44.

20 In some respects the city is a giant with feet of clay. Arthur J. Vidich and Joseph Bensman, in *Small Town in Mass Society*, show the pattern of economic dependence of the small town. In their study, small-town residents liked to think of themselves as independent of the mass society, but in fact they were controlled by industries and institutions located elsewhere. The same is often true of the city.

There are, of course, other types of urban vulnerability. New York experienced a prolonged blackout because of a power shortage. Debilitating smog alerts have occurred in Los Angeles, New York, London, and Tokyo. All cities depend upon rapid transport and are vulnerable to strikes called by national unions. Unionization and strikes are also becoming increasingly frequent in police forces and fire departments.

The city is covered over with a pall of smog and soot for much of the year, even if it is built on a wind-swept coastal plain. Its problem of disposal of sewage, garbage, and industrial waste is just as serious, tending to contaminate rivers, coastlines, and underground aquifers, threatening the health of the residents of all surrounding areas.

THE DIVISIONS WITHIN

A major difficulty of cities is that of the divisions within. There always have been, and have had to be, various sectors of the city serving diverse purposes, but there has usually been a sense of unity underlying the diversity. The ancient city-states had a quality of unity about them, holding as they did first claim on the loyalties of their people. Occupation and social class were varied, but the city was the governor and protector and the bond that held people together. The city, in this sense of the word, is a thing of the past. The great mass society, if anything, is what gives the people a sense of commonality, and the city is a thing of fragments—of business centers and high-rise apartments, ghettos, and a wide belt of suburbs, with a confusion of names, shopping centers, school districts, zoning areas, governmental agencies, and associations.

There are divisions between social classes, races, and ethnic groups as well as between inner city and outer city, of economic interest, of party and policy, and of those who belong and those who do not. There is also an important division between those who believe in the city and those who do not; and even for those who believe, there are differences. To some it is a place of culture, enjoyment, and civic pride; to others it is disagreeable but a place to make a living; to yet others it is a place for economic exploitation. The city copes with all types, or there would be no city. To understand why not enough people are committed to the city, it is important to study the implications of the divisions within.

Slum and suburb Within the city there is a general segregation of social classes that helps to keep poverty hidden. The very poor either live close to the inner circle of the city or are strung out along railroad tracks, but they tend to be separated from the middle class. Occasionally urban renewal will complicate the pattern by bringing high-rise apartments to the areas surrounded by urban blight, and poverty will become more obvious and its bite more keenly felt. Value of residence usually declines by slow degrees, however, and a cartographer could map class elevation almost as surely as contour lines. Among the lower valleys in this pseudorelief map are the slums, a place of stagnation. Just how deteriorated they should be before being designated slums and how ruthlessly they should be torn out are matters for debate.

For generations Americans have worried about slums, but slum clearance has generally been beyond the financial means of individual cities, and sometimes local taxes have risen so rapidly on reconstructed property as to make slum properties more profitable. At times the federal government has become deeply involved, although funds for such developments were cut back during the Nixon and Ford administrations in an attempt to hold down government spending. From 1949 until the late 1960s the major federal agency for slum clearance was the Urban Renewal Administration, which acquired large areas for urban redevelopment.[5] Once the property was acquired, it was developed by private enterprise with generous federal assistance. In 1966, a Model Cities program was instituted to improve some of the earlier policies of urban renewal; and in 1970 a further attempt at improvement was made through the New Towns program. The 1966 and 1970 programs have been more considerate of the poor people displaced by urban renewal but have done little to alleviate the essential racial segregation of cities.[6]

Make a study of at least one specific physical need of your community, such as public transportation, parks and playgrounds, improved zoning, or amended building codes. Draw up a plan of what could be done and submit it to a councilman for his study and response.

There are really two types of interests at stake in the process of urban renewal: human and economic. Urban renewal was once urged primarily by social reformers, who saw slums as a menace to human values and felt it would be possible to bring all slum dwellers into the common, middle-class value system of a home in the suburbs or its equivalent. Now, many of the very people who were once the supporters of urban renewal are often its critics. Such books as Jane Jacobs's *The Death and Life of Great American Cities* and Martin Anderson's *The Federal Bulldozer* have been highly critical of urban-renewal projects. Jacobs stresses the breakup of neighborhoods and community feeling, the loss of small shops that were once the meeting places of old friends and the centers of neighborhood news and small talk. Anderson questions whether the value of urban renewal is worth the cost and whether its benefits fall equitably. The problem is that it has been hard to get renewal projects to serve two conflicting interests: those of the businessmen, who are trying to prop up the values of the central city and increase its economic yield, and those of the poor people, who see the cheap rents in the run-down central areas as an economic necessity. Furthermore, until rather recently, central location of housing for people who cannot afford cars has been an advantage in getting to work. With a present trend toward business development in the suburbs, this benefit is changing to a detriment in most cities.

Not only has the increasingly dispersed pattern of industry combined with the migration of black people from the South contributed to the ghetto pattern, but much federal legislation has intensified the problem. Since the Housing Act of 1937, the most common public policy for housing the urban poor has been the construction of massive federally financed apartment complexes. Some of the largest of them, built in the 1950s, were designed with the belief that concentrating the poor would permit more efficient provision of social services. "Experience

[5]Nathan Glazer, "The Renewal of Cities," *Scientific American*, vol. 213, pp. 194–204, September 1965.
[6]Leonard Downie, "The New Town Mirage," *Nation*, vol. 214, pp. 617–621, May 15, 1972.

proved instead that packing multi-problem families together was like packing oily rags, risking spontaneous combustion."[7] Several of the 1966–1969 riots started in such concentrated areas.

Whereas the policy for the urban poor was to pack them together into apartments rented at cheap rates by the government, the white middle class was given encouragement in the form of Federal Housing Administration (FHA) and Veterans Administration (VA) loans to buy homes in the suburbs. The policy of giving local communities a voice in whether or not federal projects should be allowed helped keep public housing (largely for blacks) out of the white suburbs. In the meantime, FHA funds were not available to the poor in the inner cities until 1968; previous to that time, homes in blighted areas of the inner city could not be financed through FHA because the homes did not meet strict insurance requirements.[8] Present policies are more equitable, but high interest rates make FHA loans less attractive than in earlier days for everyone, both urban and suburban.

A case study of an ethnic community Ethnic areas in the city often develop a real sense of community. In earlier America, at a time when people believed in the picture of the American city as a great melting pot, there were many heart-warming tales of the immigrant making a success in the new land. Ethnic neighborhoods were largely poor, but they usually represented gains for people who had known greater poverty abroad.

Often urban renewal has dislocated old ethnic communities, and Italians, Poles, Czechs, Greeks, and other groups have become intermingled with older American types. In view of the cultural ideal of Americanization and the melting pot, this change would seem favorable. There are cases, though, where it has worked very great hardship and brought feelings of bitterness. It has also interfered with another important American value—the right of people to live where they wish.

Herbert J. Gans made a study of the effects of urban renewal on an Italian-American community in Boston.[9] Although the West End area he describes was popularly called a slum, Gans objects to the word in this particular case. The area had the type of community feeling and cohesion that is better described by the term "urban village"—an area in which new immigrants "try to adapt their non-urban institutions and cultures to the urban milieu."[10] The term is applicable to many Puerto Rican and Negro areas of American cities. Skid row is usually near such areas, even in contact with them, but it is an "urban jungle," a place of transience, "depressed if not brutal." In the case of the residential West End of Boston, the homes were poor, the majority of incomes low, there was a problem of dirt and garbage, but the apartments were large and kept neat and livable. Best of all the apartments were cheap, a point too often overlooked by urban planners. Children reared in the neighborhood got used to it; although small children loved a chance to get out into the country, as they grew older they found the country rather distressing; they needed people and activity around them. They placed little status importance on the type of housing, and resented having their area called a slum.

Gans suggests that areas be defined as slums only if they are harmful to their residents—firetraps, structurally unsafe, infested with rats or disease, or unques-

[7]Malcom E. Peabody, Jr., "Housing Allowances," *New Republic*, p. 21, March 1974.
[8]Michael Harrington, "Introduction" to L. A. Ferman et al. (eds.), *Poverty in America*, University of Michigan Press, Ann Arbor, 1968.
[9]*The Urban Villagers*, The Free Press, New York, 1962.
[10]Herbert J. Gans, *op. cit.*, p. 4.

tionably inclined to draw children into illegal activities. They must not be called slums simply because they do not meet the standards of taste of the middle-class suburbanite. Gans charges that the West End was not a harmful place; it was redeveloped because it was a place in which developers could foresee a large profit. Much worse areas were passed up for renewal. The Italian-American community organized "Save the West End" committees, but to no avail.

There were old people who had lived in the community all their lives, or ever since leaving Italy, and knew only their friends and relatives in the area. They were to spend an old age in exile. There were small grocers who had managed to eke out a living but could not afford to relocate in a city that already had too many small stores. There were the teenagers who found the new suburban areas boring and empty. All the families had less money to spend on groceries and doctor bills and shoes for the children. The redevelopment commission had promised that 60 percent of the people would be relocated in public housing; only 10 percent actually were. Eventually nearly all the families had to find houses on their own, in most cases less satisfactory from their point of view than the houses they had left.

This is but one story of redevelopment of an ethnic community. Many projects have been similar, and some have been better planned. It does, however, illustrate the problems that must be looked for, and the superficiality of assuming that all clearance of "slums" will bring immediate benefits to their residents. Scott Greer once summarized the problem with the statement "At a cost of more than three billion dollars, the Urban Renewal Agency has succeeded in materially reducing the supply of low cost housing in American cities."[11]

Black and white Although the example given above of replacement of the poor involves an Italian-American community, the more usual case inevitably involves blacks, since they are so highly concentrated in inner cities. As we have seen, lending policies and public housing policies have both contributed to this trend.

[11]Daniel P. Moynihan, "Urban Conditions," *The Annals of the American Academy of Political and Social Science*, vol. 371, p. 161, May 1971.

24 From 1960 to 1970, the central cities experienced a net loss of 0.2 percent of their white residents. In the same decade, the black population of the central cities increased by 32.1 percent.[12] So great has been the influx of blacks into the central city that Washington, D.C., and Newark, New Jersey, are already more than half black, with New Orleans and Richmond at approximately the 50 percent mark, and Baltimore, Jacksonville, Gary, and Cleveland nearing the halfway point.[13] The significance of this development is that blacks occupy the most congested neighborhoods, the black ghetto—an area usually characterized by economic stagnation but of high costs to the city. The per pupil-day cost of education, for example, has been increasing at an annual rate of 6.7 percent for the past two decades, but local taxes have not kept pace.[14]

The white exodus to the suburbs has been even more rapid than has the black entry into the central city. Thus the central city has declined in political influence relative to the suburbs. Although there has been an increase in the number of blacks attaining middle-class status, they have been slow to follow the trend of earlier European immigrant groups of moving out of the central city, because of prohibitive costs, unfriendly white attitudes, and real estate practices. Actually, there was a net in-migration of blacks from urban fringe areas to central cities from 1960 to 1966.

In the twenty worst urban slums, the nonwhite unemployment rate varies from 50 to 300 percent higher than white unemployment.[15] A study of Los Angeles shows that employment in the predominantly black Watts area fell by 61 percent between 1965 and 1970. There had been a major race riot in the Watts area in 1965, still remembered by Californians as the worst riot the state had ever had. Millions of dollars have been spent to fight poverty in the area since the riot. Some good has actually been accomplished in occupational training of some of the residents, but they have often moved out after receiving better jobs. For those left behind the sex ratio has grown increasingly lopsided, with the number of women exceeding the number of men by 44 percent. This helps to explain the unemployment problem, but it documents a major concern: those left behind, those unable to afford rents in other areas, seem to be involved in a vicious circle of poverty. Poverty forces them to live in jobless areas, which in turn leads to greater poverty.[16] White unemployment in Los Angeles has also increased slightly because of recession conditions. Blacks in Watts, however, show 16.2 percent unemployment compared with 4.3 percent for the Los Angeles area as a whole. Such conditions of unemployment are common in the nation's ghettos.

The urban center is becoming a poor place to find a job for either black or white. In 80 percent of the cases, new industry locates outside the central city in places hard to reach by public transportation. Racial discrimination in employment adds to the problem. The result is a high incidence of dependency. In the urban slums six nonwhite children out of ten are supported by Aid to Families with Dependent Children (AFDC) payments during at least part of their childhood.[17] On the other hand, a Cleveland study showed no such conditions for those black families living outside the slums. Although the incidence of poverty increased in the slum area,

[12]Bureau of the Census, *Statistical Abstract of the United States*, 1972, p. 16.
[13]President's Commission on Civil Disorders, *op. cit.*, p. 390.
[14]*Loc. cit.*, p. 392.
[15]Moynihan, *op. cit.*, p. 165.
[16]"Watts Jobless Rate Up," *Los Angeles Times*, August 7, 1970, part I, p. 3.
[17]Moynihan, *op. cit.*, p. 169.

the median family income rose by more than $1,000 per year for those families who had moved away.

Other ethnic groups have lived in separate enclaves of their own, but the word ghetto has not always been appropriate for other groups. The Irish, Polish, and Italians have lived in their own areas by choice and usually for one or two generations. If an area remained persistently ethnic, its people usually became the owners of their own businesses and had economic and possibly political control of their own sectors. Robert Blauner compares the black situation, on the other hand, with that of colonialism, administered from without by "foreigners." The educators, policemen, social workers, politicians, and other people who administer the affairs of the ghetto residents are typically whites who live outside the black community.[18]

There are now a few black mayors and some progress toward political control of black areas by blacks, but this is so belated and uncertain that the colonial comparison still seems apt. Several black mayors of the nation's cities have faced almost insurmountable problems because they have been elected only after the central city has deteriorated financially almost beyond hope. Mayor Richard Hatcher of Gary, Indiana, especially popular with black residents, has accomplished a little by way of housing in poverty areas but has not had the funds or the power to reduce smog or crime. The black mayor of Newark, Kenneth Gibson, has inherited a city from a political crowd recently convicted of extorting $253,000 from city contracts, and allegedly connected with the Mafia. Gibson can hardly help but run a cleaner government, but he is having to take over a city on the verge of bankruptcy.[19] Among the best-known and most-popular black mayors are Maynard Jackson of Atlanta and Tom Bradley of Los Angeles. Both are effective leaders of dynamic and financially solvent cities.

Policies for the ghetto   The President's Commission on Civil Disorders suggested three possible policies for the ghetto, and three probable consequences: (1) present policies choice; (2) enrichment choice; and (3) integration choice.

As the commission points out, the present policies are leading in the direction of an increasingly divided country. A small segment of the black population is achieving a degree of prosperity, but even they are concentrated in the central city, not far from poorer black neighborhoods. For the majority, the conditions do not improve. Because of a high birth rate during the 1950s, the black population has an increasingly large percentage of young men in the age group of 16 to 24 years. It is in this very group that unemployment and discontent is highest and explosive potential is a constant threat.

By enrichment choice, the commission refers to attempts to improve existing black communities with more job opportunities, to encourage black business interests, and to give better education and training and self-help programs. Such policies would cost much more than the government is willing to spend. For years the Vietnam War was given as the reason for inadequate funds for the cities, but despite the end of the war, funds are shrinking rather than growing. Even with adequate funds, the commission sees objections to the enrichment program. Past experience has seen only failure in separate-but-equal policies, and certainly the enrichment program would not end separatism.

[18]Robert Blauner, "Internal Colonialism and Ghetto Revolt," *Social Problems*, vol. 16, Spring 1969.
[19]"The Black Mayors," *Newsweek*, pp. 16–18, August 3, 1970.

26 Make a racial and ethnic map of your community. Is there a clear pattern of de facto segregation? Is the segregation purely a result of economics? If not, find out what policies, official and unofficial, keep segregation going.

The commission finally turns to the integration choice as the recommended solution. Since jobs are being created primarily in the suburbs, there must be a determined effort to make it possible for black people to live there and to be equal competitors for the jobs. The problem of educating ghetto children could be met best in this manner, avoiding the shortcoming of lack of experience in the outside world for ghetto children, and also the economic costs and the hard feelings of extensive busing. Finally, in the opinion of the commission, integration is the only way to avoid dividing the society. This, we might add, is the only way the blacks could learn to believe in the city as a center of promise and therefore as a place demanding their loyalty and participation.

The suburbs and "antiurbs" The suburbs are not all of one type. Some have been created as the city spills out into surrounding village areas, remaking rural villages in the image of suburbia. Others have been planned in large tracts; the Levittowns, new communities, suddenly springing into existence. In social-class level they range from an aristocratic old suburbia to monotonous rows of cheaply built "little boxes." Although the suburbs are usually characterized as middle class, as though they were all on a common economic level, there is much social-class structuring about them. With the passing of time they begin to resemble the older parts of the city. The great growth of the past two decades has been suburban. Of the largest twenty-five cities in the United States, thirteen lost population between 1960 and 1970, but there was always growth in surrounding suburban areas. The 1970 census was the first to show suburban population outnumbering combined central city and rural population. Despite the race to the suburbs to avoid congestion, both city and suburb have experienced a rapid growth in condominiums and apartments in the past decade. Such compression of populations is aimed at reducing building and maintenance costs and the costs of such services as water, sewage, gas, and electricity. Condominiums could have the ecological effect of reducing the amount of farmland absorbed by new suburban developments.

Often the suburbs lie outside the city limits, so the residents do not have to pay city taxes and do not have a voice in the city government. Although the residents are economically dependent upon the city, working there and buying there, they have an emotional dislike for it. Their aim is to find a quiet suburb, although the quiet suburb of today is often the noise center of tomorrow's growing metropolis. The poor resident of the slum is often a person who does not like the city either, but who lives there because of economic necessity.

Sometimes in old suburbia or in the "gold coasts" of the great cities there are urbanites who work to promote art and music centers, colleges, and museums. Mayors and other city politicians, along with business leaders, like to see redevelopment, and ordinary citizens call for greater expenditures for schools and playgrounds and transportation. There are not too many leaders, however, of the type of Pericles or Lorenzo the Magnificent, whose devotion is to city beautification. Prevailingly the American intellectual has not been an urbanite in truly loving and promoting the city; he has displayed a nostalgia for the rural past. In fact, he has questioned the city's democracy, its intelligence, its "Americanism," its heart, and its mind.[20]

THE MIND OF THE CITY

Old stories about the "country rube" and the "city slicker" point to a belief in strong personality differences between urban and rural types. Certainly in an age of extreme mobility and rapid communication the differences should be expected to decline, but there is still evidence of a difference. The city, whatever its problems, does have certain intellectual advantages. The urbanite is relatively free of the narrow confinement of the mind that is the function of neighborhood gossip in the small town. There are enlightening opportunities—more informative newspapers, radio and television stations, libraries, colleges, theaters, and book stores; however, these advantages are not used by all. The pace of life is faster, the nervous tensions greater, and the levels of noise and congestion more shattering. Do these characteristics lead to more mental problems for the city?

Neurosis, psychosis, and the city   In *The Intellectual Versus the City*, the Whites[21] present a long history of American opinion and the conclusions that there is something wrong with urbanism. To some extent the opinions represent nostalgia for a simpler way of life, but the criticisms come from many of America's leading intellectuals, among them such pioneers in education and sociology as John Dewey and Robert Park. There are charges of the creation of a thoughtless rabble, of rising class awareness that threatens democracy, of nervous tensions, of "homogenized" sameness, and of urban neurosis and crime. Is this mere opinion or does it have its element of fact?

Leo Srole and others[22] made a lengthy study of midtown Manhattan, including the busiest and most congested parts of New York City. They concluded that midtown Manhattan is a place of serious psychological impairment for nearly one-third of its inhabitants, and that only 18.3 percent are free of any type of neurotic or psychotic disturbance. The situation was far worse for those with less than medium incomes than for those with higher incomes.

Rates of violent crime have been positively correlated with density of population in urban centers, and some research indicates that perpetrators of violent crime have a lower than normal tolerance of crowding. Ulcers, coronary disease, and high blood pressure are also more prevalent in the city than in rural areas.[23] Professor P. G. Zimbardo[24] of Stanford made an interesting study to try to ascertain whether the level of violence and vandalism is greater in the city or small town. He had cars abandoned in the small town of Palo Alto and in New York City and secretly watched. In New York the car was vandalized by twenty-three separate persons or groups in a period of one week; in Palo Alto the car was left unmolested for the same period of time.

[20]Morton White and Lucia White (eds.), *The Intellectual Versus the City*, Mentor Books, New American Library, Inc., New York, 1962.
[21]*Ibid.*
[22]Leo Srole et al., *Mental Health in the Metropolis*, Harper & Row, Publishers, Incorporated, New York, 1970, chaps. 7 and 8.
[23]Paul R. Ehrlich and Anne H. Ehrlich, *Population, Resources, Environment*, W. H. Freeman and Company, San Francisco, 1970, p. 142.
[24]P. G. Zimbardo, paper presented to the Nebraska Symposium on Motivation, 1969.

In many cases the evidence is to some extent against the city, but one needs to ask what part of the city and what levels of poverty and neglect? Srole's statistics would argue that adequate income could be a partial solution to the problems of urban life and neurosis. It should also be added that urban life does not have to be endured in the most congested areas of the city. Various studies constitute an indictment of living conditions in the areas of greatest urban rush, but no conclusions can be drawn from them about more inviting parts of the city.

Mental versus emotional life   The early German sociologist Georg Simmel wrote on the topic of mental life and the metropolis. His conclusion was that urban life has a tendency to heighten people's intelligence in some respects because they must live in a more totally competitive world and a world in which more stimuli constantly impinge upon them. At the same time, said Simmel, there is a diminution of emotional responses. Urbanites do not respond to situations of tragedy, pathos, and love with adequate emotion. They have become rather blasé, taking everything in stride with little emotional perturbation, with a blank countenance, an unconcern.

Several recent research papers have been written on the subjects related to Simmel's hypothesis. One question approached by such a study is whether or not people in large conglomerates become less sensitive to the feelings of others and less inclined to help in an emergency. A widely quoted series of experiments demonstrated that where a critical emergency develops (for example, heart attack or epileptic seizure), the larger the group of observers, the less likely anyone is to take immediate action to help. One person alone lends help because he knows he must. When others are present, subjects of the experiment fear overreacting or doing something that others could do better. Each tends to wait for the expert. Of several variables tested in the experiment, the only important one was the number of people in the group witnessing the tragedy. There was only one other correlation—a slight negative correlation between the willingness to respond and the size of the community in which the subject was reared.[25]

Urban people are, of course, likely to be in association with other people more of the time than rural people. It is possible that the conditioning of city residents to the presence of large numbers of people and their habitual dependence on someone whose specific duty is that of handling the emergency make them slightly less responsive to emergencies than country people. Rather than grab a hose to put out the fire, they may be more inclined to ask why the fire department is so slow. There is also a rule of urban life possibly carried too far, of respecting the other person's privacy.

Stanley Milgram has examined Simmel's idea about the blasé attitude and the erosion of the emotions in the city.[26] He agrees with Simmel's description of the manifest phenomena and has new approaches to their explanation. We can think of our emotional lives and our total sensory receptivity, he says, in terms of inputs and outputs. There is a limit to the possibilities of each, and anything exceeding this limit is an overload on the nervous system. To avoid the neurotic anxiety that would develop from a concern about everyone we meet, we must select and restrict inputs by such devices as unlisted phone numbers, an unfriendly countenance, or

[25]John M. Darley and Bibb Latané, "Bystander Intervention in Emergencies: Diffusion of Responsibility," *Journal of Personality and Social Psychology*, vol. 8, no. 4, pp. 377–383, 1968.
[26]Stanley Milgram, "The Experience of Living in Cities," *Science*, pp. 1461–1468, March 13, 1970.

the distant stare. The sense of moral responsibility is shifted by setting up special institutions to handle poverty, neglected children, and the needy blind. In this way it is possible to overlook and wall out the poverty-stricken, the panhandler, the skid-row alcoholic, members of other races, and residents of the wrong side of the tracks. There are too many accidents and tragedies in the city for any one person to handle; he or she would collapse emotionally. The conscientious citizen, perhaps, takes an interest in certain charitable causes but cannot possibly participate in all. Milgram's conclusion is that the restriction of emotional inputs is a matter of response to urban conditions rather than the response of a particular personality type, although he does not rule out the possibility that there can be something habit-forming about the walling-out type of response.

Is it really true that urbanization results in a tendency to ignore other people? Discuss instances from your own community that support or refute Simmel's ideas about the urban personality.

Evidence that the handling of emotional inputs is not determined purely by city life as such is the observable difference in this respect between one city and another. In some cities, visitors are treated with more politeness than in others; observers describe cities as having differences in atmosphere, from cold and aloof to warm and friendly. Milgram explains these differences as resulting partly from (1) differences in densities, the less crowded cities being less aloof; (2) the rural populations from which the cities are drawn; and (3) specific historical circumstances of the growth of the city. Paris and Vienna, for example, have preserved aristocratic attitudes toward the arts and entertainment, based on their historical positions, and will be congenial to the visitor of similar tastes. Leaders of such European cities, and also the American city of Boston, with a sense of history, are highly cognitive of historical sights and of tourists visiting them. They are not necessarily aware of their poverty areas. Cities seem to be as selective as individuals in their inputs and outputs. The evidence, however, would suggest that there is no need to be fatalistic about the urban personality type. It can change to some extent and need not be a serious problem in the city that controls crowding and has pride in its traditions and cultural attractions.

THE PROBLEMS OF GOVERNMENT

As cities grow, so do their administrative complexities, their interrelationships with other cities and other levels of government, and the number of ecological problems that are beyond their individual control. Old city governments become cultural lags in a megalopolis that extends far beyond their jurisdictional areas. New York City and its vicinity are served by 1,400 governmental and administrative districts; the San Francisco Bay Area is an urban concentration of similar governmental confusion. San Francisco employs the residents of a dozen communities strung over the Bay Area, providing their city services and paying them for their labor but unable to tax them or to demand their participation. Precisely the same is true of most great American cities. San Francisco is an unusually good example because political decisions of a century ago restricted the City and County of San Francisco to a tiny dot of land at the northern end of the San Francisco peninsula. Many other cities as well are small incorporated islands foundering in a sea of suburbia.

30 | **The interurban entanglement** As cities spill over their boundaries and inundate the rural lands that once separated them from neighboring cities, new problems arise that are beyond the competence of any particular city government. If several cities are polluting the same river or bay, the one city that attempts environmental control is doomed to failure. Broad thoroughfares that end in narrow lands as they enter the jurisdiction of the county or the next city become useless. Air pollution emanating from the uncontrolled industries of one city spreads over the entire urban complex and well out into the countryside. Urban problems of this type have become superurban, not merely metropolitan but megalopolitan.

The highway problem is the first of the interurban problems to be attacked with great energy, although more in some states than in others. Much of the highway construction program is aided by state and federal governments, and the freeway systems become a matter of large-scale planning. Eventually the freeway problems escalate, however, with more people driving more cars for greater distances as roads improve. There is no permanent solution to the traffic problem, but in some states it can be said that the battle is progressing according to plan. Federal aid prevents the total collapse of a highway system in states unable to bear their own costs.

Whatever their defects, highways are used here as an example of one step in the solution of urban problems—the involvement of larger areas of government. The problems of smog and pollution and urban sprawl are just as much beyond the control of a single city as are the planning and support of highway systems. Action by states to prevent destruction of the environment, combined with intercity and city-state cooperation, offers more hope for the future.

State and regional cooperation In the past decade, attempts have been made to achieve regional cooperation in an effort to bring urban sprawl under control and to manage suburban environments. In the early 1960s, Hawaii started the policy of protection of scenic land areas so that not all natural beauty would fall victim to urbanization. In the early 1970s, California, Vermont, and Florida all passed acts involving the state to some degree in the planning of land use, at least in major developments or developments that might have a serious detrimental impact on the natural environment. Certain urban areas have also combined efforts in an attempt to slow the pace of unplanned urban sprawl; for example, the twin cities of Minneapolis and St. Paul, the Miami Valley, and the San Francisco Bay Area.[27]

New proposals are being made by some city planners that if widely adopted could prevent the ugly patterns of city growth now so much in evidence. Several European cities have adopted "land-banking" plans whereby the city buys up its own developable surroundings. In this way the public can have a voice in plans for future development, leave parks and open space if desired, and simultaneously profit from the rise in land values. Stockholm has used such a plan since 1904 and now owns 200 square miles of surrounding land. When the profit motive is removed from land development, there is less temptation to run roughshod over prime agricultural lands, scenic areas, or vulnerable flood plains of rivers. Admittedly, extensive municipal ownership of land is not part of American tradition, and might be thought of only as a last-resort measure. Other possibilities lie in the

[27]"Managed Growth: A Look at the Shift in Land Use Policies," *Architectural Forum*, vol. 139, pp. 42–45, December 1973.

previously indicated direction of more state or regional authority over land development, regardless of who owns the land.

FEDERAL FUNDS AND REVENUE SHARING

The Conference of Mayors meeting in San Diego in June, 1974 complained that community development programs had been severely short-funded in the past few years and emphasized their need for public-transportation and public-works funds to relieve unemployment. They also asked for more New Towns programs, which had the beneficial effect of creating jobs and redeveloping urban areas, even if they failed to end segregation. The mayors, however, made it clear that they intended to control funds; and they opposed an amendment to the revenue-sharing plan that would allocate money on the basis of greatest need.

The revenue-sharing plan, started during the second Nixon administration, has the beneficial effect of returning federal tax money to the cities and thus reducing their financial problems. Use of the money is largely a matter of local control, so that cities can determine for themselves what is most needed. Reducing control by federal bureaucracy has its appeal, but money with no strings attached becomes subject to local vested interests, real estate boards, and city officials although it also opens possibilities for political action at state and local levels. Unless poverty areas can apply political pressure, the spending may go disproportionately to help business, commerce, and tourism rather than the areas of greatest need. Urban renewal, even with a large degree of federal control, was strongly criticized for such policies. At first glance it would seem that local control might be even worse. However, in spite of local vested interests, some of the few successful public-housing projects of the past have been built by local communities,[28] so there is at least a possibility that some of the cities will make better use of the money than the federal government has done.

ROADS FROM MEGALOPOLIS

Although much has been said in criticism of the city, and more will be said about its environmental problems, there is no suggestion that the city be abandoned. Urbanism is the way of life for a majority of people living in industrial societies, and for increasing numbers of people in underdeveloped regions of the world as well. For America, the trend toward city and suburb continues to accelerate. This does not mean, however, that the city has to be an unplanned megalopolis, heedless of environmental destruction and of the urban blight and decay of areas left behind.

City size For years Lewis Mumford has spoken of the possibility of building smaller cities that will leave green belts between themselves and neighboring cities. At first glance, such an idea does not seem feasible. During his long life Mumford has seen many new cities grow to approximately the desired size and then continue to expand beyond that size. There is a kind of American tradition of growth that leads us to expect all communities to expand or die, and it is exciting to be where things are happening. Naturally the rapid growth of our cities has depended upon much more than values; growth takes place in response to economic opportunity. So far the economic opportunities seem to have called for the growth of many urban areas into gigantic size.

  The solution envisaged by Mumford is to plan in such a way that essential industries will be spread out. An age of ready transportation and communication, when central offices can provide organizational control over plants located in a dozen states, would seem to make such a development feasible. The Department of Housing and Urban Development is looking into possibilities for discouraging gigantic growth of cities and helping smaller areas. There is usually a wide gap between "looking into possibilities," however, and actually implementing policy. The federal government is such an enormous customer for industry and has so many economic favors to dispense that with determination it could probably promote small- or intermediate-sized cities and slow the growth of the giants.

NEW HOUSING POLICIES AND DISPERSAL

There are other roads from megalopolis. Malcolm E. Peabody[29] describes an alternative program which he directed experimentally in 1973, and which was later adopted as federal policy in lieu of public-housing projects. The idea is simply to pay a large portion of the rent of the urban poor. Such a policy has been tried before, but in the past it has discouraged ghetto residents from moving out of the

[28]J. S. Fuerst, "Hidden Successes of Public Housing," *Nation*, vol. 217, no. 16, pp. 593–596, November 12, 1973.
[29]Malcolm E. Peabody, "Housing Allowances," *New Republic*, pp. 20–23, March 9, 1974.

rental area stipulated by the government. What is new in the plan is to pay rent for any house within the fair-price limit prescribed within the geographical area, including suburbs as well as central cities. Where the plan was tried experimentally in Kansas City, Missouri, the results were highly favorable. Concentrated populations were considerably dispersed and recipients generally liked the system; and it was far less expensive than federal housing. Peabody admits, however, that it "cannot be used in tight markets where vacancy rates are less than five to six percent without some parallel program to expand production.[30] High interest rates are resulting in too little housing construction, so the outlook for the plan is favorable in only about half our big cities—certainly not in Washington, D.C., New York, or Philadelphia, where few housing vacancies exist. Nevertheless, such a policy is better than nothing.

Orderly development   Even within the great metropolitan area there are roads from megalopolis, for the word megalopolis implies not only size but ugly, confused, hodge-podge development. The regional governmental agencies, with orderly plans for development and redevelopment, could prevent much of what is most unpleasant about megalopolis, not only ugliness but also environmental wastefulness. Environmental impact studies can be made, mapping out the most favorable areas for housing, business, industry, parks, and playgrounds. Parks and greenbelts could be left within, making possible an internal road from megalopolis, as in the greenbelts of London.

   Barriers in the way of such orderly development are formidable. Nearly everyone in a local community can find arguments for more expansion in any direction— more jobs, more investment opportunities, more real estate sales, a better price for land. Such pressures to expand regardless of the environment can generally be

[30]*Ibid.*, p. 23.

stopped only by interurban commissions or by state planning, as in the Hawaiian Islands.

Reformers in the Department of Housing and Urban Development hope to promote more uniform building and zoning codes across the country and better legislation for acquiring land for orderly housing development and other uses. The problem of rising building costs, which has created the greatest housing shortage since World War II, might be solved by a rapid increase in factory production of houses—one of the few industries to have largely resisted assembly line techniques until very recently. If cheap and efficient houses and transportation are not provided, the future of American housing might be more in the direction of apartment living—a noticeable trend of the past ten years.[31]

There are cities in today's world that do not present a picture of disorganized sprawl, blight, and dangerous social-class division. Some are wealthy, exclusive developments, but some are cities of ordinary people—such cities as Stockholm, which has had city planning for 300 years.[32] In Stockholm many people are apartment dwellers, but the apartments are surrounded with gardens and playgrounds, are convenient to shopping, and have public transportation available. Many other European countries are concentrating on the development of garden suburbs, with careful planning and balance of human needs. No two nations can solve problems in precisely the same way, but it is good to know that countries whose per capita income is less than our own are able to build cities free of blight and with an atmosphere of well-being. The challenge of the cities is a challenge for architectural, ecological, and human engineering. The future of the cities depends upon new applications of science to solve some of the very problems that have resulted from a scientific-industrial age.

Get acquainted with the policies of your planning commission. Visit their office, attend their meetings, or invite a member to answer questions for the class. Is there a zoning adjustments board to hear complaints?

SUGGESTED READINGS

Bell, Gwen, and Jacqueline Tyrwhitt (eds.): *Human Identity in the Urban Environment*, Penguin Books, Inc., Baltimore, 1973. Readings in the human problems of cities, urban psychology, social class, and ethnic relationships. Contributors include Buckminster Fuller, Arnold Toynbee, and Margaret Mead.

Gans, Herbert J.: *The Urban Villagers*, The Free Press, New York, 1962. This book, referred to at length in the preceding pages, is excellent sociology, describing all aspects of an ethnic community and the social consequences of its dislocation.

Goodman, Jay S. (ed.): *Perspectives on Urban Politics*, Allyn and Bacon, Inc., Boston, 1970. Goodman's collection is essentially a study of political power and powerlessness in the city, including reviews of several community improvement projects, political attitude surveys, racial problems, and urban-suburban differences.

Jacobs, Jane: *The Economy of Cities*, Random House, Inc., New York, 1969. Jane Jacobs presents her theory explaining the growth of cities, how they become rich or poor, and why they become or fail to become centers of civic pride. As in her earlier *The Death and Life of*

[31]"The Great Housing Crisis," *Newsweek*, pp. 69, 71, 74, June 22, 1970.
[32]Goran Sidenbladh, "Stockholm: A Planned City," *Scientific American*, vol. 213, pp. 195–205, September 1965.

Great American Cities, she strongly supports the small entrepreneur as opposed to giant corporations or company towns.

The President's Commission on Civil Disorders, *Report of the National Advisory Commission on Civil Disorders* (The Kerner Report), Bantam Books, Inc., New York, 1968. The Commission Report, mainly a study of riots and racial problems, is also a study of the American city—housing, police policies, educational facilities, unemployment, segregation, inadequacy of recreational facilities and programs, and lack of political responsiveness.

Stewart, Murray (ed.): *The City: Problems of Planning*, Penguin Books, Inc., Baltimore, 1973. Readings in the problems of cities, especially urban planning, social and spacial structure of the community, power and influence in planning the city.

Von Eckardt, Wolf: *A Place to Live: The Crisis of the Cities*, Delacorte Press, Dell Publishing Co., Inc., New York, 1967. A well-illustrated book, emphasizing the need for beauty, expression, and individuality in building and planning. Von Eckardt's book has the merit of presenting visions of what the future could hold.

QUESTIONS

1 Today's city is referred to as a "vulnerable giant." What are some of the social, economic, and technical crises to which it is vulnerable?

2 Why are there often strong differences of opinion between upper- and lower-income groups about the desirability of urban renewal projects?

3 Evaluate the three possible choices for the ghetto described by the President's Commission on Civil Disorders.

4 What are the conclusions of studies cited about the effects of urban life on the personality? Do the conclusions apply to all types of urbanization or mainly to certain types of urban areas?

5 Discuss possible ways of dealing with the governmental, ecological, and human relations problems of the modern metropolis.

2
CHALLENGE TO EARTH, SEA, AND SKY

Various kinds of poisons are entering the bloodstream, and possibly the chromosomes, of many of the earth's species. Land, sea, and sky are threatened. What is the source of the threat? Our ancestors seem to have regarded the earth as a sacred being, not to be defiled or exploited. How did we come to think of ourselves as the masters of nature, capable of defying her laws? What are the contaminants? Are the contaminants confined to certain areas, or do they spread over the entire earth? Is the threat to the sea and the atmosphere real, or is the ecology talk something on the order of a fad? What are the policies of industry and government relative to ecological problems? Why has it taken us so long to become concerned about pollution?

There are certain products that produce pollution but are nevertheless greatly desired by the public. Automobiles are one of the best examples. Are there alternatives to the internal-combustion engine, or can a pollutant-free gasoline really be developed? Can we increase our use of electric power without threat to the environment? What about pesticides? Is there a way of controlling the insect pests that bedevil us without poisoning useful species and, perhaps, even ourselves? Can we, through modification of our habits and values and new uses of science, find solutions to the very problems that a headlong rush into science and technology have helped to cause? What policies are needed? How can the individual help?

38 An awareness of the environment, of ecology, of balance in nature, and of how human beings have upset that balance has dawned with dramatic suddenness upon the consciousness of urban-industrial societies. Naturalists have worried for decades about the disappearance of species, deforestation of the land, erosion of soil, and pollution of the rivers and lakes. But these have seemed to the public like rather isolated cases—a river here, a forest there, and the disappearance of condors or whooping cranes. Now the truth is beginning to dawn: all these problems are related. Homo sapiens is just one of the thousands of species that inhabit or have inhabited the planet. This species, too, could disappear in the very process of ecological destruction that has been embarked upon with such zest and pride. The most advanced civilizations are the source of greatest danger. As the biologist Barry Commoner[1] states the problem:

> We have come to a turning point in the human habitation of the earth. The environment is a complex, subtly balanced system, and it is this integrated whole which receives the impact of all the separate insults inflicted by pollution. Never before in the history of the planet has its thin life-supporting surface been subject to such diverse, novel, and potent agents. I believe that the cumulative effects of these pollutants, their interaction and amplification, can be fatal to the complex fabric of the biosphere. And, because man is, after all, a dependent part of this system, I believe that continued pollution of the earth, if unchecked, will eventually destroy the fitness of this planet as a place for human life.

THE HUMAN MASTER

Environmental difficulties are the result of both the accomplishments of humanity and the philosophy of mastery that has developed from those accomplishments. It may be that early hunters were humble creatures, fearful of the worlds around them, wondering in the course of hunting whether they would find a meal or be a meal. Today, whatever their anxieties, Homo sapiens see themselves as the master species. Even our religion is one of mastery over nature, and nature is largely omitted from philosophical thought patterns. With all our sophistication, we can barely imagine, much less enter, the sacred world of our forebears.

The sacred world Judging the cave painting and sacred objects of the remote past and studying living primitives, we can conclude that people once tended to see the world of nature as a sacred place, full of spirits that must be appeased and regarded with awe. Animals were hunted, but they were nevertheless thought of as kindred spirits, sometimes even as totemic ancestors. No Darwin was needed to convince primitives that they were part of the animal world. Although Homo sapiens were hunters and had to kill their prey, the prey deserved ritual respect. Even in recent years Eskimo have poured a libation to the spirit of the whale and the Ainu have treated a sacrificial bear with the highest ritual respect.

There has been not only a feeling of spiritual relationship between people and the animal world, but also between people and the land itself. The Cheyenne, for example, saw the relationship between themselves and the land as so close that an evil act on the part of a man or woman could contaminate the land and all its inhabitants. Elaborate rituals were necessary to purge the land of evil. The Pueblo Indians of the Southwest, gardeners rather than hunters, had the same feeling for the sacredness of the earth and sky. The duty of humanity was to live in harmony

[1]Barry Commoner, *Science and Survival*, The Viking Press, Inc., New York, 1966, p. 122.

with nature, never to disturb its sacred spirits in any way. The attitude is not too
different from that of Lao Tse in ancient China or, for that matter, of contemporary
peasant people in much of the world, eating the good products of the wholesome
earth and in return loving it and caring for it.

The mastery philosophy   It would not be easy to name any particular period in
history when the view of nature changed. Probably the change was gradual, as
people began to feel sure of their potential to produce an agricultural abundance.
The god of science replaced the gods of nature very slowly. Ancient Greece toyed
with science, and Renaissance thinkers reawakened the interest. In England and
America the early Puritan interest in science was stimulated by the pious thought
that the study of nature was the study of the handiwork of God. There was also a
strongly practical spirit about the Puritans, and this practical interest was pursued
by many who followed in their footsteps. Nature was seen no longer as something
to look upon with reverence but rather as a barrier to be overcome for human
good.

Nowhere was the dream of the conquest of nature pursued more diligently than in
America, where the problem of conquering a wilderness lay before our ancestors.
The wilderness was conquered, and out of the problems of such a conquest came
an intensification of the view of humankind as master. Other countries have
experienced such a sense of mastery—Russia pushing eastward across the
vastness of Siberia, and Canada gradually subduing its endless taiga and tundra.
Nowhere, however, was the success as spectacular as in the United States nor the
pace of development so rapid throughout the nineteenth century. The spirit of
conquest had served us well. It is true that we had run roughshod over magnificent
forests, and that the home of the deer and the bear, the beaver, and the quail and
pheasant had fallen under the ax, or been burned, eroded, gullied, and washed
away. A fantastic productivity had been achieved, a productivity of which we had
never before dreamed, but at the cost of alienating the human being from the world
of nature.

Our abandonment of nature is eloquently described by anthropologist Loren
Eiseley.[2] Urban man "drew back from nature. His animal confreres slunk soulless
from his presence." Man looked objectively upon the world, its animal life, and
finally upon himself: "Man's whole face grew distorted. One bulging eye—the
technological, scientific eye—was willing to count man, as well as nature's
creatures, in terms of megadeaths. Its objectivity had become so great as to
endanger its master, who was mining his own brains as ruthlessly as a seam of
coal."

In Eiseley's figure of speech, nature is our first world, and our second world is the
world of science, "drawn from our own brain." Our task today is to consciously
reenter the primary world of nature and preserve it for the sake of all terrestrial life.
With billions of people now taking the place of the scanty populations of old,
productivity can no longer be purchased at the price of the desecration of nature.
We can no longer see nature, as our forebears did, as a thousand sacred spirits to
be appeased by offerings and taboos, but we still long for the clear waters of
uncontaminated lakes and streams. Perhaps we would still thrill to the sight of the
stars if we could see them through the smog. City residents though we are, we
move to the green suburbs if we can afford it, rather that stay in the concrete city.

[2]Loren Eiseley, *The Invisible Pyramid*, Charles Scribner's Sons, New York, 1970, p. 144.

Invading the moon while earth's environment decays—the final irony of the mastery philosophy.

Along with changes in outlook, other changes must come about. A restoration of the environment may result in higher-priced goods, a squeeze in profits as industries convert to noncontaminating types of production, and much greater regulation to make sure that standards are enforced. There may even be conveniences that the public will have to learn to forego.

THE CONTAMINANTS

Reform movements have some of the qualitites of other forms of collective behavior, arriving with a degree of spontaneity and being much less predictable than established institutions. Enthusiasm waxes high at one time and wanes as new issues take the limelight. Around 1970 the movement for purification of the environment encountered an outpouring of enthusiasm. Its leaders excited many people with dire warnings of impending catastrophe and attracted attention and public support. The question is whether the movement can be transformed into action or whether procrastination and discouragement will set in, and the levels of pollution will continue their accelerating rise.

Some of the leaders of environmental movements have taken such strong positions as to make themselves subject to the charge of alarmism. Such is the case with Dr. Paul Ehrlich, probably the best-known lecturer and writer on the subject of increasing population. Perhaps an alarmist is exactly what we need. We are reminded of Sir Winston Churchill's famous quip about Clement Atlee—"a modest man, with much to be modest about." Ehrlich is an alarmed man, with much to be alarmed about.

In the summer of 1970 NBC produced a television program entitled "1985." The production sequence was similar to that of an old dramatization by Orson Welles of

an invasion from Mars, "War of the Worlds." Reporters from various cities
described the lack of oxygen and the high levels of carbon dioxide, ozone, lead, and other pollutants in the air. In several cases the reports were followed by coughing spells and then silence. The commentator explained during breaks in the broadcasts of news how the victory over nature had turned into a rout of the human species. Pesticides contaminated the land, and the insects for which they were intended built up immunities. The upper levels of the atmosphere were so filled with carbon dioxide and contaminants as to turn the earth into a hothouse. Finally, the last voice fell silent and the end of the human race was implied.

Probably the producers of the NBC program would admit some exaggeration of the time element. Even the most dour prophets of doom expect the world to die a more lingering death than was represented, but they do consider death a real possibility. An examination of the facts will indicate why.

Contaminating the earth It is hard to separate the land contaminants from those of the water and the air, since many of them spread from one element to the other. Some start primarily as pollutants of the land; these will be examined first. Every year the United States disposes of 55 billion cans, 26 billion bottles, 7 million automobiles, and 150 million tons of junk and garbage.[3] About one-third of the American population, not served by sewers, dumps sewage into cesspools and septic tanks that can contaminate underground sediments and groundwater. Another third of the population has sewers but dumps sewage without adequate treatment.

The disposal of wastes is vastly increased by the demands of industry for disposal of chemicals and slag. Although the United States makes up only 6 percent of the earth's population, it consumes 40 percent of the world's resources, and all this consumption results in more wastes for disposal. Because of the great number of "mechanical slaves" used in the United States, the total waste disposal, including all industry—extractive, manufacturing, and automotive—becomes the equivalent of the human wastes of 102.3 billion people.[4]

The amount of our solid wastes doubles every ten years, according to Richard D. Vaughn, Director of Solid Waste Management of the Environmental Health Service.[5] The national bill for disposal of solid wastes is presently $4.5 billion per year. Collection methods are unsatisfactory, with only 6 percent going to sanitary landfills and most of the remainder into unsanitary dumps, except for 8 to 10 percent converted into air pollution by incineration. Approximately 60 million tons of solid wastes are abandoned or dumped illegally per year in New York City alone, along with 50,000 automobiles abandoned on the streets.

The land absorbs pesticides in incredible amounts, along with lead, mercury, fluorides, and atomic wastes, although many of these materials become problems mainly as they are absorbed into water supplies. Atomic wastes, however, do not have to be absorbed in water to become dangerous. At Grand Junction, Colorado, and nearby communities, tailings (leftovers from the refining of uranium ore) were used as fill in the construction of at least 4,000 homes. Later tests by the Public

[3]Paul R. Ehrlich and Anne H. Ehrlich, *Population, Resources, Environment*, W. H. Freeman and Company, San Francisco, 1970, p. 128.
[4]James P. Lodge, Jr., of the National Center for Atmospheric Research, quoted by S. L. Benglesdorf, "U.S. Waste: A National Headache," *Los Angeles Times*, August 16, 1970, sec. F, p. 1.
[5]Associated Press, "Pollution Experts Say No 'Quick Fix' Exists," *Los Angeles Times*, September 19, 1970, part 1B, p. 2.

High productivity and rapid obsolescence of equipment contributes the waste equivalent of 100 billion people.

Health Service indicated that radiation levels had passed the danger mark in sixty-five of the homes, and residents are worried about all of them, fearing increased risk of cancer and leukemia for themselves and their children. In the opinion of Dr. Arthur Tamplin of the Atomic Energy Commission's (AEC) Lawrence Radiation Laboratory in California, there is no safety except in moving out of all the houses.

The trouble with an increase in the amount of atomic radiation is that no amount is safe, despite governmental decrees about how much is tolerable. The fallout created for America so far is only about 1 percent of the "normal" background radiation from cosmic rays, "but even this tiny increase may have been responsible for up to 12,000 genetically defective babies and 100,000 cases of leukemia and bone tumors."[6]

The use of atomic power plants, although they do not throw the same types of pollutants into the air as do coal or oil, can nevertheless lead to problems. The present policy is to store such pollutants in empty salt mines. At the rate of development of atomic energy, however, it is estimated that by the year 2000 a fleet of 3,000 or more 6-ton trucks will have to be in operation night and day to carry away the wastes.[7] The number of mines is not infinite, and to be safe, some of the wastes must be contained for thousands of years.

Atomic radiation sometimes becomes concentrated in peculiar ways and has often proved deceptive even to authorities. The AEC once dumped nuclear wastes into a river in the South, not expecting difficulty because of the likely dilution of the small amount involved. Later tests indicated no dangerous levels. Then it was found that oysters near the river's mouth glowed in the dark.[8]

[6]Ehrlich and Ehrlich, *op. cit.*, p. 137.
[7]*Ibid.*, p. 138.
[8]Paul R. Ehrlich, "Playboy Interview: A Candid Conversation with the Outspoken Population Biologist and Prophet of Environmental Apocalypse," *Playboy*, p. 66, August 1970.

Commoner is especially alarmed by the unpredictability of the results of scientific advances. For example, it was expected that strontium 90 (a product of atomic fallout strongly associated with bone cancer) would be fairly evenly distributed over the globe. The concentrations, however, turned out to be ten times as high in the North Temperate Zone as elsewhere—the very region where most of the world's population lives.

Another surprise occurred. Eskimo were found to have absorbed more S-90 than other people, in spite of lower fallout in their part of the world. The reason was that lichens, the main vegetable food of the area, live from the atmosphere, not from roots. From the air they absorb S-90 in large amounts; caribou eat the lichens, and Eskimo eat the caribou. In this case, as in so many others, the tests were made first, then the testers were surprised by the results.[9] Commoner likens modern science to the sorcerer's apprentice, unable to predict or control the forces it sets in motion.

The earth is also being contaminated in several other ways. Lands are destroyed simply by being paved over; cities develop in what were once the most productive lands. The earth is being contaminated by constant use of irrigation waters high in minerals that are deposited in the soil. California's Imperial Valley, watered by the Colorado River, is a good example. New methods of fertilization also contaminate the land. Nitrogen fertilizers give a quick crop yield but bypass the normal soil-building processes encouraged by organic fertilizers and leave the soil compacted. The only way to keep up production is to increase the use of nitrogen compounds, which in turn call for yet heavier use. In Commoner's words, the farmer is "hooked" on nitrates.[10] The time may come when nitrates will no longer suffice and the slow soil-building process will have to be started again. Some of the world's most productive lands could become lands of famine.

Farmers and others can become just as badly "hooked" on pesticides as on nitrates, having to develop more and stronger types as insect pests develop immunity to the ones in use. The problem of pesticides, however, is more a problem of pollution of waters than of the earth.

The waters and the sea Along the coast of southern California have lived large numbers of brown pelicans—large, comical looking sea birds with huge beaks. Generations of California children have watched the ungainly birds become airborne, raising their heavy bodies into the wind, or suddenly diving for fish with a speed and agility out of keeping with their clumsy appearance. Now, we are told, the pelicans of the Channel Islands off the coast of Santa Barbara are doomed. The reason is that large amounts of DDT, intended to kill insects, have been washed from fields and crops into streams that lead to the ocean and have been absorbed in the ocean by the plankton on which sea life feeds. Fish have eaten the plankton, and pelicans have eaten the fish, with the result that female pelicans lay soft-shelled eggs, which break under the mother's weight. In 1970 only 1 pelican was hatched from a population of 552 mating pairs on Anacapa Island. Although the use of DDT has nearly ceased, its persistence in the water and in the fish the pelicans eat is such that the species continues to decline.

If this were merely an essay on pelicans, it could easily be dismissed as pure sentimentality, but it is more than a matter of pelicans. Species are part of a natural chain, and the same chain that links the pelicans to pesticides sprayed on

[9]Commoner, *op. cit.*, p. 16.
[10]Quoted in Ehrlich, *op. cit.*, pp. 85–86.

agricultural crops extends its links in another direction straight to the dinner tables of humans. On land, the pesticides on the plants are eaten by cattle, which are in turn eaten by people. The higher up the alimentary chain, the greater the concentration of pesticides. Cow's milk is contaminated to some degree; the human mother's milk is worse. Psychologists have stressed the emotional benefits of breast feeding infants; now chemists must say "beware!"

The oceans that receive poisons from the land are the land's greatest benefactor. Although land plants give forth oxygen to replenish the air, 70 percent of the world's oxygen is given off by the plankton of the sea. Even the plankton is being killed in coastal areas and its restorative work terminated. The blanket of oxygen-containing air that envelops the earth is extremely vast, although no longer pure, so that the diminished ability of the sea to restore oxygen will not be an acute problem until well into the future. There are, however, other injuries to the sea. The great majority of marine life has concentrated near estuaries and harbors, and some of these are being so polluted as to be areas of marine death. Such is the case with New York Harbor and the ocean for hundreds of square miles around.

There are other contaminants in the sea. In 1969, undersea oil wells in the Santa Barbara Channel broke out of control and spread an oil slick over hundreds of miles of water. Later the same phenomenon occurred in the Gulf of Mexico. In 1967 the ship *Torrey Canyon* sank off the coast of England, filling the waters with 166,000 tons of oil. In 1969 the *Marpessa*, the *Mactam*, and the *King Haakon VII* all exploded mysteriously and sank off the coast of Africa, pouring their black cargo into the ocean. The damage to sea life is incalculable. In one case 170,000 gallons of oil from a wrecked tanker killed 93 percent of marine life in the area of the wreck, and ten months later the area was still not repopulated. Little is known of the deeper areas, but Howard Sanders of the Massachusetts Oceanographic Institute believes that pollution at great depths is even more disastrous than surface pollution and does more damage to marine-life food chains.[11]

The size of oil tankers increases year by year because profits can be increased and costs reduced by massive shipments. The present supertankers range in size from 200,000 to nearly 500,000 tons, and there are plans for building tankers of 1 million tons' displacement. (By contrast, the big *Missouri* class of battleships—the biggest American battleships ever built—displaced 57,500 tons.) According to Canadian writer Noël Mostert,[12] the supertankers on their voyages around South Africa spill as much as 5 million tons of oil into the sea each year by leakage, collision, and dumping. The oil is carried southward to the Antarctic, where it threatens the existence of penguins, walrus, seals, and whales. One great collision of the *Taxanit* and the *Oswego Guardian* resulted in an oil slick 65 miles long. As the shipments from the Arabic world and the size of supertankers increase, the dangers increase. Small wonder that when Thor Heyerdahl first tried to cross the Atlantic by papyrus raft, he found nearly all its surface filthy with oil and other pollution.

Danger also mounts as offshore drilling increases. Fuel shortages are leading to

[11]"Warning Issued on Offshore Oil Drilling," *Bakersfield Californian*, August 14, 1970, p. 6.
[12]Noël Mostert, *Supership*, Alfred A. Knopf, Inc., New York, 1974.

offshore drilling in many parts of the world. Although techniques have improved, they do not preclude the possibility of further oil spills. Thus we are faced with the unhappy prospect of weighing energy needs against environmental needs. Since environmental protection brings no immediate profits but supplying energy brings high profits, the environment stands to suffer.

The oceans seem to be regarded as the universal sewer. Each year the United States alone dumps 48.2 million tons of waste into them. Conservationists here and abroad were horrified in the summer of 1970 when the Army decided to dump 3,000 tons of obsolete nerve gas into the ocean near the Bahamas, over the strong protests of Great Britain. Army experts assured the world that even if the gas leaked out of its containers, chemical reaction with salt water would destroy it within a day or two. The public has become a little uncertain about official assurances, however, and there was not even any assurance as to what might happen to sea life during those days. Fish live as deep as the 16,000-foot trench into which the gas was dumped. It is believed that some fish make seasonal migrations from deep to shallow waters. We do not know for sure that poisons laid to rest in the oceans will never reappear.[13]

Jacques-Yves Cousteau,[14] the greatest of underwater explorers, has traveled 155,000 miles over and under the sea during his long career in oceanography. Recently he summarized what he has seen; "The oceans are in danger of dying. The pollution is general." Cousteau continued, "Fish have diminished by 40 percent in 20 years." Besides decrying the use of the oceans as the great refuse dumps of the earth, Cousteau deplored modern fishing techniques—electric shocks to force shrimp from their holes, destruction of eggs and larvae, and the search for marine species in their once impenetrable retreats.

Such unofficial reports as those of Thor Heyerdahl and Jacques Cousteau were officially confirmed by government scientisits in 1973.[15] The National Oceanic and Atmospheric Administration reported finding globs of oil and bits of plastic along the Atlantic from Cape Cod to the Caribbean. Half the East Coast area from Massachusetts to Florida was found to be badly contaminated, and from 80 to 90 percent of the Caribbean and Gulf of Mexico. More than half the plankton collected from the surface of the water were oil-contaminated. Plankton are the minute forms of life that constitute the first link in the long chain of oceanic life, the ultimate source of food. Not only that, but the plankton of the ocean take in carbon dioxide and give off oxygen in the same manner as do land plants. Since their abundance is much greater than that of land plants, the ocean's microscopic organisms are our largest supply of oxygen. Their destruction could mean ultimate suffocation for land animals, including human beings.

The beautiful blue Mediterranean Sea is also becoming increasingly polluted, largely by human and industrial wastes from growing cities along its shores. A Marine Pollution Conference was called for Barcelona in January 1975 to try to reach international agreements to prevent pollution. The Mediterranean is regarded as the world's most threatened sea.[16]

---

[13]Rudy Abramson, "Environmental Council Report to Urge Ban on Ocean Dumping," *Los Angeles Times*, August 17, 1970, part I, p. 1.
[14]"The Dying Oceans," *Time*, vol. 96, p. 64, September 28, 1970.
[15]Associated Press dispatch, "Massive Amounts of Oil and Plastic Found Fouling Sea off East Coast," *Los Angeles Times*, February 13, 1973, part I, p. 5.
[16]Don Shannon, "Man at Environmental Crunch Point, U.N. Told," *Los Angeles Times*, November 4, 1974, part I, p. 14.

It is not just the oceans that are being poisoned, but streams and lakes as well. Lake Erie and the Hudson River are virtually beyond recovery. Pesticides, detergents (some containing arsenic), mercury, lead, fluorides, nitrogen compounds, phosphates, and various other agricultural and industrial wastes enter the streams and filter down into groundwater reservoirs. According to the United States Public Health Service, several million Americans are drinking water that is potentially hazardous to the health. Especially in systems serving communities of 100,000 or less, samples are often unsatisfactory, containing fecal bacteria, lead, copper, iron, manganese, nitrate, and in some cases, arsenic.[17]

One of the most recent hazards to attract attention in the United States (although Sweden has been aware of its dangers for ten years and Japan for fifteen years) is mercury poisoning in water and fish. Mercury-containing sludge from factories is dumped into streams and lakes, and it is now suspected that fish from such waters are unsafe for human consumption. Japan has experienced 100 deaths from eating of mercury-poisoned fish; Sweden forbids the sale of fish from certain lakes that might be contaminated. Lake St. Clair in Canada is heavily contaminated, and so are Lake Erie and the Detroit River. For years people have been eating fish from such sources, and possibly undergoing mild forms of mercury poisoning—muscle tremors, depression, nervousness, and nausea.[18]

In the spring of 1971 the Food and Drug Administration took drastic action by withdrawing from the market the most contaminated type of fish commonly eaten by the American public—swordfish. For reasons only partly understood, some types of marine life absorb much more mercury than others.[19]

Contaminating the sky It is air pollution that is most likely to concern the average citizen, especially the urbanite. Although the word "smog" was coined by an English physician in 1905 and was long associated primarily with Los Angeles, it is now a phenomenon of virtually all cities, so much so that some doctors believe no urbanite past the age of twelve has entirely healthy lungs. Air pollution is one possible reason why life expectancy is no longer rising for the American male and rising very little for the American female. As mentioned in Chapter 1, air pollution is a problem that spills over the jurisdictional boundaries of cities; in fact, it crosses national boundaries and mountains and oceans. All the world shares a common sea of air that constantly circulates, and the smog of one locality, considerably diluted, is carried on to other parts of the globe. Air pollution even reaches the upper levels of the atmosphere and may be reducing penetration of the sun's rays. Its effects on weather are not clear, but the possibilities are worrisome. The words of Omar Khayyam take on a new significance:

And that inverted bowl they call the sky,
Whereunder crawling, coop'd, we live and die. . . .

We are cooped up under the same sky, and we can all suffer a common fate if it is polluted to the point that it can no longer support life. A nightmare for the future is the development of more and more supersonic transport planes, operating at altitudes of 50,000 to 70,000 feet. Since such heights are in the stratosphere— above the circulating envelope of air that surrounds the earth—water, carbon

[17]Rudy Abramson, "Millions Drink Contaminated Water," *Los Angeles Times*, August 18, 1970, part I, pp. 1, 13.
[18]Daniel Swedling, "And Now Mercury," *New Republic*, pp. 17–18, August 1, 1970.
[19]Leonard J. Goldwater, "Mercury in the Environment," *Scientific American*, vol. 224, pp. 15–21, May 1971.

Smog, a menacing by-product of the motoring way of life and a growing cause of death in all cities. Scene of East Los Angeles.

dioxide, and particulates could remain there almost indefinitely, forming a permanent cloud cover at certain altitudes. Some meteorologists believe that the contamination of the upper atmosphere could create a "greenhouse" effect, locking in heat and raising the earth's temperatures. We may be saved from very many supersonics, not because of environment but because of poor economic payoff.

In addition to supersonics, another threat to the upper atmosphere may be developing. A number of scientists are convinced that the gases released from aerosol sprays find their way to the upper atmosphere where they begin to destroy the ozone layer. The result could be an increase in ultraviolet radiation on the earth's surface, increasing risks of skin cancer, damaging crops, and possibly disturbing weather patterns.

Air pollution has existed in cities for many years. As long ago as 1661 John Evelyn complained that the "aer and smoak" over London made it resemble the "suburbs of Hell" rather than a civilized city. Pollution in those days came largely from coal and industry. The first American cities to take action to clean the air were also primarily concerned with coal and industrial smoke—St. Louis and Pittsburgh.

In Los Angeles, however, another type of pollution was developing, characterized by nitrogen oxides and unburned hydrocarbons and ozone, along with high levels of carbon dioxide. Los Angeles, with an abundance of sunlight, had just the catalyst for changing hydrocarbons into a complex chain of chemicals, including poisonous and plant-damaging ozone, and this city had the vast amounts of automobile travel to produce more than its share of hydrocarbons.[20] Los Angeles also is so situated as to make a perfect smog trap, with mountains to the north and east preventing the escape of air, and with other conditions that cause frequent temperature inversions, especially in the summer.

For a long time the smog conditions of Los Angeles were thought of as a subject of merriment for comedians and the boosters of rival cities, but now Los Angeles has worldwide company in her smog problem. Death rates rise during smog alerts in most of the major cities of the world. In Tokyo people sometimes wear gauze over their faces to keep out the dirt or even resort to gas masks. In Los Angeles, 10,000 people per year are warned by their doctors to move away, and children are kept from strenuous play and exercise on smog alert days because of oxygen shortage. New York City produces almost two pounds of soot and noxious gases per person per day. A medical examiner commented regarding lung cases, "On the autopsy table it's unmistakable; the person who spent his life in the Adirondacks has pink lungs. The city dweller's are black as coal.[21] Fortunately for New York, the air mass is seldom trapped as it is in Los Angeles, and temperature inversions are rare. There have been days, however, when stagnant air has resulted in sharp increases in deaths.

In one respect pollution is the same all over the world, whether in city or isolated village: the carbon dioxide level is constantly on the increase. Between 1860 and 1960 the carbon dioxide content of the air increased by 14 percent. It has been increasing more rapidly since 1960.[22]

> **Debate in class what to do about some of the issues in which environmental protection and energy needs conflict with one another—offshore drilling, strip mining of coal, and the Alaska oil pipeline, for example.**

THE CONTAMINATORS

All living creatures exert their influence on the environment, breathing air, eating the food they need, and leaving their wastes. Until the human race discovered the use of fire it was no worse a contaminator than any other animal of its size and, even with the first use of fire, it was no real menace. The development of agriculture increased our ability to contaminate, to burn and deforest the land, and to deplete the soil; but it was the industrial revolution that made human intervention a real menace. With factories came smoke and soot, mines and slag piles, sump holes, industrial wastes in waters, and eventually oil slicks, exhaust fumes, smog, detergents, lead, mercury, radioactivity, poison gases, and other lethal agents.

Obviously some segments of the human race have become worse polluters than others. The few remaining unwashed Australian aborigines are, ironically, the purest in respect to environmental pollution, and no one is dirtier than wealthy, daily bathed Americans with their high-powered, premium-fuel cars, motorboats, thousands of throwaway containers, indestructible plastics, and generally sterile surroundings—rendered so by their deadly powders and sprays.

There is no question that the average citizen is one of the polluters, and various environmental organizations and women's groups have suggested rules for

[20]A. J. Haagen-Smit, "The Control of Air Pollution," *Scientific American*, vol. 210, pp. 31–38, January 1964.
[21]John C. Esposito, *Vanishing Air*, Grossman Publishers, New York, 1970, p. 204.
[22]Commoner, *op. cit.*, p. 10.

improvement—reducing miles driven, avoiding such things as overpackaging, too many plastics, throwaway bottles, etc. At the same time, blaming the average citizen has a certain danger: it can result in mere preaching, moralizing, and wishing everyone would be good. Sociology usually looks upon change from a different perspective, that of institutional change through law and regulation. If we wait for over 200 million people to solemnly resolve to be "righteous" about environmental matters, we may have to wait until the earth is completely destroyed. The institutional approach requires merely winning over a determined segment of the public that will keep up the pressure on government and industry until proper laws are instituted. Neither approach is easy, but the latter is more apt to succeed than the former. Presently a majority of people seem to be concerned about the environment, but some are not. A Harris poll in 1970 showed 2 percent of the people suggesting that the first way to save money in government would be to cut out all expenses on cleaning up the environment. In the spring of 1974, with gasoline in short supply, a few cars had bumper stickers reading, "No gas, thanks to environmentalists." Increasing pressure began to arise, urging a relaxation of environmental controls in the interests of speedy development of abundant fuel supply and even relaxation of smog-control standards for automobiles. Meanwhile, the oil companies intensified their advertising effort to convince the public that they were the best friends the environment has ever known.

Governmental confusion　As air and water pollution problems become more complex, new agencies become necessary for handling the problems. Intercity, intercounty, and interstate cooperation is needed but hard to achieve, partly because of intergovernmental jealousy. On the federal level, a similar type of governmental paralysis takes place, according to Theodore H. White.[23] Various presidents have created a confusion of agencies for handling such previous environmental problems as reforestation, water conservation, and soil depletion, but no agency for the general supervision of the environmental efforts of today. As the present environmental crisis developed, almost nothing was done. "Cities draped their towers in acrid shawls of smog, lakes bobbed with organic sewage and plastic refuse . . . [and] scientists packaged chemicals in foods and poisons in spray cans."[24]

When the president tried to establish a master plan, he found five departments and forty-four major agencies involved in the "who has the environment?" game. The antirat program alone is handled by the Fish and Wildlife Service; Agricultural Research; Health, Education and Welfare; Office of Economic Opportunity; and six other agencies. Other problems are tied to no agencies whatever. For thirty years government scientists watched the biological death of Lake Erie, but no branch of government was responsible and none responded. In attempting improvement, various government agencies are found to be warring on each other, and congressional committees representing farm, business, and manufacturing interests are pulled in different directions. Several new agencies are now in operation under an Environmental Protection Agency with powers torn from existing departments.

The problems of the NAPCA　At present the National Air Pollution Control Administration in the Department of Health, Education and Welfare (HEW) is

---

[23]Theodore White, "How Did We Get from Here to There?" *Life*, vol. 68, pp. 36–40, June 26, 1970.
[24]*Ibid.*, p. 37.

charged with federal responsibility for air pollution control. The job is a vast one that calls for control of the entire auto and petroleum industries, the development of electric power (except hydroelectric), the burning of coal, and most activities of the chemical and refining industries. The control problem properly belongs to HEW, because air pollution has become a major threat to health. Besides causing rising death rates from respiratory diseases, pollution is now suspected for producing mutagenic effects, possibly causing genetic damage. Increase in particulate matter is associated with increase in the amount of stomach cancer, and carbon monoxide levels are high enough to account for some types of anemia and to put greater strain on the heart.[25] Emphysema, the nation's fastest-growing cause of death, is aggravated by smog and sulfur dioxide. Some doctors have even found evidence of mental damage from heavy concentrations of lead and carbon monoxide in the air.[26]

DELAY IN THE AUTOMOBILE INDUSTRY

It is estimated that 60 percent of all air pollution results from the internal-combustion engine to which the auto industry is firmly committed. John Esposito, a member of Ralph Nader's investigative group on consumer affairs describes the response of the auto industry to the need for cleaning the air as "twenty years in low gear." Alternatives to the internal-combustion engine have received very little consideration, partly because of a close relationship between autos and the petroleum industry. Henry Ford II is quoted as saying of the oil and auto industries, "Like flowers and bees, where you find one the other is sure to be near."[27]

In the 1950s, auto makers maintained that smog was not a serious problem, that the vapors dissipated too rapidly to do any damage. In the next few years, they tried to picture smog as something confined to Los Angeles. Eventually suits and government actions began to take effect and smog-control devices were required. The auto companies had long said there was no way to make such devices, so according to S. Smith Griswold of the Los Angeles Air Pollution Control Board, "We got independent companies to design emission control devices and ordered auto makers to put them on their cars. Then we discovered the auto makers *had* the devices, and when they were forced to, they put them on."[28]

Government action has consisted of trying to enforce a series of deadlines for producing more effective antismog devices and for installing them on each year's new models and then on previous models still in operation. Unleaded gasoline will eventually get much of the more dangerous of all exhaust contaminants out of the air. However, there are two remaining problems of such gravity that it would be rash to consider air pollution from autos on the way to solution. So far the antismog standards are very poorly enforced. Devices are installed on new cars, but the states have no system of regular inspection to see whether they are working properly. The other problem is that even with general compliance with emission standards, the emissions per car will fall by about 60 percent by the early 1980s; but in the meantime, if present driving trends continue (a little problematical in view of fuel problems), there will be twice as many autos on the road.[29]

[25]Esposito, *op. cit.*, pp. 11–15.
[26]Victor Boesen and Wayne Sage, "Smog in Your Head," *Human Behavior*, February 1973.
[27]Esposito, *op. cit.*, p. 35.
[28]Quoted in Ronald A. Buel, *Dead End: The Automobile in Mass Transportation*, Penguin Books, Inc., Baltimore, 1972, pp. 65–66.
[29]*Ibid.*, p. 66.

The internal-combustion engine depends upon massive consumption of petroleum, a fossil fuel deposited in the earth millions of years ago. There is endless debate about how long the oil reserves of the world will last at present rates of consumption, but there is no question that the use of petroleum involves drawing on a bank account that cannot be renewed. Furthermore, the oil reserves are unevenly distributed, with the Arabic countries being almost the only region of great surpluses. If oil continues to be burned in massive amounts for driving cars and also for generating electricity, our need for Arabic oil will increase. We have already had a foretaste of the problems of depending on foreign supplies of vitally needed resources. Oil became an instrument of international diplomacy in the spring of 1974, when the Arabs cut off supplies to countries that were too favorable to Israel. The Arabic countries have become increasingly aware of the potential power of oil in international diplomacy. They also may be planning an industrial future of their own based upon chemicals to be developed from their abundant oil reserves.[30] Such developments could make them largely independent of foreign markets for their oil, further increasing their power in world affairs. Their policies might become a model for other developing nations with raw materials that the industrial nations require.

Present policies in the United States call for an increased use of coal to meet our energy needs. Coal has the distinction of being an unusually dirty fuel, emitting large amounts of sulfur dioxide that damages lungs and corrodes buildings. A Cornell medical study concludes that several thousand people die each year as a consequence of pollution from coal and thousands more have their health impaired.[31] Over 50,000 miners are currently disabled from black lung. Both these health problems can be solved, but only at a high cost.

Present law calls for cleaning up coal emissions by means of a device called a stack gas scrubber that uses pulverized lime to remove the sulfur dioxide. Coal companies complain that the device is not very effective and will result in enough sludge to present another environmental problem. One company claims that the sludge from one large utility system would cover 10 square miles of land 5 feet deep within a year.[32] In all likelihood the statement is an exaggeration, since industries have a record of resisting governmental regulations with as loud cries as possible. There is no doubt, though, that the coal industry faces serious problems in trying to meet nonpolluting standards.

Since about 55 percent of the generating capacity of the United States depends on coal, the amounts required are enormous. The cheapest way to keep up with the demand is to increase the amount of strip-mining in the Western states, a process now underway. Some of the coal is also relatively low in sulfur dioxide. The serious problem is that strip-mining results in environmental destruction. It would probably cost about $10,000 per acre to restore the stripped land.[33] Unless the government is much more diligent than usual, there will be vast acres of environmental ruin as a result of strip mining.

Another alternative—and one that we may be forced into because the Western reserves could be exhausted by the end of the century—is more deep mining. John McCormick of the Environmental Policy Center estimates that by digging much

[30]Jim Muir, "The Arabs' Master Plan for Oil," *Atlas World Press Review*, vol. 21, no. 3, pp. 22–23, June 1974.
[31]David J. Rose, "Energy Policy in the United States," *Scientific American*, vol. 230, no. 1, pp. 24–25, January 1974.
[32]"Environment: the Scrubber Flap," *Newsweek*, pp. 84–85, June 17, 1974.
[33]Rose, *op. cit.*, p. 27.

deeper than at present, the Appalachian mining concerns could unearth all the coal we need, and coal of lower sulfur content than that produced at higher levels.[34] Such a solution, though, would require heavy investment in health and safety equipment; otherwise, the mines could be a disaster area of cave-ins and black lung.

Greater difficulty in obtaining oil and other natural resources leads to the conclusion that goods of the future can be produced only at much higher costs than now. One of the alternatives to coal and oil is that of nuclear power, but this alternative is also fraught with problems.

THE NUCLEAR ALTERNATIVE

At present the major thrust of government encouragement of energy development is in the field of nuclear energy. Nuclear power now accounts for about 2 percent of our energy needs. By 1990 nuclear power is expected to fill 22 percent of our needs.[35]

Despite all the arguments from the Atomic Energy Commission, doubts about the safety of nuclear reactors linger in the minds of many people. The fuel for a reactor consists of tiny pellets of uranium 235, each of which generates more energy than a ton of coal. After the energy source is used, it cannot simply be dumped out as can slag from a coal furnace. The heat is so intense that some authorities, including the Union of Concerned Scientists and Paul Ehrlich, consider safeguards insufficient. They think it is possible for an accident to occur, causing the central core to escape through a meltdown and release radioactive debris.[36] Such an accident has not occurred, although there was leakage of nuclear waste from a plant in the state of Washington in 1973. The other worrisome problem is that of storing atomic wastes, some of which remain contaminating for thousands of years. At present, most core wastes are being stored in concrete tanks while a study is being made of their ultimate disposal. Even if buried in mines or in deep trenches of the ocean, there is a possibility that they could be brought to the surface by some convulsion of nature. The AEC seems convinced of the safety of atomic development, and the same conclusions have apparently been reached in many other countries with nuclear power developments. Theodore B. Taylor,[37] a nuclear physicist, assures us that the radiation level in areas near a nuclear plant is less than 1 percent of the amount of radiation always present in the atmosphere. He sees a more serious problem in the possibility of fissionable materials being "secretly diverted from parts of nuclear-fuel cycles and used for making nuclear explosives for destructive purposes."[38] Now that nuclear power plants are in the hands of a large number of governments, the problem of keeping active materials from the hands of subversives or terrorist groups is outside the control of the United States. The problem of nuclear safety is worldwide and very complex. The use of fission energy is safe, says Hannes Alfven, Swedish Nobel Prize-winning physicist, only if all people in charge are thoroughly competent, and "if there is no sabotage, no hijacking of transports, if no reactor fuel processing plant or waste repository anywhere in the

---

[34]"Shortchanging the Environment," *New Republic*, p. 6, March 9, 1973.
[35]"The Uranium Problem," *Scientific American*, vol. 230, no. 1, p. 50, January 1974.
[36]Ralph E. Lapp, "Nuclear Power and Safety," *New Republic*, pp. 17–19, April 28, 1973.
[37]Theodore B. Taylor and Charles C. Humpstone, *The Restoration of the Earth*, Harper & Row, Publishers, Incorporated, New York, 1973, p. 67.
[38]*Ibid.*, p. 69.

world is situated in a region of riots or guerrilla activity, and no revolution or war . . . takes place."[39] Such requirements are hard to meet. Are there any better possibilities for an adequate supply of fuel?

What is your regional agency for environmental problems? Who selects the staff? What powers does it have over industry and the public? Information should be available at the county courthouse.

NONPOLLUTING ENERGY SOURCES

Hydroelectric power is nonpolluting, but nearly all available power is already developed. A newer energy source is geothermal heat. At present, several generators are being run by steam escaping from fumaroles in the earth, the oldest being in Calistoga County, California. For many years Iceland has used hotsprings and natural steam geysers for much of its energy and heat. Considerable exploring of geothermal sites is presently being done, and new sources are being developed. However, geothermal energy is limited now to areas of fairly active vulcanism. The only possibility for increasing this source of energy enough to make it a major contributor to our energy needs would be to find some means of boring deep into the earth to create artificial fumaroles or other heat releases, which would obviously be very expensive, if at all feasible.[40]

Wind power is another possibility. Wind was used widely for pumping water before the age of internal-combustion engines and electric energy. The full exploitation of wind power would call for extremely high windmills built at regular intervals and at great expense. Nevertheless, some authorities believe that wind power could eventually be used to generate as much as 20 percent of our power needs.[41]

By far the most important potential source of energy is the sun, which supplies 167,000 times more energy than the world consumes; but its energy is dispersed and hard to store. For a number of years a few people have managed to heat their houses with solar energy, usually using black metal collectors on the roof to heat circulating water that is eventually stored in water tanks. Solar heaters for household water supply are now used in Japan, Australia, the United States, and the U.S.S.R. Part of the useful fallout of our space technology has been the development of solar batteries capable of storing sun power. It will probably be possible to develop solar energy on a vast scale in the future, but large areas of desert territory will be necessary. Nearly 100 square miles are needed to gather enough sun energy for a large plant with a capacity of 1 million kilowatts. Glaser estimates that a piece of desert land 150 miles square could collect enough solar energy to supply the entire needs of the United States.[42] Much more speculative is a plan for gathering solar energy in a large satellite station, 36,000 kilometers above the earth, which would direct microwave energy to a receiving antenna on earth to be converted back to electricity. Much time, effort, and money will be needed to devise methods of developing large amounts of energy directly from

[39]Quoted in Donald P. Geesaman and Dean A. Abrahamson, "The Dilemma of Fission Power," *Bulletin of the Atomic Scientists*, vol. 30, p. 39, September 1974.
[40]Rose, *op. cit.*, p. 23.
[41]Peter E. Glaser, "Power from the Sun," *UNESCO Courier*, pp. 16–21, January 1974.
[42]Glaser, *op. cit.*, p. 16.

wind and sun, but such possibilities are our best hope that we will not always pollute our atmosphere and waste irreplaceable fossil fuels.

OTHER REMEDIES

In addition to the development of nonpolluting sources of energy, there are other possibilities for reducing pollution, whether in auto emissions or waste materials or pesticides.

Auto emissions could be reduced greatly by means of several alternatives. The most drastic would be simply cutting down on the use of cars, which may eventually be necessary. One of the most valid reasons why people do not cut down on car use, though, is that our cities have grown into such dispersed patterns that autos are highly desirable. It has been the automobile that has made possible the type of urban sprawl discussed in the previous chapter; but urban sprawl, in turn, has made automobiles a necessity. A future redesigning of cities might alleviate the problem. Meanwhile, the development of good, efficient, convenient public transportation systems would make it possible for far more people to leave their cars at home when they go to work.

Another promising alternative regarding transportation, and one that has been largely ignored because of the commitment of the auto industry to the internal-combustion engine, is that of developing another type of automobile. Electric cars, steam cars, and gas-turbine engines are all in use on a small scale. All of them have their problems, but the problems are not insurmountable. Despite the limitations of their batteries, electric cars are perfectly practical for city driving. At present none of the three alternative types of automobiles can be produced quickly and cheaply and made to run at the speeds and with the acceleration the public has come to consider necessary. But probably the main reason is that other types of autos have not been worked on and improved over the years. Many authorities expect eventually to find an alternative to the internal-combustion engine.

Waste   For many of the problems of waste materials mentioned previously, there are solutions. Sewage treatment will have to be greatly improved, and at a higher cost than at present. Garbage removal could be greatly improved by more sanitary landfills, but this would not constitute an adequate solution. More effort must be made to reduce the amount of garbage and trash by making more materials of easily degradable substances and by recycling. The vast piles of debris left from autos, washers, and other household appliances could be salvaged for reuse. Presently the price of such scrap materials is not sufficient to encourage their collection, a problem that might have to be solved by a certain amount of subsidization. In poorer countries nothing of the kind goes to waste.

Pesticides   Among the most serious problems are agricultural fertilizers and pesticides. Robert van den Bosch[43] reports that after years of use of pesticides, we have more species of insect pests than ever before and that over 200 of these have developed a resistance to chemicals. The situation reminds one of a comment by Ehrlich to the effect that human beings need not worry about being eliminated from the earth. A much more able and adaptable creature is ready to take over—the cockroach!

[43]Robert van den Bosch, "The Insects are Beating Us," *California Monthly*, pp. 23–27, April 1970.

One trouble in the area of pesticides is that chemical agents are developed by people in the agriculture business, people who are interested only in the immediate control of certain insect pests and not in the total picture of ecology. Their salespersons are out to sell the product, not to worry about the environment. The best product from the commercial point of view is one with wide applicability to a number of pests, saving both time and money. DDT was once the answer to everyone's need. Now that its lethal and lingering effects are known, it is being replaced by organophosphates which, van den Bosch says, are even more lethal, although shortlived. The difficulty is that they kill too wide a range of insects. Often, too there is rapid resurgence of the insect pests, with evolutionary mutations making them immune to the spray.

What you can do:
Walk or ride a bicycle
Cut down on wastes
Return items that can be recycled
Avoid pesticides as much as possible
Avoid use of spray cans
Avoid unnecessary electrical appliances
Study voting records of local politicians
Join environmental organizations, such as Friends of the Earth, 30 E. 42d St., New York, N.Y., 10017.

The insect problem is not easy to solve with chemicals; it will require a sophisticated, discrete approach to each type of pest—a more expensive method than that used today. Pest-control programs must be supervised by entomologists, not salespeople. In some cases, natural enemies can be used against insect pests, or it is possible to develop entirely sterile males so that the pest population eventually dies out.

Similar steps will probably have to be taken to restore the fertility of the soil and to avoid too complete a dependence on chemical fertilizers. Indications are that the ingenuity of modern science can rise to the task of ensuring agricultural production, provided world population does not increase to such a level as to make all efforts futile.

Implementing scientific knowledge   Whether scientific knowledge will be applied is, of course, heavily dependent upon political decisions. Many impressive political speeches are being made on the subject of environment, but it must not be assumed that political speeches and committee reports are automatically translated into action. Some local and state governments have made a creditable record, and others have done nothing. There is no doubt that at present pollution levels are continuing to rise.

Regardless of how many laws and enforcement agencies there are, much will depend upon whether strong pressures are brought upon governments and whether determined men hold office on environmental boards. Too often polluters rather than environmentalists are appointed to local control boards.

The public must always beware of false promises or statements to the effect that "at last we have pollution on the run."[44] The struggle will be long and difficult and, in a sense, can never be won entirely. As solutions to existing problems are found, new problems will arise. There is always the danger that air pollutant X will be eliminated only by increasing air pollutant Y.

A number of politicians are sincerely interested in the environment, but even the best are constantly being approached by pressure groups. There is always a temptation to yield to the side that promises the most in votes and campaign contributions. The pressures, however, will be on the side of the environment if millions of Americans join conservationist and environmentalist groups, keeping themselves informed and making their voices heard at the centers of political power.

SUGGESTED READINGS

Benarde, Melvin A.: *Our Precarious Habitat*, W. W. Norton & Co., Inc., New York, 1973. Discusses potential threats to health and quality of life resulting from misuse of our environment. Good coverage of chemicals in our foods, pesticides, and many health-related problems.

Commoner, Barry: *The Closing Circle*, Alfred A. Knopf, Inc., New York, 1971. This book effectively condemns technology for what it has done to our ecology and our chance of survival. Commoner, one of the world's most respected biologists, gives us twenty to fifty years to survive under present conditions.

DeBell, Garrett (ed.): *The Environmental Handbook*, Ballantine Books, Inc., New York, 1970. Prepared for the first national environmental teach-in, the first half of *The Environmental Handbook* contains a wide variety of essays on environmental problems, and the second half deals with ecotactics—what can be done, individually and politically. The handbook also lists all the leading environmental organizations in the country.

Ehrlich, Paul R., and Anne H. Ehrlich: *Population, Resources, Envrionment*, W. H. Freeman

[44]"Pollution: Puffery or Progress," *Newsweek*, pp. 49–51, December 28, 1970.

and Company, San Francisco, 1970. A comprehensive book that should be in all libraries. The Ehrlichs are experts at gathering the information and making a dramatic presentation. A good resource book for the three interrelated problems included in the title. (The only book on this list not available in paperback.)

Esposito, John C.: *Vanishing Air*, Grossman Publishers, New York, 1970. Esposito, a member of Ralph Nader's team, presents a study of the atmospheric crisis, with strong condemnations of policies of delay. Governmental agencies and the auto and power industries come in for some harsh criticism.

Mostert, Noël: *Supership*, Alfred A. Knopf, Inc., New York, 1974. A frightening look at the nature of oil transport in the gigantic tankers that haul oil from Arabia to the industrial nations. The superships are so unwieldy as to be a hazard at sea, occasionally colliding and making oil slicks as extensive as the famous oil spill off the coast of Santa Barbara. Emphasizes danger to sea life.

Ridgeway, James: *The Last Play: The Struggle to Monopolize the World's Energy Resources*, New American Library, Inc., New York, 1974. Explores the energy crisis, the secret manipulation of prices and monopolistic control of energy, and warns of impending shortages and economic warfare in the future.

QUESTIONS

1 Contrast the "sacred philosophy" and the "mastery philosophy," and try to explain what developments led to the mastery philosophy.

2 Give some instances showing how the entire earth is interrelated in problems of ocean and air pollution.

3 Contrast the moralizing approach and the political-institutional approach to environmental control.

4 What are the dangers of overdependence on fossil fuels? On atomic energy? What alternatives are available?

5 The chapter on pollution has suggested that all our environmental problems are subject to fairly effective control. Do you agree? What changes will be needed to bring about such control?

How successful have seventy years of pure food and drug acts been in protecting the consumer? Obviously, they have helped in eliminating some of the most flagrant conditions described in the meat-packing industry at the turn of the century; but have new deceptions entered the food business? Is the new inventiveness of chemistry turned to enriching our foods, or is it simply serving us a dangerous "chemical feast"? Are other types of products designed mainly for safety, utility, and durability, or are they designed with little regard for any of these qualities? What new perils does the consumer face in an age that is just as inventive in merchandizing techniques as it is in gadgetry? Finally, what organizations, publications, and types of legislation exist to try to help the consumer?

We shall find the answers to some of these questions far from reassuring. From infancy on, the consumer is met with many hazards to health and longevity, including baby foods, nutritionally deficient "unfoods," and potentially dangerous chemicals. His pocketbook is threatened by all kinds of deceptions—in insurance, on the grocery shelf, in time payments, and in the buying of goods that will quickly become obsolete. Bureaus have been created to aid the consumer, but there is always danger that regulator and regulated will grow too close together in association and attitude.

60 A trap is a device for catching prey by stealth and deception, whether the prey be an animal, an enemy, or a suspected criminal. Most traps of this type, however, are regarded as too cruel or unfair and are forbidden by law. On the other hand, most traps set for catching the consumer by deception are still permitted; there are often legal regulations, but they are easily evaded. Generally speaking, the consumers are fair game. They find traps in the grocery store, in loan offices, in real estate and insurance agencies, and in all kinds of televised advertisements. The foul food traps are still carefully baited, with the odor disguised by chemicals. There are other kinds of consumer traps that employ something akin to hidden timing devices, so that the products are timed to wear out rapidly or to become obsolete, as styles and models change with lightning speed.

The struggle to help the consumer is one with a long history, strewn with the wreckage of martyrs. As in the case of environmental pollution, some progress is being made, but new problems arise. New traps are set and, as the author of a book in the 1930s stated, one must learn to "eat, drink, and be wary."

THE PERSISTENCE OF THE JUNGLE

A sensation was created in 1906 when Upton Sinclair published his famous book *The Jungle*. Sinclair's intent was to portray a junglelike society of crushing poverty and despair for its industrial workers and of types of corruption, craftiness, backstabbing, and disregard for human life that belong more to a jungle than to a civilized society. The whole story is viewed through the eyes of Jurgis Rudkus and his family, non-English-speaking immigrants from Lithuania, who are exploited and cheated at every turn. The search for jobs takes them to the slaughterhouses of Chicago, an area the book calls Packingtown. It was the description of the meat-packing industry that created the sensation, and in the public mind "the jungle" meant specifically Packingtown. Thousands of people became so nauseated at reading the book that they quit eating meat and meat sales declined drastically. The meat-packing industry claimed that the book was libelous and that the public was being alarmed over nothing. What were the real facts about the jungle in 1906 and what are they now?

The jungle in 1906 So horrible was the story of the jungle that many doubted Sinclair's veracity. Major magazines ran articles written by members of the packing industry to discredit it, and threats of libel suits were made—but not carried out. President Theodore Roosevelt read the book and took immediate alarm. Roosevelt had the philosophy, at variance with that of most of his predecessors, that the federal government should play an important part as protector of the public interest. He appointed investigators to learn the true facts in the case. His investigators returned to tell him that there was no falsehood whatever in the book. Sinclair had accurately described the jungle. The entire industry crawled with filth, but the worst was the sausage-packing operation:

> There was never the least attention paid to what was cut up for sausage; there would come all the way back from Europe old sausage that had been rejected, and that was mouldy and white—it would be dosed with borax and glycerine, and dumped into the hoppers, and made over again for home consumption. There would be meat that had tumbled on the floor, in the dirt and sawdust, where the workers had trampled and spit uncounted billions of consumption germs. There would be meat stored in great piles. . . . It was too dark in these storage places to see well, but a man could run his

hand over these piles of meat and sweep off handfulls of dried dung of rats. These rats were nuisances, and the packers would put poisoned bread out for them, they would die, and then rats, bread, and meat would go into the hoppers together.[1]

As is generally known, pure food and drug acts were passed in 1907, and a Food and Drug Administration was created to make sure the public would never again face the risk of contaminated meat or other kinds of contaminated or chemically unsafe foods. In the intervening years the rats have diminished, but there are areas in which federal inspection does not take place, and there are many more miracles of chemistry than the glycerine and borax of 1906. A familiar old jingle was parodied in those days:

Mary had a little lamb,
And when she saw it sicken,
She shipped it off to Packingtown,
And now it's labeled "chicken."[2]

Whether lamb becomes chicken today we are not sure, but things still have a way of ending up with labels assuring the public that they are what they are not. Generally lambs are lambs and chickens are chickens, but their weight is greatly inflated by hormones whose safety for the consumer is extremely questionable.[3]

TODAY'S JUNGLE AND THE FOUR D's

There is still a jungle, mainly because the federal government is not as alert as it should be and, in the worst cases, because not all meat is federally inspected. Consequently, packers may be tempted to market 4-D meat (dead, dying, disabled, and diseased).[4] Despite the passage of the Wholesome Meat Act of 1967 that called for all state inspection laws to be "equal to" federal laws, they generally are not.

The concept of equal is hard to define; but worse yet, the only power the United States Department of Agriculture has over the states is to take over their total inspection systems, for which USDA does not have the personnel or the funds. The result is poor enforcement. One state meat inspector told investigators, "If I condemned an animal, I'd lose my job."[5] Another told an investigating committee that sick cows and hogs, turned down by federal inspectors, "will be taken down the road to the state slaughterhouse and get passed by inspectors at the state plants."[6] He went on to tell of one processor who sold cancerous tumors from diseased cattle to Boston supermarkets, calling them brains and sweetmeats. The date was two years after passage of the Wholesome Meat Act.

Even federal inspection is subject to criticism. The difficulty is that the federal inspectors are overworked, are under constant pressure from the meat-packers, and are not sufficiently sure of backing from higher authorities. For example, an inspector at a badly run chicken packing house found so many unfit chickens that he was forced to slow down the line in order to make an adequate inspection. The

[1]Upton Sinclair, *The Jungle*, New American Library, Inc., New York, 1960, p. 136.
[2]*Ibid.*, p. 348.
[3]Beatrice Trum Hunter, *Consumer Beware*, Simon & Schuster, Inc., New York, 1971, chaps. 5 and 6.
[4]Ralph Nader, "Watch that Hamburger," in David Sanford (ed.), *Hot Water on the Consumer*, Pitman Publishing Corporation, New York, 1969, pp. 45–47.
[5]Harrison Wellford, *Sowing the Wind*, Grossman Publishers, New York, 1972, p. 30.
[6]*Ibid.*

62 plant manager complained to the inspector's superior, who ordered him to allow the manager to set the speed of the operation, even though the law specifically gives the inspector the authority.[7]

Another problem is that the law is not particular enough about sanitation standards for workers at packing plants. In one Southern plant, it was noted that intestines, fecal matter, tumors, and heads drop into a belt over a trough of water. Employees wash their hands in the trough and then go back to handling chickens. "I guess 40-50 percent of the 'ready to cook' chickens go out in a highly contaminated form," stated the inspector.[8]

Consumers Union recently tested samples of pork sausage and found that 30 to 40 percent of the samples failed their absence-of-filth tests. One-eighth of federally inspected sausage and one-fifth of that not federally inspected contained insect larvae, rodent hairs, and other kinds of filth. Consumers Union also found much to be desired in the quality of fish sold on the market. Every month shipments of fish are ordered destroyed because of decomposition, positive staphylococci (bacterial parasites on skin and/or mucous membranes), coagulase (an enzyme causing coagulation), or parasitic cysts. Imported dried fish have been found to contain maggots.[9] Water from sewage and industrial waste can easily contaminate shellfish and other marine products. Frozen salmon from the Great Lakes had to be destroyed because of high levels of pesticides.[10]

In recent years there has been a large increase in infectious hepatitis and salmonella, and a connection between these diseases and food contamination is suspected, although difficult to prove. Oysters, clams, and mussels are often eaten raw or only partially cooked, in spite of the floods of industrial and domestic sewage that pour into the waters in which they live.[11]

There are other details of today's jungle that are almost as nauseating as those related by Sinclair. Consumers have found dozens of offensive items in soft drinks, including decomposing mice, maggots, and cigarette butts.[12] It must not be denied, though, that in the years since 1906 progress has been made. Most impurities are now killed by chemicals. Most food does not spoil—it is too full of chemical preservatives. A question remains, however, about whether the progress has been aimed at helping the consumer or primarily at fooling him.

From the jungle to the chemists   Altogether, 485 chemicals and other additives can now be used in foods *without being mentioned on the labels*.[13] Turner, a member of one of Nader's investigative teams, leads one to wonder about the safety of many of these chemicals. In his book *The Chemical Feast*, Turner savagely attacks the Food and Drug Administration, picturing its attitude toward the major food producers as friendly enough to border on collusion. He also gives a long recitation of bureaucratic rigidity, stubborness, and "group-think" that reminds one of the caricatures of bureaucracy presented in *Parkinson's Law*. In Turner's opinion, the FDA neither holds nor in any way deserves the confidence of the American public. To be fair it must be admitted that more rejection of chemical additives occurred in the first few years after Turner's book was published in 1970.

[7]*Ibid.*, p. 59.
[8]*Ibid.*, p. 129.
[9]Nader, "What are We Made Of?" in Sanford, *op. cit.*, pp. 3–9.
[10]*Ibid.*, p. 6.
[11]Nader, "Something Fishy," in Sanford, *op. cit.*, pp. 37–39.
[12]James S. Turner, *The Chemical Feast*, Grossman Publishers, New York, 1970, p. 74.
[13]Turner, *op. cit.*, p. 236.

Turner's explanation would be simply that the FDA responds to pressures. When the pressures from consumers' groups are strong, more FDA action is taken. Otherwise, the major pressures come from the food and drug interests, who constantly try to assure the FDA that there is nothing to worry about in their products. A glance at some of the examples Turner gives will show why he is concerned about the FDA and believes it will work effectively only if consumer organizations are active and critical.

In 1969, in a dramatic action taken by then Secretary of Health, Education and Welfare Robert Finch, cyclamates were recalled from the market because studies had indicated that they cause cancer in experimental animals. What the public did not know was that there had been very good evidence of this for many years before the removal of the cyclamates. As early as 1954 the Food and Nutrition Board of the National Academy of Sciences had warned against cyclamates. Eight years later the stand was reaffirmed, with the added conclusion that they do not even help in controlling weight, as they are supposed to do. Two Japanese scientists demonstrated in 1966 that cyclamates contain extremely dangerous carcinogenic ingredients. In 1968, Dr. J. Verrett found that cyclamates can cause deformation in chicken embryos. The FDA was supposed to adhere to the rule that drugs harmful to animals should be removed from use. In spite of this ruling, cyclamates continued their twenty-year position on the Generally Regarded as Safe (GRAS) list. The public eventually learned that diet drinks contained cyclamates and that cyclamates were under suspicion. It was not generally known, however, that cyclamates were added to many other kinds of products, such as jams and jellies and canned fruit, and that even children's vitamins were coated with cyclamates. Since cyclamates were on the GRAS list, no mention of them had to be made on labels.

While the FDA remained inactive on the issue, the Harvard School of Public Health made a study showing that experimental rats fed cyclamates gained more weight than control rats without cyclamates. More importantly, an investigation of diabetics, who had generally been taking both cyclamates and saccharin, revealed that diabetics have six to ten times as many grossly deformed children as the normal population. At about the same time, another doctor found that cyclamates break chromosomes in experimental rats and could be mutagenic. None of these bits of information moved the FDA to take action. It was only when NBC, the *Washington Post*, and *Newsweek* began to publicize the story told them by Verrett that the FDA and the Secretary of HEW were forced to act.[14]

The story of cyclamates would be ancient history except that attitudes and policies of the Food and Drug Administration keep it alive, with the public wondering when a similar discovery will be made—possibly another one that has been kept under cover for years. The earlier thalidomide case had resulted in favorable publicity for the FDA, but even it was more a matter of good luck than of design. Had it not been for the determined efforts of Dr. Frances Kelsey, there would have been hundreds of cases of deformed babies born as a result of the drug having been prescribed for expectant mothers. The first word of the cruel effects of thalidomide came in the form of a dispatch from Germany to our Department of State, telling of 150 babies born without arms or legs because of the drug. The head of the FDA was informed by the Secretary of State but did not bother to mention the German information to Kelsey, who was responsible for making a

---

[14]*Ibid.*, pp. 3–29.

decision on the drug.[15] Afterward the department boasted of having completely protected the public. Actually, more than 2 1/2 million pills had been distributed, supposedly for experimental tests. Ten deformed babies were born in the United States; the deformities were probably caused by thalidomide.

In his attack on the FDA, Turner leaves one with no assurance that other cases of this kind will not arise. His well-documented contention is that the FDA has several prominent blind spots having to do with chemicals, nutrition, food poisoning, and heart disease. After the cyclamate matter, the FDA took 64 other drugs off the GRAS list, admitting by implication that they had never been properly investigated.

One of the other blind spots of the agency is that it continues to assert that nutrition in America is excellent, even though congressional investigations have reported cases of malnutrition, not only among the poor but also among much of the chemically fed American public. It also ignores or minimizes the problems of food-borne diseases, such as salmonella and infectious hepatitis, which have been sharply on the increase in recent years. In fact, the National Research Council of the National Academy of Science has called salmonella "one of the most important communicable disease problems in the United States today."[16] In most people it causes only nausea and diarrhea, but for the very young or very old it can cause death. Poultry and eggs are the most frequent carriers. Often the fault is in food-serving establishments—restaurants, schools, and nursing homes; but a sizable number of cases have also been attributed to food processors.

Chemicals and animal weight   Beef production can be increased greatly and the cost of feeding reduced by several modern chemical devices. Silbesterol is very commonly used to add weight rapidly, and yet a *Farm Journal* article warned farmers that it would not be wise to admit using it because the quality of meat is not as good. The fat content is higher, making it an economic fraud. What is much worse is that silbesterol is a carcinogen, judging by tests with experimental animals. The FDA permits its use provided that no silbesterol is actually retained in the meat. Critics say that byproducts of silbesterol remain and are still dangerous. Possibly in the future, tests will determine the answer for sure; but with the long record of permissiveness toward other chemicals that were later found to be potentially dangerous, the continued use of silbesterol is not reassuring. Antibiotics and tranquilizers are also used to keep cattle quiet so that they gain weight faster. Critics fear that residues of the substances remain in the meat.[17]

STAYING ALIVE

It would seem that the problem of staying alive, barring war or other disaster, should be less serious than in earlier times. Throughout most of America's history, life expectancy has increased as childhood diseases, diphtheria, smallpox, tuberculosis, and various other ancient plagues have been virtually eliminated. Other problems have replaced the old ones, however. Cancer and heart disease increase markedly, influenced, no doubt, by foul air, chemical additives, and nervous strain, as well as by cigarettes that magazines still advertise in lyrical tones as bringing the freshness of country living and all the ruggedness of adulthood. Modern Ameri-

[15]*Ibid.*, pp. 221–227.
[16]Wellford, *op. cit.*, p. 130.
[17]Hunter, *op. cit.*, pp 115–120. See also Wellford, *op. cit.*, for a more thorough treatment of these and many other "hidden ingredients," pp. 125–186.

cans also face the need for rapid transportation, and their means of transportation are far from safe. These dangers, and other tensions of modern life, make people nervous, and they light up more cigarettes, drink more bourbon, and take more preparations to calm themselves down or pep themselves up, or ease their stomach, or put iron in their blood, or restore their vigor, or stop their headaches, or allow them to sleep. With all these marvelous inventions, their life expectancy has virtually ceased to lengthen.

> **Examine bottled drinks, fruit juices, and baby foods to see what you can learn about chemical additives. Check with** *Consumer Reports* **magazine. Report misbranded or contaminated foods to FDA, Department of Health, Education and Welfare, Washington, D.C.**

Into the mouths of babes There are suspicions that some of the additives put into foods can cause deformities, but assuming a normal baby is born, with a good appetite, what risk does it run? The baby first nurses from its mother who, as noted in Chapter 2, might produce milk contaminated with DDT. Next it is placed on a formula, sweetened by chemical additives. As it grows a little older it learns to ingest baby foods, which were once mainly fruit, vegetable, or meat. As the costs of these ingredients rose, the baby food companies began to add more and more starch and sugar—less nutritious, but cheaper.[18] Although an attempt is being made to sell cereals and other starchy foods for the small baby, the baby does not develop starch-digesting enzymes until the molar teeth erupt. The adding of starch may cause gastrointestinal troubles.[19] Strained ham and ham broth contain salt, sugar, and sodium nitrate, all of which are bad for infants. The sodium nitrate makes the color of food look right regardless of how old it is.

An early taste for too much salt can also be acquired and may be retained for life. In many cases, high salt intake is associated with hypertension. In one experiment, five out of seven rats fed on commercial baby foods developed high blood pressure.[20] Sugar helps to make babies fat, but fat babies are not as healthy as those of moderate weight. Monosodium glutamate, an artificial taste stimulant, was added to baby foods until 1969, when Dr. John W. Olney discovered it could cause brain damage in experimental animals, including rats, mice, and rhesus monkeys. The following year the FDA agreed to review the matter and removed monosodium glutamate from its GRAS list.

Our daily bread As babies grow into childhood they will, if they listen to the advertisements, learn to eat breakfast cereals, which claim to give vigor and vitality. In the summer of 1970 the FDA issued a report stating that nearly all breakfast cereals are pure calories, with almost no food value. Typical American children will, in all likelihood, learn the blessings of pure, white bread, vitamin enriched. What they and their parents will not know is that in the refining process twenty-four ingredients are removed from the wheat and only four are added.[21] They will drink a substitute for orange juice that is tangy but is really just a

[18]Turner, *op. cit.*
[19]Hunter, *op. cit.*, p. 315.
[20]Beatrice Trum Hunter, *Consumer Beware*, Simon & Schuster, New York, 1971, p. 317.
[21]Turner, *op. cit.*

collection of chemicals with no fruit juice content whatever. They will, in fact, come across a large number of "unfoods."

An ingenious example of an unfood is one company's product called "beef stroganoff." Since meat is supposedly involved, the product comes under the regulation of the Agriculture Department, which says the package must contain 45 percent meat. The loophole in the law is that only the inner container—the one actually containing the meat—must tell the true story. The problem is solved for the producer by putting four packages inside the one the housewife buys. Only one of those four must contain 45 percent meat. Others contain noodles, breadcrumbs, and sauce.[22] The whole deal is neat and legal, and the inner package that is allegedly meat is actually part meat and part soybeans.

As they grow older people may tend to put on weight. They can be sold various drugs for reducing purposes, but most of the drugs cause dehydration, thus producing only a temporary weight loss. Those that are effective appetite depressants are too dangerous to try without medical advice.[23] People may also hear that too much caffeine is bad for the health. They resolve to stop drinking coffee, struggle hard with their resolution, and win. What they don't know is that the colas they have become almost addicted to also contain caffeine, but the company does not have to mention the matter.[24]

[22]Sanford, "Unfoods: Do You Know What You're Eating?" in Sanford, *op. cit.*, pp. 53–57.
[23]Fred Trump, *Buyer Beware*, Abingdon Press, Nashville, Tenn., 1965, pp. 106–109.
[24]Turner, *op. cit.*, p. 112.

Driving a car   One of the main interests of consumer education for a number of years has been in the field of automobiles, partly from the point of view of economy, but even more for the sake of safety. Each year cars kill about 50,000 people. Each year 4 percent of the people who die in the United States die as a result of traffic accidents involving automobiles. Trains and buses also kill, but in relatively small numbers. For every 10 billion miles of travel, there are 5 train fatalities, 13 bus fatalities, 14 airplane fatalities, and 570 auto fatalities[25] It would seem only natural, then, that we would make every effort to improve the safety of cars; but for many years safety was virtually ignored. The appeal was to speed, power, beauty, style, luxury—anything but safety.

Nader documents many instances of extremely dangerous cars, his initial case concerning the sporty Corvair.[26] His major theme is that Detroit should have been much more responsible in its attitude, emphasizing safety rather than power and style. There were cries of outrage and quackery against Nader, and many auto-loving people were willing to admit a certain amount of guilt on the part of the public for having shopped more for style and power than for safety. However, public support for Nader increased as it became known that General Motors had hired private detectives to follow him, to search his record for scandals, and to snoop into his private life, views, and associates.[27] In the summer of 1970 General Motors paid Nader $420,000 in settlement of a suit brought against the company for their harassing activities.

More important, however, than the argument with the American automobile manufacturers—all are taken to task by Nader, and the manufacturers of small foreign cars even more so—is Nader's charge against the "Safety Establishment." Just as it was argued in Chapter 2 that preaching endlessly to the individual offenders does little good, so does Nader contend that preaching safety to the driver does little good. The assumption is that a person who has an accident must have been violating the law. "Manslaughter charges are hurled routinely against drivers; there is yet to be any similar charge against the manufacturer for vehicle defects."[28]

The Automotive Safety Foundation (ASF), established in 1937 by the Auto Manufacturers Association, gives grants for research work in driver training, laws, and highways, but never a cent for research on the safety of autos themselves.[29] Briefly, the Nader charge is that much of the safety effort has had the intended effect of taking pressure off the manufacturers and assigning the entire guilt to the driver. His book evoked a storm of protest but also awakened people and legislators. If interest does not die, the auto should become a less lethal device in the future, with killing not rising as fast as passenger miles.

| Before buying a car, check car safety. Write to Ralph Nader, Center for Study of Responsive Law, 1908 Q St., NW, Washington, D.C. Also check *Consumer Reports*.

The years since publication of Nader's *Unsafe at Any Speed* have seen an increase in legislative interest in auto safety. Seat and shoulder belts are now

[25]Joseph Kelner, "Highway Murder," in Sanford, *op. cit.*, p. 220.
[26]Ralph Nader, *Unsafe at Any Speed*, Grossman Publishers, New York, 1965, chap. 1.
[27]David Hawkins, "The Safety of the American Automobile," *Science, Conflict, and Society: Readings from Scientific American*, W. H. Freeman and Company, San Francisco, 1969, pp. 252–256.
[28]Nader, *op. cit.*, p. 237.
[29]Nader, *op. cit.*, p. 247.

installed, more and more dashboards are padded, for several years emergency lights have been standard features, and experimenting is being done with other features of the car. Car bumpers are now supposed to withstand a 5-mile-per-hour impact. The latter regulation saves a little money for insurance companies, reducing quite a few small claims, but has virtually no impact on car safety.

Another interest of consumers has been that of automobile cost. For many years, effective advertising plus the American feeling that every device should constantly grow bigger and better led to gigantic automobiles, sometimes called dinosaurs of the highways. The automotive industry was reluctant to give up size and weight because the larger and more luxurious the car, the greater the margin of profit. Foreign competition in the form of smaller cars began to eat into the market drastically before Detroit was able to change its habits. Eventually, though, the price of gasoline caused public interest in smaller cars to rise to the point of forcing American manufacturers into the competition. Only the future will tell whether the trend toward economy models will continue or whether the earlier status appeal of automotive giantism will bring back the old habits of fuel and metal wastage.

The license Not all the fault is with the automobile manufacturers, of course, although recently they have been getting the lion's share of unfavorable publicity. There is no denying the carelessness, insobriety, or lack of training of many drivers. The defensive driver, wishing to stay alive, must look upon the other driver's license as a license to kill. It is shocking to read the estimate of a Cincinnati neurosurgeon, Dr. F. H. Mayfield, that 6 million of the nation's drivers are subject to convulsive diseases. In thirty states licenses are renewed by mail, with no eye tests required, provided that one passed a test years ago. Most state laws are lax enough to allow a person to drive even though his or her reflexes and vision are impaired by too much drinking. The thoroughly drunk driver is usually taken off the road by friends or by the police. The half-drunk driver, the real danger, is often allowed to go on driving.[30]

Some state driving laws are almost as generous in their definition of drunkenness as the old rhyme:

Not drunk is he who from the floor
Can rise again and drink some more,
But he is drunk who prostrate lies
Without the power to drink or rise.

THE PRICE PAID

Inflated prices are a matter of serious concern to the consumer, and they are, of course, sometimes made unavoidable by the economic pressures of a large buying public competing for scarce goods. Federal fiscal and monetary policies and escalating interest rates can have strong effects on prices, and so can the presently threatening tendency to increase international trade restrictions. A full-length book on consumer economics could not leave out these problems for the consumer or hundreds of others—real estate swindles, false guarantees, insurance policies that are canceled whenever a calamity befalls, get-rich-quick schemes for

---

[30]Kelner, *op. cit.*, pp. 221–222.

As a fuel crisis developed, Detroit continued to load the high-ways and parking lots with automotive dinosaurs, luxurious but wasteful.

raising chinchillas, sweepstakes, chain letters, and many other possibilities listed in Trump's *Buyer Beware*. Many of these traps are avoided by the more wary. Our discussion has focused mainly on the types of consumer problems that are difficult for even the informed citizen to avoid: the problems of the grocery shelf and planned obsolescence, for example. To a degree the thousands of little advertising lies trap all people, even the sales resistant, with their tendency to make habitual thought patterns of their slogans.

The grocery shelf The food industry in recent decades has become a good example of oligopoly—control of almost the entire product by very few producers. Four firms prepare 85 percent of the nation's breakfast cereals. Most are bulky enough to look like a bargain, but in actual weight and nutritional value most represent a poor investment. Campbell Soup produces 95 percent of all prepared soups. Borden and National Dairy (Kraft) produce more than half the cheese on the American market. Processed foods, featuring food additives and a minimum of home preparation, exceeded sales of all other foods for the first time in 1969. The large firms making up oligopolistic control of much of the food market are very difficult for the FDA to regulate.[31]

Much of the food marketing is done by chain stores, which are fond of boasting that they work for a very small margin of profit. Based on food sales, it is true that the profit is low compared with many industries. Based on total investments, however, the story is quite different. Chain store profit on investment amounts to about 12.5 percent.[32] Usually there are many middleman transactions separating farmers and the grocery store. Farmers constantly complain of low sales prices and

[31]Turner, *op. cit.*, pp. 82–85.
[32]Sanford, "Gamesmanship in the Supermarkets," in Sanford, *op. cit.*, pp. 21–27.

rising costs. Each middleman blames the other, but for whatever reason, the price of food continues to soar.

The grocery shelf is loaded with several trick devices. Big, generous-looking packages are only partially filled. Some items are given favored treatment in a conspicuous spot at the end of the shelf, perhaps because the item is overpriced or otherwise hard to sell. Or it might be an item that people do not put on shopping lists but that might attract the housewife as an item for impulse buying. Another possible explanation is that the food brokers have worked their miracles to make sure a product is placed in a conspicuous location. Much of the food-brokerage business is done on the basis of proven sales records of goods, but when two competitors are close together in sales records, the broker might use a little "entertainment grease" to help push his product. "It can be anything from a pen with the company name on it to a broad for a week in the Caribbean,"[33] explained one very frank broker. Although the amount of entertainment grease is on the decline, it is still a sizable item that somehow has to be supported. As with the costs of other promotional schemes, the price is eventually passed along to the consumer.

Packaging techniques become more refined with the passing of time, adding not only to the trash-pollution problems but to the deception of the consumer as well. It is estimated that the average family spends $200 per year just for the packages that are eventually thrown away.[34] Packages look as though they hold much more than they do and are priced in a confusing manner. Which is cheaper, the 13-ounce package for 73 cents, or the 15-ounce package for 85 cents? It would take an hour of extra shopping to make all the decisions properly. Even college-educated women failed a test in picking the best items for the money. A study in Washington, D.C. revealed that stores in the same chain charged higher prices for food in the poorer sections of town, whether for white or black poor, and that the quality of perishable items declined.[35] The pattern of differential prices is generally true throughout the United States, although often the reason is higher costs in small, independent groceries in the poorer areas.

Check your grocery shelf for deceptive packaging, especially for empty space. Write a protest to the manufacturer about the air in your food.

Planned obsolescence The consumer, trapped by many small tricks of the grocery business, falls into a much more expensive trap in the obsolescence business. Vance Packard wrote a book on obsolescence and similar problems, entitled *The Waste Makers*.[36] It was written before the environmentalist movement was as prominent as it is today, but some of its points are very similar to those of the environmentalists. In order to keep production humming, prosperity rolling, and profits gushing in, everyone must be induced to spend more and more. Otherwise the market will be glutted. Economists frequently comment on this particular dilemma of modern production; John Kenneth Galbraith is especially

[33]David Shaw, "Grocery Shelf Psychology—It Aims to Please," *Los Angeles Times*, August 18, 1970, pp. 1, 20, 21.
[34]Hunter, *op. cit.*, p. 23.
[35]James Ridgeway, "Segregated Food at the Supermarket," in Sanders, *op. cit.*, pp. 26–29. (See also "What's Happened to Truth in Packaging?" *Consumer Reports*, vol. 34, pp. 40–43, January 1969.)
[36]Vance Packard, *The Waste Makers*, Pocket Books, Inc., New York, 1963, p. 23.

condemnatory of that characteristic of our productive system. It is Packard's book, however, that most boldly accuses much of industry of something approaching a deliberate plot against the consumer by making completely unneeded items seem like necessities of life. Their philosophy, Packard says, can be stated as "The way to end glut is to produce gluttons." Accordingly, more color matching is promoted to broaden sales of wardrobe items and matching items for the house. A one-car family is made to feel poverty-stricken, and a man pushing a lawnmower by hand is a disgrace to his middle-class neighborhood.

Another way to increase consumption is to increase the size of the items produced. We have previously noted the great increase in size, expense, and fuel consumption of automobiles until foreign competition and gasoline prices forced a change—which may yet prove only temporary. Increases in size and quantity were not enough, however. Packard quotes one writer for an industrial publication as saying, regretfully, "The more durable the item the more slowly it will be consumed." His suggestion was to make items *look* obsolete whether they were or not.[37] Other solutions to the problem were also found, such as making appliances with sealed units so that consumers could not repair their own. A prominent journal for product designers presented an article suggesting "death dates" for all products—a way of speeding up replacement. Although many engineers and producers were outraged, quite a few thought it a commendable idea or at least "realistic" in terms of marketing needs. In a chapter entitled "The Short, Sweet Life of Home Products," Packard makes it sound as though the "death date" idea is pretty well implemented and that it would be wise never to buy a home appliance without first looking up its record in *Consumer Reports*. The problem of durables that are not very durable becomes more acute with the passing of time, the exhaustion of resources, the increasing numbers of people, and the ever-mounting piles of junk for which there is no satisfactory means of disposal. Small wonder that Alvin Toffler speaks of ours as the "throwaway" society. He defends some of the disposability on the grounds of actual wearing out or replacement by superior products, but even the increase in new products is a serious problem. Each year the number of new products appearing increases, with 9,500 new consumer-packaged products added in a single year.[38] The American trend, he points out, is now becoming a trend in all industrialized nations. All the old products must be thrown away—a thought that links the entire consumer problem with the environmental problems discussed previously.

Those little lies   The Justice Department filed a $1 million suit against Geritol in the spring of 1970. For a decade the product had been advertised for people with "tired blood." Old people especially had been led to believe that Geritol was the last great medicine-man cure-all and restorer. A multimillion dollar business had flourished, making claims that the Justice Department calls deceptive and misleading.[39] The preceding year the Federal Trade Commission filed complaints against Allerest and Dristan, contending that neither completely relieves allergy as they claimed. Both companies stopped the particular advertisements. Another famous little lie on television showed a rapid shave preparation so marvelous at softening beards that it was spread on sandpaper and the sandpaper was shaved clean.

[37] *Ibid.*, p. 55.
[38] Alvin Toffler, *Future Shock*, Bantam Books, Inc., New York, 1971, pp. 51–73.
[39] Daniel Henninger, "The One-Eyed Slicker," *The New Republic*, vol. 162, pp. 17–19, May 2, 1970.

What actually happened was that sand was shaved off a glass surface.[40] Libbey-Owens-Ford auto glass was demonstrated to give fantastic clarity. One reason was that the glass was rolled down when the picture was taken.

Although in all the cases above FTC action was taken, there are numerous cases in which action cannot be taken. Many detergent advertisements stretch credibility. One merely shows a blood-stained shirt dipped into water containing the detergent and seconds later it comes out spotless. Clothes can come out whiter than white, cleaner than clean, purer than purity itself. There is no legal requirement that possible damage must be mentioned. Some types of toothpastes clean very well, but contain abrasives that are harmful to tooth enamel. Generally such truths do not have to be admitted. Many of the little lies of advertising are lies of omission rather than commission.

Most people are fed other little lies. In spite of truth-in-lending laws, there are special carrying "fees" that run up interest rates. A group of Philadelphia loan companies was found to be holding second mortgages on homes in New Jersey, with special hidden charges that made the effective interest rates as high as 58 percent.[41]

Nearly every householder is met at the door occasionally by a personable young man or lady selling magazine subscriptions. A charming girl with a British accent says she is trying to make enough money to stay in the country and not lose her visa; please help. She is really from Chicago. A sales crew in Virginia threatened to burn a woman's house if she wouldn't buy a subscription. She dropped dead of a heart attack. Sometimes the salespeople are as much victims as the customers. Deputy Attorney General Herschel T. Elkins of California reports cases in which young people were recruited in the East for magazine saleswork in California. They were given high promises of good pay but no provision for transportation home. They had to sell or be stranded. They also found that they were being charged for food, travel, lodging, and other expenses, and often ended their sales tour owing the company money.[42]

> **Have you bought a faulty appliance or been unable to get satisfaction on a guarantee? If your state has an office of consumer affairs, report the matter. Otherwise write to the Presidential Advisor on Consumer Affairs, Washington, D.C.**

The lies go on and on. Some are big; some are little. Attempts are made to deal with some of the consumer's problems, but others are fairly well ignored. The many examples given so far have included cases in which something effective is done, and some in which nothing is done. It is time to look at some of the basic causes of consumer traps and suggestions for remedies.

HELPING THE CONSUMER

There are several possible approaches to consumer problems, some calling for major institutional change, some for minor institutional change, and others for further use of the agencies now available. Regardless of the approach, the

---

[40]*Ibid.*

[41]Jonathan Kwitny, "The Money Lenders," in Sanford, *op. cit.*, pp. 141–145.

[42]Alexander Auerbach, "Complaints Rise on Door-to-Door Magazine Sales," *Los Angeles Times*, August 28, 1970, part I, pp. 24, 25.

consumer must make himself heard politically and economically; without organi- | **73**
zation and effort he will continue to be misled and overcharged.

The antiestablishment approach Sinclair was a socialist, thinking that the only solution to social problems lay in taking away the profit motive from industry. He was a gradualist, not calling for sudden and violent overturns, and at times, such as when he ran for governor of California, seeming to believe in working within the system. Nevertheless, when he wrote *The Jungle* his conclusion was that the only solution for the ills of the working man and the corruption of American society lay with socialism. In the uncompromising opinion expressed in *The Jungle*, all other attempts at reform would be mere palliatives. Sinclair believed that as long as people could make money by turning out bad products and mistreating labor, they would do so.

Using the present system Fred Trump takes a completely opposite approach. To a great extent his previously mentioned book *Buyer Beware* is practical advice to the individual consumer, warning him of the frauds to avoid. There is no condemnation of a great industry, such as the auto or food industry. There are many comments on petty swindlers, dishonest practices and dishonest practitioners, but these comments are always of evils begotten by evil people—not by an essentially evil or unworkable system.

Trump's book is very much worth reading because it is full of practical advice and has a list of the agencies and organizations to which the consumer can turn for help. Such agencies include the Federal Trade Commission, the Post Office, Consumer Advocates in some states, Better Business Bureaus, and the same Food and Drug Administration that Turner criticizes so strongly.

Consumer Reports, the publication of Consumers Union, also gives much practical advice on the rating of products and publicizes governmental actions against the food industry and various products. Its position is more critical of major industries than those books that concentrate mainly on swindlers. Most issues of *Consumer Reports* have a section entitled "The Docket" that gives a rundown of federal and state actions against false advertising, real estate and insurance swindles, and violations of truth-in-lending laws. Typical items include reports of the finding of intolerable amounts of DDT in lettuce, insect parts and cat hair in butter, shipments of contaminated seafood, and insect filth in packaged rice.

Consumer Reports and its rival magazine, *Consumer Bulletin*, are of great help in trying to beat the "consumer trap." Ratings of nearly all conceivable products are given—automobiles, furniture, household appliances, washing detergents, shaving soap, toothpaste, over-the-counter medicines, tools and hardware, and so forth.

The establishment modification approach Packard and Sanford, as well as Turner and Wellford of the Nader group, attack subsystems within modern American capitalism without attempting to attack the capitalistic system as a whole. Packard's *Waste Makers* is an appeal for industry reform, to prevent the production of shoddy goods and cheating the consumer. There is also an expression of concern with a system that will have to depend on constantly growing demand, even at the cost of waste and planned obsolescence.

Turner turns more explicitly to criticism of government and industry, but unlike Sinclair's, his criticisms are aimed at modification of the present system rather than at scuttling capitalism. Some of his criticisms pertain to the Food and Drug Administration: the policy of assigning too many products to the GRAS list without adequate investigation, denying that there are malnutrition problems, and looking upon nearly all food producers as "good guys." He recommends a system that will represent consumer organizations to speak before the FDA, rather than the present situation in which almost all consultations are with food and drug producers. He also suggests stricter use of antitrust legislation to break up oligopoly in the food industry. An even more important theme of his book is that of being sure that government regulators honestly regulate.

The regulators and the regulated The problem approached by Turner and Wellford has wide-ranging implications for the consumer, whether the Food and Drug Administration or any other regulatory commission is under consideration. The first efforts of regulated industries are aimed at getting their friends onto commissions. If they fail, the next attempt is to make friends with existing members of the commission, helping them to understand and be "reasonable." Only one important director of the FDA was caught in actual, provable conflict of interest, but there has been a tendency to develop an official attitude of implicit trust of the entire food and drug industry, whose bad actions were the original cause for creating the FDA.[43] It is difficult to have long conferences with the representatives of a regulated industry without becoming somewhat sympathetic. The industry's representatives, naturally, make every effort to be ingratiating, which no one can claim is either illegal or unethical. The trouble is that over a period of years too many representatives of industry become looked upon as old friends; but the consumers, whose interests are the reason for the existence of the agency, are never seen. Head commissioners attempt to reform the system but find themselves enmeshed in a rigid, self-perpetuating system of thought and action, including listening to scientists friendly to department views and dismissing others as eccentric. Turner alleges that defense mechanisms are developed for congressional investigating committees, hiding much information on the grounds of protecting "trade secrets," justifying previous records, and covering up what cannot be justified.

There are bureaus and legislative acts to protect the consumer, but they can fall into relative disuse unless public pressure is placed on them. When the alarm bells are rung, as in the days of *The Jungle*, or as in the recent case of cyclamates, action is taken. What is needed is a more permanent, ongoing system for making sure that the consumer is represented. A suggestion to this effect would be a much larger representation of consumer organizations in meetings with the FDA, the Federal Trade Commission, and other agencies directly concerned with consumer problems. Such a policy would give consumers countervailing power relative to the food and drug interests.

The current age of alarms has caused legislators and congressmen to push for more safety regulations on cars than we have had in the past. There is a tide of legislative talk and a trickle of legislative action on environmental problems. The danger is that the public may resume its usual pendulum swing from panic to complacency, and the pressure will be off, which is why it is important that new institutional means are developed for representing the consumer. Some states now have consumer advocates. Representation of consumer groups on regulatory

---

[43]Turner, *op. cit.*, p. 218.

commissions is a hopeful possibility. For reasons of consumer complaints and various other complaints against government, an office of ombudsman would be very much in order.

The ombudsman is an official in Scandinavian governments whose duty it is to hear complaints from citizens against governmental bureaucracy. The first state to have a strong office of ombudsman was Hawaii. There the ombudsman is empowered to investigate all bureaus and commissions and subpoena and publicize findings, to the great discomfort of agencies and bureaus. There is always the fear, of course, that the ombudsman will simply become another bureaucrat, but from a structural point of view he has a degree of independence from other bureaus and has no direct tie-in with the interests that they regulate.

One of the major proposals of consumers' groups is for the establishment of a Department of Consumer Affairs in the President's cabinet. Such a department would give more prominence to consumer problems and more power to deal with them. To date, however, Congress has not approved such a proposal, although it has been introduced repeatedly. Obviously, many producers have a vested interest in defeating proposals for such a department.

No system is immune to corruption or stagnation, be it bureau, consumer advocate, or ombudsman's office. Along with legislative and institutional reform, public action groups and alarmists are needed to trouble the placid waters of institutionalization. Sinclair would have thought of these solutions as mere palliatives to a system that is fundamentally sick. Like many socialists of his time, he greatly underestimated the amount of improvement that would come about in working conditions and pay, but he properly criticized a system easily given to the production of shoddy, deceptive, and even dangerous goods. The only way to avoid solutions that would shatter the free enterprise system is to work out better means for correcting such abuses.

SUGGESTED READINGS

Buel, Ronald A.: *Dead End: The Automobile in Mass Transportation*, Penguin Books, Inc., Baltimore, 1973. Although primarily a book arguing for mass transportation, much of the first part is concerned with the manner in which the public has been exploited by America's gigantic "auto-highway-petroleum complex."

Hunter, Beatrice Trum: *Consumer Beware*, Simon & Schuster, Inc., New York, 1971. Like several other writers on consumer problems, Beatrice Hunter is alarmed over the types of chemicals fed to chickens, cattle, and other animals to increase their weight—chemicals that may pose health hazards for human beings. The book also contains much useful information on avoiding the tricks of the marketplace.

Margolis, Sidney: *The Innocent Consumer versus the Exploiters*, Pocket Books, Inc., New York, 1968. Particularly good on such consumer problems as unfair credit practices, garnishment and repossession, home-improvement traps, and waste of money through brand names rather than generic names of pharmaceuticals. The book also has a useful final chapter on where to get help and advice.

Nader, Ralph: *Unsafe at Any Speed*, Grossman Publishers, New York, 1965. This is the book that finally roused the sleeping public to the realization that their autos are unnecessarily dangerous. A little bit of safety action has resulted; more will result if more of the public learns the facts presented by Nader.

Turner, James S.: *The Chemical Feast*, Grossman Publishers, New York, 1970. As indicated by references in the previous pages, Turner's book is a well-aimed attack at the food industry, chemical additives, and the public agency responsible for pure food and drugs in America. *Time* magazine said "it may well be the most devastating critique of a U.S. Government agency ever issued."

Wellford, Harrison: *Sowing the Wind*, Grossman Publishers, New York, 1972. Wellford looks into the difficulties of enforcing pure food laws, laxity in inspection, and shortage of qualified personnel for inspecting, especially in the meat and poultry industries.

Magazines: be sure to look over copies of *Consumer Reports* and/or *Consumer Bulletin*, especially if you are going to make an important purchase.

QUESTIONS

1 How do modern chemical techniques tend to parallel the older problem of contamination of meat as described by Upton Sinclair in *The Jungle*?

2 Starting with infancy, describe the hazards to long life and health that confront a person as part of the consuming public.

3 The driver was once considered the sole reason for high death rates from automobiles. Where else does much of the fault lie?

4 In what ways is rapid obsolescence of products and the throw-away society geared to the American economy?

5 Discuss the problems involved in trying to set up regulatory commissions to protect the consumer.

It is probably inevitable that educational institutions should garner more than their share of both praise and blame. Schooling is praised because America has always placed very great faith in education both as the prime mover behind national development and as the potential solver of the majority of personal and social problems. But schools are also sharply criticized, because the faith placed in them is too great; some of their assigned tasks are impossible of accomplishment. Moreover, the schools are criticized because they have accumulated such a burden of size and administrative complexity that the students, for whom they are intended, have become anonymous numbers to be processed, grouped into ability levels, graded, and passed along to the next institution. Along with the overloading of the school facilities themselves goes an overloaded, creaking curriculum, straining to teach the fundamentals, to discipline, to indoctrinate, to provide for upward mobility, to meet state requirements, to avoid ruffling local interests, to cope with new needs such as driver education and sex education, and to give the impression that everyone who graduates has really received an education.

The educational system is ideally the servant of the people, but it has been forced to serve a large number of masters who do not speak with one voice. Furthermore, new burdens are being added as each generation of students varies in composition and interests and as their future needs and prospects change.

How well are the schools coping with their current tasks? Is there a clear consensus about what they are supposed to achieve for the individual and society? One of the points on which public opinion is fairly well agreed is that the schools should equalize opportunity; but have they really achieved this, especially in the secondary and college systems, for the economically deprived elements of society? Is there any remedy for the great size, impersonality, and bureaucratic structure of our schools? Are the secondary schools, colleges, and universities geared mainly to student needs, or do they serve other masters? What are the characteristics of the changing student populations with which the colleges must deal? What new requirements stem from the increasing percentages of students who enter the colleges, and how are the requirements being met?

THE CONFUSION OF AIMS

The educational policies of the early Puritans of Massachusetts centered first on the idea of frustrating the Devil by giving everyone the ability to read the Bible. In later years, those who could read were also likely to be more successful in life than those who were illiterate, and the old Puritans had little use for people who were failures. In Puritan philosophy, it was abundantly clear that people who failed in life were not of the elect of God and probably deserved the low status they received. The Puritans, then, could be said to have seen a certain amount of education as a religious necessity and also as a practical matter of worldly success.

Throughout the nineteenth century, American elementary and secondary education had its patriotic counterpart to the Puritan ethic. Learning to read and write would equip people for the economic struggles of life; but the whole process of going to school would do much more. Schooling, it was hoped, would indoctrinate people in Americanism and would exorcise the devils of radical and alien ideas just as surely as it had exorcised Satan for the Puritans. The norms of a highly competitive free enterprise system would be absorbed in the schools, along with classes in reading and writing and lessons in temperance and morality.

Serving industry Several recent writers on the development of the American educational system contend that mass education at the primary level began in the nineteenth century "to meet the needs of capitalist employers for a skilled and disciplined labor force and to provide a mechanism for social control in the interests of political stability."[1] Since workers were thrown together in large numbers, often in sweatshop conditions, the possibility for trouble was much greater than it had been when the same class of people worked the land in relative isolation from one another. Many manufacturers and business people saw school as a good place for indoctrination of workers to the view that the economic system was fair and honest and the best possible. Teachings in the old readers were intensely patriotic and moralistic. Regarding the need of industrial workers for schooling, the chairman of the Massachusetts State Board of Education said in 1841, "The ignorant and uneducated I have generally found the most turbulent and troublesome, acting under the impulse of excited passion and jealousy."[2] Apparently the discipline of the schools was expected to lead to greater docility.

To be fair, though, it must be admitted that much of the agitation for free public education came from reformists dedicated to ending the abuses of child labor. Education helped indoctrinate workers with the values of the industrial system, but

[1]Samuel Bowles, "Getting Nowhere: Programmed Class Stagnation," *Society*, vol. 9, pp. 42–49, June 1972. This is also the theme of Michael B. Katz, *Class, Bureaucracy and Schools: The Illusion of Educational Change in America*, Frederick A. Praeger, Inc., New York, 1971.
[2]*Ibid.*, p. 43.

it was also a reformist cause. Furthermore, parents increasingly supported the idea of schools for their children, especially as the nation became urbanized and there were fewer home chores for children than there had been on the farms.

Although diverse groups supported the idea of schooling, futurist Alvin Toffler concludes that school organization came to resemble the factory. The labor force learned to work in large masses under the discipline of the employing company and its schedule, and more and more children of the labor force went to school and accepted a discipline and regimentation that mirrored the factory system. According to Toffler, "the whole idea of assembling masses of students (raw material) to be processed by teachers (workers) in a centrally located school (factory) was a stroke of industrial genius."[3] He goes on to say that such a model of a school was quite acceptable for an assembly line age when a majority of people had to be trained to hold factory jobs. It hardly fits in a society that calls for increasing numbers of creative thinkers, scientific researchers, organizers, and planners; but often the school remains the same as before.

The critical function The educational system, of course, had aims other than training and disciplining workers. An ideal of the Founding Fathers was that of promoting an enlightened citizenry. Despite the heavy hand of discipline and indoctrination into the principles of a free enterprise system, the schools have had the effect in many cases of creating independent thinkers. Especially in the colleges, sharp critics of society have emerged, even though they have often been looked upon as enemies of society, trying to subvert a system to which it is felt they should give warm-hearted agreement.

Down to the present day, the majority opinion of local boards of education controlling primary and secondary schools has been that the schools should teach the cultural traditions without too much criticism. Student radicals of the 1960s and their supporters, on the other hand, think of the schools as a battleground for new ideas. They cannot see how a society constantly faced with new challenges can survive without constant confrontation of new issues and ideas.

Another conflict in aims is over the very pragmatic idea of learning reading, writing, and arithmetic in preparation for a specific job, on the one hand, and of emphasizing courses aimed at life enrichment, on the other. Should schools be merely centers for learning course materials or should they provide a place of enjoyment during the long years of primary and secondary education? In the public mind, fundamental instruction is apparently more important; when funds are short in a school district, recreation, athletics, and life-enrichment programs are trimmed so that courses in basic skills can be retained. These conflicts in emphasis are mentioned only briefly. Many more could be added, but enough has been said to illustrate the idea that schools cannot possibly conform to the expectations of everyone.

The equalization ideal Another very important function of education, as most people have seen it, is that of providing a path for upward mobility. Horace Mann (1796–1859), generally considered the most important figure in the promotion of free, compulsory education in America, spoke of education as "the great equalizer." Our previous comments about the schools as a means of training and disciplining a labor force and indoctrinating them in free enterprise values may

---

[3]Alvin Toffler, *Future Shock*, Bantam Books, Inc., New York, 1970, p. 400.

seem to contradict the equalization motive, but not entirely. Seymour Martin Lipset[4] presents evidence to show that people who advocated the equalization function of education, including even nineteenth-century captains of industry, have been perfectly sincere. American society, and not just its liberal members, has placed a strong emphasis on the ideal of giving everyone an equal start. What society has failed to note, however, is a fact first commented on by the New York Workingmen's Party as early as 1829: hours spent in school cannot create equality among children from homes of the rich and poor, the educated and uneducated, the English-speaking and non-English-speaking, the Americanized and distinctively foreign.[5]

Neighborhood schools versus integration Some of the minority groups of the days of the Workingmen's Party were eventually able to become upwardly mobile, but only after a generation or two of contact with the American culture, both inside and outside the schools. The largest minority group was not even thought of in terms of education in those days, but the time came when the education of the black minority became an important issue. The Supreme Court ruled in 1954 that segregated education was inherently unequal. The struggle for desegregation was fought long and hard, with a far-from-successful outcome. It was at first assumed that the South would be the area of greatest resistance, but by the mid-1970s it became clear that some of the areas hardest to integrate were the extremely segregated cities of the North. As noted in Chapter 1, the Northern black population is concentrated mainly in certain inner-city areas and the white population in outlying neighborhoods. The most practical means of meeting the integration requirements of the courts has appeared to be that of busing students from one section of town to another.

In some cities, busing has taken place without much complaint. In the places of greatest storm and stress, however, the argument is used that schools, especially elementary schools, should be neighborhood institutions. Actually, much busing has been done in the past for other purposes. Children have been transported from crowded schools to less-crowded schools in a district, and very small communities have bused their children to unified schools. Since the neighborhood issue seems to be of only minor importance in such cases, it is hard for black people to believe in the sincerity of white neighborhood-school advocates, although some blacks also oppose busing out of the neighborhood. Although there are arguments against busing, such as fuel costs and the time and expense involved, it is apparently the only way of complying with desegregation orders short of ending the entire pattern of de facto housing segregation in the cities, which would probably upset the neighborhood-school advocates even more. Much ambiguity is displayed throughout the country. During Boston demonstrations over the busing issue, President Ford called upon the city to obey the law, but in the same breath expressed his disagreement with court decisions. Many politicians have found busing a paying issue to campaign against, but in other districts pro-busing candidates have won. The advocates of busing feel that despite its problems, it is a necessary step toward ensuring mobility through the school system to blacks as well as whites. (See Chapter 7 for more information on the traditionally underprivileged position of minority groups.)

---

[4]"Education and Equality: Israel and the United States Compared," *Society*, vol. 11, pp. 56–66, March-April 1974.
[5]*Ibid.*, pp. 57 and 58.

Ask several black students and several white students for their opinions on busing for the sake of racial integration. Be sure to ask why they approve or disapprove. Look for differences in opinions among blacks and whites; and also try to guess whether the reasons given for the opinions are genuine or merely what is considered socially acceptable.

MOBILITY OR STAGNATION

The first American high school opened in 1820; by the middle of the century, there were forty; and by 1890, high school enrollment had risen such that 3.5 percent of the people were high school graduates. The whole problem of equality of opportunity was answered rather simplistically: those who went to high school had taken full advantage of the opportunity and the others had not. Granted, it was harder for some people to forego early entry into the labor market than for others, but that was thought of as an individual, not a social, problem. It is the thesis of Samuel Bowles, cited above, that the real result of the system was virtually social-class stagnation. The lower classes were allowed to become sufficiently literate to serve in society, but high school and college were for the upper classes, so that the sons and daughters of the rich could remain in their inherited class position. With the great influx into the high schools in the twentieth century, the situation changed. Increasingly, nearly all young people from all strata of life were entering high school; 94 percent of all fourteen- to seventeen-year-olds were in school by 1970. Some were the academically prepared offspring of well-educated homes, but there were also many for whom entry into high school was a unique family experience. They were generally not prepared to keep up with those from the more educationally elite backgrounds.

Under such circumstances, an educational system has only three alternatives. The first is that of the old European model of separate schools for the upper classes and academically gifted and trade schools for the nonacademic masses. In the United States, though, time-honored custom has put all students into the same schools. Classifying them into different school systems would have been too much of a shock to the egalitarian ethic. The next possibility would be to leave all the students in the same classes and greatly increase the effort put forth on the less able, using such means (admittedly expensive) as having several teachers to a classroom or hiring special outside tutors.

Tracking systems   The other possibility, and the one generally settled upon, was to turn the high school (and sometimes even the grammar school) into an ability-grouping, or tracking, system, with classes for the academically gifted, for the middle range, and for the less able. After all, if state laws require high school attendance, it would be unmerciful to set standards that were beyond the reach of many students. At first glance, the idea of different academic levels within the same school seems fair and reasonable. The problem of teaching is simplified, since students compete with others who are virtually their equals in ability. The brightest students are stimulated by competing with other bright students, and the less intelligent are spared the utter discouragement of hopeless competition.

The seemingly ideal system of placing each student in his or her proper track has been subject to much criticism, however. Some have commented that it is an almost perfect model for a rigid class system, much more fitting for an aristocracy than a democracy. In his famous novel *Brave New World*, Aldous Huxley undoubtedly had the school tracking systems in mind when he presented a future society in which all people were conditioned to become alphas, betas, gammas, deltas, epsilons, and epsilon minuses, the last being almost utterly devoid of human intelligence. Each class of children is reared separately and led to expect very different rewards out of life. Critics of the tracking systems in our schools feel that exactly the same thing is happening here. The students who enter high school with low scores on their IQ tests are considered lost causes and are placed in an academic level with other educational "losers." Unless the school has a dedicated teacher who tries hard with such students, they may be assigned a teacher who is unhappy with his or her job, equipped with unchallenging teaching materials, and possessed with a general sense of hopelessness. Even if the IQ test scores were originally in error (as they sometimes are, particularly with students for whom English is a second language), the scores can still become self-fulfilling prophecies. Being placed in the lower tracks of a school system is discouraging at best; at worst, it is mentally stultifying. The tracking system can, in short, be thought of as an unintended means of perpetuating social-class stagnation. The unforeseen results of well-intended programs often lead to new problems.

College accessibility Regardless of whether the poor are of native or foreign background, black, white, or brown, highly intelligent or not, their chances of entering college are far less than those of the well-to-do. Bowles presents data showing that even among high school graduates, those from economically poor backgrounds have less than one-fourth the chance of graduating from college as do those from well-to-do families.[6] Furthermore, less than half the students in the top quartile of intelligence go to college if their families are in the bottom income quartile. The consequence of such a distribution of college graduation reveals another injustice in social class and education: state-supported colleges and universities draw their tax money from all the people, but it is largely the wealthier half of the population that reaps the benefit. In the statistics presented by Bowles, the child from the 90th percentile of income distribution can expect to receive 4 1/2 more years of schooling than a child from the poorest decile. Putting the case in its most extreme form, we can say that the child of the poor family is likely to be placed in a lower track or ability grouping in school, likely to be given a poorer education than the wealthy, and very unlikely to go to college yet expected to pay his or her share of the tax money that supports the entire system.

To each his own One of the proposed solutions to the dilemma is the adoption of a philosophy that says that "not all children are equally capable, but the school must develop them all along the lines of their own special capacities and limitations." Such a philosophy has resulted in several real improvements. The federal government is now funding programs to help the physically handicapped, the emotionally handicapped, and also the mentally retarded. However, a danger lurks in the philosophy of each according to his special needs. It is too easy simply to counsel children to pursue the lines of work that are traditional to their social class and ethnic group. Children of lower-class families are often advised to elect majors that seem to fit with their home background. A study of Mexican-American students and their teachers indicates that Chicanos are generally given less praise

[6]Bowles, op. cit., p. 47.

and encouragement than Anglo students, which lowers their hope for achievement.[7] Such students can easily be encouraged to set very limited goals, regardless of their ability.

Class background The thesis that family background affects economic success
far more than does IQ has been commented on increasingly in recent years. It was
one of the major themes of the Coleman Report of 1966[8] and of the more recent
research of Christopher Jencks and associates,[9] and it figures heavily in some of
the writings of Richard Hernstein.[10] All three of these writers as well as several
others have come to the conclusion that schools make very little difference in
success, that the real difference is a matter of family background, motivation,
and/or an inherited IQ.[11] In their conclusion, they would be in agreement somewhat with Samuel Bowles, except that Bowles sees class stagnation (the inevitable
result of capitalist control of industry) rather than biologically or socially inherited
differences in ability as the key factor. In any case, the conclusion is that the school
system does not function very effectively for upward mobility. One can quarrel with
this conclusion to some extent. Even though, as we have already noted, the
chances are much better for the offspring of college-educated parents, there are
many families whose young people are now going through college even though
neither parent had any college training. Additional evidence that a certain amount
of educational mobility actually does take place, despite the gloomy conclusions of
Coleman and Jencks, is that for the first time in history, in 1973 the number of black
students entering college (generally community colleges and state colleges) was in
direct proportion to their percentage of the total United States population.[12] In
spite of this gain, research has consistently shown that the black college graduate,
although better off than the nongraduate, does not achieve as high an income as
the equally educated white, although the difference is narrowing.[13] Even in
minority groups, individuals from family backgrounds of approximately middle
class status or above are the ones most likely to go to college. Hernstein goes so
far as to suggest that our society is becoming a hereditary meritocracy based on
IQ. Jencks objects to such a possibility and suggests a way out. In his opinion, we
must make pay for work much more equal than at present, whether the jobs call for
college training or not. Since any large amount of upward mobility through
education is impossible, such a wage policy would be the only just solution to the
dilemma.

The apparent inability of the schools to upgrade the social class status of more
than a small minority of people from lower-class backgrounds may have something
to do with the bureaucratic structure of the schools. The impersonality of the
school systems results in treating students in terms of categories rather than
personalities.

[7]United States Commission on Civil Rights, *Teachers and Students: Report V, Mexican-American
Education Study*, Government Printing Office, Washington, March 1973.
[8]James S. Coleman, et al., *Equality of Education and Opportunity*, Government Printing Office, Washington, 1966.
[9]Christopher Jencks et al., *Inequality: A Reassessment of Family and Schooling in America*, Basic Books,
Inc., Publishers, New York, 1972.
[10]Richard Hernstein, "I.Q. and the Social Class System," *Atlantic*, vol. 228, pp. 43–64, September 1971.
[11]Godfrey Hodgson, "Do Schools Make a Difference?" *Atlantic*, vol. 231, pp. 37–46, March 1973.
[12]Lipset, *op. cit.*, p. 59.
[13]Melvin Borland and Donald E. Yett, "The Cash Value of College for Negroes and Whites," *Transaction*,
vol. 3, pp. 44–49, November 1967.

Urbanization and well-meaning laws to prevent students from dropping out of school (often resented by high school students as too dictatorial), have increased the number and size of our public schools, and often crowded them beyond their capacity to do an effective job. Along with size has been an increase in administrative staffs and bureaucratic rules and regulations.

As previously noted, the number of high school graduates in 1890 represented only 3.5 percent of the population. By 1970, over 55 percent of all adults were high school graduates; but this figure really underrepresents the trend, because it includes people who were born as long as seventy or eighty years ago. Of the young adults, aged twenty-five to twenty-nine, 75 percent were high school graduates by 1970 and 16 percent had completed four or more years of college.[14] On the college level, enrollment increases in the decade of the 1960s were dramatic, with 476,000 baccalaureate degrees or higher awarded in 1960 and 1,165,000 in 1970. Approximately 13.6 million college degrees will be awarded in the 1970s. Community-college enrollments have increased even more than those of four-year colleges, up 280 percent in the decade of 1960–1970.[15] In the 1970s, community-college enrollments continue to increase, but mainly among adult students attending part time. The high point for college entrance by white high school graduates was reached in 1968, when 57 percent entered college. The absolute numbers of college students remained about the same in the middle 1970s, as in the late 1960s; but late in the decade the percentage of college entrants will increase or enrollments will decline, since the crest of the 1950s baby boom will have been reached by 1974–1975.[16] Despite some decrease in the age group, crowding of high schools continues because of the crowding of urban populations and a reluctance to vote money for new schools.

Effect of large enrollments　In the mind of the average layman, the occupational function of the schools is their major reason for being. School is explained to children from their earliest years as the means to "amounting to something"; but the admonition is not always followed, partly because the beginning of schooling is remote from ultimate occupational goals. For children from educated family backgrounds, and for a few others who are academically gifted, the learning of literature, history, and the arts is interesting and worthwhile, provided that the subjects are well taught. For many others, though, such subjects seem to be only a waste of time. In the days when it was perfectly respectable to drop out of school once the essentials of reading, writing, and arithmetic were learned, no major problem was posed. With the almost universal requirement of a high school diploma, and with nearly half the high school graduates entering some kind of college, the problem is much more difficult now. For many, the time spent in school has become an extremely long sentence. Standards are being relaxed, tracking systems are being used, more attention is being paid to teaching methods, and more counseling is being done—but often to no avail. Junior high and high school students have become unruly; and in some campuses violence has erupted. Often the only disciplinary measure open to the school is that of suspending students for

[14]Jencks, et al., *op. cit.*, p. 63.

[15]Michael F. Crowley, "Professional Manpower: The Job Market Turnaround," *Monthly Labor Review*, pp. 9–14, October 1972.

[16]Nelson F. Foote, "Putting Sociologists to Work," *The American Sociologist*, vol. 9, p. 125, August 1974.

a period of time, very often students whose chief aim is to get out anyway. After the students are suspended for a period of time, school authorities must round them up and bring them back to school to meet state attendance requirements. Why is there such determined resistance to the processing of students?

Mass education often has too little time for the individual who needs help. Join a tutorial program and help a child. Contact local schools to see what can be done.

High school resisters Part of the problem of many high school and junior high school students is simply a matter of age—the time in life when adult status has not yet been achieved but childhood has been left behind. They are years of objection to being herded about like children, years when important decisions about occupation, dating, sex, and status with one's peers become increasingly worrisome. The transition to adulthood is being made in the context of a large school, often with a terribly impersonal bureaucracy at a time when individual attention is needed. These problems apply to all, even to the most conforming students. They become much more perplexing to individuals who have met mainly failure at school and for whom the school holds no promise. A study by Nathan Caplan[17] concludes that the greatest single factor contributing to delinquency is the student's belief that academic and occupational success will never be achieved, whether or not the appraisal is realistic. Often, too, conditions outside the school have a very great bearing on whether discontent will lead to delinquency and violence.

A study of New York City high schools shows that political disorders, such as mass picketing and presentation of demands in the high schools, are influenced by racial distribution of students and teachers.[18] A high concentration of black students and teachers correlated with political protests, which in turn correlated with political events outside the school. (The data are for the school year 1968–1969 when political protests were more common than they are now.) The presence of a considerable number of black teachers on the faculty might have encouraged political demonstrations while reducing the number of nonpolitical disturbances. Free-for-all fights and gang rumbles become less frequent when students have political objectives on which to focus their attention.

A much more thorough study of violence in California high schools shows the same correspondence between political disturbances on the campus and outside events as was noted in New York, with such disturbances declining after 1970 along with the general decline in urban riots and college demonstrations.[19] However, vandalism has been increasing rapidly, not only in California but nationally. A Senate subcommittee in 1970 reported a 36 percent increase in vandalism over a period of four years—a total of 250,000 cases in the 110 school districts studied. The California study found that "the incidence of vandalism, fighting, and drug-alcohol offenses in the schools was directly related to the size of the school."[20] Also, the lower the socioeconomic level of the school, the more

[17]Nathan Caplan, "Delinquency and the Perceived Chances for Conventional Achievement," unpublished paper presented in the sociology department, University of Michigan, 1974.
[18]Paul Ritterband and Richard Silberstein, "Group Disorders in the Public Schools," *American Sociological Review*, vol. 38, pp. 461–467, August 1973.
[19]*A Report on Conflict and Violence in California's High Schools*, California State Department of Education, Sacramento, Calif., 1973.
[20]*Ibid.*, p. 5.

Vandalism increases in the city high schools, especially among the poor, the unsuccessful, and the alienated.

vandalism and other crimes. Vandalism is the type of crime noted by two well-known sociologists (Albert Cohen and James F. Short) as a symptom of alienation, angry hopelessness, and bitter antagonism. It is a type of malicious, nonutilitarian behavior aimed at expressing resentment, found mainly among the alienated poor, but sometimes also among segments of middle-class youth. The New York study indicates that resentment is mainly directed toward society itself; the California Department of Education study indicates that much of the resentment reflects on the schools. The California report states that the most frequent protest theme could be called the "ethnic-low-income-alienation complex," characterized by segregation of minority and low-income students within the school via clubs, tracking, and other subtle mechanisms. Other problems of the same type are courses and teaching practices that do nothing to enhance the esteem of low-income students. The increasingly poor prospects for students who drop out of school causes many to remain who would like to get out and sometimes the practical, vocational courses they want, as well as the individual instruction they need, are not available. They are too expensive for the school district to support.

The college bureaucracy   The very word college sounds old-fashioned today; even the term university is becoming outdated. This is the age of the "multiversity." The school years are spent in institutions that have become a preview of the mass bureaucracies that lie in the future for the graduate. Jacques Barzun speaks of World War II as the great divide between the old university and the new. Before World War II the administration of Columbia University by a single president was possible; now, even though there is still a single president, he can no longer function except through a mounting hierarchy of intermediaries, to administer scores of departments, hundreds of faculty, and tens of thousands of students.[21]

The increase in the student body of the great university is well known, but such is only part of the problem of school size. The university must now train scientists and engineers, contribute to medical, war, psychological, sociological, and economic research, and provide a home for the arts and theater. The degree of specialization is increasing. The individual of broad interests is an anachronism. Once a renowned scholar might teach a variety of related subjects; now he teaches a subdivision of a subdivision of a discipline. The result is that the proliferation of staff outpaces the proliferation of students. "What one man would have taught in 1880 required three in 1920 and from ten to thirty in 1960."[22]

The specialization is, of course, a result of several kinds of social changes. As the society becomes more scientifically oriented, it must spend more time on new research, which calls for high levels of specialization. One of the major themes of books that attempt to probe the future (Alvin Toffler's *Future Shock* and Daniel Bell's *The Coming of Post-Industrial Society*, for example) is the increasing amount of effort that goes into the production of knowledge, which is a slow, tedious process, calling for much experimentation and mathematical verification. One unfavorable consequence of the research effort, seen from the point of view of the undergraduate student, is that it does not necessarily result in good teaching.

The decline of teaching   In college the research-oriented bureaucracy often pays little attention to teaching. The question "Is Professor Schwartz an interesting lecturer?" only displays the naiveté of the questioner. The "right" question would be "Is Professor Schwartz eminent in the field?" Nothing is so damaging to one's academic reputation as to be known as a good teacher but a poor researcher. The fear of such reputational damage has "led many a naturally good teacher to deliberately hide this particular light under a bushel lest he thereby be thought of as without promise as a research man."[23] One clever assistant professor is quoted as saying that he is careful not to get tagged as being "good with undergraduates" for fear all promotions will cease.

To the ordinary student, the ability to teach is much more important than is the ability to do research. In answer to the question "In what ways would you bring about improvement in your school?," 46 percent of all students questioned in a college poll asked first for better teachers. Typical comments were "What good are

[21]Jacques Barzun, *The American University*, Harper & Row Publishers, Incorporated, New York, 1968, pp. 6–8.
[22]*Ibid.*, p. 18.
[23]Robert A. Nisbet, "Sociology in the Academy," in Charles H. Page (ed.), *Sociology and Contemporary Education*, Random House, Inc., New York, 1964, pp. 63 and 64.

Long waiting lines and inadequate registration systems symbolize the low rank of undergraduate students in the university bureaucracy.

degrees or academic reputations to me? I need a teacher." One student complained that his best teacher had been fired because he did not want to do research.[24]

This is not to say that professors shirk their duties. A recent study of the University of California indicates that work has actually increased but the amount of time devoted to undergraduate students has declined. The additional hours have gone to graduate students and research.[25] The system sought for becomes one that is economically productive: one professor with a student assistant lecturing to auditorium-sized classes and giving examinations that will be read only by an assistant, or, better yet, a computer. The total impact reinforces the image of the withering individual in the mass society.

Another frequent student complaint concerns a grading system that has no court of appeal. Of the 10,000 students interviewed by a college poll, 54 percent complained about the grading system. There were also complaints of an overloading of the curriculum with courses that seem irrelevant or display no clear relevance to the student. The students voiced other strong complaints about red tape, cumbersome communications systems, and the slow pace of reform.[26]

[24]James A. Foley and Robert K. Foley, *The College Scene*, McGraw-Hill, New York, 1971, pp. 78 and 79.
[25]Daryl Lembke, "UC Professors Fire Back at Work Critics," *Los Angeles Times*, October 5, 1970, pp. 1, 22.
[26]Foley and Foley, *op. cit.*, pp. 79 and 80.

Make a survey of college opinion at your school about what improvements are most needed—in grading, size of classes, remedial courses, psychological counseling, vocational counseling. Present results to the administration.

89

The university as a corporation   In the late 1960s the college campuses were aflame with protests over the Vietnam war and the military establishment. By the mid-1970s, the major concern of college students has become the job supply, which will be discussed in the next chapter. The protest generation uncovered an unpleasant fact about the relationship between the university and the outside world that did not fade away with the signing of the peace treaty in Vietnam: much of the university research work is paid for by vested interests concerned with many things besides the pursuit of pure knowledge or the furtherance of education. James Ridgeway[27] documents a whole series of ways in which the multiversity has become the handmaiden of business, politics, and the military establishment. He starts by pointing out that the average board of regents is made up for the most part of wealthy men who hold important positions in major corporations. Racial minorities, women, labor interests, and other nonestablishment groups are conspicuously absent. Add to this type of "general staff" for the university the fact that much of its income is derived from grants and it becomes clear that there are possibilities for corruption.

According to Ridgeway, the pharmaceutical companies have ingratiated themselves with medical schools by paying large sums of money for research. In return, professors have testified for their products before the Food and Drug Administration, even in cases where the research has been hasty and inadequate. Young doctors going through medical school and receiving favors from the drug companies are expected to remember their benefactors when writing prescriptions in later years. For many years the innumerable tests of cigarettes were called inconclusive largely because the tobacco companies were paying for the research work in some of the universities. Columbia University even became involved in promoting a filter-tip cigarette. According to Ridgeway, many very thorough tests of safety features were made in autos, but little or no negative publicity was given because of the close connection between research grants and the auto industry.

The defense establishment has received much more publicity than the other promoters of research. Responding to defense requests, the universities have become the major developers of atomic and hydrogen bombs and nearly every device of military importance. The result is that the Pentagon has often been the largest source of university funds. Under such circumstances one wonders how research scientists and university administrators can keep an open mind about issues of defense, war, and peace, and the international espionage of the C.I.A. In connection with the defense establishment, large amounts of secret research work in psychological warfare have been carried on to learn how to manipulate unfriendly (and even friendly) populations and how to propagandize in the underdeveloped world—secret activities that ill-befit institutions dedicated to the dissemination of knowledge.

Our schools, both high schools and colleges, have grown too vast, like the toad in Aesop's fable that tried to puff itself up to become an ox. Size and the complexity of tasks has almost led to the neglect of the primary function of administering to the

[27]James Ridgeway, *The Closed Corporation: American Universities in Crisis*, Ballantine Books, Inc., New York, 1968.

needs of the students. More attention needs to be given to the students, their changing characteristics and needs. What are the students of the 1970s like?

COLLEGE AND NONCOLLEGE YOUTH

The picture of college youth changes rapidly, so that assessing their needs is difficult. In the 1950s the general description of college students was that of individuals devoted mainly to their own personal careers, of getting positions in business, industry, and the professions. The 1960s, in contrast, were characterized by strong student involvement at the major universities in the civil rights movement, the student rights movements, and especially the antiwar movement. Along with the protests went a general political radicalizing of college students. They become more radical not only in opinions about the military-industrial establishment and business and the unresponsiveness of government but also in a number of attitudes regarding life-styles. There was a great increase in demand for sexual freedom, more use of marijuana, new styles in music and art, and extremely casual dress and appearance, the latter of which was in strong contrast to the grey-flannel-suit stereotype of the 1950s. As the new environmentalist movement and the women's liberation movements developed, they found ready support on the college campuses.

Compromise with the establishment The decade of the 1970s has shown a reaction by college students in the direction of compromise with the establishment. In a study made by Daniel Yankelovich,[28] and sponsored by several foundations, important changes in attitude were found among both the college youth and the noncollege youth of comparable age. Among college students, an interest in new life-styles continues, but the interest in radical politics is quiescent. There is much more commitment to the traditional idea of education and hard work as a means of getting ahead. The generation gap has narrowed as the older generation has become more tolerant of new fashions and life-styles and as college students have become more willing to reenter the mainstream of the technological society. The New Left has become a negligible factor on college campuses. There is less involvement in the cause of minority groups, with the strongest expressed sympathies being for the American Indians.

Persistence of new values Some of the attitudes of the 1960s have been retained, such as a belief in the new sexual morality, sympathy for the women's liberation movement, a decline in conventional religion, and a desire to find self-fulfillment. The attitude now seems to be that self-fulfillment can be found in the context of a conventional career. Comparing 1968 with 1973 (the year of the Yankelovich study), it was found that the young people expressing primary interest in a career increased from 55 to 66 percent, and those looking for a challenging job increased from 64 to 77 percent. Those emphasizing a desire for self-expression also increased from 56 to 68 percent; and those wanting greater sexual freedom increased from 43 to 61 percent. One of the earlier political attitudes also intensified: those believing patriotism to be a very important value declined from 35 to 19 percent. A strong conflict of values appears in the survey, with a general feeling that ours is too much of a money-grubbing society but, conversely, a strong

[28]Daniel Yankelovich, *Changing Values in the 70s: A Study of American Youth*, McGraw-Hill Book Company, New York, 1974.

interest in well-paying jobs. In an assessment of our society, opinion remains pessimistic, with little faith in the honesty of government or of the political parties. In the personal sphere, however, the outlook is optimistic, with the feeling on the part of college students that they are "training themselves for positions in an elite group which is peculiarly necessary in an advanced industrial society."[29]

Noncollege youth In some respects the more interesting and possibly more significant part of the study has to do with the opinion of noncollege youth. "What we find today is an astonishingly swift transmission of values formerly confined to a minority of college youth and now spread throughout the generation."[30] The noncollege youth of the 1970s—not the majority but significantly larger percentages than four years before—seems to be increasingly accepting the viewpoints of college youth of the late 1960s on such subjects as sexual freedom, abortion, patriotism, and religion. They did not, however, accept the ideas of the women's liberation movement. Self-expression and self-fulfillment were accepted as important values by three-quarters of the noncollege youth, and they considered interesting work just as important as job security.

Pessimism rather than optimism characterizes the noncollege youth in their outlook about their own personal futures. The pessimism is particularly pronounced among minority youth and Vietnam veterans. A majority of both groups say they cannot make ends meet. The veterans, in 25 percent of the cases, felt that they were only second-class citizens. Alcohol and drug use were twice as high among the veterans as among the nonveterans. Yet in spite of pessimism regarding personal lives and society, a majority of the veterans were more likely than others to approve of suggested reasons for going to war, such as stopping aggression or stopping communism.

More than six out of ten young adults, college and noncollege, believe that special interests run the political machinery of the nation and that the society is democratic in name only. New ideas of fundamental rights are also emerging in both groups. A majority felt that the best medical care should be available to everyone regardless of ability to pay. A majority also felt that there should be greater worker participation in job decisions. Almost a majority (48 percent) thought that all people should be able to send their children to college whether they could afford to bear the costs or not. Further details of the attitudes of young adults toward education are particularly interesting. Asked if they thought one year of their schooling should be devoted to career planning, 76 percent of the noncollege youth said "yes." Seeing their lack of educational background and vocational training as the source of their failure to get satisfactory jobs, 71 percent said they would consider a six-year combined work-college program; 68 percent were interested in new technical schools; and 66 percent were interested in new types of apprenticeship programs.

Implications of attitude change The optimism expressed by college students in the survey is not entirely justified. In the next chapter we shall look at the problems of employment in more detail; but stated briefly here, the Labor Department projections into the mid-1980s indicates that more college degrees will be earned than are needed to fill the positions usually awarded to college graduates.

[29]*Ibid.*, p. 22.
[30]*Ibid.*, p. 23.

92 Currently, the surplus is especially great in the teaching field. The result will probably be that college graduates will absorb many jobs previously held by people who have completed only high school or one or two years of college. The Labor Department predicts more job changing and discontentment among college graduates who cannot be absorbed into their fields but no serious unemployment.

Obviously, if people with college training are to occupy jobs now open to noncollege people, the result could easily be even fewer interesting jobs for the latter. The solution being taken by many of the noncollege group is to improve their education by course work while continuing their jobs. Much of the course work is in evening school, especially in community colleges. Four-year colleges and universities, jealous of their reputations as academic institutions, are only beginning to adjust to the part-time vocational student. Since the rush to college has not been as great in the 1970s as it was in the 1960s, chances seem good that more programs for the part-time student will develop.

A study of attitudes among noncollege youth could easily lead to the conclusion that there will be increasing demands on the part of laborers for a role in decision making along with general discontent and radicalism. The first conclusion—about the demands of labor—is probably warranted, but caution should be used in making further conclusions from statistical studies. There is often a gulf between what people say in questionnaires and what they actually do, and attitudes are easily changed by the events of the day. The attitudes of college youth are not as radical as they were during the Vietnam war. Perhaps a change in philosophy in Washington will be able to dispell the aura of corruption and manipulation of the Watergate period and political attitudes will be less alienated than the 1973 studies showed. Daniel P. Moynihan has even theorized that the future society might become rather conservative, partly because of a lowered birthrate and a high average age of citizenry. "A society whose population is barely growing tends to be curiously straitened and strict in its behavior,"[31] Moynihan says, but he admits that his opinion is based more on historical impressionism than on sociological research.

The strong support given by noncollege young adults for much greater attention to career planning, combined with the previously cited demands of discontented high shcool students for better vocational counseling, suggests that more attention should be turned in the direction of advice on employment. The complexities of the current occupational scene call for counselors who can devote their full attention to the needs of the labor market rather than to the testing of ability and interest done in most schools.

Equality of results Daniel Bell confronts us with an important dilemma of modern education in America: the demands of a meritocracy versus the demand for equality of result in education.[32] The word meritocracy is borrowed from the English sociologist Michael Young, who used it to describe a society of the future with leadership held by an intellectual elite, selected purely as a result of merit in intelligence and training. There are, says Bell, many characteristics of the late twentieth century that call for such a meritocracy. Increasingly greater effort is being put into the production of new knowledge, and the need for bright, imaginative, well-trained, scientifically oriented leaders is greater than ever before.

[31]Daniel P. Moynihan, "Getting Back to Earth," *The Public Interest*, Summer 1973.
[32]Daniel Bell, *The Coming of Post-Industrial Society*, Basic Books, Inc., Publishers, New York, 1973, pp. 408–433.

At the same time, the philosophical requirements of equality of opportunity have taken root very strongly in the society. Not only have we increasingly insisted on equality of opportunity, but the current ideology begins to call for equality of result, especially with respect to minority groups. One of the consequences of the demand for equality of result has been affirmative action programs, first started by executive orders during the Johnson administration and strengthened in the years since. At first, the policies called for employment of members of minority groups, especially blacks and Chicanos, in approximately their proportion to community membership. More recently, affirmative action programs have come to apply to women as well. The results have been the opening of many positions for minority-group members who have college degrees and much greater encouragement for minority-group members to enter college.

Affirmative action programs have done the very great service of raising hopes and aspirations for minority people and giving them more of a share in America. At the same time, the new policies have thrown another task onto the schools, which is to try, in a single generation, to bring the sons and daughters of the poorly educated up to the same level of academic competence as the offspring of the middle and upper-middle classes. In many individual cases, the results have been favorable. On the general average, however, the job has proved extremely difficult.

Both primary and secondary schools have tried a number of innovations, some of which have proved helpful to minority students and some not. More teaching assistants to give individual attention have proved beneficial. On the other hand, attempts at open classrooms and more student self-direction have been more successful for students from well-educated homes than for others. Children from poorly educated families can hardly be expected to take over much self-direction. Richard Endsley, coordinator of the experimental schools in Berkeley, California, says of nonwhite children from poverty areas, "Non-white kids tend not to function well in open classrooms because they simply aren't used to that type of behavior from what should be adult authority figures."[33] What seems to be in order is emphasis on basic skills, taught by kindly but insistent adults, at least in the all-important years of primary education. Otherwise the task of remedial work in high schools and community colleges becomes formidable—if, indeed, it can be accomplished at all.

The transformation of higher education Martin Trow agrees with the opinion commonly held that the present trend toward larger and larger percentages of college students from each high school graduating class will continue,[34] despite temporary downturns. Although there will be no law forcing attendance, public pressure and the unavailability of jobs for people without any college training will act as compulsive forces. To a degree, what has happened to the high schools will happen to the colleges: the student body will continue to lose its elite status; the common-man level will have to be absorbed. In order to make college available and meaningful to the new students, many new directions will be needed, some of which are already partly in evidence.

When colleges attracted only a small percentage of the college-age group, it was assumed that those who attended were motivated to do so. The problem of motivation will become increasingly pronounced in the colleges; in fact, it is

[33]Quoted in "Back to Basics in the Schools," *Newsweek*, p. 94c, October 21, 1974.
[34]Martin Trow, "The Expansion and Transformation of Higher Education," General Learning Press, Morristown, N.J., 1972.

The transformation of higher education provides for the return to school of people of all ages.

already much more manifest than in the past. Possibilities being tried in many community colleges include a certain amount of field work rather than a total concentration on class hours. Students who volunteer to work in poverty areas or at other welfare-oriented tasks can receive credit for doing so, especially in the social sciences and humanities. The Carnegie Commission on Higher Education recommends a greatly increased use of delayed entry into higher education as well as "stopping out" periods. Many high school graduates, especially those who are not strong in academic subjects, would be well advised to delay college entry for a year or two, thereby giving themselves a chance to work, to mature, and to think over possibilities. Even though a few might choose not to go on to college as a result of this delay, the majority will probably do so. After entry, it has been suggested, reentry should be made easy, in case a student wishes to take more time out, which might be necessary for financial reasons or because of indecision about goals.

At present, late entry, stopping out, and reentry are quite common practices in community colleges. If Trow is right in his analysis, such practices will be more common in the future in four-year colleges as well. Moreover, large numbers of adults will be returning to college from time to time or taking evening courses. Part of the consequence will be that of erasing the boundaries between community and college. The charge that the colleges use tax money from all the people to serve just a few will not be as valid as heretofore. Undoubtedly new problems will arise, and the old problem of trying to maintain standards of excellence in a mass educational system will probably be more serious than at present. It must be added, too, that there will continue to be college dropouts just as there have always been high school dropouts; and for those who complete college, the task will be rewarding only if the demand for highly trained personnel remains strong. Far

more counseling, career planning, and close cooperation between schools and the
job market must develop or society could wind up with large numbers of well-
educated malcontents.

What courses offered in your school help to erase the boundaries between college
and community? What new offerings could you suggest?

SUGGESTED READINGS

Foley, James A. and Robert K. Foley: *The College Scene: Students Tell It Like It Is*,
McGraw-Hill Book Company, New York, 1971. Student attitudes and opinions based on
interviews about race, sex, riots, drugs, God, the faculty, business, and war are all included.
The authors appeal also for the paternal generation to read it, "for it is possible that the
generation gap can be closed with greater ease than either side imagines."

Glasser, William: *Schools without Failure*, Harper & Row, Publishers, Incorporated, New
York, 1969. Glasser presents an alternative to school systems that inevitably pronounce a
number of children as failures. His alternative involves attempts to increase the student's
awareness of his own responsibility, along with setting realistic goals to be mastered step
by step. Advocates a democratic atmosphere, learning by problem solving, free discussion,
and student participation in planning.

Page, Charles H. (ed.): *Sociology and Contemporary Education*, Random House, Inc., New
York, 1963. Selections by such prominent sociologists as Bierstedt, Bressler, Chinoy,
Nisbet, and Paige. Deals with the relationship between sociology and education, the
broadening aspects of sociology, the challenges to the conventional wisdom, and popular
sociology in contrast to academic research.

Ridgeway, James: *The Closed Corporation: American Universities in Crisis*, Ballantine Books,
Inc., New York, 1968. A powerful indictment of the universities for maintaining too close a
collusion with business, government, and the defense department. Also protests the use of
graduate students as "a pool of cheap labor."

Toffler, Alvin (ed.): *Learning for Tomorrow: The Role of the Future in Education*, Vintage
Books, Random House, Inc., New York, 1974. A collection of essays dealing with ways to
better equip schools and curricula for preparing the younger generation for the future
world. Includes curriculum considerations for humanities, social sciences, and physical
sciences. Considers all levels of education and the future of women and minority groups.

Useem, Elizabeth: *The Education Establishment*, Spectrum Books, Prentice-Hall, Inc.,
Englewood Cliffs, N.J., 1973. Concerned with the groups that control our schools and
colleges, largely business, male, white, and elitist. Consequences to education of the
present groups in control. Contends that the system perpetuates inequality.

QUESTIONS

1 What problems prevent us from accomplishing the equalization ideal of education?

2 What are the reasons for and objections to tracking (ability-groupings) systems in the
schools?

3 What have been some of the undesirable consequences of large size and bureaucratic
structure in high schools and colleges?

4 What are the contrasting opinions and outlook for the future of college and noncollege
youth, according to the Yankelovich survey?

5 What does Trow mean by the transformation of higher education?

5

WORK FOR THE NIGHT IS COMING

What has happened to the old ethic of hard work? Has it defeated itself by turning out too many goods, or by making types of work for which only a minority of people have the required talents? Is there truth to the charge made by Goodman that many jobs facing youth are meaningless and unrewarding? How closely connected are the realities of the employment market and the educational system described in the previous chapter?

Whatever the case about replacement of certain types of unskilled and semiskilled work, much blue-collar labor still remains. Have the problems of alienation of labor been solved? What about the practical problems of mine safety, adequate workmen's compensation laws, and attempts to lessen occupational diseases and health hazards? What is automation doing to jobs, and what will it do in the future? Is job security for the educated likely to be increasingly threatened by economic slowdowns and shifts in governmental policies? Are there any jobs to prepare for that are absolutely safe against declining need and layoff?

Finally, what are some views of the consequences of the changing nature of work in increasingly technological, bureaucratic societies? Will there be more work satisfaction or less? Can leisure activities give purpose to life if the amount of human labor needed continues to decline? How will leisure be used?

One reason the educational system is overburdened with responsibilities is that such intensive training is now needed to meet the nation's work requirements. It is frequently said that there are no longer any jobs whatever for the uneducated and unskilled. The statement is a little exaggerated, but it is certainly in line with the trends that have been observable for several generations. In colonial America and throughout the first half of our independent existence as a nation, the majority of people simply inherited their occupations from their parents. The occupation was usually farming, a type of job that called for hard work and frugal living but that was uncomplicated by the specialties of botany, zoology, entomology, soil chemistry, farm management, and marketing. The majority of nonfarm work was also manual labor that called for no advanced training or specialization.

Today the problem of occupational choice is one of the most trying of life, although it is seldom given the consideration it deserves in school curricula. Students going to college worry about occupational choice, frequently change majors, and dread the possibility of preparing for blind alleys or overcrowded fields. From their high school days they are told how only a college education can guarantee them jobs that pay well and are personally rewarding. Many skeptical students wonder not so much about the self-realization value of an education but about whether the modern computerized society is producing the types of jobs that give a sense of fulfillment. Will the jobs prepared for in college be available, or will less satisfying alternatives have to be accepted? Will occupational life be a useful, creative process, or will it consist mainly of developing salesmanship for unloading surplus goods on an unwilling public?

THE WORK-ETHIC CYCLE

In a thought-provoking documentary film presented by NET in the early 1960s, the main musical theme in the background was the old American hymn "Work for the Night is Coming." The theme was used, the commentary said, because no other country had made hard work so much of a national ethos as had the United States. There may possibly be exceptions to the statement, but there is no doubt that we are products of what Max Weber called the Protestant ethic—an ethic of hard work, frugality, and striving. It can be said with little fear of contradiction that we have long since abandoned much of the frugality of which Weber spoke, but to a great degree the ethos of hard work continues. Even the wealthy people of America have not been idle; they have busied themselves at becoming wealthier than before. There has also been an unusually strong tendency (as will be explained further in Chapter 10) to view poverty as almost entirely the product of laziness and evil. For generations we have repeated Poor Richard's admonitions: "waste neither time nor money; an hour lost is money lost." Our homespun philosophers and poets have told us "procrastination is the thief of time," and "Act, act in the living present, heart within and God o'erhead!" And we have made heroes of the giants of production, so much so that Aldous Huxley imagined a *Brave New World* in which all events would be dated from "The Year of Our Ford."

The nemesis of the work ethic The work ethic consists not only of hard work but also of frugality. When such an ethic is applied to an entire society, and especially one with a rich domain to exploit, the time comes when there seems little point in being frugal. In fact, the work ethic and the frugality ethic become mutually

The work ethic and the conquest of a continent. Work on the transcontinental railroad proceeded night and day.

99

incompatible. Unless people spend their money freely, there will be no market for the mountain of products ground out by an efficient technology and a work ethic. More attention must be turned, then, to consumer goods and to salesmanship and services. Nowhere else in the world is such a large part of the population engaged in the processes of producing services as in the United States, and this has a pronounced effect on the types of jobs available. The production ethic has nearly defeated itself.

The nemesis of the competition ethic Competition has been a major force moving the American economy toward greater productive efficiency, but competition eventually begins to defeat itself. The most efficient competitors run the less efficient out of business or make merger arrangements with them. Eventually the overwhelming amount of business is concentrated in the hands of a few giant corporations in each field of production, a condition referred to as "oligopoly." The result of the change in the competitive economy is that more and more people must be hired to work for gigantic concerns. Many years ago the gigantic concerns were opposed by the labor unions, but now union labor finds it more convenient to bargain with large concerns than with small ones. Now a new type of criticism arises, this time from higher echelons. It is feared that the human being is dominated by the organization for which he or she works—a condition described in such books as *The Organization Man*[1] and *Up the Organization*.[2] Large numbers of people, and especially college graduates, become organization men of the type described in these books—well treated in many respects but with their lives, thoughts, aims, and values, circumscribed by the organization. Only an insignificant number work for small concerns or for themselves.

[1] William H. Whyte, *The Organization Man*, Simon and Schuster, Inc., New York, 1956.
[2] Robert Townsend, *Up the Organization*, Alfred A. Knopf, Inc., New York, 1970.

| **Ensuring perpetual motion**   It has long been assumed that with vastly increasing productivity and with the growth of large organizations able to produce the goods and, to quite a degree, regulate the market, the need for workers would decline drastically. Sometimes it seems to do so, especially during economic recessions, but unemployment never rises to anything like the levels of the Great Depression or as high as would seem logical in terms of machine and worker productivity. Techniques have been developed for keeping up a fairly frantic pace of production regardless of how glutted the market would have seemed to people of an earlier age.

One of the techniques for maintaining production has already been mentioned—planned obsolescence. Another technique for keeping consumption going is good advertising that will cause people to feel a need for previously unheard of commodities. By one means or another, a technique is developed for increasing consumer demand sufficiently so that all products will be sold. The result is what two generations of beatniks and hippies have called "the rat race." Many of the most talented people in society devote their lives to making others realize they need something they have never heard of before.

The great supervisor   Even with great effort devoted to keeping the perpetual-motion machine running, there is always a feeling of danger. What if Mr. Smith should decide not to try to keep up with the Joneses? What if a million Mr. Smiths decided not to keep up with a million Joneses? There could be a major depression. To avoid the possibility of such a disaster, many people are employed by the government, analyzing the economy, deciding whether to give it a shot in the arm by deficit spending or to slow it down by raising rediscount rates. Or should there be price and wage controls? Or should the government step in with makeshift jobs? Decisions of this kind, and the public knowledge that the government has to wrestle with such problems, gives a permanent atmosphere of uneasiness about the whole world of work. In earlier times man's work was much harder and often from sunup to sundown. Today the hours are shorter and the rewards higher, but the uncertainties are greater.

Besides regulating the economy through money supply and government spending, the government may act as an employer of last resort in times of recession. Even in good times the government is the largest single employer of manpower, and the individual may find that the best area of employment is in a government job. Opportunities might be found in private industry, but a type of private industry that is mainly geared to meeting governmental requirements—supplying the war machine, building airports and government edifices, designing bridges, highways, and aqueducts. Or the individual might be the representative of industry, working to get the contracts that ensure financial survival and affluence. Whatever the job, it will be increasingly perceived as part of a giant, interlocking organism of public and private sectors. The ethic of hard work not only has rendered frugality obsolete but has subordinated individual enterprise to a mighty enterprise in governmental-industrial cooperation.

In the old hymn "Work for the Night is Coming," night symbolized the end of life and the path to one's heavenly reward. Now night seems to symbolize the end of the individual's effort on his or her own shop or plot of ground. Rather than reach the heaven of traditional Western theology, we have evolved a system reminiscent of Eastern philosophy, in which the individual must merge with the oversoul. The oversoul in this case is a bureaucratic society, increasingly planned, dominating, and inescapable. Worse yet, no one is convinced that government economists know what to do, or whether there is, indeed, any way of simultaneously coping with unemployment and inflation.

Perhaps the problem transcends all national economies. Multinational corporations, operating in many nations and with stockholders and managers of many nationalities, now dominate some of the high-technology industries. More than 200 such corporations, with minimum assets of $100 million each, are growing more powerful than many of the nations of the world.[3]

RELUCTANT YOUTH AND THE BUREAUCRATIC SOCIETY

The emerging society is called by various names: the technical society, the bureaucratic state, the administrative state, or even "technological totalitarianism." Whatever the emerging form of society might be called, it is one that promises abundance for people who plunge wholeheartedly into its mainstream. For the foreseeable future, however, not all people can enter the mainstream, for some will be swept into little side channels and some into scum-laden pools of poverty. Moreover, the main course often shifts, and one can end in a backwash that will dry up unless fed again by waters of life in the form of federal money. Such is the occasional fate of much of the aeronautics industry. The shipping industry has always depended on subsidization for survival, and for years the same was true of the agricultural field.

The encircling system   Years ago school readings books had stories in which boys grew to young manhood and then went out to "seek their fortune." The work world had a spirit of adventure. The talented and lucky individual could have innumerable experiences of life, from factory worker to typesetter to railroad brakeman, and he could eventually work his way up. Now there is something called "the break in the skill hierarchy," the point beyond which the individual lacking special training can never go.

The possibility of having various vocational experiences still exists, but on a diminishing scale. Employment for the young is not encouraged. Labor laws make such jobs difficult, and there are also other biases against youth. In a time of job shortages, people feel that all available jobs should be given to the heads of households. There is also uncertainty about how steady an employee a young person will make, although a recent Labor Department study shows them doing about as well as adults. Especially if they seem capable and ambitious, the young workers will be thought likely to look for "greener pastures" as soon as possible or for a return to school.

The net result of the employment bias against youth is an unemployment rate of 17.5 percent for eighteen- and nineteen-year-olds with one to three years of high school. Ironically, those with only an eighth-grade education show a slightly lower unemployment rate of 15.7 percent.[4] The probable explanation is that eighth graders are seen as the stable lower class, not likely to change to better jobs.

The personal future of employment, then, becomes a curious contradiction for a freedom-loving society. One should be free to investigate a great variety of

[3]Irving Louis Horrowitz, "Capitalism, Communism, and Multinationalism," *Society*. vol. 11, no. 2, pp. 32–43, January-February 1974.
[4]William Deuterman, "Educational Attainment of Workers, March 1969 and 1970," *Monthly Labor Review*, pp. 12–13, October 1970.

Actual and projected demand for new elementary and secondary school teachers compared with number of college graduates, 1963 to 1978 (numbers in thousands) *Manpower Report of the President*, Department of Labor, transmitted to Congress, March 1970

Year	Total teachers employed	Number required for growth and replacement	New teachers required*	Total number of college graduates†	New teachers required as percent of graduates
1963	1,806	209	157	444	35
1965	1,951	208	156	530	29
1967	2,097	222	166	591	28
1968	2,178	239	179	667	27
1969	2,225	209	157	755	21
1970	2,245	190	142–190	772	18–25
1973	2,286	189	142–189	859	17–22
1975	2,304	183	137–183	928	15–20
1978	2,334	187	140–187	1,029	14–18

*Figures for 1963 to 1969 represent 75 percent of the total number required for growth and replacement, with a conservative allowance for the numbers of teachers who returned to the profession. Since the return flow of experienced teachers may possibly decline during the 1970s, the ranges shown indicate the numbers and percents of new teachers that would be required with a return flow ranging from 0 to 25 percent.
†Includes bachelor's and first professional degrees awarded.
SOURCE: Based on data from the Department of Health, Education, and Welfare, Office of Education.

interests and viewpoints. One should investigate philosophies, political ideologies, and religious experiences. Also, before marrying one should date a number of different people, gaining experience before making decisions. But in the field of employment, one should take a battery of intelligence tests and occupational preference tests, go to a vocational counselor, and then set one's course without deviation and definitely without experience!

THE UNCERTAINTIES

The dramatic growth in the number of people graduating from college indicates an increasing concern about the diminishing number of jobs requiring lower levels of skill and training. People have turned to more schooling not only in an attempt to ensure jobs but also in an attempt to find more interesting and rewarding work. Surveys taken in the 1940s and 1950s found people ranking steady work first on a list of job requirements. By the end of the next decade, interesting work ranked first.[5] Partly as a consequence of the search for more interesting and satisfying life work, the number of college graduates more than doubled from 1960 to 1970. Unemployment among college graduates remained very low, and pay averaged almost twice as high as that of high school dropouts.

In spite of generally better employment prospects for the educated, uncertainties have crept into the occupational picture. By 1970 it was becoming apparent that there were more people with teaching credentials than there were teaching positions, partly as a result of a downturn in birthrate that was already affecting the

[5]George Strauss, "Worker Dissatisfaction: A Look at the Causes," *Monthly Labor Review*, vol. 97, no. 2, p. 57, February 1974.

lower grades. One could argue that a really excellent educational system could absorb more teachers, but the shortage of tax dollars limits the number who can actually be hired. Education has been a preferred field for women, partly because there has been less sex discrimination in pay than in many other occupations, and partly because working hours correspond fairly well with the school hours of their children. Two-thirds of the women graduating from college in the late 1960s prepared for teaching jobs.[6] Although there continues to be a need for new teachers to replace those who are retiring, the need declines each year. Whereas 35 percent of all college graduates were needed for teaching in 1963, the estimated need by 1978 is for only about 14 percent.[7] The outlook will be good for those with the very highest credentials and with certain special skills. There will also be "jobs in rural districts and in all geographical areas where teaching salaries are low and better paying positions are available in other field in the community"[8]—not a very happy prospect!

| In the *Monthly Labor Review* or in the annual bulletins of the Department of Labor, look up the prospects for your own chosen area of employment.

Just as the problem for teachers developed, it was becoming apparent that certain technical fields were, at least temporarily, oversubscribed. Not many years before, there had been speculation about whether we could produce enough talent to fill all the technical positions needed, and the United States was causing a "brain drain" by hiring too many foreign experts, especially from developing nations. Then came a turnaround in the job market even for some types of engineers and scientists, partly because of reduced government expenditures for scientific research.[9] Increasingly the government becomes the decision maker on whether certain categories of specialists will be hired or not.

The general problem for college graduates, as seen by the Labor Department is that the years 1972 to 1985 will call for a total number of 14.5 million jobs for college graduates, but the number of graduates will be approximately 15.3 million. The oversupply of graduates is expected to be more severe in the 1980 to 1985 period than in the 1972 to 1980 period.[10] One reason for this is that more women than previously are not only graduating from college, but actively entering the market for the best jobs.

Despite the problem of oversupply, the rate of unemployment among college graduates is expected to remain very low. A survey of recent college graduates finds one-half in work "directly related to their major field of study, almost one fifth in work somewhat related, and about one third in work not at all related."[11] The latter group includes a large number of graduates in the humanities and social sciences.

What is happening is that the college students are finding jobs, but often not the

[6]U.S. Department of Labor, *U. S. Manpower in the 1970s*, November 1970.
[7]U.S. Department of Labor, *Manpower Report of the President*, pp. 169–170, March 1970.
[8]*Occupational Outlook Handbook for 1970-1971*, U.S. Department of Labor Bulletin 1650, p. 198.
[9]Michael F. Crowley, "Professional Manpower: The Job Market Turnaround," *Monthly Labor Review*, p. 12, October 1972.
[10]Neal H. Rosenthal, "The United States Economy in 1985: Projected Changes in Occupations," *Monthy Labor Review*, p. 24, December 1973.
[11]Vera C. Perrella, "Employment of Recent College Graduates," U.S. Department of Labor Special Labor Force Report 151, 1973, p. 42.

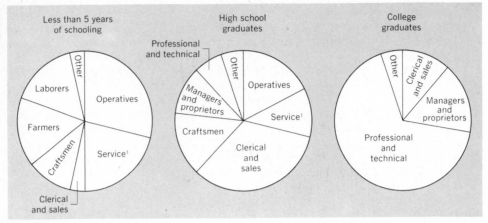

| Less than 5 years of schooling | High school graduates | College graduates |

¹Includes private household workers

ones they prepared for. Since the supply of college graduates is greater than the demand for the usual types of jobs requiring a college degree, more will be absorbed in other types of work—a situation variously called "occupational upgrading" or "college graduate downgrading." With college graduates having to settle for jobs previously held by high school graduates, the latter will find themselves somewhat less employable than before. As stated by a Labor Department researcher,

College graduates are expected to continue to have a competitive advantage over those with less education in competing for employment. Despite the apparent surplus of college graduates for the 1980-85 period, which is generated by statistics based on past patterns, it is unlikely that the unemployment rate of college graduates will be affected significantly. Rather, it is likely that college graduates will obtain jobs previously held by individuals with less than 4 years of college. In general, graduates have reacted to changes in the job situation in the past by taking the best available job, and there is no reason to assume that this will change. Problems for college graduates will more likely be underemployment and job dissatisfaction, resulting in increasing occupational mobility rather than unemployment.[12]

The college experience should not be measured solely in terms of employability. The individual's life is enriched by college experiences and formal studies not directly concerned with the job. Nevertheless, men and women who make the effort and bear the costs of four or more years of college can be forgiven for expecting a financial as well as an intellectual award.

Another important question has to do with the types of jobs and conditions of employment that will exist in fields that are subject to rapid technological change. Such fields of employment tend to hit the blue-collar worker first, but they are eventually of concern to the white-collar worker and the technician.

CHRONIC PROBLEMS OF INDUSTRIAL LABOR

The society that is moving in the direction of greater rationalization of production, closer linkage between government and industry, and greater giantism and

[12]Rosenthal, *op. cit.*, p. 24.

efficiency in its techniques of production is even less reassuring to the common laboring man than to the college graduate. The increases in automated processes have been an incessant worry to labor union leaders and workers. There have been predictions of doom for the laborer, and there have also been predictions of shorter hours and improved wages, working conditions, and other benefits. The actual fact seems to be that automation has not taken away as many jobs as had been feared, but neither has it produced a generally happy, contented worker.

The middle-class labor myth It is often said that the worker of today is so well paid that he no longer identifies with the working class but regards himself as middle-class, happy, and immune from industrial alienation. The statement cannot be refuted in all cases because conditions of labor differ greatly from industry to industry. To weight the scales badly, one could start with a study of migratory agricultural labor, which is so depressed and so little changed over a period of time that its discussion must be left instead to a later chapter on poverty. Factory work is not nearly so depressed as agricultural labor, but studies of factory workers do not indicate a high level of satisfaction with the jobs. The authors of *Man on the Assembly Line* found that 90 percent of the workers hated their jobs, largely because of pace, noise, and inability to communicate with fellow workers.[13] Although workers were better paid than on their previous jobs, they generally disliked the assembly line jobs more. Harvey Swados expresses the assembly line worker's view succinctly when he says that although the working man possibly desires all the same commodities as the middle class,

> He works like a worker. The steel mill puddler does not yet sort memos, the coal miner does not yet sit in conferences, the cotton millhand does not yet sip martinis. The worker's attitude toward his work is generally compounded of hatred and resignation.[14]

Swados continues to comment on the sense of being outside the system, of not counting, of not being quite human as long as one is a common laborer. Another commentator makes almost precisely the same contrast between laborer and white-collar worker. The white-collar worker, sitting in an office, identifies with the company, almost feels like part of management, even though his wages may be lower than those of the skilled laborer. Patricia Sexton[15] comments on her experiences of three years on the assembly line. The average person who has not faced assembly line work, she says, finds it hard to imagine some of the causes of strikes, but they often boil down to a denial of human dignity. "Comes lunch time, there's a good cafeteria for the office staff, but it's too far away for the plant workers." Anyway, plant workers just don't belong there. The pace of the line is so antagonizing, she says, that many workers try to get on as sweepers, even though the job doesn't pay as well. She also mentions such little indignities as being timed for a trip to the restroom, and "no doors on the johns." With the work pace as wearing as it is, anger can mount over a slight speed up or refusal of a coffee break, or the decision to no longer have coffee carts on the factory floors. In spite of complaints about the union, workers rally around the union when a strike is called;

[13]Charles Walker and Robert H. Guest, *Man of the Assembly Line*, Harvard University Press, Cambridge, Mass., 1952.
[14]Harvey Swados, "The Myth of the Happy Worker," in Eric and Mary Josephson, *Man Alone*, Dell Publishing Co., Inc., New York, 1962, pp. 105–113.
[15]"The Auto Assembly Line: An Inside View," *Harper's*, vol. 224, pp. 54–57, June 1962.

and a strike—though it entails hardship—has certain excitement about it, since it is a way of striking back at the high and mighty.

Make an informal survey of worker satisfaction, interviewing blue-collar and white-collar workers and professionals.

Not all studies of blue-collar labor report as strong feelings of alienation as Swados and Sexton described in the early 1960s, but there are a number of problems that are growing more and more severe. Income, which seems adequate for a young couple, becomes increasingly inadequate as children mature and high school expenses must be faced.[16] Blue-collar laborers are aware of declining status and, much worse, the decline of their line of employment. Steel, railroading, auto-assembly lines, and many other fields of blue-collar employment decline with the advance of automation. Economically, the rapid gains of the 1950s were not maintained in the 1960s; and by the 1970s, blue-collar workers experienced an actual decline in income relative to inflated prices. Not only that, but the laborers felt discriminated against in the tax structure as they became aware of the ability of the rich to evade taxes.

The children of blue-collar workers, it is true, receive more education than their parents; but often the education process is a case of running hard just to stand still. The sons and daughters now need at least a community-college education to be eligible for the jobs that were once given to high school graduates, or even high school dropouts.

As costs rise, the only alternative is to have the wife work. In an age of increasing status and employment for women, this seems a satisfactory alternative, but the wives of blue-collar workers are usually not employable at very desirable jobs.

Much has been made of the occupations of the post-industrial age—the age in which the majority of jobs are in the professions, sales, or services rather than in industry—but many of the new jobs can be as boring as the old. Perhaps the biggest compensation for the new types of jobs is that they are generally not as physically exhausting as were some of the old, nor do they present the same kinds of health hazards.

Health and hazard   Studies of social-class differences have consistently revealed a difference in life expectancy between classes. One reason concerns differences in working conditions. Much of the current interest in problems of the poor has centered on those without jobs, as though a person with any type of fairly regular employment has no serious problems. As a matter of fact, many Americans still work at jobs that are lethal. During the twentieth century, 100,000 men have been killed in mines, and 1.5 million serious accidents have been reported since 1930. The deaths do not stop. In 1968, seventy-eight were killed in a single mine disaster at Farmington, West Virginia. In the 1940s Harry Truman called on Congress to improve mine safety legislation. Nothing was done, and more than 200,000 miners have been killed or injured since then.

Another killer that awaits the coal miner is much slower than cave-ins and explosions but just as sure, and that is black lung. The lung tissue becomes increasingly scarred and useless, until the miner is laid off for being unable to do a

[16]Richard Parker, "Those Blue Collar Worker Blues," *New Republic*, pp. 16–21, September 23, 1972.

The new jobs in automated plants, although less hazardous to health, can be as tedious and boring as the old.

full day's work; later he begins to gasp for breath. The Surgeon General of the United States estimates that we have 100,000 cases of black lung among miners.[17] In 1969 a new safety law was passed for miners that should eventually bring improvement, although the first year the law was in effect the accident rate was higher than the year before.[18] Five years later, the major issues in a prolonged strike in Kentucky were the failure of employers to enforce mine safety standards and to provide hospital benefits. Men were scrambling for jobs in the one new mine in the area that had a good record for almost no accidents and deaths.[19]

One foundry in Michigan has only 1,000 employees, but is faced with suits from 350 of them—all over silicosis, a crippling disease of the lungs caused by inhaling the fine silicon dust from sand used in casting. The foundry is old and not in line with modern standards. The lawyer representing the plaintiffs contends that since the maximum liability per worker is only $12,500 plus medical care and funeral expenses, the company has been unconcerned. Similar types of lung diseases result from work with asbestos, but New York City is the only place with safety standards regarding its use. A condition called "brown lung" has developed among 100,000 textile-mill workers as a result of breathing fine cotton dust. Many

[17]Robert Coles and Harry Huge, "Black Lung: Mining as a Way of Death," *New Republic*, January 1, 1969.
[18]Ward Sinclair, "Confusion in the Coalfields," *New Republic*, pp. 17–18, July 18, 1970.
[19]Eliot Marshall, "Bloody Harlan Revisited," *New Republic*, pp. 14–16, June 8, 1974.

accidents are also caused by moving vehicles; some would be difficult to stop, but too many are the result of indifference.

Unfortunately, there are many other unsafe industries in the United States, and many seem to be growing more dangerous. The Bureau of Labor Statistics shows increasing accident rates during the past decade in ten industries. Each year there are 14,000 deaths and 2 million injuries in industrial accidents, and 500,000 workers are disabled by industrial diseases.[20]

Most of the types of accidents and diseases discussed are far from inevitable. Several plants have worked hard for safety, and the work has paid off. Labor unions are agitating for strengthening of safety regulations, but so far nothing substantial has happened. In spite of the quadrupling of the appropriation for mine-safety inspections, Nader charged that the Bureau of Mines was conducting only one-eighteenth as many inspections in 1970 as it did in 1969.[21] The health problems of the laborer are definitely remediable but have not received the publicity needed to ensure strong action from the government.

AUTOMATION AND THE WORKERS

The development of automated processes in industry is both a source of hope and of fear. The majority of laborers have looked upon it with apprehension, as well they might. Many men of middle age or past have been replaced by automation and have found new jobs nearly impossible to obtain. At the same time automation brings certain types of promise to the world of labor.

> Study such features as workmen's compensation, safety regulations, and retirement pay in a job you know at first hand or the occupation you intend to enter.

The advantages   Hardly anyone in a country geared to industrial progress would assume that automation could be delayed indefinitely. Rapid advances in automation have helped the United States maintain a competitive advantage in some areas of foreign trade, although the race for such an advantage is constantly tightening. For the laborer, one of the encouraging developments of automation is the tendency to replace some of the more tedious jobs with those that require higher levels of training. Assembly line jobs are the types most easily replaced. Automation is leading to an economy in which the majority of jobs are in the white-collar or service categories rather than in the mines and mills. Even on the factory floor, the worker in the more automated plant is generally better integrated into the production system and less alienated from management and fellow workers than in the older type of plant.[22]

Automation and the unskilled   The opposite effect of automation is to make the unskilled even less employable than in the past. At a time when the public conscience has been roused to some degree about the problems of poverty and hard-core unemployment in the inner cities, it develops that the unemployed are harder to help than ever before. Even the high school dropout could easily learn an

---

[20]"A Matter of Life and Death," *Newsweek*, pp. 64–66, August 17, 1970.
[21]*Ibid.*
[22]Michael Fullan, "Industrial Technology and Worker Integration in the Organization," *American Sociological Review*, vol. 35, pp. 1028–1039, December 1970.

Computers, **109**
the
redistributors
of jobs,
give to the
trained,
take from
the
untrained,
and count
people as
inanimate
objects.

assembly line job, but such jobs are declining. Retraining programs have been instituted, but they can succeed only if jobs are actually available. Only a very small fraction of the unemployed are able to pass the tests for entering the training programs.[23] Another disturbing question is whether the new jobs prepared for will not also become obsolete in a short period of time. Or is it possible that automation is creating jobs in new fields as rapidly as it replaces them in old fields?

Employment   The argument that automation creates as many jobs as it replaces would be quite naïve if we assumed that it takes as much manpower to produce the automated devices as the total number of hours they will replace. If that were true, there would be no economic advantage to automating a plant. The more subtle arguments are: (1) Automation makes its products available in enormous quantities at reduced prices; consequently, far more products are sold than in the past. Perhaps it takes only half as much manpower to produce the goods as it did before automation, but more than twice as many goods are sold. The result should be an increase in employment. (2) Although automation may replace workers in one industry, it adds so greatly to prosperity and the general level of consumption of goods and services that new jobs are generated in other areas of the economy to compensate for the ones lost through automation.

In regard to the first argument, Charles Killingsworth[24] analyzes employment rate as a consequence of the particular stage of development an industry has reached. For example, Ford introduced movable assembly line techniques during the infancy of the automobile industry while it had an unrealized capacity for expansion. The new process, making possible an expansion of production, resulted in bringing the price of cars down to a level that the majority of people

[23]Michael Harrington, "The New Lost Generation: Jobless Youth," *New York Times Magazine*, May 24, 1964.
[24]Charles Killingsworth, "The Automation Story: Machines, Manpower, and Jobs," in Charles Markham (ed.), *Jobs, Men, and Machines*, Frederick A. Praeger, Inc., New York, 1964, pp. 15–47.

could afford. Now that there is a car for every three people, it is doubtful whether even a revolutionary change in technique could result in a comparable increase in production. In the case of Ford, the production increase was great enough to vastly increase employment, in spite of increased worker efficiency. In a hypothetical modern case, the total sales might increase slightly, but not enough to add to the total demand for labor. This, says Killingsworth, is the essence of why for a number of years Western Europe progressed rapidly in production and had full employment. The people of Europe are in the youth of the automotive age, which we reached long ago. Almost exactly the same is true for various kinds of household appliances and television sets. In present-day Europe, new techniques stimulate production enough to increase total employment; in the United States they are unlikely to do so.

A recent study of computer control offers much the same conclusion as Killingsworth. In several industries the introduction of more computers created new jobs and replaced only a few workers, but this seemed to be a temporary situation. It was expected that as process computer applicatons increased and spread into more industries, "their displacement effect may become even more pronounced."[25]

Leaving the picture of automation at that state, it would be easy to conclude that massive and permanent unemployment is in the offing. Over a period of twenty years from 1952 to 1972, unemployment averaged a little over 4.5 percent; but by the latter part of the period, it was rising as the country entered a depression. Figures are hard to compare because the Labor Department, in an apparent effort to make the record look good, has changed its definition of unemployed. Previously all people between fourteen and sixty-five who were looking for work within the last sixty days were considered unemployed. Now the fourteen- and fifteen-year-olds have been dropped from the list.[26]

Looking at the overall picture of employment in the United States during the last decade, we can see that jobs have been created in some areas to compensate for the ones being lost elsewhere. While agriculture and mining have declined as areas for hiring, certain services have increased greatly. Education is one of these services; entertainment, recreation, and medical care are others. As the society has felt the increasing need for education, it has supplied the jobs for teachers. As it has become affluent enough to afford more and more entertainment and recreation, it has provided jobs in those fields. The question remains, however, "Will such areas of employment continue into the future in strong enough demand to compensate for any losses taking place in mining, railroads, steel, and automotive industries?" Or will new jobs, possibly hundreds of millions of hours devoted to improving the environment, take up the slack? Or will the job slack be handled simply by having people work fewer hours and retire early. A slackening demand for workers has caused some industries to turn to an early-retirement policy, sometimes without full retirement benefits for workers.

Leisure: prospect and problems   Since labor first demanded a ten-hour day, there has been concern over what the worker would do with spare time. Opposition to shortened hours has even taken the form of speculating about whether idle time

[25]Arthur S. Herman, "Manpower Implications of Computer Control," *Monthly Labor Review*, vol. 93, pp 3–8, October 1970.
[26]John C. Leggett and Claudette Cervinka, "Labor Statistics Revisited," *Society*, vol. 10, no. 1, pp. 99–103, November-December 1972.

will lead to drink and degeneration. What usually occurs seems to be more investment of time in home improvement or in driving the family car much greater distances than before. There has been a long decline in the hours of work for the wage earner, and so far it has not resulted in any drastic moral deterioration. In 1962, Local No. 3 of the International Brotherhood of Electrical Workers made news headlines by signing the first twenty-four-hour week contract. There was public reaction against it, but its results have not been catastrophic. The necessary work is accomplished, and there is no sign of increasing family problems as a result of too much leisure.[27] There has been no rush elsewhere to the twenty-four-hour week. A more common development in the past ten or twelve years has been toward a four-day week. Sometimes hours remained forty per week but were planned in such a way as to give the worker three days off and increase the possibilities for leisure.

The psychological problems of nonwork The real psychological problem is not so much a matter of hours of work as it is having some kind of job to organize time and to give a person a sense of importance. Bayard Rustin sums up the importance of work with a statement that says much about the work ethic with which this chapter is concerned:

What is man? A man is his work. If I ask you Who is Beethoven? you will all say "Composer"; Picasso, a painter; Nat Hentoff, a writer. But if I look at a list of people on relief and ask you, "Who is Mrs. Jones?" [You will tell me] "Nobody!"[28]

Even for some retired persons the same problem often exists. A man who has spent his life thinking of himself as a worker can easily come to think of himself as nobody after he retires. Stuart Chase tells of a group of white- and blue-collar workers in New York on a system of mandatory retirement at age sixty-five. The majority said farewell to New York and headed for the land of their dreams— Florida, California, or Arizona. Within six months most were back. Those with previously developed hobbies and outside interests adjusted fairly well. Several others had mental breakdowns, and one person committed suicide. The man whom Chase designates as the saddest case of all set his alarm clock for the usual hour and went to the shop every day to watch his old friends work.[29]

The President's Council on Aging confirms the conclusion that many people cannot adjust to retirement and even regard it with shame. Especially among the least educated, hobbies may be regarded with contempt. Often the retired man sits around the house, restless and irritable, and relations between the older married couples begin to deteriorate. Another indication of the American's uneasiness with a life of leisure comes from a questionnaire in which a nationwide sample of workers was asked whether they would continue to work even if they had the good luck to be handed enough money to get along without work. Eighty percent said "Yes."[30] The very same people often defined work as "something you have to do because it's good for you," or "something you don't like." The explanation for wanting to work has to be found in a puritan ethic or in an inability to otherwise

[27]Theodore W. Kheel, "How the 24-hour Week Has Worked," in Markham, op. cit., pp. 100–106.
[28]Bayard Rustin, "Education," in Robert Theobald (ed.), Dialogue on Poverty, The Bobbs-Merrill Company, Inc., Indianapolis, 1967, p. 59.
[29]Stuart Chase, The Most Probable World, Penguin Books, Inc., Baltimore, 1969, pp. 136–137.
[30]Ibid., p. 140.

find meaning in life. For very few people is industrial work anything but drudgery, but the alternative of uselessness seems to be worse.

For those who have developed other interests and hobbies, the impact of a short work week and early retirement is quite different. Society obviously has the problem of finding recreational activities not only for those with the ability to be creative but for many others as well. For nearly everyone it also remains vitally necessary that some kind of meaningful employment be found for at least a considerable part of one's life. The employment might occasionally have to be created by the government, but it must be something worth doing. Chase uses a quotation from Dostoyevsky about the importance of a meaningful job. Dostoyevsky was no product of the Protestant ethic, but he states the case for meaningful work eloquently. Perhaps the work ethic could be called the ethic of meaning, in which case it belongs to the entire human race. Dostoyevsky wrote: "If it were desired to crush a man completely, to punish him so severely that even the the most hardened murderer would quail, it would only be needed to make his work pointless and absurd."

WORK AND ALIENATION

The idea of the alienation of labor is not a new one. When the hard conditions that are still found among some of the poorest migratory farm laborers were common to nearly all workers, the alienation of labor was equated with poverty. Early nineteenth-century reformists wrote of how the worker was turned against government and church and society generally by long hours of labor, unwholesome conditions, and such abuses as the employment of women and children in factories and mines.

Marx was a little more sophisticated in his analysis of the reasons for the alienation of labor, but he also attributed it largely to poor conditions and an unequal share in the product of toil. To Marx, the roots of alienation and the factors that made the poor workingman of the industrial period more alienated than the medieval peasant had been was his relationship to the production process. The worker no longer owned the tools of his labor, but worked away from the home in a factory owned by others and at the production of goods in which he had no financial stake. He also became part of a long production process in which he was only a minor instrument, so that he had none of the feeling of pride in workmanship that had belonged to the master craftsmen of the earlier guilds.

Whatever the truth of the Marxian picture, it described primarily industrial labor and did not anticipate the tremendous growth of a white-collar class or of vast bureaucracies that would be rather similar in both socialist and capitalist states. It was for later writers to turn their attention to new aspects of the technical system, first to white-collar labor and then to something called the technocratic, or cybernetic, state.

Mills and the white-collar world   The late C. Wright Mills was one of the sharpest critics of the conditions that produce and mold the character of the white-collar worker. Throughout modern societies, a majority of people rate white-collar work above industrial labor. A white-collar job is the upward-mobility dream of industrial workers for their children. It has been the American dream of success for millions of immigrants entering the country. Mills nevertheless finds much to criticize in the white-collar class, almost exactly the class of people that politicians are now referring to as "middle America." Mills saw the white-collar worker as part of a class that had gained the whole world but lost its own soul. Centered in a society beset with innumerable social problems, the white-collar worker (Mills includes professionals in this category) loses all social concern in a search for status, a "status panic."[31]

Mills was convinced that the future was not bright for the lower echelons of white-collar workers. Too proud of their status differentiation from that of manual labor, they would not organize. Even more than the common laborers, they could easily be manipulated by what Mills later identified as "the power elite"—the top ranks of government, industry, and Madison Avenue. Since almost everyone now completes high school and becomes eligible for at least the lower ranks of white-collar status, increased effort and strain are required for entering and advancing in the middle class. The white-collar class, or middle America, becomes a battleground of status striving and anxiety. Heart attacks are common among those who have had to fight hardest to work their way up. One recent study found heart attacks three times as common for male white-collar workers from farm backgrounds as for those who remained on the farms.[32] The greater risk seems to be for the upwardly mobile, not for those born of wealthy families. Along with the striving of the white-collar world, Mills finds a very limited concern for social problems and a narrow kind of social-class ethnocentrism. Writing in 1951, he asked questions that were heard more frequently in the years following. Is the end of the struggle a status ambiguity? Is the world manipulated by a powerful and inexorable technology? In answering the first question, we could say that changes have taken place since the time of Mills. More occupational groups—clerical workers, teachers, police officers, firefighters, and many others—now identify with labor sufficiently to unionize and even to strike. In answer to the second question, opinion inclines more to the side of Mills. Some writers even question the morality of many aspects of modern employment.

From meaninglessness to immorality In *Growing Up Absurd*, Goodman stresses the number of pointless and meaningless jobs in modern society. In his later book, *Like a Conquered Province*, he goes into the problems of the amorality of many jobs, particularly research projects. Science, in its pure research, claims to be neutral, neither good nor bad. Yet, says Goodman,

> What is striking is that the doctrine of pure science and its moral neutrality always come to the fore when scientists are assigned an official status and become salaried and subsidized, as in the German universities in the nineteenth century or in America today.[33]

The great industrial machine can be geared to purposes that individual scientists or researchers disapprove, but they can always explain that science is neutral. Industry is also neutral. It simply produces what the market demands—harmful drugs, tobacco, dangerous toys for children. The political process also becomes neutral, simply marketing the candidate the best way possible, so that he can feel out public demand and satisfy it or do a good enough public relations job to give the public the illusion of being served.

[31]Wright Mills, *White Collar: The American Middle Classes*, Oxford University Press, New York, 1951.
[32]George Getze, "Successful Men Run Greater Heart Attack Risk," *Los Angeles Times*, July 13, 1970, part I, pp. 1, 5, quoting Berkeley scientist S. L. Syme.
[33]Paul Goodman, *Like a Conquered Province*, Vintage Books, Random House, Inc., New York, 1968, p. 302.

The technological society Probably no critic of modern society is more severely pessimistic than Jacques Ellul. In his book *The Technological Society*,[34] he pictures the course of events in terms somewhat similar to those of Goodman. The essence of the technological society, in Ellul's thinking, is that technique has replaced purpose. The important achievement is efficiency, but efficiency for no particular end. The danger in fascination with efficiency is that it leads one to admire such things as giant engineering projects that desecrate nature, organizations that submerge the individual, and even such marvelous achievements of science as hydrogen bombs. The technological society is essentially immoral. What, then, is its impact on labor?

An illusion is created, says Ellul, that we are moving in the direction of humanism in the world of work. What we are actually doing is studying the physiology of work, the organization of labor, vocational guidance, and techniques for keeping people contented on the job. These, though, are all techniques aimed at serving the cause of efficiency of production, not human happiness. The dream is to create a society in which each worker is fitted and measured for an occupation in such a way that he or she will be as content as the worker in the bee colony, knowing nothing else, dreaming of nothing else. We shall have attained "technological totalitarianism." This is the type of planning we have criticized in the Soviet Union; yet, says Ellul, it is typical of the development of all technological societies and can be anticipated as an increasing trend in the future.[35]

Conflicting interpretations Such writers as Mills, Goodman, and Ellul point to dangers under the surface of the social system. It cannot be assumed that the partial winning of the struggle against want and the development of a more thoroughly schooled population means that all is well. On the other hand, none of the critics would expect us to resign ourselves to despair. Is there any way to resist a system that puts each person into a tiny, fairly isolated little cubicle, where he or she can spend life worrying about such irrelevancies as status?

Buckminster Fuller, inventor of the geodesic dome, is a Renaissance-type man with a wide range of interests and ideas. He sees our way out of eventual destruction as a reversal of the present trend toward narrow specialization. He even presents the argument, based on both biological and anthropological studies, that human tribes and animal species that have been most vulnerable to extinction are those that have grown most specialized.[36] Applying the same perspective to the modern world, he sees danger in the nationalistic rivalries that keep some types of learning secret and exclusive and the academic specializations that cause even the most capable minds to be narrowly channeled. In his opinion, we must all belong first to the entire world, not the specialist world. Only after relating ourselves to our entire space ship earth should we devote part of our time to work specialties.

Fuller's generalist view is actually very much in line with what many members of the younger generation seem to be seeking—a life in which art, music, and poetry are examined at least as much as business and technology. There is also the wholesome tendency to relate to the entire society and even to the total natural environment, rather than merely to the white-collar world of which Mills complained.

---

[34]Alfred A. Knopf, Inc., New York, 1967.
[35]*Ibid.*, pp. 349–361.
[36]Buckminster Fuller, *Operating Manual for Space Ship Earth*, Pocket Books, Inc., New York, 1970, pp. 35–36.

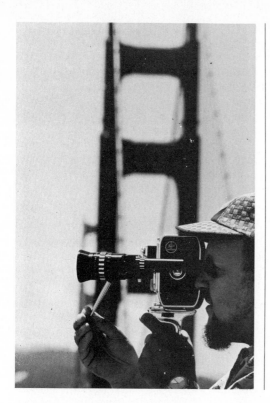

The development of leisure-time activities is an alternative to future empty hours of idleness.

115

Whether such interests are merely passing fads and we shall eventually channel ourselves into the narrow ways Ellul warned of remains to be seen. What is definitely true on the positive side is that the world of work does not have to be the compelling sunrise-to-sunset routine that it was for our ancestors. If the world of work is to become a new form of slavery, it will be unnecessary slavery, of our own making.

Survey your community resources for meaningful nonwork activities—the arts, sports, recreation, entertainment, causes to pursue. Once again you might want to write suggestions to the city council.

Education for the new life   In the previous chapter many criticisms of education were made. Actually, in spite of these complaints, there are new trends at work in education that could well prepare people for an age in which work is no longer the major part of their lives and the source of their self-concept. For more than a century adult education has been prominent in parts of the world, especially in Denmark. Presently, adult education of all kinds is a very important part of community- and state-college systems. Often the return to school is mainly a diploma quest, but it serves other purposes as well—cultivation of the arts, literature, drama, and the general enjoyment of life. The same sources of social change that have created a utilitarian need for technological education are perhaps now just as surely bringing about a need for education in the creative use of leisure. Ralph M. Goldman of San Francisco State College has made a proposal for Life-Span Educational Insurance, which could conceivably meet both occupational and leisure-time needs.[37] The main selling point for such a policy would be to make retraining immediately available for people whose jobs are replaced by new techniques. It could also be used to pay the educational costs of women who wish to train for jobs after their children are in school. Finally, since all people could take out such an insurance policy, the insurance could be used for leisurely, creative college pursuits for people not seriously in need of its retraining features. Such a proposal would need considerable thought and study, but it at least points to new possibilities for meeting the dual training needs of an industrial system with changing employment patterns and with increasing time for leisure.

SUGGESTED READINGS

Ellul, Jacques: *The Technological Society*, Alfred A. Knopf, Inc., New York, 1967. Ellul's book is concerned with much more than work in the future but has great bearing on it. He sees the demands of the technological society as overwhelming to the individual, making him a card in a great computer.

Goodman, Paul: *People or Personnel* and *Like a Conquered Province*, Vintage Books, Random House, Inc., New York, 1967. The first of these two books (published in one volume) is addressed to the problems of working for the impersonal corporation, the dehumanization and powerlessness of the individual in our most gigantic concerns. The second book, on education, democracy, city planning, and ecology, is equally readable, but only secondarily concerned with work.

Pavalko, Ronald M.: *Sociology of Occupations and Professions*, F. E. Peacock Publishers, Itasca, Ill., 1971. A broad introduction to sociological implications of the role of work and occupations in society; presents empirical findings and sociological theory.

Terkel, Louis (Studs): *Working*, Pantheon Books, Inc., New York, 1974. Terkel's book consists of conversations with people in all lines of work—truck drivers, hair stylists, executives, garbage collectors, waitresses, stockbrokers, and scores of others. The questions asked are: "What is your work like? What do you learn from it? What stories do you have to tell?" Easy reading; informative about other lines of work, their attractions and drawbacks.

U.S. Department of Labor, *Occupational Outlook Handbook for 1974-5*, Bureau of Labor Statistics Bulletin 1650, Government Printing Office, Washington, D.C. The Labor Department's *Occupational Outlook Handbooks*, published every two years, are an invaluable source of information for persons trying to guess the future of job security. Although all predictions are risky, the handbooks review the situation and present the best available information on professional, managerial, clerical, sales, service, skilled manual, agricultural, commercial, governmental, and other types of employment.

U.S. Department of Labor, *Monthly Labor Reivew*. This frequently overlooked magazine gives all the latest information on wage and price trends, changing retirement age and retirement pay, significant court decisions in labor cases, blue-collar versus white-collar opportunities, female employment, and many other topics of concern to the wage-earning public.

Wallick, Franklin: *The American Worker: An Endangered Species*, Ballantine Books, Inc., New York, 1972. An indictment of our national carelessness about worker health and safety. One of the final chapters gives good information on what steps the worker can take to obtain legal action in dangerous and substandard employment situations.

[37]Ralph M. Goldman, "Life-Span Educational Insurance: A Proposal," *Educational Record*, vol. 51, pp. 60–65, Winter 1970.

1 What has to be done if the work ethic defeats itself by turning out too many goods?

2 What are some of the characteristics of the work world that cause uncertainties and reluctance on the part of the young?

3 In spite of better wages and unionization, many problems remain for blue-collar labor, such as . . .

4 Explain differing views of the ultimate effect of automation on employment.

5 What are some of the conflicting interpretations of the effects of technological society on meaning and purpose in life?

In an older agricultural society the marriage relationship was held together by economic necessity. Economic change and greater female equality have changed the marital relationship into one that is held together almost exclusively by affection. What are the consequences to family stability? Are there peculiarly heavy strains on a marriage relationship that is born in romance and based almost singly on the expectation of happiness and fulfillment? If more marriages dissolve, is the trend a subject for alarm, or is public alarm merely a matter of cultural lag? How realistic are the divorce laws of most states?

The family bond is a loosening one in respects other than an increased divorce rate. Why are we talking increasingly of a generation gap? In the following pages, an examination of the family will suggest that age-grades are becoming more important than kinship in one's psychological location in society. But are there dysfunctions to separate youth subcultures, middle-America subcultures, and old-age subcultures? What happens to the aged in such a society? Are we drifting into a system of minimal family care for the young and more and more public upbringing of youth? Is there any way to strengthen the psychologically protective features of the family in spite of institutional changes that at present seem to weaken it? Is there any means to prevent further loosening of the kinship bond?

There are great contrasts in family types, and both sociologists and anthropologists have theorized considerably about the connection between family type and societal needs and values. For example, strong lineage systems develop where many of the functions of education, law, and government are carried on by the family or where inheritance is extremely important. Polygamous families have a special value for societies with a high death rate among males (usually caused by war) or in societies that place great importance on male dominance and on the increase of certain lines of descent. Some extremely warlike societies, such as ancient Sparta, found it useful to downgrade the importance of family duties for their young warriors, especially if the warriors belonged to an upper class with servants to care for the household.

The family in modern industrial societies also needs to be structured in ways congenial to societal requirements. The family must give enough freedom to the young so that they can adjust to changing norms, customs, and occupational roles. The family is less bound by tradition and a wide range of duties than were many families of the past but compensates by the idealization of romance and strong affection between mates and between parents and children. The modern middle-class family also has the difficult task of defining the right balance between intergenerational solidarity and growing independence for the younger generation. A need exists to create personality types with a sense of direction and also with the capability of changing to meet everchanging circumstances. For this reason the typical middle-class family cannot be rigid and authoritarian, with its statuses and relationships tightly structured. However, if the family goes so far to the other extreme as to lack cohesion and is unable to produce a generation of children who feel secure and confident, both the individual and society will suffer. At present, more than 500,000 children per year see their parents separate, and the divorce rate is slowly increasing. The reasons given by people who break the bond of marriage are numerous, but underlying the individual reasons are certain basic characteristics of the marital tie in a mobile, industrial society.

SOCIAL CHANGE AND THE MARRIAGE RELATIONSHIP

Certain distinctive characteristics of the family system in the Western world, and in the United States in particular, are the results of economic change, reduced family size, and equalization of status. The economic change of the last century or so has resulted in jobs outside the home for the father, and more recently for the mother. The family no longer earns its living together on a family-type farm as it once did. As a consequence, children learn their occupational roles not from parents but from the school and other institutions.

The family is smaller than it used to be, with fewer children and rarely any outside relatives. Along with the exclusion of relatives from the home, there has been a decline in the feelings of responsibility for elderly grandparents. Social security and medicare take care of the aged, and they are less the family's concern than in the past.

The status of family members grows more nearly equal with the passing of time. Only a few grandparents can remember a time when the rule "children should be seen and not heard" was rigid doctrine. Male and female are expected to be companions on a more or less equal footing within the household. Since the children must be reared with a view to independent decision making, their status comes very close to equality with that of the parents.

The old-style family, bound by status, propriety, and a marriage vow that says "as long as ye shall live."

121

A few other significant changes have been going on in the family, such as a declining educational role within the home, less of a role in the teaching of religion, and usually a diminishing role in recreation, especially as the children reach the age for driving automobiles and as age specialization in entertainment grows.

Growing role of affection   Students of the family are in fairly close agreement about the types of changes that have come about, but not in the evaluation of the changes. It is true that the family is less concerned with as many functions as it once performed, but is that necessarily bad? Possibly the family of today, with more privacy and with less anxiety about getting a day's work out of all its children is better geared to affectivity and enjoyment than it once was. Philippe Ariès[1] pictures the family of medieval Europe as one with less of an affectionate bond between husband and wife, with far less privacy, and with different attitudes toward children from those of today. Although not neglected, children were in no way made central to the family as they are now. The special psychological needs of children were not recognized. Portraits showed them as quite undifferentiated in appearance and proportioned exactly as adults. "Most people probably felt that children had neither mental activities nor recognizable bodily shape."

Women likewise were given less of the special consideration of later times. For the upper classes, few in number, there was a cult of chivalry. Centuries later, women of more common birth were also supposed to be accorded chivalrous

[1]Philippe Ariès, *Centuries of Childhood*, Alfred A. Knopf, Inc., New York, 1962, p. 39.

The new-style family, with equality and individual fulfillment and bound only by "as long as ye shall love."

treatment; but women were seldom considered as people with minds worth developing or capable of carrying on an intelligent conversation. Close emotional relationships between husband and wife were unimportant. Even if they could barely tolerate each other, the family continued, upheld by law, village opinion, relatives, and the church.

In the modern family, by contrast, emotional feelings are particularly intense because of the small number of people sharing a common household, not intruded on by many guests or to any great extent by neighbors or relatives. Under these circumstances preservation of the marital relationship seems especially valuable. Yet it is in this very type of family that the preservation of that relationship presents unusual difficulties.

The unstable family   To speak of the modern, nuclear family, centered only in the parents and their offspring, as an unstable family is, admittedly, to use a biased term. It is the term devised by the French sociologist Le Play to describe such a family in contrast to the extended, or stable, family—the type of kinship system that linked large numbers of relatives together. Le Play's contention is that the European family of an earlier time had been a large, consanguineal family, rather like the Oriental families of more recent times. Such a family held together and was an ongoing institution, never coming to a close because of the death of any particular member or married couple. The link between generations was stronger than the husband-wife link.

In modern America we think of the ideal marriage as involving the closest link between husband and wife, definitely not to be interfered with by kinsmen. Not all families fit the model, of course. In many old-money families the proper marriage is made with family position in mind. In other cases, even in this age of legal abortions, premarital pregnancy of the woman rather than romantic devotion is the reason for marriage. Some people marry for money or to escape from home, but all such marriages are looked upon as less than ideal. The emphasis on money and position belonged more to Le Play's old-fashioned stable family than to the modern type.

The modern type of family has evolved to meet the requirements of an economic system that places the father's job far from the household and that often needs women too for work outside the home. Partly in response to economic and educational realities, the society has become equalitarian in its sentiments. A society that educates and makes fairly equal demands on both men and women calls for a high degree of equality between husband and wife. In an equalitarian situation, marriage must be based on consent and that consent must be won through love and romance. There are other interests too, of course—children, a home, and possibly many common interests and values—but romantic attachment is vital. Leo Zakuta[2] notes that in this respect there is still a contrast between the European and the American marriage. European marriages are also based on mutual consent and usually follow a romantic courtship, but the idea of singleness of devotion is not played up to quite the same degree. Far more European women, if confronted with the knowledge that their husbands have been having affairs with other women, will take the "boys will be boys" attitude. If American women are becoming more tolerant, it is not because of ready acceptance of more prerogatives for men than for women but because of acceptance of more freedom for both sexes.

The problem is that the very characteristic that has made the modern American marriage a particularly intense state of bliss, with full love and gratification for both partners, also makes the marriage more vulnerable to friction than an arranged type of marriage. When the husband had a status far above that of the wife, sometimes relations were very free and easy for him. The greater the difference of status between mates, the greater the freedom of the husband to have a mistress and, concomitantly, the more acceptable the status of mistress. Even prostitution was tolerated and defended as "ultimately the most efficient guardian of virtue." The idea was that the prostitute not only protected good women from being attacked by evil men but even protected wives from too frequent demands from their husbands.[3] Now that women are no longer expected to be so inhibited as to not enjoy the pleasures of sex, love and romance are much stronger and are almost the total center of marital stability. However, love is such a powerful emotion that it can turn to hate if neglected. The husband as authority figure could be respected, or at least accepted, if not loved. The husband as lover may be hated if no longer loved.[4]

The consequences of the equalitarian and romantic marriage are certainly not to be condemned entirely. Certainly no one, including sociologists who analyze the virtues of older systems, wish to have their marriages arranged by wise parents, and only occasionally are people willing to be paired off by a wise computer. The

[2]Leo Zakuta, "Equality in North American Marriages," *Social Research*, vol. 30, pp. 157–170, Summer 1963.
[3]Christopher Lasch, "Divorce and the Family in America," *Atlantic Momthly*, vol. 218, pp. 57–61, November 1966.
[4]Zakuta, *op. cit.*

modern wife is not willing to trade her position of equality or near-equality for the guarantee of a permanent marriage to a domineering man. It is important, though, to see the contrast in sociological perspective and to know that a high divorce rate will not fall under the hammer blows of constant preaching and scolding or of outmoded laws that try to force people to stay together.

The marriage that places high value on equality and companionship, however, is probably more stable in today's society than the one that insists on male dominance and rigid division of labor. The nonequalitarian family might have had stability in an earlier age, but for modern America it is in a state of strain.

The anachronistic family The family that rejects equality and companionship between the spouses begins to seem out of date, an anachronism. Mirra Komarovsky describes her research in a group of such homes, consisting entirely of white, Anglo-Saxon, blue-collar workers, generally of very limited education. In such a family the male role is an isolated masculine role, not at all concerned with companionship with wife or with other women. "Regular guys don't mess around with women except when they want what a woman's got to give them" said one of the wives. The man was not expected to help around the house, and it was all right for him to be "out with the boys." The situation was uneven, with the woman staying at home with the children. She did not worry about the social adjustment of the children or their psychological problems, but found lots of worries about making them behave and obey.

In pursuing the question of whether such a family is actually happier than the middle-class family with more ambiguous norms, Komarovsky's conclusion is "no." The amount of complaints and general unhappiness seems to be greater. A possible explanation is that in the modern world it is more or less necessary for husband and wife to be good company for each other and share interests and confidences. In the old days such a relationship was hardly necessary because people stayed in the same neighborhoods, close to their kinsmen and friends. Now they move frequently and neighborhoods are not emotionally close. The consequence seems to be that the wife of the blue-collar worker in Komarovsky's study is isolated from the old-fashioned female gossip of earlier days, and also has no role in the mixed company so typical today. The husband is often unhappy because his wife is moody. Neither realizes that the source of trouble could be their belief in a God-given, impenetrable wall between the psyches of men and women.[5] It should be added that Komarovsky's study, published in 1964, describes a declining number of blue-collar families. The shift in point of view in the 1970s is dramatic, according to Social Research, Inc.,[6] and in the direction of more participation by women outside their families, fewer children, and greater equality between the sexes.

DIVORCE

The right to divorce is recognized in nearly all societies, although Italy did not pass a divorce law until 1970. The grounds for divorce and statistics on divorce vary greatly the world over. There are some tribal societies in which divorce rates are even higher than in the United States; and Egypt and a few other Islamic countries

[5]Mirra Komarovsky, "Blue Collar Families," *Columbia University Forum*, no. 7, pp. 29–32, Fall 1964.
[6]Burleigh B. Gardner, "The Awakening of the Blue Collar Woman," *Intellectual Digest*, pp. 17–18, March 1974.

have sometimes had higher divorce rates than ours; otherwise, the United States has the dubious distinction of being the world leader in divorce. In some tribal societies the reason for high divorce rates bears an accidental resemblance to our own: people marry very young in a kind of trial-marriage situation, not expecting to achieve marital stability until later in life.[7] In parts of the Islamic world the husband still has full authority about divorce, and this custom results in a very high divorce rate.[8]

DIVORCE STATISTICS, UNITED STATES

The divorce rate has increased gradually in the United States along with the more mobile, urban way of life. In 1900, about one marriage in twelve ended in divorce; at present the rate is close to one in three. The divorce rate reached a high point in 1946, at the end of World War II, mainly as a result of many young marriages made on short acquaintance during the war years. After the war, the divorce rate declined for several years and remained fairly steady until the 1960s. In 1960 there were 35 divorced persons for every 1,000 married persons living with their spouses. By 1970, the number of divorced persons had risen to 47 per thousand married persons, and by 1974 to 63—the highest rate in United States history, and a figure showing a sharper increase in four years than in the previous ten. As of 1974, there were 2.3 million divorced and unremarried men and 3.6 million divorced and unremarried women in the United States.[9]

There are 7.9 million children in families headed by women, largely a reflection of a high divorce rate, although births to unmarried women account for a small portion of the number. Whereas the total number of children under eighteen years of age declined in the years 1970 to 1972, the number in homes headed by women increased by 1.2 million.[10]

DIVORCE AND SOCIAL CLASS

William J. Goode[11] finds that, with rare exceptions, in industrial countries people with higher incomes, higher levels of education, and occupations that are given community respect are the least likely to divorce. Highest divorce and separation rates occur at the bottom of the socioeconomic scale, although desertion is sometimes used as an alternative to divorce if a divorce is hard to obtain or too expensive. One reason for the difference is that the higher-income family is more likely to have future commitments: that is, divorce entails heavy economic loss. There is also considerable evidence that marital relationships are more satisfactory among middle- and upper-class people than among people living in poverty. In all cases, divorce rates are increasing, causing concern about the children of divorce; but the fact of the greater prevalence of divorce among poorer families might influence statistics about the relationship between divorce and the problems of children.

---

[7]M. F. Nimkoff, *Comparative Family Systems*, Houghton Mifflin Company, Boston, 1965, pp. 337, 359.
[8]Even in the Islamic world, the custom is changing, and sometimes there are subtle devices by which a wife can defend herself against the husband's intent to divorce her. See Lawrence Rosen, "I Divorce Thee," *Transaction*, vol. 7, pp. 34–37, June 1970.
[9]Associated Press report based on Bureau of the Census figures, November 8, 1974.
[10]Anne M. Young, "Children of Working Mothers," Special Labor Force Report 154, U.S. Department of Labor, March 1972.
[11]William J. Goode, "Marital Satisfaction and Instability, A Cross-Cultural Analysis of Divorce Rates," *International Social Science Journal*, vol. 14, no. 3, pp. 507–526, Summer 1962.

Children of divorce   Early studies of children coming from broken homes indicated that the home broken by divorce was the direct cause of much delinquency. For example, a study made in 1950 found that 60 percent of the troublemakers came from broken homes. A study in Denver in the 1960s found that 75 percent of delinquent black youth were from broken homes. Such statistics, however, leave two questions unanswered: (1) Would the children be better behaved if their parents remained together even in a quarrelsome, unhappy marriage? (2) Are there factors other than divorce that account for the delinquency? In answer to the first question, most studies agree that a bitter, quarrelsome, intact home is certainly no better an environment for the young than a broken home. In answer to the second question, it must be recalled that divorce and separation rates are highest in the very social-class strata where delinquency rates are highest.

Howard N. Bahr[12] reviews some of the above data on broken homes and concludes that often they are more of a comment on results of poverty and bad living conditions than of family breakup. In his own study, Bahr investigates the relation between adult homelessness and excessive drinking to early family breakup. Of the alcoholics and vagrants in his study, 30 to 40 percent came from broken homes, but so did the same percentage of nonalcoholics from the same area and social-class background.

Many delinquency studies end in statistics similar to those of Howard Bahr's. Others do show some correlation between broken homes and delinquency, higher for girls than for boys and for younger than for older delinquents. The difference is not very great, however, and the figures do not answer the question "What would have happened if an unhappy family had remained intact?"[13]

A study of middle-class college students found less general happiness, less self-confidence, and more difficulty with the opposite sex among students who came from homes broken by divorce.[14] A later study on self-concept concludes that people reared in broken homes are more likely to have derogatory feelings about themselves than those from intact homes. Women from broken homes agreed with such statements as "sometimes I feel that I haven't much to be proud of" in 71 percent of the cases, and men in 58 percent of the cases, as compared with only 49 percent of people from intact homes. The self-derogatory statements were strongest for those who had experienced family breakup at ages five to nine and at ages thirteen to sixteen.[15]

Divorce laws: legal fiction versus reality   Divorce laws are slow to change to meet modern realities. One reason is that the majority of states still define marriage in terms of a "legal fiction"—a point of law that has little bearing on reality. The legal fiction is that marriage is a contract set up under civil law and its maintenance is therefore a business of the state. Unless it can be proved that one person has sinned against another, there are no grounds for breaking the contract; the married couple must remain in holy wedlock, which someone has aptly called "holy deadlock."

---

[12]Howard N. Bahr, "Family Class and Stability as Antecedents of Homelessness and Excessive Drinking," *Journal of Marriage and the Family,* vol. 21, pp. 477–483, August 1969.

[13]Sophia M. Robinson, *Juvenile Delinquency: Its Nature and Control,* Holt, Rinehart and Winston, Inc., New York, 1960, pp. 108–112.

[14]Jack Harrison Pollack, "Are Children of Divorce Different?" in Judson R. Landis, *Current Perspectives on Social Problems,* Wadsworth Publishing Company, Inc., Belmont, Calif., 1966, pp. 190–193.

[15]Howard B. Kaplan and Alex D. Pokorny, "Self-derogation and Childhood Broken Homes," *American Journal of Family and Marriage,* vol. 33, pp. 328–337, May 1971.

What constitutes grounds for divorce in your state? Are the divorce laws consistent with modern realities? Try to get a lawyer experienced in divorce cases or a marriage counselor to speak for the class.

127

Since marriage and divorce regulations are made by state rather than by federal government, the nation has a confusion of divorce laws. Nearly all states accept adultery and cruelty as grounds for divorce and often stretch cruelty to mean "mental cruelty," which can mean almost anything from fiendish mistreatment to mere incompatibility. Most states also recognize a variety of other grounds for divorce: desertion, incurable insanity, criminality, "loathsome disease," frigidity and impotence, among others. In many states, however, someone has to be at fault in order for a divorce to be granted. Fourteen states have followed the example of California, which in 1970 changed its law to make divorce possible simply on the grounds of mutual consent without anyone having to accept the blame. Such a practice lowers court costs and prevents the bitter court fights that often accompany divorce.

Many of America's divorce laws were passed in the late nineteenth century as a response to women's protest movements. The idea of the laws was to protect women against cruel and tyrannical husbands. Previously, divorces were granted by state legislatures on an appeal that usually came from a man of means and influence. Divorces were virtually impossible for the poor or for women, except occasionally on grounds of adultery or cruelty. Present laws in the majority of states still reflect the idea of protecting the woman from a cruel husband and often result in the husband's feeling victimized by the proceedings. They are also strongly criticized for encouraging long court duels, high lawyers' fees, and a struggle that is a bitter experience for the divorcing couple, friends, relatives, and particularly the children.[16]

There are no present indications that the divorce rate will decline in the future. Donald J. Cantor[17] predicts a situation in which first marriages will be regarded almost as trial marriages. In fact, at present large numbers of young people cohabit for awhile without marriage. One small survey among college students[18] found a large majority approving of such arrangements, although less than one-third of the women said that they personally would accept such an arrangement. The most frequent reason for approval was approximately what Cantor suggests: to try out living together before making the stronger commitment of actual marriage. There may be enough arrangements of this type to account for a slight increase in average age at first marriage rather than a continuation of the long-term downward trend in age.

The only types of loosening bonds discussed at length in this chapter have been those of marriage. An offhand impression of the society makes it look as though the bonds holding generations together are also weakening and that the society is becoming increasingly age-graded.

THE AGE-GRADED SOCIETY

Much has been written by anthropologists about age sets in the primitive world, but only a few have commented on the parallel between primitive and modern

[16]Christopher Lasch, *op. cit.* See also, Donald J. Cantor, "The Right of Divorce," *Atlantic Monthly*, vol. 218, pp. 67–72, November 1966.
[17]Cantor, *op cit.*
[18]Survey by author conducted at Bakersfield College, Spring semester, 1974.

societies in this respect. In societies that make a strong issue of rites of puberty, those who have gone through the rites together form a bond for life, linking them almost as closely to age mates as to family. Jomo Kenyatta's *Facing Mount Kenya* gives an interesting picture of this strong emotional bond, as remembered by Kenyatta from his youth. In Yoruba society the young initiate into the Egungung fraternity went much further in making his primary link one to the fraternity rather than to family. The initiate was asked, "Are you prepared to go even against your brother? Your father? Your mother?" The answer in each case had to be "yes."[19] Totalitarian states of modern times have deliberately used youth groups for the same purpose.

At first glance, American society seems to bear no resemblance to the African societies mentioned or to totalitarian states. What, then could be the reason for a similar development? One trait that all the societies have in common is that the major role-training for life is taken over by agencies outside the family. In some cases, the role-training was largely military. In American society economic change has necessitated role preparation through the schools (the same is the case with other industrial countries, and youth subcultures are very much in evidence). The other trait that all age-graded societies seem to have in common is the necessity of learning universalistic principles.

No antifamily purpose is intended, of course, in the promotion of age sets in American society, but it can be argued that the age-grading system of modern education produces a latent function that is antifamily. It is impossible to understand part of the strain within the modern family relationship without turning to the problem of age-grading. S. N. Eisenstadt has made a thorough study of age-grading.[20] Most of his book is an anthropological study of age-grading and the varieties of the custom in the primitive world. His basic principle is that age-grading occurs in societies with universalistic as opposed to familistic values and where major statuses are acquired outside the kinship group. In primitive societies the universalistic values are learned from the process of initiation into the age sets rather than from the family, and the age sets are a fully institutionalized phenomenon. In modern societies, the very term age sets is seldom used, and there is no deliberate attempt to institutionalize such groups, but age sets nevertheless exist and are very important. Even small children are aware of multitudes of their peers. In their adolescent years, they will be more fully aware of their own generation and develop a strong identity with it and a loyalty that often flies in the face of family solidarity.

Make an observational study of a junior high school or grammar school subculture. What changes have come about since you were the same age?

There are various reasons why the age set takes on a strong identity and loyalty function. For one thing, as Eisenstadt points out, the child in modern society is learning universalistic norms that are not always part of family norms. The children from families with old-fashioned, puritanical norms will be thrown into contact with a society and generation that is much more permissive. The family with strong racist feelings will probably have its children reared in an atmosphere of increasing racial equality and acceptance. The family that believes strongly in thrift and

---

[19]Eugene Victor Walter, *Terror and Resistance*, Oxford University Press, New York, 1969, p. 84.
[20]S. N. Eisenstadt, *From Generation to Generation*, The Free Press, New York, 1956.

avoidance of debt will have no choice but to see its children indoctrinated by an age set in which the old Benjamin Franklin ideas are not even a cultural memory.

The occupational function   The school rather than the family is charged with the responsibility of preparing the young for future occupations. The family in modern industrial society prepares youth for an occupational role only indirectly by sending the young to school. Often the occupation being prepared for is so far from family knowledge that no useful parental advice is possible. Consequently, a gulf opens within the family and leaves the young person looking for advice but unable to find it.

The inability of the family to prepare the young for an occupational role is one of the traits that has caused it to be designated an "inefficient institution." Bright children born in families of low socioeducational status are seldom prepared realistically for the roles for which they are equipped by native ability. Even the age set is of little help in this respect because it is divided along social-class lines, so that those least able to find their way to high status are usually thrown together.

The rites of puberty   In strongly age-graded preliterate societies, there are often extensive and severe rites of puberty or coming-of-age ceremonies, marking the passage from childhood to adulthood. Childhood is left behind, and the new initiate is nearing the age for marriage. Often there will be considerable sexual experimenting before marriage, but eventually a marriage will be arranged. The family usually cooperates in the process by raising money for bride price.

There are no such institutionalized rites of puberty in American society. Instead there are sports, rock sessions, drinking and marijuana parties, fads of all types, and general defiance of convention. Such informal rites have the function of bonding young people together and giving them a sense of collective identity just as surely as do the rites of the primitives. Both the age set and the school take over much of the function of instruction in sex that is the prerogative of the home in many societies. Our schizoid attitudes toward sex make frank discussion between parents and young people difficult. School instruction is sometimes opposed by a vocal minority of parents, leading to rather timid and superficial treatment of the subject (if any) in junior high and high school. Part of the consequence of ignorance, coupled with permissive youth norms, is an increase in the amount of venereal disease, inexcusable in an age of medical knowledge.

DATING AND EARLY MARRIAGE

As of 1972, the average age for the first marriage in the United States was 20.9 years for women and 23.3 for men, representing a decline of about two years for women and four years for men as compared with 1900, but showing a slight increase in age for both sexes compared with the period 1950–1960.[21] Marriages usually occur at a younger age in the lower socioeconomic class than in the middle class. Regardless of social class, those who start dating before fifteen years of age are inclined to marry younger than the average.[22] The earlier the marriage, the more likely all kinds of marital troubles. According to Mervyn Cadwallader of San José State College, 40 percent of all brides are between the age of fifteen and

[21]Statistical Abstract of the United States, Bureau of the Census, 1973, p. 65.
[22]Arthur A. Campbell, "Early Dating and Early Marriage," *Journal of Marriage and the Family*, vol. 30, pp. 236–245, April 1968.

Modern rites: defiance of convention.

eighteen, and half their marriages end within five years.[23] The years that have passed since Cadwallader's study have seen a slight increase in age at first marriage but no decline in the divorce rate.

There was a time when the older generation decided the order of maturity. The first step to maturity was economic independence and the second was marriage. Now the first step seems to be marriage. "The Masai becomes an adult when he kills a lion," says Cadwallader, "and an American becomes an adult when he gets married."[24] This statement is hardly a joke. The status of adolescence tends to be long, confusing, and of indefinite termination, except through marriage. A difficult status is terminated by a status that is even more difficult at that stage of life.

Age sets and ideologies The intergenerational drift is very pronounced and important in many other respects. New fashions and designs, vocabularies, and vices, such as substituting drugs for alcohol, arise. New ideologies also arise, differing from generation to generation, but never the same as those of the parental generation. There was "flaming youth" in the 1920s, radical youth in the 1930s, delinquent youth in the 1940s, conformist youth in the 1950s, and, again, radical

[23]Mervyn Cadwallader, "Marriage as a Wretched Institution," *Atlantic Monthly*, vol. 218, pp. 63–64, November 1966.
[24]*Ibid.*, p. 64.

youth in the 1960s and the "hang-loose" ethic. Politically, the 1970s are outwardly less radical than the 1960s but no return to an earlier age in style of life. Although many college students take less interest in politics than their counterparts of a decade earlier, enough make radical changes in religion, morals, and philosophy to cause ideology to remain a major factor in the generation gap.

In most places where age-grading is part of the institutional policy of a society, it reinforces the religious aspects of life by ritualization. In modern societies, especially in the last decade or two, there has been a strong tendency for youth, especially college youth, to reject the old-time religion, sometimes becoming frankly agnostic and sometimes looking for something new. Again the age-grading tends to divide the family.

> **What do you believe to be the stereotypes of middle-aged Americans about college youth? Put your stereotypes in question form and see whether a sample of middle-aged Americans actually holds the assumed attitudes.**

Middle America The age set of the parental generation is now referred to by politicians and the mass media as middle America. Age-grading is really not a phenomenon of the middle years, but a stereotype has developed in our society that makes it so. Just as the elders, with the help of the mass media, have stereotyped the young as a generation of purposeless hippies, the young have stereotyped their elders. Middle America is supposed to be conservative, hypocritical, money-grubbing, and definitely past the age for any fun or spontaneity in life. Actually, middle America's enjoyments do seem to be widely separated from the young and not sufficiently concerned with them.

The Struldbruggs For the oldest age set there is something equivalent to burial without death. At first there are the activities of elderly groups such as senior citizens' clubs, but the groups are set off into a world of their own. The wealthy can even retire to communities of their own, the most famous of which are the Leisure Worlds in various parts of the country. In these cases the idea of age sets is again strong, just as it was in youth, because the aged are fairly well isolated from the mainstream of the culture.

Since people no longer die after enjoying a few years of retirement, and only a few can afford to live in a Leisure World, the majority eventually become a burden on society. They also become pitiful to look upon and must be hidden away from sight. Some of them reach a state of decrepitude that reminds us of the Struldbruggs in *Gulliver's Travels*. When Gulliver visited the land of the Luggmaggians, he found that some of their people, the Struldbruggs, did not die at all but lived for century after century. Gulliver's first comment was that it must be wonderful to have such long life and to be able to learn, to remember, and to advise others. He discovered, though, that longer life means not longer memory or greater wisdom but only people that are "opinionative, peevish, covetous, morose, vain, talkative, and . . . dead to all natural affection." They enjoyed nothing, had no amusements, no memories. They couldn't even occupy their time reading because "their memory will not serve to carry them from the beginning of a sentence to the end."[25]

Swift did what we are all inclined to do about the extremely aged—looked upon them as stereotypes rather than as people. We do this because we wish to avoid

---

[25]Jonathan Swift, *Gulliver's Travels*, The Pocket Library, New York, 1957, pp. 210, 212.

Age and
the lonely
years of
low income,
declining
health,
and aban-
donment
by family.

thinking of ourselves as we may sometime be: that is, we think of the old as something of a very different order from our own, rather than as part of a continuum to which we belong. Simone de Beauvoir, in her passionate plea for better treatment of the aged, elaborates on this psychological compulsion to stereotype rather than to see human beings. If we wish to be kind, we speak of the white-haired and venerable aged, mellow and wise. "The counterpart of the first image is the old fool in his dotage, a laughing stock for children." In any case, says de Beauvoir, "they [the aged] stand outside humanity. The world, therefore, need feel no scruple in refusing them the minimum support which is considered necessary for living like a human being."[26] Elsewhere she speaks of our discarding the aged like scrap as revealing "the failure of our civilization. . . . If we were to look upon the old as human beings, with a human life behind them, and not as so many walking corpses, this obvious truth would move us profoundly."[27]

Simone de Beauvoir's conclusions are that with the rare exceptions of Norway, Sweden, and Denmark, the wealthy Western nations handle the aged in a disgraceful manner. The aged make up the largest category of poverty-stricken people in America and much of Europe. Those who need care are put in institutions euphemistically called convalescent homes, some of which are in disgraceful condition. A New York reporter found rest homes badly run in many of the cases he investigated—"abominable . . . filthy rooms, roaches in glasses, dirt in water pitchers, and indescribable conditions in bathrooms."[28] No doubt the large amounts of money spent on Medicare and Medicaid have resulted in improvements, but much remains to be done.

[26]Simone de Beauvoir, *The Coming of Age*, trans. Patrick O'Brian, G. P. Putnam's Sons, New York, 1972, p. 4.
[27]*Ibid.*, p. 6.
[28]David H. Pryor, "Somewhere between Society and the Cemetery: Where We Put the Aged," *New Republic*, vol. 162, pp. 15–18, April 25, 1970.

The Senate Subcommittee on Nursing Home Care in 1974 characterized the institutionalized care of the aged as a national disgrace, saying good homes are still in the minority. The report speaks of an alarming number of known cases of "abuse and physical danger, including unsanitary conditions, fire hazards, poor or unwholesome food, infections, adverse drug reactions, overtranquilization and frequent medication errors."[29] Senator Frank Church, chairman of the subcommittee, accused the Department of Health, Education and Welfare of lack of attention to nursing homes and of an attitude "characterized by neglect, indifference, and ineptitude."

The Senate subcommittee report is not to be construed as universal condemnation of rest homes. Some are well run, those in which care is considered more important than profit and where the elderly are thought of as human beings. There are still far too many institutions, however, in which the aged are considered not as human beings but only as Struldbruggs.

> **Study rest homes in your area; talk to some patients. Do you find that some are almost completely abandoned by their relatives?**

CURRENT CHANGES IN FAMILY AND MARRIAGE

Attitudes about the institution of marriage have changed in some respects but not in others. In a Harris poll of 1971, 88 percent of the people questioned indicated that the family is still necessary, and 84 percent of the young people intended to marry and have children.[30] On the other hand, 72 percent thought the family was becoming weaker. Another poll in 1972 found 45 percent of the respondents thinking that "the institution of marriage as we know it is becoming outmoded." Nevertheless, most of them were married or intended to marry.

The young people in the surveys were more in favor of women working than were the old. The young also favored the possibility of a woman president, smaller families, and premarital sex. *Society* magazine editorializes that the youth vote of the present is probably predictive of future attitudes of older people as well, since age does not necessarily make people more conservative. For example, those people in the thirty- to forty-year age group in 1945 were opposed to having women work outside the home; thirty years later the same group gave majority approval. The shift with age was toward modernity, not toward the past.

If the same gradual change toward the opinions of the young continues to take place, we can expect more support for living together on a trial basis before marriage. Children will be born only after trial marriages are legalized, the years of child care will occupy only a small part of the lives of the parents, and whether people remain together after the children are grown will depend entirely on how satisfactory is the marriage relationship.

FUTURE POSSIBILITIES

The family, admittedly, is beset with problems. We could add to all the previously mentioned complaints that the family is in some respects a terribly undemocratic

[29]Associated Press, "Nursing Home Abuses Told in Report," *Los Angeles Times*, November 20, 1974, part 1, p. 4.
[30]These and following statistics are summarized in the "Roundup of Current Research," *Society*, vol. 11, no. 3, pp. 6–12, March-April 1974.

institution for an age of equalitarianism, because a powerful family cannot resist exerting its influence in the direction of special favors for its own members. This is one reason why families have often been seen as enemies by totalitarian regimes. This very trait of a family, which can easily turn into a vice, is also its greatest virtue. Irving Goffman makes the extremely significant comment in his book *Asylums* that the family is the greatest possible enemy of total institutions. By total institutions he means jails, prisons, armies, asylums, orphanages, monasteries—any institution that takes total control of the individual. In this sense, an entire state can become a total institution, crushing individual decisions, and even turning son against father and brother against brother. Such a state is antifamily, and the family, battered though it may be, attempts to act as a refuge against such a state.

The family is a prescientific development that gives difficult tasks to the novice, often links incompatible people together, even occasionally gives dull parents bright children, or vice versa. The family provides for the performance of the extremely vital task of early socialization by anyone who happens to be a parent—frequently a disaster of unskilled labor. But anachronistic though the family seems in a scientific age, it is still amazingly popular, as evidenced by the prevalence of early marriage and a 98 percent remarriage rate for the divorced. Flying in the face of our concerns over population explosion, the majority of couples want children, and family-planning agencies are almost as busy prescribing remedies to the infertile as they are trying to stem the tide of babies. Whatever its ills, it is better to think of the family as in need of a doctor than as in need of an undertaker.

Worldwide trends in the family   Nimkoff concludes his book on different family types with an essay on the future of the family.[31] A major change is in the direction of more public upbringing of children through schools and nursery schools and, in some cases, through public boarding schools. The public rearing of children is especially pronounced in the Russian boarding schools and in the government communes of China. On a small, voluntary scale, the Israeli kibbutzim represent the same type of development. The age-grading tendency previously discussed is promoted by such institutions.

The second worldwide change that Nimkoff mentions is toward a minimization of function, as is the case with the family of the United States. To a considerable degree, the family loses its secondary functions of economic production and protection but maintains its psychologically supportive function. It also gains function in the realm of planning, both for children and for the budget.

A third change is the one most central to our discussion—a change in stability pattern. The rising divorce rate in the United States can be expected to be duplicated elsewhere. However, Nimkoff says that the family is simply reacting to social systems that are in a state of flux. Despite its marital instability, perhaps the family remains more stable than most other social institutions. In times of human storms—war, depression, or revolution—the family, despite its frictions, gives what little protection it can and often provides people with their only reason for survival.

In Nimkoff's opinion, the trend of the family is toward play rather than work as an integrative principle. With more leisure and more recreational activities, he argues, the family can spend more time together. In times of less prosperity, parents are

---

[31]Nimkoff, *op. cit.*, pp. 357–369.

often so busy scratching out a living that they have little time to devote to children. Even the working parents of today often have more leisure time than did earlier generations. In the context of other statements in Nimkoff's book, however, there are a few exceptions to his conclusions about the integrative functions of leisure time. He mentions, for example, that when the American family had one car, the car served an integrative function. People had to plan their activities together in order for them all to get a ride. Now that there may be several cars in the family, the possibility of going separate ways for recreation increases. Such an instance can be multiplied by examples from many kinds of specialized recreational activities.

Conflicting proposals   Proposals for helping the family can be based on opposing viewpoints of what is desired. Some would argue that great efforts must be made to preserve the marriage bond. Few would any longer advocate making divorces impossible, but many persons would suggest family counseling before a divorce is considered. Others would not object to attempts at counseling but would take more of a roll-with-the-tide attitude. If many young marriages are likely to end, then, why not make divorce easy and free it of stigma as much as possible?[32]

The process of readjustment after divorce is a difficult one at best, entailing new life habits, new social relationships, and often financial problems. Every attempt should be made to prevent adding further problems. At present, although many divorces are arranged without a court scene, they are often bought through bargaining over custody of children, property, alimony, and so forth.

Another proposal for making the marriage relationship more stable is to be more restrictive about marriage. It is possible to imagine a science-fiction situation in which geneticists would examine the applicants for a wedding license to make sure their mating would be in the interests of human perpetuation, and in which psychologists or computers would study their personality profiles to make sure they were compatible. Actually, a certain amount of genetic counseling is already being done, and computers have been used extensively for matching people for a first date. They may someday be a substitute for the old marriage arranger of Asiatic and Eastern European tradition. Obviously, though, the computer's judgment would be merely a suggestion, not an order. It is also hard to see how any type of counseling system could be entirely effective, since it would always be possible to leave one's own state or country to get married and since marriages are sometimes a result of premarital pregnancy.

Communes and other alternatives   The proposals most frequently discussed for care of children in the future all tend to emphasize nursery school, preschool training, summer camps, and every conceivable way of taking them away from home and keeping them with peer groups. It is this tendency of parents to want to be free of their children as much as possible that led Barrington Moore to ask if there is not some better alternative to the family.

It would be reactionary and unrealistic to propose that child care be returned completely to the home. The question is whether there is not some way of keeping parents and children more emotionally close than is often the case in modern societies. Some persons contend that the Israeli kibbutz does precisely this task. For those not familiar with the kibbutz, it is the name for a type of small cooperative

---

[32]Cantor, *op. cit.*

A universal trend: public rearing of children.

community in Israel in which both the mother and father are freed to work in agriculture or to follow military duties by leaving child care entirely to specialists. Parents visit with the children, but only in a fun and enjoyment capacity. The problems of discipline are not theirs. The result seems to be the production of bright, capable, cooperative children who, upon maturity, usually remain in the kibbutz system.[33]

It is unlikely that communes will ever account for as large a portion of child-rearing in the United States as in Israel, in spite of our historic record for experimental communes. As Margaret Mead observes,

> You can get rid of it [the family] if you live in an enclave and keep everybody else out, and bring the children up to be unfit to live anywhere else. They can go on ignoring the family for several generations. But such communes are not part of the main world.[34]

Nevertheless, American communes are important as social experiments and even more important in that their present numbers show a discontent with the traditional family. Nineteenth-century communes were largely of a religious or utopian type.

[33]Stuart A. Queen et al.: "The Minimum Family of Kibbutz," in *The Family in Various Cultures*, J. B. Lippincott Company, Philadelphia, 1961, pp. 116–136.
[34]Margaret Mead, "Future Family," *Transaction*, pp. 50–53, September 1971.

Numerous modern communes are similar in dedication, but others are dedicated simply to escaping the rigid family and the urban-industrial society. Altogether there are about 2,000 communes, not including many urban cooperatives and collectives.[35] Many of them fail; but in spite of the problems of inexperience and untrained leadership, many also survive. The more dedicated they are to an ideology, whether religious, Marxian, or merely countercultural, the more likely they are to survive. They fulfil certain needs that the isolated family finds difficult to fulfil. In spite of her dim view of their survival value, Mead concedes them this point. There are more people around to take an interest in babies and children, more playmates for the children, more helpers in an emergency, and more people involved in cooperation. Some of the communes are fairly strict and rigid; some are poorly organized; some are based on free love; some are puritanical; but all provide some of the needs that many people find hard to fulfil in the small, isolated family.

There are a number of family systems that are neither communal nor strictly orthodox. A few researchers have found an increasing amount of "coupling," that is, two married couples living in close association. Such an arrangement has the advantages of furnishing help in child care as well as brothers and sisters for companions.[36]

The more conventional solution to the problem of children in the isolated family is that of public upbringing, as discussed previously. Surveys of the American public show 73 percent of working mothers in favor of improved child-care centers, but only 35 percent of younger respondents aged 16 to 21 supported the idea.[37] Child-care centers appear to be acceptable only on a pragmatic basis after mothers have felt a practical need for them, not as the preferred method of child care. Can child-care centers and more public upbringing be made to harmonize with the objective of close parent-child relationships?

Urie Bronfenbrenner discusses a possibility that might resolve the dilemma to some extent.[38] His proposal is that business and government cooperate more with families by providing for child and infant care at or near centers of employment. Communities, he says, should also establish neighborhood family centers, with cooperative efforts at child care and projects in which both young and old could cooperate. The schools, he thinks, could prevent too much separation of ages by finding projects for children in the adult world and for getting older youth interested in helping children. The present efforts of many college students are in line with such ideas, and so are recent clean-up-the-environment movements that have involved all age groups.

It is hard to argue with Nimkoff's conclusion that the trend in the world today is toward greater public upbringing of children. To a degree it is inevitable, but means must be found to prevent the total institutionalization of childhood found in some totalitarian regimes, or imagined in Huxley's *Brave New World.*

SUGGESTED READINGS

Fairfield, Richard: *Communes USA: A Personal Tour*, Penguin Books, Inc., Baltimore, 1972. A sympathetic survey of the commune movement, based on the author's visits to large numbers of communes in the United States and Europe. Communes of many types are

[35]Richard Fairfield, *Communes USA: A Personal Tour*, Penguin Books, Inc., Baltimore, 1972, p. 3.
[36]*Society*, "Roundup of Current Research," *op. cit.*, p. 12.
[37]*Ibid.*, p. 10.
[38]Quoted by Marelene Cimons in "Our Children: Love Them or Lose Them," *Los Angeles Times*, December 13, 1970, sec. F, pp. 1, 21.

included—religious, service, youth, and group-marriage communes. Interesting interviews with members.

Glasser, Paul H., and Lois N. Glasser: *Families in Crisis*, Harper & Row, Publishers, Incorporated, New York, 1969. A good collection of articles, generally based on empirical research. The general topics covered are family poverty, disorganization, illness, and disability.

O'Neill, Nena and George O'Neill: *Open Marriage: A New Life Style*, M. Evans and Company, Philadelphia, 1972. The O'Neills contend that as people enter into marriage, they gradually reshape their personalities to conform to traditional role expectations. *Open Marriage* calls for the right of marital partners to be themselves and have their own careers, friends, and interests, which will make them more interesting and attractive to one another.

Queen, Stuart A., et al.: *The Family in Various Cultures*, J. B. Lippincott Company, Philadelphia, 1952. A fascinating, well-written book that traces the historical roots of the Western family. It also gives interesting comparisons with different traditions—the Hopi family, for example, and the Israeli kibbutz.

Wiseman, Jacqueline P. (ed.): *People as Partners: Individual and Family Relationships in Today's World*, Canfield Press, San Francisco, 1971. A good collection of articles by authorities on family. Parts 5, 6, and 7 on family partnership, children as junior partners, and marital crises are particularly applicable to the preceding pages.

Yorburg, Betty: *The Changing Family*, Columbia University Press, New York, 1973. Particularly good at explaining the underlying sociological changes affecting the modern family. Yorburg's book is also good as a discussion of the social-class and ethnic variations on family types encountered in the United States.

QUESTIONS

1 How can a greater cultural emphasis on love, romance, and equality actually make a marriage relationship more vulnerable to breakdown than in the days of arranged marriages?

2 Why is the type of family described by Komarovsky less satisfactory now than in the past (see "the anachronistic family")?

3 In what ways are the divorce laws of most states unrealistic?

4 Why has our society developed such strongly age-graded characteristics?

5 What are the worldwide trends in family as described by Nimkoff?

II
THE
INCONGRUITIES

There are many incongruities that contribute to the worries of our troubled land, such as the paradox of poverty in the midst of plenty, and race and sex discrimination in a society that claims to believe in equality. Another incongruity is that of maintaining fairly rapid population growth at a time when human population is reaching the limits of the earth. The first of these problems has troubled societies since ancient times, and even population growth has been seen as a potential source of danger since the early nineteenth century. What, then, is new about the incongruities?

WHAT IS NEW

In many cases what is new about the problems discussed in the next four chapters is the increasing social awareness of their implications. Racial inequality has been inconsistent with our declared social norms throughout our history, and we find it hard to understand how our ancestors could have been blind to the fact. It is only recently, however, that we have become aware of some of our other incongruities. We thought we had been good to the blacks because they were eventually freed from slavery. We were good enough to allow large numbers of immigrants to come to our shores, including the impoverished, the refugees, and ironically, the draft dodgers from lands of compulsory military service. Only in an age of protest, however, did we begin to realize the full meaning of second-class citizenship for black Americans and a vastly uneven welcome for the immigrants entering our land. The problem of women's rights is similar. We have long believed women achieved equality when the Nineteenth Amendment was passed and have spoken with complacency of an age of female equality. The employment discrimination facts now being publicized have taken much of the nation by surprise.

The problem of poverty is not new, but it is relatively new to have a society that could actually afford not to have poverty. The problem of overpopulation has been perceived by a few people for many years, but by only a few. As recently as the early twentieth century, Theodore Roosevelt was decrying our declining birthrate, fearing "national suicide." Now, with the birthrate much lower, most people are worried about the crowding of the earth.

MEETING THE SOCIAL PROBLEMS CRITERIA

All the problems discussed in the next four chapters involve large numbers of people. All are seen primarily as normative problems, and all are amenable to solution; and, as a matter of fact, at least some progress has been made with many of them. The racial problems, however, still present a threat. So little has been done about the racial problems of the ghetto that we could continue to have the bitter, divided society warned of in the *Report of the President's Commission on Civil Disorders*. Persistent poverty is also a threat, for it is costly and alienative, and tends to undermine belief in the viability of our economic system.

As for the problems of male and female, we do not anticipate any literal battle of the sexes, but we do anticipate increasing complaints about the confusion of role requirements of both men and women, and about women's relative deprivation in both the political and occupational spheres. Finally, the potential threat of the population explosion is very great—more so in already crowded parts of the world than here, but potentially dangerous everywhere.

INTERRELATIONSHIPS

The problems of minority groups, female employment, and poverty are intricately related to economic and social change. Poor immigrants from Europe were once able to find jobs in the factories and mines of America. Recent immigrants from the rural South to the urban North, however, have not been able to find work. Increased efficiency and automation have eliminated many jobs for the unskilled and semiskilled. Even when norms change enough to make us realize the need for greater racial equality, our tradition-bound institutions—schools, labor unions, industries, and political parties—respond slowly.

The problems of minority groups and poverty are closely related to alienation and deviant behavior. Those whose experiences of life have caused them to feel unwanted and unworthy are not closely bound to the norms of the property-owning middle class. Craftiness is sometimes the price of survival. Outraged feelings can also lead to acts of hostility or a retreat into the world of drugs.

The problems of women's rights are closely connected to economic change as well as to normative change. Women were once employed only in poorly paying sweatshop jobs or in domestic tasks. Even now women's jobs tend to be low paying, but educational equality and opportunities for the skilled and educated have greatly increased the number of women in the occupational world and the number who feel cheated in pay and in opportunities for advancement.

THE INCONGRUITIES PERSPECTIVE

Incongruities always exist in societies to some degree. All societies hold certain social sentiments or values—idealizations of what is believed to be right. Practice seldom lives up to the cultural ideal, and the difference between ideal and practice is referred to as normative strain. There are also cases in which old cultural ideals are outmoded by new events and needs, and normative change becomes necessary.

Managing normative strain   As noted in the introductory chapter, societies develop means for the management of normative strain. They learn to explain away inconsistencies or to so completely compartmentalize their thinking that they do not even notice them. Men of the Victorian age could glorify and sentimentalize women much more than modern men do, but nevertheless confine them to the kitchen. Whites, without the slightest touch of irony, could speak of how they liked black people just as well as anyone else "as long as they know their place." A country boasting of being a land of refuge for the poor was hardly aware of its inconsistency in passing an Oriental Exclusion Act. The poor were to be helped with charity, but only the deserving poor, and those who were unfamiliar with the rules of the middle-class world were not considered deserving.

Education in the social sciences, more travel and acquaintance with other people and customs, an awareness of world opinion, and more experience with the heterogeneity of the city have helped to broaden attitudes. Technical change has had its effect by moving people away from stagnant rural communities. Even these developments, though, might not have produced as much normative strain as is now apparent if our society had not already held sentiments about equality. The inconsistencies between ideal and reality have become abundantly clear and have led to an age of protest.

Value conflict   Whereas normative strain refers to an inconsistency between norms and practice, value conflict refers to a real difference of opinion as to what the values should be. Value conflict is often involved in what is called deviant behavior, but it applies to other situations as well. Most Americans believe in democracy, a certain degree of equality of opportunity, the elective process, and other time-honored American ideals and customs. They do not, however, agree in values about poverty. Some think the poor should be given very little for fear they will be happy and content with social parasitism; others believe that poverty is seldom the individual's fault and that welfare payments should be sufficient to prevent degraded status. Similar conflicts occur in the next problem to be considered: population. Most Americans believe in birth control; some do not. Many Americans believe in almost any method to achieve birth control, including abortion. Many others believe this is wrong. Consequently, population issues become involved in value conflict.

Conflicts in values make it impossible to prescribe solutions to which all will agree. There are a few guidelines to take into consideration, though. Are proposals consistent with the needs of a modern industrial society, and will they bring a degree of normative consistency to the culture? Will the solutions leave the society less threatened by internal dissension; will its incongruities be reduced?

Relationships between the majority group and racial and ethnic minorities have long constituted one of our outstanding normative incongruities. The United States takes pride in having been a place of refuge for large numbers of immigrants drifting in from many parts of the world; but why was the welcome so uneven? Why did the descendants of the "old immigration" object so strenuously to the "new immigration"? Why have some of the new immigrants objected to the northward and urban emigration of black Americans?

What are the various accommodations that have come about between the black and white races in America? Is the next accommodation going to be one of full equality, or will American institutions continue to show racial separation and bias? How much real progress has been made by the black race in job equality, housing equality, and educational equality?

What special problems have been encountered by Hispanic Americans, especially those of Mexican descent? What are the characteristics of the present Chicano protest movement? Finally, what are the special problems of the American Indians? How are we to understand the ambiguous attitudes of many toward becoming full-fledged members of the white man's society? Do our values call for cultural homogeneity or for pluralism?

146 At the base of the Statue of Liberty is an inscription in honor of the immigration policies of the United States, reading in part

Give me your tired, your poor,
Your huddled masses yearning to breathe free,
The wretched refuse of your teeming shore,
Send these, the homeless tempest-tost to me,
I lift my lamp beside the golden door!

America has had a right to such an inscription on her Statue of Liberty, for her record of welcoming the stranger has been far more generous than is usual in this ethnocentric world. As with so many idealistic sentiments, though, there have been contradictions between ideal and reality. The "teeming masses" referred to have generally been those of Europe, not of Asia. Preferably, too, they have been those of Northern Europe, not of the South and East, and Protestant rather than Catholic or Jewish. In spite of the preferences made clear in the immigration acts of the 1920s, the gates have actually swung open at times for the latter groups as well as for the former, and many have found America to be their promised land.

A much more serious contradiction to the ideal of a welcoming "lamp beside the golden door" was the exclusion of certain other groups from the implied equalitarian philosophy of the goddess of liberty—the red, the brown, and the black. The red race was already here, but eventually driven away, exterminated, or starved on reservations. The Mexicans occupied much of the Southwest and were brought into the union by conquest. Their numbers swelled over the years by new entrants, but they were truly welcomed only for work that no one else wished to do. The Africans were brought in chains, welcomed only as chattels. For both red and black, a determined effort was made to exterminate all previous culture and, regardless of their external color, to make them culturally white.

Regardless of the fate of the excluded minorities, the people of Europe came by the millions—more than 40 million altogether, escaping hard times and oppression, escaping debtors' jail, escaping wars and conscription, and looking for a future for themselves and their children. America needed people to fill its vast domains, to build its railroads, and to work in factories and mines. However, even with the Europeans, some were better received than others; and the people of Asia were eventually excluded. The recent emphasis on the problems of black America, and on the Indians and Chicanos, has superseded an interest in the immigrants from the Old World, but an examination of the immigrant record is still important. The record will tell us much about why the ideal of the great American melting pot applies to some but not to others. So before turning to the more distressing problems of the racial minorities, it will be good to review the story of the Anglo-Saxons and the "white ethnics," for the mingling of ethnic streams was often turbulent, even when they flowed mainly from the same European source.

JOINING THE NEW SOCIETY

Joining the new society was not always easy even for the European, and especially not for the poor. The ocean passage was long and often accompanied by sickness that killed the aged and the weak. Many of the poor came over as indentured servants and had to work for years to pay off their passage. Sometimes their children likewise became indentured servants and had to work for masters until they reached their majority. After the indenture was paid, they were not always prosperous, and many had second thoughts about having left Europe. Generally however, the time came when financial improvement was possible for most of the early immigrants. They came largely from Northwestern Europe, resembled the dominant racial type already here, and were overwhelmingly Protestant. In the census of 1820, the United States numbered 9 1/2 million Americans, one-fifth of whom were blacks and most of the remainder of Northern European descent. Indians were not counted.

There were a few early protests against the immigration of Quakers, Unitarians, and Catholics; and after the 1820s, there were protests against the Germans and Italians who were migrating into the country. It was not until later in the century, however, that feelings against foreigners began to rise to fever pitch. As the pace of immigration increased, people became less willing to welcome "the wretched refuse of your teeming shore."[1]

American racists in the late nineteenth century listened to such writers as Madison Grant, author of *The Passing of the Great White Race*. From overseas, John Stuart Chamberlain of England and Gobineau of France were writing of the dangers of the "bastardization" of races by intermixtures. Their use of the word "race" was different from the meaning given the word today. To them, Mediterranean and Eastern European people were of a different race from those of the West. It is also discouraging to know that learned authorities, including sociologists, anthropologists, and psychologists, were inclined to give credence to the racist view. A Senate immigration commission of 1911 drew on the writing of the learned authorities in concluding that "the new immigration as a class is far less intelligent than the old, approximately one-third of all those over 14 years of age when admitted being illiterate."[2]

Obviously, lack of education was being equated with lack of intelligence for the white ethnic groups. President Wilson did not agree with such an assumption and opposed restriction of immigration on a literacy basis.

The offenses of the new immigrants   Often the offenses of the new immigrants were merely those mentioned in an old Irish national song, "And denouncing us for being what we are." What the new immigrants were was something a little different from the American tradition. Many were Catholics, a few were Jews; some were Greek, Russian, or Romanian Orthodox. Their customs and appearance seemed strange, and it was assumed that they could never become really Americanized. They were accused of coming just to save money so they could live prosperously back home. In fact, some did not intend to stay permanently. Many young immigrants from Greece and other parts of Eastern Europe came to earn dowry money so that their sisters could get married; only then could they marry with a clear conscience. Most eventually decided to stay and wrote home for brides to be sent to them. Some lived very frugally and had a hard time in the New World, but most Eastern Europeans were inured to poverty, knew how to live more cheaply than native Americans, and managed to flourish in the New World.

Seen from the point of view of the racist, the real offense of foreigners was simply "being what they are." From labor's viewpoint, their offense was often a willingness to work for low wages. Manufacturers and builders of railroads seemed like paragons of racial liberalism, urging more immigrants to come over. Laborers

[1]Peter I. Rose, *The Subject is Race*, Oxford University Press, New York, 1968, pp. 21–25.
[2]*Ibid.*, p. 24.

An outcry arose against the so-called "New Immigrants" from southern and eastern Europe and Asia: they were guilty of being different.

protested immigration, seeing immigrants merely as competitors for jobs. To this day a perceived economic threat can rouse hostilities against the outgroup, and there is a slight parallel between the urban migration of black Americans today and the transoceanic migration of Europeans in the past.

Melting temperatures   W. Lloyd Warner and Leo Srole[3] have analyzed the rates of assimilation of various ethnic groups into American society and described the sharp contrasts in rate of "melting" in the great melting pot. To no one's surprise, those who were white, Protestant, and English-speaking faced the least difficulty in assimilation. Those who were white and Protestant, but non-English-speaking (Dutch, Germans, and Scandinavians) came in a close second. Behind them were those who spoke English but were Catholic, mainly Irish. Then came Czechs and Poles and various others who physically resembled the Western Europeans, but were neither English-speaking nor Protestant. After them were Southern Europeans and Near Easterners, also non-Protestant, and darker in complexion. In the long run, it seemed that physical appearance was more important than cultural difference in the rate of absorption into American society. Afro-Americans, having been deprived of all their African cultural inheritance, were culturally part of America since the seventeenth century, and yet their real assimilation was still in the indefinite future.

It might be argued that the Chinese and Japanese, although of different appearance, have been well received at times; but animosity against them can be aroused easily. The antiforeign protests of labor in the late nineteenth century were aimed more at the Chinese than at any other minority, and they were the first people to be excluded from migration to the United States.

[3]W. Lloyd Warner and Leo Srole, *The Social Systems of American Ethnic Groups*, Yale University Press, New Haven, Conn., 1945, pp. 283–296.

The inscrutable Occidental   There is a whole body of Western literature filled with clichés about the mysterious, inscrutable Oriental. Surely the Occident must have been even more inscrutable to the Chinese who arrived in California during the Gold Rush. They had been told of opportunity and were welcomed to work in mines and on railroads. It soon developed, though, that they were highly competitive in both labor and business, and this fact changed the good, diligent men of the Far East into the "yellow menace." They were excluded from the country, and those who were already here were not allowed to bring their wives. In 1890 there were more than 100,000 Chinese men but only 3,868 Chinese women in California, and white America wondered why there was prostitution in Chinatown! The Chinese were not allowed to own land or to farm, nor were they allowed to enter any businesses except laundries and restaurants.[4]

The Japanese also came to California, and their arrival too was protested. They were partially excluded in 1907 and completely excluded in the 1920s. When World War II came, the Japanese had the honor of replacing the Chinese as the Oriental peril, even those who were United States citizens. For the safety of the West, they were incarcerated in relocation centers, sustaining hardship and heavy financial loss, while their sons fought for America in Europe. They were poorly compensated for property loss in 1973 after nearly thirty years of litigation. Oddly enough, in Hawaii, where Japanese were much more numerous than in California, they were left free. Inscrutable, indeed, is the Occidental!

THE UNEVEN RECORD

Even for those people who entered America years ago in answer to the call of opportunity, the record of success has been very uneven. One reason is connected with the reception given them, although the less-preferred position has not been an absolute barrier to upward mobility. A fair percentage of Catholics succeeded quite well, even in the days when anti-Catholic prejudice was strong; and many Jews, Eastern Orthodox, and Buddhists have also succeeded in American life. An analysis of why some groups succeeded better than others may cast light on the current problems of the racial minorities whose opportunities seem so severely limited.

The criteria of success   Obviously, one criterion of success was being of the "right" type—culturally, socially, and religiously. Another important aid to success was possessing the right kind of skill for working in the new land. The type of skill required differed from time to time, and what was helpful in one period was not necessarily helpful in another. For example, the hardy European peasants were well equipped for facing the clearing and developing of land before the closing of the frontier. Many others, common laborers, found their strong backs greatly needed for building railroads, working the mines, and developing the resources of the country. Both farm experience and physical strength decreased in importance as the economy of America became less purely extractive and more urban-technical. Almost the only exception has been that of farm laborers from Mexico, sometimes encouraged to enter either legally or illegally to help keep down farm labor costs and frustrate efforts at unionization.[5] More typically, after World War II, the people most strongly desired were scientists, engineers, rocket experts, and

[4]Charles Hillinger, "Why Chinese in U.S. Had to Be Laundrymen," *Los Angeles Times*, February 20, 1971, pp. 1, 24.
[5]Alejandro Portes, "Return of the Wetback," *Society*, vol. 11, no. 3, pp. 40–46, March-April 1974.

doctors. Manufacturers by that time could easily agree with union laborers in seeing no need to bring unskilled migrants into the system. Often today, the unskilled migrant entering the city is a black person looking for the type of job that is disappearing.

There were definitely other criteria for success, which were closely connected with the values of the people arriving in the new land. Many of the early arrivals from Northwestern Europe represented the basic, hard-striving ethic that Max Weber describes in *The Protestant Ethic and the Spirit of Capitalism* (and which we shall say more about in Chapter 10). There were certain traits about the early Protestants that made them compulsive in their struggle to get ahead rapidly, but many non-Protestant people had similar values. A study by Bernard Rosen,[6] which compares several immigrant groups, finds the Jews and Greeks doing particularly well in achieving middle-class status, and also finds that they stress the values of success striving and independence training in the rearing of their children. Included in Rosen's study is the idea that a slight handicap acts almost as a goad to greater effort; an overwhelming handicap in prospects for the future leads to discouragement. The Jewish admonition to children has been "Remember you must do a little better than others in order to get the job, because you are a Jew." The much-stronger prejudice against hiring the black has, in the past at least, been more of a discouragement than a goad to increased effort.

Other immigrants tilled the same American soil but reaped little harvest. Many early arrivals, even from the preferred British Isles, settled in marginal agricultural regions where a handful of their descendants continue to live in poverty. Many miners from Europe entered American coal mines, devoting their lives to an unwholesome task that has declined in manpower requirements. Generally speaking, the Europeans found America to be a land of opportunity. The opportunity for the later arrivals—the white ethnics—was not quite so great, however, as it had been for the original settlers.

> By conducting a few interviews, see what you can find out about differences in success orientation of different minority groups. How demanding are they of their children in school work? What would they consider an adequate life goal?

The WASPs   Fears are sometimes expressed that the white ethnics (Italians and Greeks, Poles and Czechs, Jews, Armenians, and others) are increasing their economic stake in America and about to "take over"; but the evidence indicates that the WASPs (white Anglo-Saxon Protestants) are still doing extremely well. The WASPs are still a majority of the population, although not so large a majority as in former times. The figures[7] for 1968 were approximately as presented in the table on the opposite page.

Economically, the advantage of the WASPs is more impressive than their numerical majority. Of the directorships of the fifty largest corporations, 88 percent are held by WASPs. Of the ten largest commercial banks, WASPs hold 83 percent of the directorships; Roman Catholics come in second in directorships, and Jews third. Even the Bank of America, founded by Amadeo Giannini, and with many Italian holders, is said to be "infiltrated" by WASPs. The WASPs hold 80 percent of

[6]Bernard Rosen, "Race, Ethnicity, and the Achievement Syndrome," *American Sociological Review*, vol. 24, pp. 47–60, August 1959.
[7]Fletcher Knebel, "The Wasps: 1968," *Look*, pp. 69–72, 75, July 23, 1968.

Total population	200,000,000	
minus	50,000,000	Roman Catholics
minus	22,000,000	Negroes
minus	6,000,000	Jews
minus	4,000,000	Eastern Orthodox
minus	1,000,000	Oriental and Polynesian
minus	550,000	American Indians
minus	650,000	Others
equals	116,000,000	WASPs

the directorships of the five largest insurance companies in America. Minority proprietors are common in clothing stores, entertainment, construction, and even in research laboratories, but the big, basic production industries are still largely WASP. Occasionally one encounters an anti-Jewish fanatic convinced that the Jews control most major industry. Actually, they make up only about 7 percent of big-business executives, although they constitute 3 percent of the population and 8 percent of college graduates.

For the WASP descendents it would be comforting to believe that the reason for the difference in economic power is a matter of basic ability. The prevailing opinion of the nineteenth century was that such superior ability was the obvious explanation. Recent investigators such as Mills (*The Power Elite*), Gabriel Kolko (*Wealth and Power in America*), G. William Domhoff (*Who Rules America?*) and Ferdinand Lundberg (*The Rich and the Super-rich*) present no such explanation. They perceive a class of inherited wealth descended from people who inhabited this land when the foundations of industrial empires were laid. More so than the equally able members of ethnic minority groups, their ancestors were "in on the ground floor." Mills presents evidence that the ascent from rags to riches has been growing more and more unlikely for nearly a century. Of the early arrivals who were allowed into the competition, the majority were white Anglo-Saxon Protestants. The other early arrivals—Africans and the indigenous Indians—were not allowed into the game.

The first backlash The word "backlash" came into common use in the days of strong racial protest movements, but it could easily have been applied at an earlier time to the opposition of the old-type Americans to the new immigration of the late nineteenth and early twentieth centuries. Antiforeign sentiment became so strong that restrictive laws were passed in the 1920s to stem the tide of immigrants. There had already been acts to exclude the Chinese and nearly all the Japanese, but the Immigration Act of 1924 was much more thoroughgoing. The aim was to keep the ethnic composition of the population the same as it had been in the past. Using surnames as an index to the lands of origin of the people already in the country, a quota system was adopted to limit the new immigrants on a national origins basis. By the new law, approximately half the people allowed to enter the United States each year were allocated to the British Isles and about one-quarter to Germany and the Netherlands. Eastern and Southern Europe had to be content with very small quotas, and Orientals were completely excluded. Although occasional modifications of the law were made in order to admit hardship cases after World War II and after the Hungarian uprising of 1956, the quota system remained the basic law until its revisions in 1965 and 1968.

The Immigration Act of 1924 had clearly negated the old American value of equality in favor of preferential treatment for Nordic and Protestant areas. The law reflected not so much a reversal of American opinion as a set of circumstances that allowed political control to be gained by the narrow, provincial elements of American society.[8] It was during a decade of backlash against United States involvement in world affairs, of uneasiness over the increasing urbanization of society, of fear of subversive influences creeping in from Russia, and of a new type of puritanism that insisted on preventing people from drinking. It was the decade of the Scopes trial, aimed at defeating evolution in the name of fundamentalism. It was a decade of revival of the Ku Klux Klan in a form at least as much antiforeign and anti-Catholic as it was antiblack. Apparently reactions against the inevitable onrush of world events can, under some circumstances, call forth authoritarian sentiments that have long lain dormant.

> **Make an opinion survey of racial attitudes. Do you find age and social-class differences? Do you find antiblack prejudice among white ethnic groups? Are the white ethnics of your study actually any worse than the WASPs for prejudice?**

The ethnics and the new backlash   Ironically, a new kind of backlash is said to exist among the very ethnic minorities who were once the victims of a backlash that led to discriminatory immigration laws. In their case there is uneasiness about the entry of the black racial minority into the competitive labor market. Such anxiety was heightened by the presence of fairly frequent racial riots in the 1960s. At such a time it is sobering to recall that the Irish, Poles, and other minorities have had their episodes of violence. In 1870 and 1871 the Irish turned New York City into a battleground between the Orangists and the Catholics,[9] and the Molly Maguires employed terrorism in their labor demands of the 1860s and 1870s. When feelings run high and discrimination occurs and hopes for progress are thwarted, any group can riot.

Another idea that bothers white ethnics (and some WASPs) almost as much as the threat to jobs is a feeling about traditional success striving. Many whites see themselves as having started poor but having nevertheless worked their way up in a competitive labor market without special legislation or special aid. Why, they ask, can't the black minority of the poor urban ghettos do the same? To answer that question requires a glance at black history and at the present condition of our labor requirements.

RELUCTANT JOINERS: BLACK AMERICA

More than any other racial minority, the blacks point out the mythological element in the great melting pot story. To a very great degree the same can be said for two other minorities, the Mexicans and Indians. All three are distinct from the minorities we have previously discussed. Throughout most of American history the

---

[8]Seymour Martin Lipset, *The First New Nation*, Doubleday & Company, Inc., Garden City, N.Y., 1967, pp. 289–301.
[9]Thomas N. Brown, *Irish-American Nationalism, 1870–1900*, J. B. Lippincott Company, Philadelphia, 1966, p. 80.

Indians have not been admitted into the dominant society, the Mexicans have lived only on its fringes, and the blacks have lived only in a symbiotic relationship to it, working for it but not belonging to it. All three groups must be examined before leaving the myth of the melting pot, but the case of the black Americans must be examined first, partly because of their vast numbers and partly because they alone endured centuries of slavery.

The stages of accommodation   Accommodation, in its sociological meaning, is any arrangement for reducing conflict between groups that are potential enemies. A slave-to-master relationship is one kind of accommodation, the most unequal kind possible, in which the potential conflict is settled by giving all the force and all the rights to one side. The story of slavery in America is sufficiently well known to need little repetition, except to point out that it was an unusually severe type of slavery. In many slave systems encountered in the world, slave status is not absolute; even the slave is given certain rights, such as the right to marry, and sometimes even the right for his children to be born free. In the earliest days of the American experience, there were actually such limitations on slavery, and the slave condition was not expected to be eternal. As slavery became increasingly profitable, however, it became increasingly permanent and absolute. Field hands in particular had no rights whatever—no right to family life, to eventual freedom, or to learn to read and write; and various publications gave good advice on how to keep them firmly under control. The beginnings of social-class differentiation within the slave system arose with household domestics and craftsmen, who had a better chance at life than the field hands. Their descendants, along with those of freed slaves, were to be the forerunners of what black sociologist E. Franklin Frazier called the black bourgeoisie.

With the end of the Civil War and the beginning of freedom, it looked as though an entirely new type of accommodation was coming about, one of both freedom and equality. In the early years of freedom, black people could vote, ride the trains, and enter any part of town they wished. In fact, there was a period of twenty years when it seemed that interracial feelings were improving and equality was near.[10] Then in rapid succession the Jim Crow laws were passed, to help divide poor whites from poor blacks and prevent an overturn of the old upper class of the South. In many states the black man had to ride in separate train compartments, keep off the sidewalk, stay out of public parks, avoid white restaurants and theaters, stay out of white quarters of town after dark, avoid glancing at white women, and learn to say "Yes sir, you're right, boss," regardless of how humiliating the circumstances. He could not be a man; he must be called boy all his life.

Nevertheless, the chains had been partly broken. A few blacks were able to get an education. Men left the South and found *de facto* rather than *de jure* segregation and situations that were more bewildering than ever, but not quite so hopeless. Events occurred that began to upset the accommodation. Two world wars took place, and black troops saw other parts of the world and other conditions. Especially in World War II, many knew a temporary taste of prosperity and hope for the future, and all heard lectures on the evils of racism overseas, in spite of the fact that they were fighting in a segregated, racist army. The irony of their situation became more and more apparent and galling. "There comes a time when people get tired," Martin Luther King said; "We are tired of being segregated and

[10]C. Vann Woodward, *The Strange Career of Jim Crow*, Oxford University Press, New York, 1966.

Total segregation in the 1950s. Even after railroads had complied with ICC orders to end segregated waiting rooms, state and local authorities attempted to keep them.

humiliated, tired of being kicked about by the brutal feet of oppression."[11] The Montgomery bus strike had started, and it signaled the beginning of a revolt which has not yet died.

Since 1952, leadership and methods have changed. From Dr. King's completely nonviolent methods there was a change to occasional violence. A nonviolent method is particularly infuriating to some of the opposition. Nonviolence, as Mahatma Gandhi once observed, depends on an opposition with a sense of humanity, and not all the white opposition had a sense of humanity. Several of the outstanding pacifist leaders were assassinated, and an escalation of passions took place.

Eventually the American public became accustomed to riots in the cities, to Eldridge Cleaver and H. Rap Brown, to Malcolm X and the separatist Black Muslims, and to the Black Panthers. There was talk about a white backlash—something that was measurable to a degree, but hardly enough to swing elections in most parts of the country. There came also the cry of Black Power, and the very words were electrifying to many black Americans, even though the expression was never clearly defined.

The search for identity One reason the cry of Black Power had considerable force for rallying support was that it gave a sense of importance to people who had

[11]Quoted in Louis Lomax, *The Negro Revolt*, Harper & Row, Publishers, Incorporated, New York, 1970, pp. 101–102.

long suffered ego destruction. The works of such black writers as Richard Wright, James Baldwin, and Ralph Ellison are full of references to the problems of identity. People can seek a feeling of identity in various ways. They can look to their own achievements and to those of people in their group. They can look to the past and identify with their ancestors and the land of their origins, or they can turn inward, developing their intellectual and contemplative powers. But in none of these ways could the black American find a sense of identity. Accomplishments were seldom possible, and when they occurred, they were erased from the history books. They could not look backward to Africa, for all their roots had been torn out in the days of slavery, and old lineages, clans, and tribes were as foreign to them as they were to the white world that surrounded them. Spiritual contemplation was not admired in American society. Power was respected, however. One has a sense of identity if he can make his presence felt. For the black person with the strongest sense of the mark of oppression, a new identity came through violent protest.

The next accommodation Much was won in the years of protest. The poll tax was brushed aside by court decision, and so was most of the Jim Crow legislation, and black enrollment in colleges began to rise. New civil rights organizations supplemented the old ones, and what had once been largely black bourgeoisie organiza-

Family income by race and Spanish origin

Race and ethnic group	Percent of white income	Percent of families in poverty*
White	100	8.6
Black	60	29.8
Mexican	70	21.1
Puerto Rican	58	29.0
Cuban	89	13.8

*Poverty level varies with family size and with inflation. At the time of the survey, the poverty level was $4,200 annually for a family of four.
SOURCE: Adapted from Paul M. Ryscavage and Earl F. Mellor, "The Economic Situation of Spanish Americans," *Monthly Labor Review*, p. 4, April 1973.

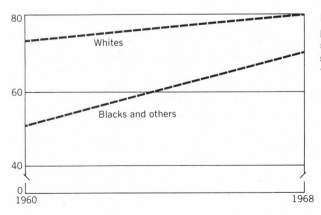

Percent of persons leaving school as high school graduates, 1960–1968

tions now became mass movements of the poor and lower class. White leadership of civil rights organizations, which had generally been well meaning but too patronizing, was replaced by black leadership in all cases. A new identity, a new drive, and new purposes were found.

In spite of progress, dangers remained. The country began to argue increasingly about whether busing should be used to integrate the schools or whether children should always be sent to schools in their own neighborhoods. The observant realized that the whole argument evaded a much more embarrassing question: why were all the neighborhoods segregated? Was not the society basically hypocritical as long as such segregation not only existed but continued to grow? How could educational, economic, and occupational integration come about while the blacks continued to be segregated in the ghetto?

The institutionalized segregation of neighborhoods is very costly to society. The present course is leading to what the President's Commission on Violence characterized as "two societies, separate and unequal." What the commission should have added is that we have always had two societies, separate and unequal. The first inequality was slavery; the second was (and to a degree still is) Jim Crowism; the third accommodation is that of the ghetto and its attendant deprivations, and of essentially racist institutions. The real fear for the black person in modern American society is that the third accommodation will have the degree of permanence that the first and second have had. One of the dangers is the argument that says "Look, you've got a civil rights act, the right to go to school, and the right to vote. What more do you want?"

The institutions of racism Some of the worst atrocities of racism have declined; there is a growing white consensus that blacks are not, after all, inherently inferior and subhuman. A majority at least speak the sentiments of racial equality, especially a majority of the young; and most of those who are somewhat racist do not consciously realize they are. Nevertheless, ingrained habit and institutionalization continue to be racist. Economically, as we have seen, the real power is in the hands of whites, generally of Anglo-Saxon descent, but it is not only in the main economic power centers that the black people have no foothold. They live in run-down ghettos that are owned mainly by whites, and usually buy at stores with white proprietors. In proportion to their share of the population, black Americans own only one-tenth as many businesses as do whites, and what they own are mainly very small concerns. The reason does not seem to be bad management; the Small Business Administration has been very successful in collecting on loans to black proprietors.[12] For the most part such businesses are located in poor areas, patronized only by the poor, and must buy wholesale from major producers—all white—and generally must pay very high interest rates on loans. Furthermore, most starts in small businesses have occured at a time when most small proprietors, black or white, have a hard time continuing to exist.

For the consumer the same kind of economic disadvantage is present and is well documented in David Caplovitz's *The Poor Pay More*. Prices are higher, interest rates are much higher, and the goods are more apt to be shoddy. An FTC study found that an item selling wholesale for $100 would sell in a high quality store for $165, but in a store in a low-income area for $250.[13]

[12]Louis L. Knowles and Kenneth Prewitt (eds.), *Institutional Racism in America*, Prentice-Hall, Inc., Englewood Cliffs, N.J., 1969, pp. 16–17.
[13]*Ibid.*, p. 25.

Have you been discriminated against because of race, color, or creed? Write to Equal Employment Opportunity Commission, Department of Labor, Washington, D.C., if it is a job covered by federal law. Otherwise take your case to a minority group organization such as NAACP.

157

Employment practices continue to discriminate against blacks. In a study of large corporations in fifteen Northern cities it was found that blacks held 20 percent of the unskilled jobs, but only 2 percent of the skilled jobs and 1 percent of professional positions. The same study found that 40 percent of black students attended schools that were at least forty years old, whereas only 15 percent of whites attended schools of equal age.[14] The ward politician in the black community finds it hard to do anything for his area because he must buck strong white economic interests.

More and more blacks are graduating from high school, but the unemployment rate among blacks and whites remains the same—twice as many black dropouts as whites are unemployed. The police watch the boys of the ghetto area more closely, frisk them more frequently, and break up their gatherings more often than in other parts of town.

The schools are, on the average, of poorer quality. And the black child feels left out of the reading books, especially the history books. A study in California found some schools still using history books that failed to mention a single black person after the time of the Civil War. This is the type of neglect that has led to demands for courses in black history. Black students are incensed that more than 20 million Americans should be treated as though they have no historical existence.

The officer corps of the armed forces remains overwhelmingly white, especially in the Navy and Marines. Blacks make up 12 percent of the Marine Corps, but just over 1 percent of its officers. In the Navy, they fare about the same and in the Air Force, slightly better. The Army is the branch of the service that comes closest to having black officers in the same proportion as black enlisted men, but even there the officers number only about one-third as many (11.2 percent enlisted men to 3.2 percent officers).[15]

In spite of this fact, considerable political progress has been made. In 1970 there was a 22 percent increase from the previous year in the number of black officeholders in the United States, and a fourfold increase compared with 1966. Even with this dramatic increase, blacks still held only 1 percent of the public offices in America in 1970, although they make up 11 percent of the population.[16]

No institution remains more rigidly segregated than the church. Proper sentiments are often expressed, ministers meet in integrated ministerial associations, church conventions pass resolutions in support of an integrated society, but on Sunday morning, black is black and white is white.

The contrast The discussion of the institutions of racism fairly well answers the question "Why haven't the black Americans succeeded as well as the white ethnics, and why do they still complain?" It is only in recent years that blacks have even come close to educational equality and the opportunity to enter the competition of American life. They have entered the competitive market for jobs at a time when high skills are required but are at a disadvantage in attaining those skills.

[14]David Boesel et al., "White Institutions and Black Rage," *Transaction*, vol. 6, pp. 24–30, March 1969.
[15]Ray Cromley, "Military: Too Little, Too Late," *Bakersfield Californian*, p. 23, February 18, 1971.
[16]"Blacks Show 22 Percent Rise in Officeholders," *Los Angeles Times*, May 3, 1971, part 1A, p. 6.

They carry a burden of generations of educational and cultural neglect and of discrimination that has embittered them and vitiated their creative energies. Their subcultural background has provided them with neither the knowledge, the habits, nor the strongly competitive attitudes in monetary matters that are needed for success in the capitalistic world. Against these barriers they have done remarkably well but must still struggle in education, in politics, in community action, and in propaganda in their own behalf or be stopped at what has been described as the third level of accommodation—a step above Jim Crow but a long step below equality.

RELUCTANT JOINERS: THE BROWN AND THE RED

African people were brought to America in chains and slavery. The Indians were equally reluctant to join our society, having been brought in largely by conquest and treaty violation. The Mexicans are of several types historically, differing from those who were already in the Southwest before acquisition of the territories from Mexico to those who have entered the country of their own volition. For them the reluctance is not so much over the joining of the society as over being totally engulfed in it. They would like to retain an identity of their own. Just as the blacks call an individual who is too deeply involved with the whites an Uncle Tom, so do the Mexicans sometimes use the word Tio Tomás, or Tio Taco, and the Indians sometimes refer to an Uncle Tom-ahawk. Sometimes the Indian who is too thoroughly assimilated into the white society is called an apple—red on the outside but white on the inside. The meaning of all such terms of derision is quite clear: there are differences of opinion about how far assimilation should go. Does one want to leave all that is African, all that is Mexican, or all that is American Indian and become a total *asimilado*?

Who are the Chicanos? Choosing the right terminology for the American of African descent is difficult, but for the American of Mexican descent it is nearly impossible. Such terms as Spanish-American, Spanish-speaking, Mexican-American, Hispanic, and Spanish-surnamed have all been used and would be a little more inclusive than the term Chicano; but they are not liked by the young militants. To some members of the younger generation the older names seem to imply that a polite euphemism must be found for Mexican, as though the word itself denotes some type of inferiority.[17] Many Americans of Mexican descent refuse to abandon Mexican in favor of Hispanic and even prefer the newer word Chicano. The word Chicano omits many people of Hispanic culture—Puerto Ricans, Cubans, and other Latin Americans. It is not acceptable to the descendants of many old Spanish families of the Southwest or to many middle-class business and professional people of Mexican descent; but it is the preferred term for a significant group and is coming into wide use. As one Chicano student states the case:

It used to be that it was a put-down for a Mexican-American to be called a Chicano, but today the new breed Mexican-American has learned to identify with the adjective in much the same way the Afro-American has learned to identify with Black. It's their thing, and because it's their thing they are proud of it.[18]

[17]Ruben Salazar, "Who is a Chicano?" *Los Angeles Times*, February 2, 1970, sec. 2, p. 1.
[18]Angel Campos, Letter in *The Renegade*, Bakersfield College, Bakersfield, Calif., March 5, 1971.

La huelga (the strike) of California grape workers brought a new sense of solidarity and power among Chicanos. A protest march to Sacramento is shown here.

Those who call themselves Chicano identify more with the poor than with the middle class. Their parents have brought some of the values of the Mexican peasant—a strong sense of family, and a sense of manhood that comes from the type of work which makes men hard and muscular but wears them out early. In many cases they are farm laborers, especially those most recently arrived from Mexico, and a life in the fields starts in childhood. For the urban majority, segregation is prominent and increasing, unemployment rates are high, and school dropout rates are equally high. The average educational level for the younger generation is tenth grade, although it is somewhat higher in New Mexico and California and lower in Texas.

Educational problems In older generations, when race was taken for granted as an explanation for all cultural differences, little thought was given to the fact that Chicano children did not generally do well in school. At times their deficiency in English has been a convenient excuse for segregation, and such segregation has served mainly to perpetuate a set of values that could fit them for nothing but lower-class existence. To this day, they are still stereotyped as candidates for the stable lower class, or at best lower-middle class, and are often counseled into programs that terminate with a high school diploma but are not intended for college preparation.

The explanation for a rather poor record in school, which was once blunt racism, has now changed to bilingualism. George I. Sanchez points out the partial falsity of such an explanation.[19] Many ethnic groups have done well in school in spite of bilingualism. If a foreign language is learned at the right time it can even increase a person's perception of language and linguistic principles and broaden his thought patterns. If, however, the child's mother tongue is looked upon with scorn, not understood by his teachers, forbidden, and treated as though it is purely an

[19]George I. Sanchez, "History, Culture, and Education," in Julian Samora (ed.), *La Raza, Forgotten Americans*, University of Notre Dame Press, Notre Dame, Ind., 1966, pp. 1–24.

instrument for expressing evil thoughts, bilingualism presents serious problems. It is also well known that children can best learn the art of reading if they first learn to read in their native language rather than in an acquired language. For the Chicano, the learning process is reversed, just as it is for American Indians.

Sanchez further says, however, that even though the language problem is important, even more important problems are often ignored. In Texas, where the socioeconomic condition of the Chicano is particularly depressed, the Mexican child needs far more attention to enculturation into American ways. A good school for such children should keep classroom size to a minimum and employ teachers who understand Spanish and are familiar with the Chicano subculture. They should understand the kinship loyalties that tend to hold Chicanos close to their own culture and should encourage them to think of improving conditions for their people, not just for themselves. Too often the individualized Yankee norm is taught: try to rise above the level of your family and friends. To people of one ethnic background this might seem admirable; to others it is the mark of an ingrate, if not a traitor.

Above all, a school system should not leave Chicanos out of its books and its accounts of history and it should not vilify their ancestors for having tried to defend their territory against Yankee imperialism. It also should not judge them and start them on the path to a "failure syndrome" by assigning an IQ score based on tests in a language they understand poorly.

Conflicting cultural backgrounds   Organizations of a political activist type have been formed by the Chicanos, although there have been some strongly retarding problems. One problem is that the people are not all of a kind. Some are strongly Americanized; at the opposite pole are those newly arrived from Mexico speaking little or no English. There are also old rural communities, dating back to Mexican rule in the West, where leadership has been of a traditional patronlike type, and where the family is so strong as to virtually preclude other types of organization. One Texan community study says, for example,

> The strength with which a person is bound to his family so overshadows all other bonds in importance that it contributes to the atomistic nature of the neighborhood. Socially, if not spacially, each household stands alone.[20]

Some Mexican leaders are offended by studies done by Anglo-American social scientists; these studies tend to picture Mexicans as of one particular cultural and psychological type or as uniformly tradition-bound people. Octavio Romano and Rudolfo Gonzales both stress the multiple origins of La Raza and the cultural range from tradition to modern sophistication. There was, for example, a great exodus of Mexican intellectuals following the Mexican Revolution of 1911; the exodus brought in a type very different from the peasant who has been studied so much by anthropologists. An interesting contrast in interpretation is offered by two translations of a fairly common Chicano saying. The American anthropologist William Madsen[21] explains the term *cada cabeza es un mundo* (literally, "each head is a

[20]Arthur J. Rubel, *Across the Tracks: Mexican-Americans in a Texas City*, University of Texas Press, Austin, p. 25.
[21]William Madsen, *The Mexican-Americans of South Texas*, Holt, Rinehart and Winston, Inc., New York, 1964, pp. 20–21.

world'') to imply the Chicano's sensitive nature, his resistance to probing questions, and his right to his own opinion. Octavio Romano[22] interprets the saying quite differently. He relates it to the great multiplicity of the Chicano culture, but not to any distinctive psychological patterns. The people came from all parts of Mexico and from all classes, the exploited and the exploiters, the educated and the illiterate, Michoacans, Chihuahuans, and Aztecans, the Hispanicized and the pure Indian; each has his own mind. He cites the expression in connection with the movement to get all together as part of *La Raza*—no longer *cada cabeza un mundo*. Parenthetically, it should be added that many Chicanos have never heard the expression, a good illustration of wide cultural differences.

The complaints summarized   Some of the most common complaints have already been mentioned: treating Spanish as an inferior language, judging children on the basis of unfair IQ tests, and segregating them educationally on that basis. All that has been said about the institutions of racism for blacks applies to a degree to the Chicanos. There is de facto segregation of the Chicanos into their own barrios; there is no treatment of Chicano culture or history; there are complaints of unfair treatment by police and courts; like the blacks, Chicanos tend to be the last hired and the first fired; their children go to the oldest schools in the district; and their sons died in disproportionate numbers in the war in Asia. They also feel themselves to be left in an ambiguous position between citizen and foreigner.

This last complaint needs a little elaboration, for it is true that the more militant Chicanos want a certain degree of cultural self-determinism, but not as foreigners. Their feeling is that the goddess of liberty can accept ''your tired, your poor'' despite considerable cultural differences. Defining how far cultural differences can extend in a nation of nations is a problem for all Americans; finding the right fit between pride in *La Raza* and in United States citizenship is a problem for the Chicanos. They wish to be judged as individuals not as ethnic categories, but at the same time they do not want to be completely cut adrift from their mother culture.

Chicano organizations are becoming much more active now than formerly in trying to achieve economic advancement for their people, while retaining an interest in their culture. The college-entrance rate for Chicanos is on the increase, although still inadequate. The University of California at Los Angeles had only 300 Mexican-American students as of 1970, but even this number represented an increase from the mere 79 of 1967. The number increased to over 1,000 by 1974. The number (less than one-tenth of 1 percent in a state where people of Spanish surnames number nearly 10 percent of the population) is pitifully small, but it still represents progress. The Los Angeles situation is typical. Throughout the Southwestern states there is a rising demand for more access to college and jobs and, it seems, the beginning of a new identity and a new spirit and militancy.[23]

The red dilemma   We have long been told that the ''vanishing American'' is no longer vanishing, but many Indians feel that they are vanishing in a spiritual sense. Even in a physical sense the plight of Indians is extremely bad. In both educational

[22]Octavio Romano, ''The Historical and Intellectual Presence of Mexican Americans,'' *El Grito*, vol. 2, p. 37, Winter 1969.
[23]Editors of *Newsweek*, ''Tio Taco is Dead,'' *Newsweek*, pp. 22–25, June 29, 1970.

achievement and in income they rank far below either the black or the Chicano. The average income of the Navajo reservation family is just under half the government's official poverty level.

There has not been the close identity between Mexicans and Indians in the United States that is sometimes found in Mexico. South of the border, the leaders who were most Indian are often the most idolized—Juárez, Zapata, and even Pancho Villa. In the United States nearly every barrio has someone nicknamed "El Indio." There is a resentment of the way Indians are depicted in American movies, but it is only recently that there have been attempts to make this a common cause.[24] Although many Anglo-Americans feel a strong sense of sympathy for the Indian, no Indian leader has ever been elevated to the rank of national hero in the United States.

Warped history   The story of the American Indian is an oft told tale, but it has been told with little attention to detail. Most Americans know that the Indians were somehow cheated out of their land, that they were moved westward, that they were defeated and broken in spirit. We know the fight was an uneven one, with heavier force of manpower, weapons, and technology on one side than the other, but we like to think it was otherwise fair combat, and often our histories lead us to think it was. Histories are more likely to be written by winners than by losers and to give an implied blessing to superior power. "History, in its written version," says the Mexican writer Miguel Méndez, "is a vulgar prostitute who disdains those people who do not adore gold and power."[25] Hence, many details have been omitted. The Negro has been forgotten, the Mexican has been vilified, and the Indian has been recorded as a strange combination of romantic, villain, and madman. There have been historians who have told the story truthfully, but the garbled folk history that comes through our children's texts and motion pictures fits the characterization Méndez assigns it. Nothing is told of giving the Indians blankets contaminated with smallpox germs and of the indiscriminate killing of women and children as late as 1890.

In the tragic episode known as the Trail of Tears, in which five civilized tribes were exiled to what is now Oklahoma, 4,000 Indians died from exhaustion and cold on the way. Yet President van Buren told the nation on December 3, 1838, "The measures [for Indian removal] have had the happiest effects. . . . The Cherokees have migrated without any apparent reluctance." To this day aged Cherokees, Creeks, and Choctaws tell their grandchildren what their grandparents told them—that history is a lie.[26] The President did not bother to tell the country, either, that Chief Osceola was seized while approaching under a flag of truce and died of mistreatment.

White children learn the history of Kit Carson, the wilderness scout, the hero, the knight of the West. Aged Navajos tell their grandchildren how he encouraged the Utes to plunder their land and steal their women and their horses, and how his troops destroyed their wheat and corn and their animals until they were starved into surrender and captivity. Then there was the Long Walk to Fort Sumner, 300 miles away, where preparations for detention were so poor that many died, and the

[24]Romano, *op. cit.*, pp. 37–39.
[25]Miguel Méndez, "Tragedias del Noroeste," *El Grito*, vol. 2, Winter 1969. "La historia en su version escrita es un puta vulgar. Desdena a los pueblos que no otorgan la lisonja del oro y del poder."
[26]John Collier, *Indians of the Americas*, Mentor Books, New American Library, Inc., New York, 1957, p. 125.

funds appropriated for their care were swindled. After four years in captivity they were sent home to a land in ruins, where they spent more years in malnutrition and misery.[27]

Soon, however, the government showed its protective hand and supplied sheep and seed. A treaty was drawn up making the Navajos (the same as nearly all other Indians) wards of the state. If they would obey and let the government think for them, plan for them, show them how absurd their religion and their customs were, and send their children off to school to learn to develop contempt for their parents, then all would be well. There is no better way to create a dependency syndrome; many Navajos are now on welfare, as are many other tribal Indians. At first the Indians hid all their best children and sent only the lame, the unintelligent, and the misfits to school; but eventually more and more children were rounded up by the authorities and sent to school. A society that told all immigrants they could practice their own religion set about determinedly to stamp out the Navajo religion. When the religious education succeeded, and a young Navajo "followed the Jesus trail," he would find himself rejected by his own people, but still regarded as a "dirty Indian" by the whites.

It must be admitted that the Navajos had been raiders and a nuisance to the surrounding Pueblos and the whites. The Pueblo Indians had never made any trouble, and were not even supposed to be considered wards of the state, according to Supreme Court rulings in 1910. Yet every possible type of deception was used by white raiders to try to seize the Pueblo lands. Religious prejudice was roused against them. All members of the governing board of the Taos tribe were imprisoned for "religious crime"—a strange type of crime to reconcile with the First Amendment to the Constitution.[28] Eventually the Pueblo tribes united, hired lawyers, and saved their liberty and most of their land.

The legacy of history   These historical episodes may seem a digression, but they have an important purpose. It is necessary to know the legacy of bitterness that has been left, or the white man can never understand the phenomenon of "blanket Indians"—Indians who are given all the blessings of being dragged away from home to a white man's school but eventually return home to their old people and their old ways. It is necessary to know a little history to know why the Indian has not jumped eagerly at the white man's ways, why 40,000 Navajos have never learned English, and why they look with hostility at the tourists who drive through their reservation and stare at them as though they are animals in a zoo. It helps to explain why they have resisted assimilation, even though their economic future would seem to require such a solution.

This does not mean that all people who have worked with the Indians have been either stupid or villainous. Many have meant well, and there are Indians who have seen the benefit of becoming urbanized and have been glad for what education has been supplied. The majority, however, even when necessity drives them to Chicago, or Los Angeles, or Oakland, are lonely persons, torn from their people and their gods, but far from being assimilated. They seek the company of their own kind, and they seek a new identity that is neither that of their autochthonous origin nor of modern urban America.

[27]Ruth M. Underhill, *The Navajos*, University of Oklahoma Press, Norman, 1956, chaps. 8 and 9.
[28]Collier, *op. cit.*, pp. 143–154.

164 | **The new mood**   White America has been a little shocked at such episodes as the seizure of Alcatraz and the much more tense and dramatic seizure of Wounded Knee. A people long considered to be either dead or changed into whites is again making its presence known. Stan Steiner was the first to write a book on Red Power.[29] Like all power terms, it sounds a little threatening, but the essence of Red Power is the idea of allowing the Indians to control their own destiny, to bring to a long-delayed halt their status as wards of the state. The young warriors returning after World War II expected a new status in American life. They had been praised for their service to their country. Then they had returned to find themselves "not the last hired and the first fired, but never hired at all."[30] They found the old complaints about the Indian who had tried to become white but found no place. They witnessed a case or two of Indian soldiers being refused burial in white cemeteries. They found that even the Indians with high academic potential were likely to drop out of college, not for intellectual but for emotional reasons. They believe that Indians have a compelling need for an independent identity, one that will fit them for the modern world but not swallow them in the white society.

At one location in the land of the Navajos—Window Rock, near the center of the reservation—is a school completely run by the Indians. There are other persons present, but they too speak Navajo and have a feeling for the traditional ways of the tribe. There the children can learn in a manner that acquaints them with the needs of the white man's world but does not alienate them from their essential Indian identity. There they can learn to read and write both English and Navajo. There they can practice Christianity if they wish, but they need not be told that the sacred views of their ancestors are madness or evil. They can gaze in reverence at the sacred San Francisco Peaks; they can learn the legends of First Man and First Woman, and of Changing Woman—the inner being of the earth, who gives life and renews life. They can learn the healing ceremonies of the Beauty Way and the Enemy Way and know what it is like to live in harmony with the holy people and all the wondrous spirits their ancestors have known.[31] They can belong to the land that is sacred to them and have some type of psychological moorings, regardless of how far the search for jobs may take them. They can eventually find a place in the modern world, but in their own way and at their own pace.

Unfortunately for the cause of the Indians, tribal and ideological issues still divide them. Tribal leaders among Pueblos, Sioux, Navajo, and others wish to retain tribal organization and their own prerogatives. Leaders of the American Indian Movement want to unite all Indians, including urbanites who have never experienced tribal life. The latter group, although more integrationist than the tribal leaders, has demonstrated in favor of the preservation of Indian lands, as in their celebrated seizure of Alcatraz Island and their later occupation of Wounded Knee. More so even than either blacks or Chicanos, the Indians have the problems of division and of too little concentration of numbers to make their weight felt politically. Nevertheless, Indian activism seems to have produced an upturn in morale. The Census Bureau reports an interesting sidelight to the new feeling of Indian pride. The reported Indian population increased from 523,000 in 1960 to 792,000 in 1970, a jump of more than 50 percent. Census Bureau officials speculate that many people are now reporting the Indian identity they once tried to hide.

[29] *The New Indians*, Dell Publishing, Inc., New York, 1968.
[30] *Ibid.*, p. 24.
[31] "The Long Walk," National Educational Television documentary, 1969.

Wounded Knee, South Dakota, the scene of the last great massacre of Indians by white troops, was seized and held by Indian militants in the spring of 1973.

THE PROSPECTS

Over a period of years the distinctions between the Anglo-Americans and the white ethnics have become less important. Legal discriminations against Chinese and Japanese have been removed, and hard feelings have declined. Anti-Semitism is also on the decline, although it still exists among extremists of both the right and left wing. Unless international events or some other crisis cause an unpredictable shift in public opinion, we can probably look forward to a continuing decline in prejudice aginst most of the groups included under the term new immigrants.

The distinction between the majority group and the three minorities just discussed, however, continues. Although public opinion polls show a marked decline in prejudiced beliefs, the actual pattern of segregated neighborhoods, churches, clubs, recreation halls, and schools makes the society look more racist than stated opinions would indicate. The three major minorities, although they have their differences, have a number of problems in common.

Common ground   Mexicans, black Americans, and Indians all find difficulties in the attempt to follow the upward-mobility pattern of both the old immigrants and the new. They see a need for intense effort in education, and they are calling for an education that not only prepares them for economic life but gives their people dignity and pride. They are all entering an economy that has a decreasing need for the untrained and that because of its pace of change makes the catching-up process in technical and scientific fields more and more difficult. They all have a backlog of bitterness that only time, social justice, and new opportunities can heal. They are all tempted to confrontation, sometimes of a violent sort, if they find no other way of making their grievances known.

Collectively, however, the three minorities are a potent political force. The future depends upon their learning to use their political and legal powers more fully in order to overcome the wiles of some whites and the complacency of others. The future depends also on the majority group's willingness to understand the plight of the minorities and not block their progress by neglect, indifference, or parsimoniousness about supplying education and the other necessary opportunities.

> **If you live in a big, multiracial city, work with minority-group children through a Head Start or school tutorial program.**

SUGGESTED READINGS

Brown, Dee Alexander: *Bury My Heart at Wounded Knee: An Indian History of the American West*, Holt, Rinehart and Winston, Inc., New York, 1971. An impassioned account of the events in the rapid decimation of the Indian tribes of the West, ending with the final massacre at Wounded Knee. Although the Indians occasionally attacked, the determined drive of the whites to wrest the last of their territory from them left them no alternative but the actions of desperation, followed by collapse, surrender, and the death of their culture.

Knowles, Louis L., and Kenneth Prewitt (eds.): *Institutional Racism in America*, Prentice-Hall, Inc., Englewood Cliffs, N.J., 1969. Knowles and Prewitt show us that even though public attitudes have changed, the consequences of ingrained institutional policy keep our society strongly racist in such areas as education, justice, politics, health care, housing, and employment.

Pettigrew, Thomas F.: *Racially Separate or Together*, McGraw-Hill Book Company, New York, 1971. One of the several books by Pettigrew, a social psychologist of great knowledge and experience and strong moral conviction about the need for a united society. Covers housing, police relations, education, societal attitudes, and possibilities for political action.

Samora, Julian (ed.): *La Raza: Forgotten Americans*, University of Notre Dame Press, Notre Dame, Ind., 1966. Many books are now appearing on the problems of the Mexican-Americans. This is one of the best, especially on educational problems and employment. It strips away considerable mythology about the complacent Mexican. (Not available in paperback.)

Steiner, Stan: *The New Indians*, Dell Publishing Co., Inc., New York, 1968. A loosely structured account of travels, meetings, and conversations with Indians in many parts of the United States. Steiner allows the Indians to explain their attitudes in their own terms. The book gives a feeling of the emergence of a new awareness and self-concept.

Young, Whitney M., Jr.: *Beyond Racism*, McGraw-Hill Book Company, New York, 1971. An eloquent plea for an open society by the late president of the Urban League. Presents a program of action for government and individuals to ensure democracy, justice, and equality.

Magazines: people unacquainted with the publications of other racial groups should examine a few issues of *Ebony*, and also one of the Chicano magazines, of which *El Grito* (Berkeley, California) is a very good example.

QUESTIONS

1 Why were the immigrants to America given an uneven welcome?

2 Compare the causes of the backlash of the WASPs against the white ethnics with that of the ethnics against the blacks.

3 Describe the type of racial accommodation known as Jim Crowism.

4 Explain and give examples of institutions of racism.

5 What are some of the special problems faced by the Chicanos?

5 Why have many American Indians been slow to integrate into the general culture of the United States?

The incongruities between ideal and practice noted in Chapter 7 are applicable also to a discussion of male and female. Why had we assumed that once the Nineteenth Amendment was passed, women should have no further complaints regarding equality of opportunity? What are the actual grounds for women's complaints about employment, promotion, and social acceptance as equals? What are the demands of most of the leaders of the women's liberation movement? Does social change, through its influence on employment opportunities, have a bearing on the case of female equality? Since most social roles are reciprocal, can we expect greater rights for women to have a negative effect on the position of men? Will the role expectations of men become more difficult, or will men be relieved of certain role burdens they would be glad to discard? Are there any demands of the women's movement that could be helpful for both sexes? What will happen to the traditional roles of women? Will the women's liberation movement add considerably to the pressures that are even now resulting in more public rearing of children?

We shall note that by no means do all women show a great interest in the demands of women's liberation. Nevertheless, the movement is very strong and vocal. New adjustments are being made, and even more will have to be made in the future if we wish to remove the incongruities existing between our professed belief in human equality and the actual case of male monopoly of the most important leadership roles in society.

As the values of society change in the direction of greater equality, it seems only natural that the increasing equality should apply to women as well as to men. The preponderance of societies, of course, have rated man as superior to woman and have given higher status to the work done by men than to work done by women. The unequal status assigned to work roles was noted by Ralph Linton in his definitive essay on status and role. In one society women make the pottery and in another men are the potters; in the former society the potter's trade is a lowly one; in the latter, a high art. In modern society there has been an equivalent point of view, holding that the routine, tedious tasks are best performed by women but the more creative tasks are best performed by men. Philip Goldberg gave a test to women students in which they judged the quality of written articles bearing the pseudonyms John T. McKay and Joan T. McKay. Although the articles were all written by the same person, even the women students rated the articles they believed to have been written by John as superior to those by Joan.[1] Apparently even women have been sold the idea that men are more creative.

The attitudes of inequality used to be more marked. Ancient societies generally had little use for female liberation. Even the creative period of the French Enlightenment found Condorcet almost alone in pronouncing women the intellectual equals of men. As recently as 1873, Dr. Edward H. Clarke wrote that a boy could study for as much as six hours per day without injury, but if a girl spent that long studying, her "brain or special apparatus will suffer . . . leading to grievous maladies which torture a woman's earthly existence, called leuccherea, amenorrhea, dysmenorrhea, chronic and acute ovaritis, prolapsus uteri, hysteria, neuralgia, and the like."[2] Not only were study and thought too much of a strain for a woman but other activities as well. Apparently her "brain and special apparatus" could easily suffer from too much sexual activity or from any employment outside the home. Of course, there were a few bad women who seemed able to entertain any number of evil men and even to break the employment rules.

Attitudes have changed, of course, but there is a women's liberation movement today that contends attitudes have not changed very much. There are other groups that question unshakable tradition regarding male and female, including the free sex movement, the gay liberation movement, and zero population growth. All have one point in common: they tend to challenge the traditional idea that male and female differences should serve solely for species perpetuation and a division of labor primarily structured to serve that ancient cause.

THE INCONGRUOUS ROLES OF WOMEN

In the early days of the Women's Rights Movement it was supposed that the right to vote would be the key to full equality. High political office would be within the grasp of women, and woman suffrage would usher in a great period of reform. Actually, by 1970 there was only one woman in the Senate and a mere ten or twelve in the House of Representatives, none in the Cabinet, none on the Supreme Court, and certainly none looking like candidates for President. In India, Ceylon, and Israel women have served as Prime Ministers. In the United States high offices seem to be securely in the hands of men.

Women are also grossly underrepresented in the professions of law, medicine,

[1]Cited by Jo Freeman, "Growing Up Girlish," *Transaction*, vol. 8, p. 37, December 1970.
[2]Quoted by Marijean Suelzle, "Women in Labor," *Transaction*, vol. 8, p. 56, December 1970.

	Women as proportion of	
Year	Labor force	Professions
1900	13.3	34.2
1910	19.9	41.2
1920	20.4	44.1
1930	22.1	44.4
1940	24.3	41.3
1950	28.0	39.3
1960	32.7	38.1
1970	37.8	40.8

SOURCE: Rudolph C. Blitz, "Women in the Professions, 1870–1970, *Monthly Labor Review*, p. 35, May 1974.

and divinity, in music, art, and architecture, and even in such fields as dress design. The schools are filled with women teachers, but few are administrators and even fewer are members of boards of education. On the university teaching level, women not only are few in number but have declined in percentages between 1940 and the early 1970s, although affirmative action programs on behalf of women are now reversing the trend. Women are generally credited with being more religious than men but seldom seem to be considered capable of the ministry. One must look hard in any church for women ministers or priests. Religious leaders, like archangels, are masculine, and the masculine image in religion is irritating to many feminists. Combining the issues of race and sex equality, one feminist leader, Bernice Sandler, has on her desk a sign reading "Trust in God—She will provide—She is black."

Stopping the bias   Much of the reason for few top positions for women in business, politics, education, or religion is that of lingering prejudice. Men do not like to see their occupational realms invaded. A woman can be accepted as a clerk or typist, or even as a coworker, but seldom as a supervisor. William F. White's investigations of worker relations in industry indicated worker dissatisfaction in any case where a woman stood superior to men, even in conveying orders from elsewhere. Women can be given jobs, but not the best jobs, and not too many of those that pay well. They are numerous in the ranks of ill-paid nurses, but almost nonexistent among well-paid doctors. In nearly all occupational areas, the pay of women is lower than that of men, but more important is the disparity in types of jobs held by the two sexes. In a study of several hundred occupations, only one of the forty-two jobs in the top-paying decile (dental hygienist) was held mainly by women. Of the bottom decile in pay, women made up the majority of jobholders in twenty-five our of forty-three occupations.[3] The figures in the table above show that although women have steadily increased their percentage of the labor force, they have shown no advance in percentages of professionals in 1970 compared with 1910–1940.

[3]Dixie Sommers, "Occupational Rankings for Men and Women by Earnings," *Monthly Labor Review*, pp. 34–51, August 1974.

In 1960, of all the families headed by women and having children at home, 28 percent were below the poverty line. By 1970, the same types of families headed by women and below the poverty line had increased to 47 percent.[4]

The reason for lower pay for women is only partly a matter of their entering lower-paying jobs; in many cases, it has been a matter of unequal pay for the same job. Finally, beginning slowly in 1972 with the enactment of an Equal Employment Opportunities Act, and with a Supreme Court ruling of 1974 that women must be given equal pay for essentially equal work, a change began. A rash of suits against such concerns as Standard Oil, AT&T, and Corning Glass Works were won, allotting millions of dollars in back pay to women who had been discriminated against in wages since the passing of the act.[5] Even more important than the court cases themselves was the realization that the government was determined to act in such cases. The result was a change to rapid negotiations with women to change discriminatory practices, including the bias against promotions for women.

The 1972 act calls for equal opportunities for racial and ethnic groups as well as for women and is the source of affirmative action programs in their behalf in industry and in the schools and colleges. It has often been noted by sociologists that well-enforced laws begin to change the way people think about things. When women or ethnic minorities are placed in positions superior to the ones they have held in the past, they are eventually accepted, and a once-reluctant public begins to think of the new norms as right and proper.

The sex role Some early feminists were enemies of marriage because the woman's role in marriage was seen as that of an inferior. The woman took the husband's name, implying, they said, that she was his property. Women had been placed on a pedestal in the Victorian age, but a pedestal is a confining spot to occupy. There was little equality and no occupational and sexual freedom. The feminists insisted that women should not be limited completely to the glories of the female sex role, with its attendant duties of maintaining the household, having babies, and being pleasing to men. They must have full equality, said the feminists; what is permitted for men should be permitted for women. The experience of two world wars had demonstrated that women could serve in any occupational role. In fact, during the Second World War women were praised in such songs as "Rosie the Riveter" for doing a man's work. In peacetime they were expected to return to the kitchen.

Little by little a single standard in sex matters is being approached. Some early studies indicate the beginnings of the change. In 1920, Dr. Gilbert Van Tassel Hamilton made a study of one hundred women. Of the fifty born before 1890, only seventeen had ever had pre- or extramarital sexual relations; of those born after 1890, thirty had had pre- or extramarital relations.[6] Later, Lewis Terman made a similar study of American women, comparing those born from 1890 to 1899 with those born from 1900 to 1909 and after 1910. The percentage of women who were virgins at the time of marriage gradually declined from 74 to 51 percent for the 1900 to 1909 group, and to 31.7 percent for those born after 1910. Kinsey's reports on the American female follow the same trend, showing a particularly rapid change

[4]Robert L. Stein, "The Economic Status of Families Headed by Woman," in Nona Glazer-Malbin and Helen Youngelson Waehrer (eds.), *Woman in a Man-Made World*, Rand McNally & Company, Chicago, 1972.
[5]"The Job Bias Juggernaut," *Newsweek*, pp. 75–76, June 17, 1974.
[6]William L. O'Neill, *Everyone Was Brave: The Rise and Fall of Feminism in America*, Quadrangle Books, Inc., Chicago, 1969, pp. 297–298.

toward sexual permissiveness in the 1920s.[7] Equally important as a change was the recognition that respectable women should have the right to enjoy sex as much as men. Victorian ladies simply yielded to their husbands' "animal nature," supposedly with great reluctance. Now women are also allowed to have an animal nature, and every sex manual emphasizes the point. The greater emphasis on the woman's role as a partner in love, however, had a tendency to reemphasize basic physical differences. In some ways woman had gained, but perhaps in some ways she had lost in her battle for entry into the status of equality.

> **Study employment situations for women in your own chosen field. (If your chosen field is teaching, up to high school level you'll find fair equality but tally the ratio of women to men administrators.)**

Enter Dr. Freud   The awareness of freudian psychology had a profound effect on the relations of male and female. We are not concerned here with whether or not the great Vienna psychiatrist was correct in all his interpretations of dreams; what is important is that he was heeded. Freud was able to convince much of the Western world that it was suffering from a puritanical hang-up that was causing frigidity, impotence, and neurosis. The forbidden subject of sex came to the fore, and it threw a roadblock in the way of liberated women. Why did women want to be doctors, lawyers, engineers? In freudian writings was the implication that they desired such careers because they were sexually frustrated, not normal, not able to bask in the glory of sexual attractiveness. In a freudian phrase detested by the feminists, they were suffering "penis envy."[8] Friedan makes a strong point of the effect of Freud. Women turned too frequently from reading liberation journals to reading sex manuals.

   An equally important reason for the decline of the earlier feminist movement was a change in breeding habits. Some militant feminists interpreted the change as a deliberate attempt to sell out the cause of womanhood; others more plausibly interpreted it as a reaction against the dislocations of war. Whatever the reasons, the 1940s and 1950s showed a renewed interest in the home. The idea persisted that the normal woman, the one not rendered neurotic by suppressed desires, should be interested mainly in the blessings of husband, home, and children. The old German phrase *Kinder, Kirche, und Kuche* (children, church, and kitchen) was almost applicable. Those who remember the end of World War II will recall the enormous prevalence of pregnant women and baby carriages. Woman, in spite of her relative sexual freedom, was still linked strongly to her traditional role. Its demands had increased in various ways, but basically it was still a home role. In the 1920s the college coed was looking for liberation and a career; in the 1950s she was looking for a husband.

The impossible role   What had actually happened was a type of liberation that in some ways increased frustration. Now it was granted that woman should be educated, but not for a life career. She should be educated in order to help her husband earn a living, if necessary, and to keep up with her husband intellectually and make a good companion for him. At the same time, her household role had

[7]*Ibid.*, p. 300.
[8]Betty Friedan, *The Feminine Mystique*, Dell Publishing Co., Inc., New York, 1962, chap. 5.

The baby boom—a roadblock to liberation.

diminished but little. There were more labor-saving devices, but there was also more labor. Baby care had become more demanding, including considerable reading about child care, more fussing with formulas and psychological needs, and greater attention being given to diet and vitamins and more permissive training. At the same time she was not permitted, as her grandmother had been, to put on weight and recognize age. She was expected to be fascinatingly beautiful and shapely. There is an old Chinese saying that a man's needs are three: a wife to keep house and bear children, a concubine for sexual pleasure, and a friend with whom to communicate his philosophy and dreams.[9] The American wife must be all three.

THE FEMALE STEREOTYPE

One of the serious psychological problems of any minority group is that the stereotypes of what they should be like have long existed in the minds of most people. Like the happy-go-lucky stereotype of the black American and the complacent, fatalistic stereotype of the Chicano, the submissive stereotype of the woman had to be challenged. The point of view that all women conform to a type because of inborn traits flies in the face of one of the first principles of social psychology: people tend to conform to the roles society expects of them. The well-bred Victorian woman was expected to be delicate; the Spartan woman was expected to be hard and strong; the Mundugamor woman was expected to go on

[9]David Mace and Vera Mace, *Marriage East and West*, Dolphin Books, Doubleday & Company, Inc., Garden City, N.Y., 1959, p. 224.

head-hunting raids; the Tasmanian woman was expected to swim out to the seal rocks and club seals over the head. Somehow society interferes strongly with what folk wisdom has assumed to be inborn temperamental differences between the sexes. It should not be surprising that a society that no longer has a need for keeping its women busy bearing children, that educates its women and gives them a good knowledge of the world outside the home, and that even expects them to work outside the home when need arises, should find its women demanding greater equality. Much of the rebellion is against what one woman sums up as the idea that "if they [women] know their place, which is in the home, [they] are really quite lovable, happy, childlike, loving creatures."[10] As more and more women display their competence in any line of work from truck driving to surgery, the falsity of the stereotype becomes increasingly apparent.

THE MALE STEREOTYPE

Since social roles are generally complementary, societies have exaggerated male and female differences, stereotyping the two sexes at opposite poles. Men, so the stereotype goes, are aggressive, dynamic, and logical rather than emotional, and they love to lead, just as women are said to love to follow and play a subordinate role. The stereotype has been preserved by making men, and only men, eligible for all the highest positions of leadership. And to make doubly sure that the male domain is maintained, it is said that men cannot achieve self-realization, that is, they cannot develop their masculinity, on any other grounds. Hendrick Ruiten-beek,[11] for example, tells us that the present trend toward sex equality amounts to a psychological castration of the male (a view not accepted by sociologists). He sees impending disaster for men, contending that the consequence of lowering male status in the home is increasing anxiety and alienation, especially in the United States, where the man's role was previously a very active one.

Even in the realm of sexual activities, the old stereotype defined the male as in greater need of sexual outlets, and, in turn, condoned philandering on the part of the man but not on the part of the woman. Within the bedroom it was the man who was to be pleased. Consistent with a position that women's liberationists call "male chauvinism," Ruitenbeek contends that the new equality in sex affairs, and the man's knowledge of the woman's greater demands on him, is damaging to the male ego. He also worries over the idea that the man must be dominant in the home for the sake of his son's male image. Merely being a pal to his son will not do. The lack of strong role differentiation, in Ruitenbeek's opinion, can lead to a type of alienation on the part of both men and women. Such are several of the conclusions that flow from an old-fashioned stereotyping of the two sexes. The constructs fail to fit a large percentage of the members of the groups they are supposed to describe; and even when they do, it is hard to say what is natural temperament and what is simply response to social expectation. An examination of a society that avoids any strong role contrast between the two sexes seems to demonstrate that traditional stereotypes can be abandoned without any serious personality problems.

[10]Naomi Weisstein, "Psychology Constructs the Female," a paper delivered at the meeting of the American Studies Association, University of California, Davis, Calif., October 1968.
[11]Hendrick Ruitenbeek, *The Male Myth*, Dell Publishing Co., Inc., New York, 1967.

A study of the Israeli kibbutzim does not confirm the dire predictions made by Ruitenbeek. The ideal in the Israeli kibbutz has always been one of complete equality between the sexes. In a study of male and female roles within the kibbutz, Yonina Talmon[12] shows that a certain degree of status differentiation does take place, but only a minor one. Although children are reared in age groups by individuals other than their parents, they spend time every day visiting with their parents. Both mother and father love to see them, play with them, and show great affection toward them. The mother plays the larger role in the very rare cases where any disciplining by the parents is necessary. Men help with the housework, but not as much as women. Both sexes do a man's work in the commune, in agriculture, handling trucks and tractors, or whatever is necessary, although women do less of that kind of work than do men. Since most economic matters are handled by the kibbutz rather than by the mating couples, very little budgeting and planning at home are necessary; but what little is done is usually taken over by the woman. Men are more likely to go to meetings of the kibbutz and assume leadership, although the difference herein is not very great.

Women more than men tend to gravitate toward occupations having to do with child care, not because they are pressured into doing so by rules or by the expectations of others. A traditionalist might take comfort in noting that domestic choices are taken by women quite frequently even when there is no social requirement to do so, but the point is really irrelevant. Women's liberationists say not that all women must avoid housekeeping but merely that they must not be pressured into it as the only choice or thought of as odd and unfeminine if they prefer more rewarding (to them) lines of work.

What develops in the kibbutz, then, is a situation in which children mature in an atmosphere of little if any male dominance or even competitiveness. The results have been by no means a disaster for the male self-image or for the growing children. The evidence seems to be that happy, generous, cooperative children mature in a society based on sex equality and cooperation. Productiveness and creativity survive; and both sexes appear to be capable of rising to the defense of their territory.

LEADERSHIP

For believers in traditional roles it may be comforting to know that large numbers of American women hold beliefs almost as ancient as the Chinese principles of Yang and Yin. Yang, the male principle, is active; Yin, the female principle, must be passive or the harmony of the universe is upset. A recent Gallup poll found that the wives of workingmen generally saw their Yin role as quite satisfactory. The role might be too passive, but only 30 percent thought men have an easier time than women; 46 percent thought women have an easier time than men.[13] However, as was previously noted, the wives of blue-collar workers were changing their attitudes rapidly by the mid 1970s.

Among college women there was more discontent with the woman's lot. Whereas

---

[12]Yonina Tulmon, "Sex Role Differentiation in an Equalitarian Society," in Thomas Lasswell, John Burma, and Sidney Aronson (eds.), *Life in Society*, Scott, Foresman and Company, Glenview, Ill., 1965, pp. 145–155.

[13]"Life is a Toil," *Transaction*, vol. 8, p. 10, December 1970.

the national sample showed 65 percent saying that women get as good a break as men in this society, only 50 percent of college women agreed. It is obviously the 50 percent in disagreement who are the most vocal on the matter of male-female relations. The women's liberation movement may not express the convictions of the majority of women, but what makes it important is that so many of its champions are among the most capable and active members of society. They are the cutting edge of the blade, as were their female counterparts in the first Women's Rights Convention of 1848. As mentioned previously, the earlier movement for women's rights was less productive than might have been expected, but more sweeping goals are now being pursued with a renewed zeal and at a time when equalitarian norms of various kinds have been proclaimed more loudly than ever before.

Attitude survey. By a simple questionnaire, see if you can find differences between generations and social classes in what are considered proper male and female roles. (For example, should men be nurses? Would you vote for a woman for President?)

The demands In an earlier age the primary demand of women was for voting rights and the secondary, for the right to jobs. Today the demand for equal rights to jobs and equal rights to pay and promotion has moved into first place. Women's groups do not all agree about their demands, but they nearly always include jobs and certain other rights that will increase a woman's employability—for example, the right to child-care centers, and the right to abortions if babies are unwanted or are due at unacceptable times. A recent scholarly book on the history of women's movements in America attributes their failure primarily to the basic female problems of child bearing and infant care.[14] If women are to succeed in careers, they must find means of regulating these basic demands. The possibility is greater now than in the past. Family planning is almost universally accepted, but child-care centers leave much to be desired.

Several European countries, especially Sweden and Denmark and the Soviet Union, have concentrated much more on child-care centers than has the United States. Since Russia has long had a manpower shortage (there are 18 million more women than men, largely because of World Wars I and II), the U.S.S.R. has to rely upon women's labor and has provided day-care centers and boarding schools. The Scandinavian countries are much more comparable with the United States, and in those countries equal employment opportunities have been aided by low birth rates and readily available infant- and child-care centers. Recently the American government has recognized the need for child-care centers, but mainly to make it possible for women to hold jobs that will get them off welfare. The demand of the women's rightists is for child-care centers for all working mothers, even those receiving good pay and married to men with good jobs. They see child care as a right that is necessary to guarantee equality.

Perhaps progress will become fairly rapid in child-care centers. The 1970 White House Conference on Children heard a series of demands for infant- and child-care centers and for schooling at an earlier age than at present. So far, however, child-care facilities have remained inadequate in number and poor in quality, hardly keeping pace with the worldwide trend noted in Chapter 6. There are

[14]O'Neill, *op. cit.*

Occupational equality for working mothers depends upon a much larger number of adequate child-care centers.

about 5 million children of preschool age with working mothers, but the highest estimate of day-care facilities available is 640,000, most of which will not take children under three years old.[15] Research in New York led to the conclusion that many people take care of children because they are too sick physically or emotionally to handle other types of jobs. The majority of child-care centers are run by people who seem fairly pleasant, and the researchers found no cases of real abuse; the major problem was that the centers were run by people interested in business rather than in children. The facilities were physically adequate, but the atmosphere was usually one of unrelieved boredom. It takes trained and imaginative people to keep children busily occupied and happy and to see that they have the types of learning experiences that prepare them for school and for life. The majority of working mothers cannot feel assured that their children's needs are

[15]Joseph Featherstone, "Kentucky Fried Children," *New Republic*, pp. 11–16, September 12, 1970.

being met in these respects.[16] In the meantime, figures from the Department of
Labor show the increased need (see page 000). In the decade of the 1960's, women
in the labor force with children aged three to five increased from 25 to 35 percent;
for those with children under three years old, the increase was from 15 to 24
percent.

Another important demand of the women's liberation movement is for the right of
abortion. Although the right for abortions in the early months of pregnancy was
upheld by the Supreme Court, the issue continues to provoke argument, being
involved as it is with conflicts in values. The strongest statement in favor of fully
legalized abortion is that a woman should have the full right to determine what
happens to her own body. The opposite view is that a fetus has equal status with
developed human beings and must be considered just as much a living individual.
Daniel Callahan[17] has written about the results of opposite philosophies regarding
abortion in various parts of the world. All countries with either moderately or highly
restrictive laws, he found, show high rates of illegal abortion and higher rates of
maternal deaths than do countries that make abortion easy. On the other hand,
countries that.make abortion easy have a harder time with contraceptive programs,
especially among the poor. Callahan, a moralist, is not happy with easy abortion
but feels that restrictive laws are worse. He recommends at least formal counseling
on the matter and, following abortion, counseling on contraception. Few feminists
would take issue with such a recommendation.

The total right of the woman to decide on an abortion, of course, runs counter to
a man's rights in the matter. In an article titled "Adam's Rib, or the Woman Within,"
Una Stannard[18] shows how strongly men are involved in the desire for children.
She even demonstrates that many cases of "womb envy" are apparent in the
anthropological world. Nevertheless, the woman can always argue that a child not
desired by its own mother is brought into the world with a very poor start in life.

Women against myth   Going beyond the immediate and practical demands for
equal opportunity are others that get into the fields of emotions, self-image, and
conceptualizations of reality. Kate Millett,[19] for example, generalizes beyond mere
occupations to the description of a society that has been insensitive to woman's
basic humanity and has systematically subdued her politically, by which she means
in all power-structured relationships. Males are still given a "birthright priority" to
rule females, and the right is perpetuated by fables about the natural abilities and
temperament of woman.

> **Does your school have a special program in women's studies? Such classes are
> becoming increasingly common. Take up the matter with your dean of instruction or
> equivalent administrator.**

Suelzle,[20] a little less vehement than Millett, also gives a number of the generalized complaints about inferior status (as do most women leaders). She lists several

[16]*Ibid.*
[17]Daniel Callahan, *Abortion, Law, Choice, and Morality*, The Macmillan Company, New York, 1970.
[18]Una Stannard, *Transaction*, vol. 8, pp. 24–32, December 1970.
[19]Kate Millett, *Sexual Politics: A Manifesto for Revolution*, Doubleday & Company, Inc., Garden City, N.Y.,
1970.
[20]Suelzle, *op. cit.*, pp. 52–60.

myths about females that are antagonizing to militant women. The idea that few women really want a career she considers a myth. Women are, in fact, taught that they should not want a career, and they are treated as though they should not desire one. Women are taught always to underestimate themselves—a reason why they start out well in school but often lag in the college years. Suelzle also presents some statistical evidence for attacking the myth that women are absent from the job more than men. A Women's Bureau study found them doing slightly better than men. She also spikes the statement that most women are working only for pin money and that women control a majority of the wealth of the country.

Another myth about which women have complained increasingly is a myth regarding rape.[21] Rape, it is said, very seldom occurs; most charges are false. Actually, large numbers of forced rapes occur, but not too many are brought to court because of a feeling that court procedures show a bias against women in such cases. Since it would be easy for a man to be a victim of false charges, precautions are taken in behalf of the accused. The precautions, in the opinion of the American Civil Liberties Union, go much too far. The judge starts by cautioning the jury that rape charges are easy to make and hard to defend against—a statement that immediately places doubt about the veracity of the woman making the charge. In all other trial cases, the only instruction is to weigh carefully the testimony of all witnesses. A much more serious defect of the present law is that a woman's previous sexual conduct is considered highly relevant. If she has had premarital or extramarital sex relations with anyone, such conduct, the law assumes, tends to indicate that she actually consented to the alleged rape. Such a law is archaic and grossly one-sided. It would be almost as logical to say that any man who has had pre- or extramarital relations can be presumed to be a rapist! Changes are gradually being introduced in state legislatures to ensure that only *relevant* evidence of previous sexual conduct can be introduced into court, and that the judges admonish the jury in the usual manner, by simply telling them to weigh all evidence with care. There is no doubt that false charges of rape are sometimes made. Neither sex has a monopoly on truthfulness. The important point is that the weighing of evidence, and the determination of what can be used in evidence, should be even.

If the stereotyping myths that have always assigned the male a dominant role are brought to an end, and if full equality in occupation and in law become the norm, will there be any ill effects on the male of the species? Will coexistence be more or less harmonious than in the past?

COEXISTENCE

One consolation about a battle of the sexes is that the two must ultimately arrive at some form of accommodation. The major demands repeated most frequently by women would not be impossible for men to accept. The emotional tone of the women's liberation movement is at times antagonizing to men, but movements are seldom led by the calm and complacent. Equality of employment and pay seem reasonable, and it can be argued that bringing women's pay to the same level as men's prevents the possibility of replacing male workers with cheaper labor. Similarly, the provision of better care centers for children is hardly a male-versus-

[21]Mary Saylin, "ACLU Seeks to End Victimization of Rape Victim During Trials," *ACLU Open Forum*, pp. 3 and 5, June 1974.

female issue. If the care centers are to be subsidized by the government, they are a political and monetary issue, but an issue along which people divide on partisan more than sex lines. The issue of abortion presents more normative difficulties, but again, opinion differences are probably more a matter of religion and ideology than of sex. When it comes to the last types of demands, the ones that insist upon equal status for women and for discarding all the old stereotypes, there will be strains in the immediate future, especially for the older people, both male and female. Ruitenbeek, the psychologist previously quoted, concludes that both sexes suffer from types of alienation as their old identities are challenged by modern realities. No doubt such feelings of alienation do occur temporarily when old role sets are disturbed, but they constitute a very weak argument for postponing social justice. Human beings are capable of adjusting to new role definitions.

If we use the word "anomie" rather than alienation to describe the situation of modern sex roles, we shall be looking at such roles in more clearly sociological terms. Anomie is a situation that exists when roles are rapidly changing or are not properly internalized, or when they call for contradictory demands. In this sense the roles of both male and female have become anomic. Although women complain of having been assigned too many conflicting roles in the modern family, men can complain about a large degree of role loss. Men are often bewildered to find themselves attacked for their inhuman domination over women at a time when they often consider the situation to be almost the reverse. This is one of the many perplexing problems of modern American society. At present there is more family breakup than in the past, which superficially seems to argue that relationships between the sexes are less harmonious than they once were. It is likely, though, that marriages that do persist and are based on equality are happier than many of earlier times. It is possible that we stand on the threshold of improved relationships between the sexes, if new status adjustments are made and internalized.

Mutual liberation   Mary Calderone, director of the Sex Information and Education Council of the United States, reminds us that we are living in an age of increasing sensitivity to human relationships. Different groups and races are more aware of each other than in the past and more capable of viewing each other as human. Possibly the stereotyped roles of male and female are more persistent even than those of race and ethnic group, but we do know that different societies stereotype the sexes differently. Certainly in the Western world the female has changed greatly from the faint and delicate creature of Victorian literature. Certainly, too, the American man has changed from the various stereotypes of several generations ago: the six-shooting Westerner, the ignorant backwoodsman, or the hearty farmer or blacksmith.

Calderone contends that man is just as much a victim of stereotypes and myths as is woman—"stereotyped grooves of earning, governing, and fighting and . . . compulsively fixed patterns for masculinity in dressing, professions, recreation, and life style."[22] She cites a case in which men had to listen to half an hour or more of women's comments on what they would like. The final conclusion was that the men admitted having been asked to express sentiments that were part of their inner lives but that they had not dared express because of social conventions. Men, she concludes, could stand to be released from some of their self-imposed demands of impassivity and stoicism; and all learning of social processes should

[22]Mary Calderone, "It's Really the Men Who Need Liberating," *Life*, vol. 69, p. 24, September 4, 1970.

relate primarily to being human rather than to being of a particular sex, color, or race. Calderone can, of course, be accused of mere sermonizing, but she states a position in line with modern trends when she suggests that the "iron-man" view of masculinity is declining.

Husbands and wives It has been pointed out, too, that the traditional type of family life—which requires the man to support the family and the woman to stay home—can be enslaving to the man as well as to the woman. The situation is summed up in the man's description of his wife as the "ball and chain." In spite of both sexes looking upon the marital relationship as a confining one, nearly everyone marries. Modern couples who simply live together without marriage, especially when young, often eventually succumb to a legally sanctioned relationship. The dilemma is that too little attachment to other people, especially to a spouse, leaves life rather empty, and too rigid an attachment seems like a form of slavery. Will greater egalitarianism help to resolve the dilemma? Marya Mannes[23] concludes that the answer is "yes."

In the days before family planning, when most women had a brood of children to care for that kept them at home, their personal identities were buried in those of their husbands and children, Mannes notes. The husband, expected to be the sole breadwinner, was equally absorbed in his work. Since children were unplanned and frequently arrived late in the lives of the parents, both were preoccupied all their lives with taking care of children or working for their support. Now the new possibility, already realized by about half the people, is that the wife can have many years of a career or involvement in other interests after her few children are grown, or even long before if there are child-care facilities. The husband in such cases does not have the full economic burden of support. Especially after the children are reared, why should he have to be the sole support of his wife? And why should she have no other interest in life but that of cooking and keeping house for him? The possibilities of new interests for both man and wife become much greater. Another advantage to the man in having a wife with career interests is that women who have more experience of the occupational world are generally more interesting people to know. They are harder to dominate, but who in the late twentieth century would hold that love can be based on dominance or the frustration of opportunities?

USING THE NEW FREEDOM

Although women failed to hold their own in the professions in the 1960s, the decade of the 1970s may be the beginning of a change. The first change is in part a result of a response to the demands for equality in the educational system; the second change is partly a consequence of the new hiring practices mentioned previously.

The Department of Health, Education, and Welfare delayed for about two years on policies for the schools that flow from the Equal Opportunity Act of 1972, but eventually new rulings were insisted upon. The rulings applying to education make the school experience for women more satisfying than in the past; the insistence on equality in employment makes the long struggle through college seem worth-

[23]Marya Mannes, "How Men Will Benefit from the Women's Power Revolution," *PTA Magazine*, January 1971.

while, unless the job market is too seriously oversubscribed. An obvious reason that the percentage of women college graduates had hardly increased for decades was that many women who attained college degrees still earned only about what a man with a high school diploma could earn.

Now the elementary and high school districts, which have been the largest occupational area for women college graduates, are required to open administrative positions for women. Colleges have been severely criticized for having too few women on their staffs, especially with the rank of full professor. Affirmative action programs aim at correcting the discriminations of the past.

Even the woman's status in athletics is improving. If athletic programs for women in college are demanded, they must be financed and supported on a scale equivalent to programs for men. Other campus changes include equal rules about curfew hours in dormitories. The custom has been undergoing change for several years, but many colleges had thought of themselves as the guardians of their students and had set strict rules about curfew hours and visiting hours for women, but not for men.[24]

Along with the freedom to enter vocations on an equal-opportunity basis, women will have to plan better about future jobs. While total professional employment in the 1960s rose by 4.4 percent, women's employment in the professions rose by only 1 percent. Of all professional women, 36 percent were teaching in elementary and secondary schools, a field with insufficient openings to continue to absorb so many. A difficulty with female employment has been that half of all women workers are concentrated in only twenty-one occupations; one-fourth are in only five occupations—secretary-stenographer, household worker, bookkeeper, elementary school teacher, or waitress.[25] Rapid growth in opportunities for women seems likely in employment as physicians, architects, and draftsmen. Women are grossly underrepresented in science and engineering, fields that are expanding only slowly; but affirmative action programs may result in more openings for women. In medicine, it was distressing for women doctors to note in 1969 that of the twenty-nine countries reporting to the Tenth Congress of the Medical Women's International Association, in only three—South Vietnam, Madagascar, and Spain[26]—did women constitute a smaller percent of physicians than in the United States.

> **Have you been discriminated against in housing or employment on the basis of sex? Write to Equal Opportunity Office, Department of Housing and Urban Development, or Health, Education, and Welfare Department, Washington, D.C.**

The Equal Rights Amendment Passage of an Equal Rights Amendment (ERA), removing all employment and other discriminations against women, is an important goal of the women's liberation movement. In 1972, Congress passed the ERA by overwhelming votes—354 to 23 in the House of Representatives and 84 to 8 in the Senate—but ratification by three-quarters of the states was still required. At first, state ratifications came in rapid succession; but just as victory seemed assured, organized opposition arose, especially from extremely conservative

---

[24]"Sex and the Schools," *New Republic*, vol. 171, nos. 1 and 2, pp. 8–9, July 6 and 13, 1974.
[25]Janice Heipert Hedges, "Women at Work," *Monthly Labor Review*, pp. 19–29, June 1970.
[26]*Ibid.*, p. 24.

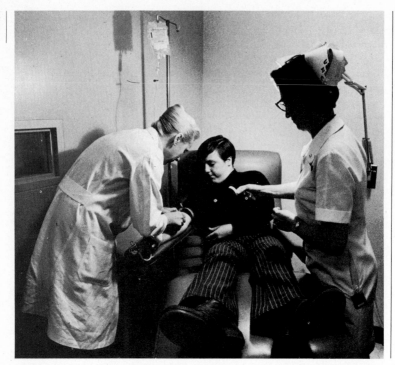

The woman doctor, unusually rare in the United States, is discouraged by prejudice, false stereotypes, and restrictive medical school practices.

groups. The right-wing opponents of the measure scored a major success in Utah, where they formed an organization called Humanitarians Opposed to the Degradation of Our Girls (abbreviated HOTDOG). The HOTDOG organization used highly emotional appeals to tradition, saying that the amendment would degrade women from their God-given role of mother and housewife to a "status contrary to the very laws of the universe."[27] The attack was loud and hysterical and apparently served to frighten the state legislature. Utah voted against the amendment. Since then, the opposition to the amendment, encouraged by success, has launched effective campaigns in other states.

As of 1975, the ERA needs to be ratified by only five more states to become part of the Constitution, but the remaining fight has promised to be difficult. Besides the right-wing opposition from such organizations and individuals as HOTDOG, the John Birch Society, and Phyllis Schlafly, another type of opposition has come from certain labor circles. The fear on the part of labor is that the amendment could undermine laws protecting women from long hours and heavy and dangerous work. Supporters of the amendment reply that the protective legislation for women has served more to exclude them from desired occupations than to actually help them. They can quote one or two federal court cases in which the invalidation of special laws for women has resulted in extending benefits to men as well as women. The Senate Judiciary Committee has rendered the opinion that "those

[27]Margaret I. Miller and Helene Linker, "Equal Rights Amendment Campaigns in California and Utah," *Society*, vol. 11, pp. 40–53, May-June, 1974.

laws which confer a real benefit, which offer real protection, will, it is expected, be extended to protect both men and women."[28] Such policies should stop labor opposition, but the ultraconservative opposition will undoubtedly continue until the amendment is ratified or defeated.

FUTURE PROSPECTS AND PROBLEMS

Already the women's rights movement has made a strong impact on society. Judging by the experience of a country such as Sweden, which has had sex equality longer than the United States, one would not predict that all women will take an interest in careers, but many more will do so than in the past. The family will be affected in the ways previously noted: more equality and independence for members and a shorter period of child care. The sex-typing of jobs is already declining and will probably continue to do so in the future. With more automation, the number of jobs requiring heavy lifting and loading will decline, which will help to bring more sex equality in blue-collar labor. Suzanne Keller[29] predicts that along with these changes will go greater community organization, not only of caring for children but also of cooking, laundering, and marketing, thus reducing further the need for a full-time housewife role. Along with other changes, she expects to see the elimination of texts that portray the old sex-and-personality stereotypes (a sore point with many women leaders at present). There will be further changes in the socialization pattern of boys and girls, with both sexes taking cooking, woodwork, household repair, and other courses of value to both (already a trend in some schools).

There are already indications of a reduced difference between the sexes, not only in terms of superior-inferior relations, but even in terms of hair style and manners of speech and dress. It would seem rather natural in a society that no longer has a wild West, and wherein increasing numbers of jobs can be held by either sex, that sexual dimorphism would decline. The ambitious young woman, who previously has been mainly negatively portrayed, will be pictured in a better light, just as is the ambitious young man. At present, as we noted in the study of the family, the treatment of the aged, unless they are well-to-do or have unusually dutiful sons and daughters, is very neglectful. Keller suggests that part of the consequence of present changes will be much better provision for the aged in communities that are interesting and not completely isolated from the main currents of the world. She suggests that such a change will be necessary so that people will not continue to depend upon their children in their old age and therefore feel a need for having several children.

New problems will arise along with the future improvements. Women will have to watch the labor market much more than now rather than prepare for only a few traditional jobs. Since equality of opportunity applies increasingly to racial and ethnic groups as well as to women, there will be increasing competition for the best jobs.

Along with the other changes in family life goes a greater amount of sexual freedom. New ideas were strongly championed by a sex liberation movement that was particularly prominent around 1969 and 1970. If the movement is less

[28]*Ibid.*, p. 47.
[29]Suzanne Keller, "The Future Role of Women," *The Annals of the American Academy of Political and Social Sciences*, vol. 408, pp. 1–2, July 1973.

prominent now than previously, it is probably because yesterday's advocacy is in large part today's reality.

The sex liberation movement An age of greater freedom of expression and equality and decline in respect for conventions is almost sure to be accompanied by open criticisms of the old moral standards. The Sexual Freedom League goes much further than most people would countenance, with nude parties, swapping of spouses, and a general attitude that everything is right as long as it is not conventional.[30] Some policies advocated by the Sexual Freedom League are in line with the thinking of the modern age: abolition of laws that invade the privacy of the bedroom, legalized abortion, abolition of most kinds of antipornography laws, more humane treatment of homosexuals and lesbians, allowance for transsexual operations, and less falsity about standards. The 1957 Wolfenden Report to the British Parliament advocated abolishing laws against homosexual practices between consenting adults. The report was eventually adopted in England and its point of view has influenced other countries as well. In the United States many cities show the same tolerance as England. Although the majority of American states have much more restrictive laws than England, California passed a law in 1975 legalizing all sex relations in private between consenting adults, including homosexual relations.

The pornography laws have been entirely eliminated in Denmark, and on a de facto basis are nearly nonexistent in many American cities. In 1970 the President's Commission on Obscenity and Pornography presented its report to former President Nixon. The report advocated abolition of laws against the reading or viewing of pornographic materials by, adults. Three members objected to the report, and much was made of the fact. What received almost no newspaper attention was that two members (Larson and Wolfgang) believed the recommendations were still too restrictive. Whatever the case, the President, Vice President, and Senate turned down the report's recommendations. The commission had done its duty of gathering facts, but facts do not necessarily influence political leadership. The constant reassurance of the commission that there was no connection (or possibly a negative connection) between sex crimes and pornography seemed to impress no one.[31] Commissions often experience the same fate as sociologists!

Similarities in protest movements In an age of protest over inequalities, it seems likely that a women's liberation movement will continue in one form or another, as will many movements aimed at greater equality. So far the women's protest movement has convinced many people that the sex equality once believed to have been attained with the Nineteenth Amendment has fallen far short of its goal. Now, with less compulsion about reproduction, with limited family size, with considerable public rearing of children, and with many years of life left after the children are grown, women are much less restricted by their traditional biological roles. The possibilities for greater liberation are at hand.

The women's protest movement is very closely linked to, and was probably partly inspired by, the protests of racial and ethnic minorities discussed in the previous chapter. In both cases there has been a wide gap between the ideal and reality; and

[30]Jack Lind, "The Sexual Freedom League," in Walt Anderson, *The Age of Protest*, Goodyear Publishing Company, Pacific Palisades, Calif., 1969, pp. 181–197.
[31]Clive Barnes (ed.), *The Report of the Commission on Obscenity and Pornography*, Bantam Books, Inc., New York, 1970.

in both cases, society has been only vaguely aware of the incongruities and has even prided itself on having handled the situation well. Complaints about employment have been prominent in both types of movements, but the issues have gone deeper than mere economics. Even more important has been the desire for a new self-concept of full equality and a denunciation of anything vaguely resembling second-class citizenship. Protests will probably continue as long as the normative incongruities continue.

SUGGESTED READINGS

Barnes, Clive (ed.): *The Report of the Commission on Obscenity and Pornography*, Bantam Books, Inc., New York, 1970. The work of the commission suffered an even worse political fate than that of most such commissions, but many of its findings are very interesting. See especially Sections 1, 2, and 3 on findings, recommendations, and the impact of erotica.

DeBeauvoir, Simone, *The Second Sex*, Vintage Books, New York, 1974. A thorough, authoritative book by one of the leading voices in the modern women's movement. Deals with both history and contemporary positions of women in Western culture, from the point of view of social, biological, and sexual roles.

Friedan, Betty: *The Feminine Mystique*, Dell Publishing Co., Inc., New York, 1962. The first volley in the present feminist movement. Analyzes the problems of inequality and their causes; refutes large numbers of myths and stereotypes about femininity, working mothers, and educational and occupational opportunities.

Millett, Kate: *Sexual Politics*, Doubleday & Company, Inc., Garden City, N.Y., 1970. The position of the two sexes has always been the result of a power struggle, says Kate Millett; "women are sometimes idolized, other times patronized, always exploited." This book, covering women in history, the earlier women's rights movement and reasons for its failure, and women in the arts and professions, has been one of the most influential books in the present women's liberation movement.

Morgan, Robin: *Sisterhood is Powerful*, Random House, Inc., New York, 1970. An anthology of writings from the women's liberation movement.

Packard, Vance: *The Sexual Wilderness: The Contemporary Upheaval in Male-Female Relationships*, Pocket Books, Inc., New York, 1970. Vance Packard has a flair for sensational titles. He is not a sociologist by training, but he documents his studies well. His book deals with changing sex norms and male-female roles, as well as with the problems of marriage and speculations about the future. As with all of Packard's books, it is very readable.

Ruitenbeek, Hendrick: *The Male Myth*, Dell Publishing Co., Inc., New York, 1967. This book, probably intended as an answer to Betty Friedan, shows a real perception of the problems of both sexes but is particularly concerned with what the author sees as the demasculinization of men.

Transaction, vol. 8, December 1970. Entire edition is devoted to the Women's Rights Movement. Excellent articles on occupations, feminine and masculine self-image, need for child care, and need for greater political activity.

QUESTIONS

1 Explain how some of the attitudes resulting from Freud's writings and the baby boom slowed down the attempt for female equality.

2 Compare the role problems of women and men in contemporary society.

3 What are three specific demands of many members of the women's liberation movement, and what are their more generalized demands (referred to as "the metaphysics" of women's demands)?

4 What are the facts about the increase in total employment of women? How does this contrast with the quality of jobs they hold and their pay and promotions?

5 What changes in attitude and what policies in employment could possibly bring benefit to both men and women?

6 How prevalent is the tendency to reject traditional feminine roles of marriage and family?

9
THE EVERLASTING POOR

Nowhere is the disparity between possibility and accomplishment more worrisome to well-meaning reformers, to critical taxpayers, and to the poor themselves than in the area of poverty and dependency. Progress has been made, but the big question is "Why has progress against poverty been so limited?" Why does poverty appear so everlasting? Why have we not done at least as well in developing a rational, uniform approach to poverty as many Western European countries have done? What are the characteristics of the poor—age and sex distribution, regional distribution, and racial and ethnic distribution? Poverty includes many besides the unemployed. What are some of the occupations that pay so poorly that they leave their workers in poverty? In particular, what are the conditions of seasonal labor in agriculture? Is "Poverty U.S.A." merely relative, or do we have actual malnutrition, ill health, and early death resulting from poverty?

We shall look at all these questions and also at various programs that have been tried or are being advocated for improving welfare and/or ending dependency. Can education and retraining do most of the job of ending dependency, or must we look more deeply into characteristics of the economy? What will have to be accomplished to prevent the poor from being "the everlasting poor"?

In an age of abundance and in a particularly wealthy society, it is easy to think of poverty as a purely relative matter—the lack of funds for a new car or fashionable clothes or the inability to keep up with the neighbors or to reach that ill-defined plateau called "the American standard of living." It is easy to rest in the assurance that Americans are well off compared with the poor of bygone times and distant places. There is a certain amount of truth to such a viewpoint, of course. The impoverished are a smaller percent of the total population than they were decades ago.

The poor have not disappeared, however, nor is there any prospect that they are about to do so. The poor are very much with us—often unobserved, it is true—but nevertheless in our midst. They suffer not just from relative deprivation; they suffer from absolute deprivation, from a lack of medical care, from a lack of housing and privacy and good food. They suffer from an inability to aid their children to find a place in the mainstream of life and from deprivation of a sense of self-worth and dignity. Even more than the numerous and hungry poor of the past, they are the "poor in spirit," pushed into the backwashes of life, more than ever before stigmatized as the inept, the retarded, the subhuman. Many are of the everlasting poor because they have no way of helping themselves and no future; such is the case with many of the aged and sick, the blind, and those crippled in body and mind. Many more of the poor are children; and unless society does better in the future than in the past, they will perpetuate the poverty of their parents; they too will be the everlasting poor.

Not only does poverty exist in America, but it exists on a scale not commonly found in the other prosperous countries. The phenomenon is puzzling to much of the world, for even the most caustic foreign critics of America generally give us credit for being a people with a heart, with a fair measure of generosity and charity in our character. Why is it that a people well known for their generous efforts to rescue Europe from poverty after two world wars, a people with a sense of mission, a people who have sent generous amounts of aid to relieve historical crises in China, India, Latin America, and Biafra are unable to cope with poverty at home? What kinds of lenses make it possible to see suffering more clearly in foreign lands than at home—in slums, ghettos, reservations, and such rural backwashes as Appalachia?

THE INCORRIGIBLE AND THE DAMNED

Certainly part of the reason for the different appraisal of poverty abroad and at home is a matter of awareness. Sudden tragedies such as floods, hurricanes, and wars receive vast amounts of publicity and sympathy. The undramatic, monotonous accounts of domestic poverty do not attract the same attention. However, the difference in dramatic quality and publicity is but a minor part of the problem of focusing public attention on poverty. Much of the problem has to do with values that are held more strongly by the American public than by much of the rest of the world.

The achievement ethic   The achievement ethic runs strong in American literature and viewpoint. In essence, it is the attitude that Max Weber characterized as the Protestant ethic . Originally the Protestant ethic was based on a religious belief in the value of hard work and thrift, and the resulting prosperity was viewed as a sign of the Lord's blessing. Those who failed to achieve success were, according to

Weber's interpretation of early Protestantism, obviously the incorrigible and the damned, not partaking of the grace of God. Such a philosophy is not believed in literally today, but it has a long carryover effect. The modern equivalent can probably be stated as the conviction that those who have not succeeded are, with very few exceptions, highly deserving of their poverty. To help such people may be commendable but by no means morally necessary.

The achievement ethic was well summarized at the turn of the century by the stalwart conservative sociologist William Graham Sumner:

> In general, however, it may be said that those whom philanthropists and humanitarians call the weak are the ones through whom the productive and conservative forces of society are wasted. They constantly neutralize and destroy the finest efforts of the wise and industrious, and are a dead-weight on the society in all its struggles to realize any better things. Whether the people who mean no harm, but are weak in the essential powers necessary to the performance of one's duties in life, or those who are malicious and vicious, do the more mischief, is the question not easy to answer.[1]

Not all Americans agreed with Sumner's viewpoint. A social reformer of the same period, Robert Hunter, wrote an impassioned book about the conditions of the poor. A quotation of his on child labor is enough to demonstrate why some people grew up weak:

> For ten or eleven hours a day these children of ten and eleven years stoop over the chute and pick out the slate and other impurities from the coal as it moves past. The air is black with coal dust, and the roar of the crushers, screens, and rushing mill-race of coal is deafening. Sometimes one of the children falls into the machinery and is terribly mangled, or slips into the chute and is smothered to death. Many children are killed in this way. Many others, after a time, contract coal-miner's asthma and consumption, which gradually undermines their health. . . . There are in the United States about twenty-four thousand children employed in and about the mines and quarries.[2]

In the long years since Sumner and Hunter wrote, there has been a softening of the tone of the Sumner philosophy, and there has been a softening of the conditions of child labor described by Hunter, but both philosophy and conditions have their counterparts today.

The philosophy of "benign neglect"　Robert L. Hielbroner[3] notes the striking contrast between the United States and many of the other highly industrialized nations of the Western world. In no other prosperous country that he has visited has he found anything like the squalid living conditions of parts of American cities, nor so much neglect of the conditions that exist. Apparently the reason for the bad showing of the United States is not that the Scandinavian countries, the Netherlands, Switzerland and others have no poverty potential to deal with; the reason is that they devote more effort to coping with the problems. Welfare expenditure in the United States is 6.5 percent of the gross national product (GNP). For the nations of the European Economic Community (France, Belgium, Luxembourg, West Germany, Italy, Great Britain, and the Netherlands) the average expenditure is

[1]William Graham Sumner, *What Social Classes Owe to Each Other*, Harper & Row, Publishers, Incorporated, New York, 1900, pp. 19–20.
[2]Robert Hunter, *Poverty*, The Macmillan Company, New York, 1904, pp. 237–238.
[3]Robt. L. Heilbroner, "Benign Neglect in the United States," *Transaction*, vol. 7, pp. 15–22, October 1970.

14 percent of the GNP; for the Scandinavian countries it is about 13 percent; for Canada, 9.9 percent.

Our neglect of poverty shows in many areas. Since 1950 we have fallen from fifth to eighteenth place among the world's nations in the prevention of infant mortality. Our relative position in life expectancy has declined, and our tuberculosis rates are higher than in Western Europe. We also have diseases of malnutrition, "including kwashiorkor—long considered a disease specific to underdeveloped areas."[4] We have not actually moved backward in most criteria of health and longevity, but we have failed to make as rapid progress as much of the technically advanced world has done.

Explaining neglect Heilbroner explains next the relative neglect of welfare and juvenile rehabilitation in the United States. He explores two major possibilities, but partially rejects the first one. It is sometimes assumed that the problem in the United States is that of a more heterogeneous population. Yet Canada and Switzerland both have the problems of ethnically heterogeneous populations but have not neglected the problem of poverty to the extent we have. Heilbroner at this point, perhaps, makes too little of the problem of racial prejudice in the United States, but he is certainly correct in pointing out that neglect exists regardless of race. Some of the all-white communities of Appalachia are among our most neglected poverty areas.

His final conclusion is similar to the one mentioned as the Protestant ethic or the achievement ethic. Heilbroner, however, proceeds to explain why this particular ethic has remained much stronger in the United States than in many other countries once thoroughly imbued with the same point of view. His conclusion is that we have suffered from too much success. The rags-to-riches myth has had a degree of plausibility in the past, and we have failed to note that the plausibility has declined in an age of economic giantism, bureaucracy, and restructuring of the employment situation.

> **Attitude survey. Is poverty mainly the fault of the poor themselves, or is it usually beyond their control? Ask this question of young and old groups, Democrats and Republicans, Catholics and Protestants, church members and nonchurch members, blacks and whites. Note differences in attitudes.**

There is yet another twist to the American norms regarding poverty. With our emphasis on democracy and belief in the possibility of nearly universal middle-class attainment, we have had little of the same noblesse oblige attitude that has generally prevailed in societies of recognized inequality. It has not seemed a part of the role of government to dispense charity to those in need. The equality ethic has, in fact, been so strong that it has been hard to believe that any but the wicked or the lazy can possibly remain in need. It is for this reason that many Americans characterize the welfare effort much as Sumner would have done—an attempt to reward the lazy, the weak, and the indifferent. In fact, many are unaware that the overwhelming majority of welfare aid goes to the aged, to needy children, and to the disabled. They do not realize that in nearly all states needy children cannot receive welfare aid if they have an able-bodied father at home,

[4]*Ibid.*, p. 16.

The costs of neglect: dilapidated housing, high infant mortality, tuberculosis, and the incurable damage of childhood malnutrition.

even if there is a high rate of unemployment in his area and he is unable to find work.

The functions of poverty   It is also possible for a society to have a vested interest in poverty. Such a condition exists when wages and working conditions are so bad that only poverty will drive people into accepting jobs. Vested interest in poverty is a diminishing reason for its existence in industrial societies, but, as we shall see, there are a few places where it is still evident.

Frances Piven and Richard Cloward[5] show how in the past the amount of relief given the poor was regulated by two principles: giving enough money to prevent riots and disorder, but little enough so the poor would be forced to take any jobs available, regardless of how low the wages or how bad the conditions of labor. Elaborating on the idea that poverty can serve the interests of some members of society, Herbert J. Gans[6] lists thirteen "uses of poverty." The first is the provision of cheap labor, already mentioned. Other points Gans makes include the provision of jobs for a large bureaucracy hired to minister to the needs of the poor and check up on the legitimacy of welfare claims. The poor can be exploited by loan sharks, narcotics peddlers, landlords, and unscrupulous merchants of all types. The poor can serve several prestige functions for the well-to-do, differentiating high and low status very clearly, providing grounds (valid or not) for moralizing about laziness and vice, and giving an opportunity to display a sense of noblesse oblige by doing charity work. The urban poor in some cases can become pawns of the underworld, doing the riskiest types of dirty work that the king-

[5]Frances Piven and Richard Cloward, "The Relief of Welfare," *Transaction*, vol. 8, pp. 31–39, May 1971.
[6]Herbert J. Gans, "The Uses of Poverty: The Poor Pay All," *Social Policy*, July-August, 1971.

pins of crime avoid. These are a few of the uses of poverty that Gans finds. He admits that the costs of poverty are high, outweighing its functions, but not for all elements of society.

The equivalent conditions When Hunter wrote *Poverty* more than seventy years ago, he was writing a bitter denunciation of a total system. Poverty was more abject, and it included a much larger part of the population than it does today. In one respect, however, poverty is the same: its worst victims are the young, and they are the ones who will perpetuate its pattern in later years. For example, compare the above quotation from Hunter's *Poverty* (1904) with the following quotation from Senator Mondale (1970):

> Nearly a million of them (the impoverished children) live in families which subsist primarily on migrant or seasonal farm work . . . the child is physically unable to attend school regularly. He begins working at a very early age. He not only suffers from malnutrition, but moves in a never-ending cycle of bending, lifting, and carrying. By the time he is 10 or 11 he has stopped going to school. He is often married at 14 or 15. Soon his health deteriorates. His back shows the damaging effects of constant stoop labor. . . . [7]

THE DIMENSIONS OF POVERTY

Poverty concentrates more in some parts of the country than in others, and more in periods of economic decline than in periods of prosperity, but there is still a stubborn omnipresence about it. John Kenneth Galbraith[8] was the first to use the descriptions "case poverty" and "insular poverty" to describe the situation of today. Case poverty is in all communities and is usually related to characteristics of the person in poverty—physical disablement, sickness, mental deficiency, alcoholism, or old age. Insular poverty refers to the islands of poverty existing in exhausted coal-mining regions of West Virginia, worn-out agricultural areas of the rural South, and Appalachian hamlets that have never known the affluence of the twentieth century. There are also islands of poverty in the ghettos of our large cities, in the Mexican communities of the Southwest, and on the Indian reservations. The word "insular" must not be construed to imply "few in number" or "vanishing."

WHO ARE THE POOR?

As of 1972, the Census Bureau listed 25.6 million people below the poverty line, or 12.5 percent of the total populaton. Racially, the composition of the poor is very uneven, comprising 9.9 percent of the white population and 30.9 percent of the nonwhite. Hispanic Americans are also numerous among the poor, with 28.9 percent of Mexican-Americans and 32.2 percent of Puerto Ricans listed as in poverty.[9] The total percentage of people in poverty has declined by nearly half since 1959, when it stood at 22.4 percent, but there has been a slight increase in poverty since 1969. In racial composition of the poor, much has been said about

---

[7]Walter F. Mondale, "Think of These Children," *New Republic*, vol. 163, p. 15, December 26, 1970. Reprinted by Permission of THE NEW REPUBLIC, © 1970, Harrison-Blaine of New Jersey, Inc.
[8]John Kenneth Galbraith, *The Affluent Society*, Houghton Mifflin Company, Boston, 1958.
[9]Bureau of the Census, *Statistical Abstract of the United States*, 1973, pp. 335 and 339.

Race and ethnic differences

White	9.9%
Nonwhite	30.9%
Mexican-American	28.9%
Puerto Rican	32.2%

Sex of family head

Male	8.0%
Female	39.0%

Education of family head

Eight years or less	18.0%
High school	6.0%
College	2.0%

Rural-urban

Rural farm	20%
Rural non-farm	15%
Central city	12%

Age

Under sixteen	16%
Sixteen–sixty-four	8%
Sixty-five and over	12%

*SOURCE: Race and ethnic data from Bureau of the Census, *Statistical Abstract of the United States*, 1973. Other statistics from Sar A. Leviton, *Programs in Aid of the Poor for the 1970s*, Johns Hopkins University Press, Baltimore, 1974.

the progress of black people in the last decade. It is true that much educational progress has come about and that more are hired for good jobs than before, but the poverty rate among black Americans is still three times as high as among whites. In 1959, 56 percent of all nonwhites were in poverty, showing that the 1972 figure of 30.9 represents progress. However, poverty among whites has declined proportionately a little more, from 18.1 percent to 9.9 percent. Whites are still being lifted out of poverty slightly faster than nonwhites. There is also evidence that progress for all impoverished groups is slowing down in the 1970s.[10]

Some people would also call into question the amount of improvement that has taken place in the percentages of the poor, holding that it is based on an unrealistic definition of poverty. A poverty income in 1959 was anything below $3,000 for a family of four; by 1973 it was defined as $4,200, which takes inflation into account but probably not adequately. In one respect there has been very little change in the past fifteen years, with the poorest 20 percent of the population earning a fairly consistent 5 percent of the total income.[11]

[10]"Rich and Poor," *New Republic*, pp. 8–9, August 11, 1973.
[11]Richard Parker, *The Myth of the Middle Class*, Liveright Publishing Corporation, New York, 1972, p. 99.

One of the 6.4 million poverty-stricken aged Americans.

In addition to being concentrated among blacks, Indians, and Hispanic Americans, poverty is concentrated in other groups. Households headed by women are five times as likely to be impoverished as those headed by men. Households whose heads have only an eighth-grade education or less are three times as likely to be impoverished as those whose heads have a high school education. Among the aged, one in five is listed as in poverty, but the situation is undoubtedly becoming worse because of inflation. Poverty also affects a disproportionate number of children, with one child in six being of a poor family, and with 60 percent of the poor children belonging to families of four or more children.[12]

Poverty cases can also be divided into the working and nonworking poor. Well over half the family heads of poverty families work, but half of them work at poorly paying service jobs, farm labor, or other unskilled labor, and many of them find only part-time jobs. More than one-third of the poor drift into and out of poverty, depending on job availability; but rising above poverty is much more difficult for female-headed households than for others.

The defined poverty level is determined in very Spartan terms. The original formula in 1959 called for food expenditures of $1,000 per year for a family of four, or approximately $0.75 per person per day. Multiplying the food budget by three, the government arrived at a "correct" figure for a minimum of health and decency income, but it is an amount that leaves absolutely nothing for emergencies, sickness, or educational expense.[13] Since then the budget has increased, but only in proportion to inflation. On only one point is there no argument with the

[12]Sar A. Levitan, "The Poor: Dimensions and Strategies," *Current History*, vol. 64, pp. 241–246, June 1973.
[13]Parker, *op. cit.*, pp. 192–195.

government's definition of poverty: those living below the poverty line are indeed poor.

The children of poverty   The majority of the poor children of America, those who live in the urban slums and ghettos, must face some of the worst conditions and institutions the nation has to offer. Infant mortality for the poor is about four times as high as the national average. In the twenty largest city school systems, children are, on the average, a year or more behind the national achievement norms. The schools become "dropout factories." Hospitals are crowded, with long waiting lines. Venereal disease is epidemic. Welfare is at its most inhumane and degrading.[14] There is much less safety from violence, robbery, or rape in the urban slums than elsewhere, and much of the theft is of the meager possessions of the poor, to be hocked for the price of dope. Drugs are everywhere, and the pressures toward drug use are greater than in any other part of society.

Many poor children of America are Indians. Seven thousand Navajo children under nine years old are in boarding schools run by the federal government; several have frozen to death trying to escape to get back home during the cold winter. Alaskan Indians are sent as far away as Oregon or Oklahoma to federal boarding schools. Most Indian children sent to Bureau of Indian Affairs schools have no knowledge of English, and their chances are only one in twenty of having a teacher who knows anything of their language. Their culture is ignored.[15]

A million or more Chicano children are sent to school without a knowledge of English and no effort is made to compensate for their language difficulties. In one school in southern Texas, Chicano children are made to kneel and beg forgiveness if they are caught speaking Spanish. Neither in educational skills nor in attitudes are they being taught how to pull out of the poverty of their parents. The culture of America remains not only foreign but hostile as well. The language difficulties of Chicano children will probably be less severe in the future, as a Supreme Court decision of 1973 becomes effective. The decision, rendered in behalf of Chinese children in California, calls for special instruction for children whose language problems make instruction in English incomprehensible.

> **Visit and see if you can cooperate with agencies, public or private, dealing with poverty—welfare offices, Office of Economic Opportunity, Salvation Army, and various Catholic and Protestant charitable organizations.**

The greatest concentration of poor whites is in Appalachia, where family size is also much larger than the average. More than 900,000 of the children of Appalachia are poor; only 6 percent receive welfare assistance. If the father is at home, no welfare assistance is given. The system encourages fathers to desert for the sake of their families.[16] In most of Appalachia, however, there is a father and there is a home. For the child of the ghetto the father is frequently missing. For many poor children, the home is missing.

Children of migratory labor   During the past few years newspaper comments on migratory labor have been mainly about Cesar Chavez and the determined attempt

[14]Mondale, *op. cit.*, pp. 16–17.
[15]*Ibid.*
[16]*Ibid.*, p. 16.

to organize farm laborers, especially in California. Elsewhere, farm labor makes no news because it is the same virtual peonage it has always been. In 1960 the late Edward R. Murrow presented a televised program, called "Harvest of Shame," showing the conditions of migratory labor in America. Ten years later, in August 1970, NBC televised a program titled "Migrant." The commentator was different, and scenes of the prosperous parts of Florida were different, but otherwise, as NBC pointed out, the two programs were virtually interchangeable. The migrant laborers pictured in the Southeastern United States were 55 percent black, 35 percent Mexican, 10 percent Anglo-American, and 100 percent wretched. On a national scale the migratory laborers' families account for nearly 1 million of the children of poverty. They go to school from four to seven months per year, but never to the same school throughout that period. The teachers find them "uneducable." The other children make fun of them. "They think I am a bum," said one of the children interviewed; "Well, I guess I am!"

Such is the self-image imposed. Dr. Robert Coles, a psychiatrist who has spent years among the migrants, says that the children eventually become "dazed, listless, numb to everything but immediate survival," with special psychiatric problems of "extreme confusion, disorientation, depression, and even suicide." They also have specific physical diseases, often resulting from the pesticides to which they are constantly exposed. For those who stereotype the poor as shiftless or lazy, Coles says that

No group of people I have ever worked with—in the South, in Appalachia, and in our Northern ghettos—tries harder to work, indeed travels all over a country working, working from sunrise to sunset, seven days a week when the crops are there to be harvested.[17]

Not only do adults work, but children work. Child labor laws are evaded, and childhood ceases at the age of nine or ten. It is no exaggeration to call the conditions those of peonage, for various devices are used to keep the laborers constantly in debt. "Many of these families are owned for all practical purposes," says Coles, "by crew leaders who transport them around the country, sometimes with guns at their sides."[18]

Coles is especially concerned with the psychological effects of the depressed, rootless life on the children. "I do not believe the human body and the human mind were made to sustain the stresses the migrants face," he says, "worse stresses than I have ever-seen anywhere in the world, and utterly unrecognized by most of us."[19]

His evidence of psychological damage to children is extremely convincing and damnatory. The child is born not in a hospital but by the side of the road, in a field, or in a one-room shack without running water or electricity. No doctor is at hand. To go to any authorities—hospital, sheriff, or welfare agency—is "just like asking for trouble" The people take care of themselves, and have correspondingly high death rates.

As the children grow up they have only negative experiences of school and of the

---

[17]Robert Coles, M.D., Research Psychiatrist, Harvard University, in testimony before the Senate Subcommittee on Labor and Public Welfare, *Migrant and Seasonal Farmworker Powerlessness*, part 2, U.S. Government Printing Office, Washington, D.C., pp. 334–335.
[18]*Ibid.*, p. 353.
[19]*Ibid.*, p. 335.

Nomadic children, home-
less and unschooled, are
destined to repeat the
cycle of migratory farm
labor if neglect of rural
poverty continues.

great society outside. Psychiatrists are interested in the self-portrayals of children and the subtle stories they tell. One of the children, an eight-year-old girl, when asked to draw something, couldn't think of anything to draw except her birth certificate. Why? That was the one special thing she owned, her one source of identity. She had no house. The children do not normally draw houses, as other children do. One girl drew only Yo-Yos, because they were just like her, she said, always bouncing around but with nowhere to land. The people in the children's pictures are faceless. The outstanding feature in one boy's picture is a high, forbidding fence. Questioned, the boy told of a conversation with his parents in which he said he would like to go to other places than just the fields:

> But mother said we had better be careful; we can't keep asking to go here and there. We should close our eyes and imagine there is a big fence on each side of the road and we can't get off even if we wanted to because of the fence. That is why I put the fence in, to keep the car from getting into trouble with the police.[20]

There is probably no better symbol than the little migratory boy's high fence to sum up the effects of a childhood of degrading poverty. The child is fenced into the limited world of his subculture and fenced out of the world of opportunity and hope.

Coles asks why such conditions continue in a country whose wealth and values should have made them obsolete decades ago. To a degree, Heilbroner's essay on benign neglect answers the question: we have tended to exclude some groups in the heterogeneous society and, even more important, we have blamed the poor for their poverty. In the case of migratory farm labor there is, however, yet another reason: the poverty of some subsidizes the affluence of others. Farms are highly

[20]*Ibid.*, p. 342.

competitive, and the depression of wages gives a competitor an advantage over his rival. The market is competitive too, and affluent Americans keep down the prices of their vegetables by tolerating the conditions that produce what Murrow so aptly called America's harvest of shame.

HUNGER

In 1967 a committee of doctors sent to Mississippi by the Senate subcommittee on poverty was shocked to find that they were looking not at mild cases of malnutrition but at starvation. They saw children suffering from damage to bodily tissues, with eye and ear diseases, skin diseases, physical weakness and fatigue—all associated with a lack of food.[21] There was considerable publicity about the matter in Mississippi and about similar conditions discovered in the Carolinas and Texas.

In 1970 Dr. Arnold Schaefer of the Department of Health, Education, and Welfare reported findings in line with the previously cited ones from Mississippi. His studies were conducted among poverty groups in Texas and Louisiana. He found high rates of anemia, vitamin deficiency, and protein deficiency, especially among those of lowest income. He also found that large numbers of people were not able to pay enough money to get the food stamps that have been thought of as a cure-all for malnutrition.[22] At about the same time, two young army officers, Capts. Terrence P. Goggin and Clifford Hendrix, were sent to conduct an investigation for the President's Urban Affairs Council. Their report concurs with many others. Only 16 percent of the poor were receiving food stamps in the counties they studied. They blamed failure largely on racial prejudice, political blackmail, and inept or underfinanced local governments. They have also accused official Washington of suppressing their report.[23]

There is reason to think the hunger problem is now less severe than in 1970. A food stamp program was greatly expanded because of publicity on hunger in the late 1960s. Under the food stamp program, people qualifying can buy food stamps for only a fraction of the cost of the food they will receive. The amount paid ranges from zero for families with no income to more than 80 percent of the value of the stamps for those at the top of what is defined as a poverty income. For many years local politics, stingy officials, and racial prejudice prevented some counties from entering the food stamp program. As recently as the end of 1973, 790 counties still refused to participate and help their poor, but federal law required full participation as of January 1974. Over 12.5 million people were using food stamps as of late 1973, but it will be noted that this is only about half the 25.6 million poor.[24] Senator Hollings does not think the hunger situation has improved sufficiently to be very encouraging, especially among the rural poor. Not only is nutrition bad, but 10 percent less is spent on education for the rural poor than for the urban, 50 percent less on welfare and sanitation, and 33 percent less on health and hospitals. Hospitals for the urban poor are overcrowded; for the rural poor they often do not exist.[25]

[21]Elizabeth B. Drew, "Going Hungry in America: Government's Failure," *The Atlantic Monthly*, vol. 222, pp. 53–61, December 1968.

[22]Dr. Arnold E. Schaefer, in *Nutrition and Human Needs*, Hearings before the Select Committee on Nutrition and Human Needs of the United States Senate, U.S. Government Printing Office, Washington, D.C., 1970, pp. 764–779.

[23]Robert Rawitch, "Food Stamp Survey," *Los Angeles Times*, September 9, 1970, part II, p. 4.

[24]"Twelve Million on Food Stamps: A Lot More to Come," *U.S. News & World Report*, vol. 75, pp. 55–56, September 10, 1973.

[25]Senator Ernest F. Hollings, "The Rural Poor," *Current History*, vol. 64, pp. 258–260, June 1973.

A cheap source of protein People in poverty look for bargains, and often the search is self-defeating. The well-to-do can explain that it is foolish to buy shoddy goods, even when the price is low; but when there is virtually no money there is no alternative. Malnutrition is often the obvious result of food shortage, as we have seen. It may also be the result of very inferior food or food that is potentially dangerous.

Two officials of the Lexington Rendering Company of Lexington, Nebraska, testified before the Senate Committee on Nutrition. The Senators were surprised that their testimony concerned pet food rather than human food. The men testifying were incensed that their state allowed careless handling of meat for animal food and permitted the use of dead and putrefying animals, some of which had died of botulism, salmonellosis, anthrax, or rabies. But what bearing has this on the problem of human nutrition and food bargains for the poor? The testimony reads:

> A portion of this nation's canned pet food is consumed by humans. The economically disadvantaged, particularly those in the South and Southwest—I speak here of the Negro, Indian, and Mexican population—receive little benefit from the small print on the labels of cans which say, "Not for human consumption." Our moral and medical responsibility to this nation's 30 million poor demands further protection, especially in view of the current "humanization" approach by the pet food industry in promotional campaigns.[26]

By the "humanization" approach, the spokesmen referred to advertisements, making it sound as though the pet food is just as good as any other food in the store. They presented many examples of advertisements to this effect. They also complained that the loathsome meat used for pet food is stored so close to meat processed for humans that some of it could easily end up in the wrong category. Four years after the statement from concerned officials of the Lexington Rendering Company, the Senate nutrition committee found that as the price of food rose steeply, the sale of pet food rose by 12 percent in one year, although there was no 12 percent increase in the number of pets. Chicken and beef were vanishing from the diet of the poor and pet food was being substituted, especially among the aged and those in impoverished ghettos.[27]

Do the poor really pay more? Do a study of your own community, comparing quality and prices of groceries in the poorest parts of town with middle-class areas. Also check on appliance stores, especially on rates of interest and other special charges.

Physical and mental effects A number of efforts have been made to prove a relation between physical inferiority and such problems as criminality and dependency. A famous old study by Lombroso is often mentioned in psychology and sociology classes, mainly as an example of faulty research work. Lombroso made a study of inmates of prisons and found a surprising number of physical defects, which he interpreted as genetic in nature. Many years later, E. A. Hooton made a similar study in the United States and found similar results. Neither study is now believed to have proved what was expected, namely, a genetic factor in criminality.

[26]David E. Gauger and Clifford L. Johnson, in *Nutrition and Human Needs, op. cit.*, part 13A, p. 3913.
[27]Jack Anderson, "Report Says Elderly Eat Dog Food," syndicated column of July 7, 1974.

What had been demonstrated is quite apparent: more poor people than rich people are sent to prison, and the poor are more likely to have been malnourished. The poor do not have their teeth straightened or their eyes and ears inspected and corrected, nor do they pay careful attention to well-balanced meals and vitamins. Most of the poor cannot afford private medical care, and often public facilities are too far away or too crowded. Some fragments of testimony from the President's Commission on Poverty illustrate this point:

> It took me nine months to get a man in the nursing home. He fell and broke his hip and injured his foot. He was ninety-two years old. When we finally got an opening he had died because the foot had already become infected, gangreous [sic], and it was too late.

> I can't get a dentist appointment for my two children. "We don't take welfare patients"—and these are people that the Welfare recommended. . . .

> I went in [to the County Hospital] and told the head nurse about it [his son was hit by a car], she said, "Well, we can't take him." Of course he was in pain. His leg was just smashed all to pieces where the bumper hit him.

> The only place we can refer for charity hospitalization is in University Medical Center in Little Rock [150 miles away]. But even then, they are so crowded that the doctors always have to make prior appointments and make sure space is available.[28]

Small wonder the poor often seem physically inferior! What about the mental effects of malnutrition and lack of medical care? More study must be done, but present indications are that malnutrition takes a heavy toll. Brain growth in the fetus can be retarded by poor nutrition of the expectant mother. Protein deficiencies can also retard brain growth in early childhood. We need to know much more than we do about ways to keep poverty from being self-perpetuating, but there is no doubt that the first step is to feed the children.

Studies among black children in impoverished areas of the South found 54 percent and 80 percent of the two school populations tested suffering from intestinal worms. The roundworms consume much of the skimpy food supply of such children. A 1968 study also found cases of scurvy, pellagra, rickets, kwashiorkor, and marasmus. Kwashiorkor is a result of protein deficiency; marasmus is a result of caloric deficiency—less politely called starvation. Schaefer showed a Senate committee the result—a film of an emaciated baby with "staring eyes and match-stick arms." The film was not of Biafra, but of Mississippi.[29]

Several prominent Senators have been startled at the findings of their committees on poverty and are determined to improve our methods for the relief of poverty and malnutrition. What legislative progress has been made in the past? Why is previous legislation inadequate? What kinds of new proposals are under study?

PROGRAMS AND PROMISES

Consistent with the achievement ethic, past programs have been geared to exclude the undeserving. Even in the New Deal period of the 1930s, when it was abundantly clear that hard-working people had been laid off by the millions through no fault of their own, attempts were still made to prevent giving a direct handout. Makeshift jobs were provided under WPA (Work Projects Administration), the CCC (Civilian

[28]The President's Commission on Income Maintenance Programs, *op. cit.*, p. 18.
[29]Robert A. Liston, *The American Poor: A Report on Poverty in the United States*, Dell Publishing Co., Inc., New York, 1970, pp. 122–126.

Conservation Corps), and various other agencies. Some work projects were severely criticized, but they at least made it possible for people to remain at work, and some made remarkable improvements in the type of environmental and conservation work advocated today. Such projects may again become means of coping with unemployment.

Social security   The major New Deal accomplishment for coping with poverty was the Social Security Act. The old age and survivor's features provided benefits for the aged and for widows and children. Later the program was extended to aid disabled workers and to provide health insurance for the aged (Medicare). One trouble with the Old Age, Survivors, and Disabled (OASDI) benefits is that they are proportionate to a person's earnings. The poorer a worker is at retirement, the less retirement pay he receives. The retirement pay is low enough so that many of the aged on social security fall below the poverty line. Another problem is that the aged find it very difficult to supplement their social security incomes. Until they have passed the age of seventy-two, there is a limit to how much they can earn without having their earnings deducted from social security benefits. In 1973 the limit was $2,100 per year, but an escalator clause geared to inflation became effective in 1975.[30] This places the aged in a position where they cannot necessarily collect all the retirement pay they are entitled to; and it flies in the face of one of the otherwise enlightened features of the act—the principle that payments are rights earned by the worker's own tax contribution to the system, not merely charity. There is no equivalent to a pauper's oath.

State unemployment insurance laws (supplemented by the federal government) add benefits to those laid off from their jobs, but such benefits are uneven and short-ranged, with a maximum of twenty-six weeks in most states. During recession periods the length of time of payments is insufficient. Twice in the 1960s Congress extended the period of payments at federal cost. With high unemployment in the 1970's, Congress extended payments for one year and was considering further extensions. Such special legislation takes care of one problem of unemployment but does nothing about certain others. The amount of payment depends on wages but ranges widely from a low of $49 per week in Mississippi to $90 in Hawaii.[31] As of 1968 almost one-third of the labor force was exempted from unemployment insurance. Some (state and government employees in most cases) had other insurance policies. Others, especially migratory agricultural workers and domestic workers, had low pay, no private insurance, and no state unemployment insurance. To those with comfortable incomes and just below, insurance is provided. To the poorest it is denied.

AFDC   Because social security leaves many gaps in aid to the poor, other programs have been developed. The largest in cost is Aid to Families with Dependent Children (AFDC). Although an indispensable aid, AFDC has many shortcomings. Consistent with the ethic of "no work, no pay," most states do not provide benefits to children whose fathers are able-bodied. If the head of a family of four works at the federal minimum wage, his family will still fall below the poverty line. (The minmum wage was set at $2.00 per hour for 1974–1975, at $2.20 for 1976, and at $2.30 for 1977 and after.) No provisions are made to supplement

---

[30]"New Changes in Social Security," *U.S. News & World Report*, vol. 74, pp. 38–41, January 29, 1973.
[31]Joseph Hickey, "State Unemployment Laws: Status Report," *Monthly Labor Review*, vol. 96, pp. 37–44, January 1973.

the wage earner's income. If the father is able-bodied but cannot find work, his children are ineligible for aid in twenty-five states and actually receive such aid in very few cases. As of 1970 only 100,000 families with men present were receiving aid for dependent children. The present policy makes it seem that children should be punished if there is the slightest hint that their fathers are indolent. It also makes it seem better for fathers to desert than to stay at home when they are unable to find jobs.

The definition of able-bodied is often extremely strict. In Wolfe County, Kentucky, 5,000 of the 6,500 inhabitants were below the poverty line in 1968, but few received welfare. Johnson, a typical case, suffered from silicosis, which results from years of coal mining and which causes shortness of breath and a feeling of smothering. However, his family could not receive welfare because Johnson was not regarded as "permanently and totally disabled." In his case, at least, food stamps were provided. The Johnson family was permitted to buy $82 worth of food stamps for only $3. Sometimes not even $3 was available, but it was paid by the Office of Economic Opportunity (OEO).[32]

The welfare system also assumes that "employment and receipt of assistance are mutually exclusive. This view is untenable in a world in which employable persons may have potential earnings below subsistence standards."[33] It is this policy that gives rise to a peculiar social injustice by which an unemployed family head can make more money than one who is employed full time.

Another difficulty with existing systems is that AFDC payments are very low in most states and do not increase sufficiently to keep up with prices. Between 1961 and 1971 the average AFDC payment per family in the United States increased from $116.68 to $183.40, but in the five poorest states it increased from $37.28 to only $59.84.[34] As of 1970, New York paid the highest amount per child—$77.90 per month; the lowest payments were $15.20 in Alabama, $12.10 in Mississippi, and $9.25 in Puerto Rico.[35]

The Office of Economic Opportunity   The Johnson Administration launched what it called a "war on poverty," the major feature of which was the creation of the Office of Economic Opportunity. The effort was not the type of war that called for drastic institutional changes, but it did launch a number of experimental programs that have been helpful. More than 1,000 Community Action Agencies were created in various cities, with such aims as establishing industries, building rental houses, establishing cooperative buying organizations, providing child care and job training, exchanging information on employment, and repairing houses. The philosophy of the program called for participation by the citizens of the poverty areas themselves.

Another widely acclaimed policy of OEO was the establishment of Head Start programs aimed at giving children of depressed poverty areas a better start in school. Studies of its results indicated only partial success in spite of general agreement that a real effort was made. While he was Secretary of Health, Education, and Welfare, Robert Finch concluded that an even earlier time of help was needed; the development of mentality can be damaged at an extremely early

[32]Liston, *op. cit.*, pp. 78–79.
[33]The President's Commission on Income Maintenance Programs, *op. cit.*, p. 5.
[34]Richard M. Pious, "Nationalizing the Welfare System," *Current History*, vol. 65, pp. 66–70, August 1973.
[35]The 1973 World Almanac, Newspaper Enterprise Association, New York, 1973, p. 148.

age.[36] He could have well added that good mental development starts with proper nutrition of the mother while she is carrying the child.

One of the most promising services of OEO has been provision of legal assistance in many states. Lawyers serving the poor have done much to help them from being denied their rightful earnings, overcharged by merchants, victimized by garnishment proceedings, or forbidden the right to organize. Although bitterly opposed by former Governor Reagan, the California Rural Legal Assistance Program (CRLA) has been particularly successful in handling cases for the poor. The victimization of people who have no schooling, no influence, and no knowledge of how to obtain their rights is often accomplished with virtually no resistance. Dr. Hector Garcia tells of an interview with a law-enforcement officer who worked thirty years among Mexican-American migratory workers:

> I said, "In this 30 years or so of your law officer's work, have you ever got a search warrant, have you ever gone to the justice of the peace or the judge and gotten a search warrant?
>
> And the answer was "No."
>
> And this is fantastic, that this ranger would have worked 30 years and arrested thousands of people and never been able to get a search warrant—or arrest warrant![37]

The importance of legal assistance can hardly be overemphasized. A number of enclaves of poverty have taken their first steps toward a feeling of human dignity and mastery over their fate when they have learned that access to justice is possible.

The Nixon administration steadily cut back on funds for the OEO programs, refusing even to spend money appropriated by Congress. The last director of OEO before Nixon's resignation was Alvin J. Arnett, whose duty was to terminate the programs. Arnett dutifully set about the task, but as he traveled throughout the country he heard mainly notes of praise for the programs from both poverty groups and community leaders. Target Area Projects were being run increasingly well, lifting many out of poverty and giving hope to others. Arnett concluded that OEO programs should be encouraged rather than terminated. He was immediately asked for his resignation.[38]

The Family Assistance Program   All the aids and programs discussed omit many people and result in uneven benefits throughout the United States. Hardship and hunger and child labor still continue. There is a tendency for the very poorest areas to be helped least, and there is no effective floor for family income.

Mainly on the advice of Patrick Moynihan, then of the Department of Health, Education, and Welfare, former President Nixon became convinced that a new approach to welfare was needed. The result was the report of the President's Commission on Income Maintenance Programs, which advocated income supplements to be federally administered and to provide for the same minimum income level in all states. The original committee recommendations were for a floor of $2,400 per year for a four-member family, which was even then a little below the

---

[36]Liston, *op. cit.*, pp. 155–156.
[37]Hearings before the Senate Subcommittee on Labor and Public Welfare, *op. cit.*, part 4B, p. 1528.
[38]Alvin J. Arnett, "Director of the OEO Tells Why He was Fired by the White House," *Los Angeles Times*, August 5, 1974, part II, p. 5.

poverty line. The actual administration proposal to Congress cut the ceiling to $1,600 per year for a family of four.

A secondary feature of the proposal was to supplement existing income on a graduated scale. If, for example, a family of four received no income whatever, by the original commission proposal, the government would provide $2,400. By the same proposal, if a family earned $1,800, the government would supplement its income by $1,400, making it worthwhile to work in order to earn more than the bare minimum, and also reassuring the taxpayer that there would be work incentives. The proposal passed the House of Representatives but was bottled up in the Senate Finance Committee. The Family Assistance Program had received widespread support, but it was opposed by both conservatives and the National Welfare Rights Organization. The NWRO was opposed mainly because of the low level of pay. Actually, the intention was to set a federal floor under income that would probably have benefited the rural poor of the South the most. There was no intention of doing away with the food stamp program or of eliminating AFDC or any local welfare programs, but NWRO undoubtedly feared such a result, anticipating the prospect of families being left with a bare $1,600 per year.

Eventually the Nixon administration lost interest in the Family Assistance Program, but the idea is not entirely dead. A program that would greatly reduce administrative costs has its adherents. More work needs to be done on such a proposal to make sure that the income floor is not too low or does not also become an income ceiling.

OTHER ATTACKS ON POVERTY

In our later discussion of population, it will be pointed out that considerable headway against poverty can be made by policies that discourage a high birthrate. In recent years family planning and birth-control devices have been made available to the poor, and abortions, although not free, have become legal. The result has been a decline in unwanted pregnancies. The old stereotype of the poor family with large numbers of children is less valid than it was years ago; but still, as was noted previously, 60 percent of the impoverished children come from large families. Present indications are that poor families are declining in size to almost the same level as those of other classes in society. Although the birth-control approach to poverty is helpful, it must not be thought of as the final answer. Small families are also poor if they experience sickness or disability or long periods of unemployment.

The education panacea   The United States places great emphasis on education as an answer to all problems, but as we saw in Chapter 4, there is considerable debate about how well the schools have done in promoting upward mobility among many groups of the poor. Whatever the reason, many children from poor families become involved in a vicious circle of educational failure, leading to discouragement that in turn leads to further failure. The failure expectations are further enforced in neighborhoods of poverty where little opportunity is seen for anyone. Despite these problems, however, the poor are now going through high school in larger numbers than in the past, and some of them are doing well academically. However, the high school graduate is not in a position to compete for the most desirable jobs, and the families of the poor are unable to help with a college education. It will be recalled that in the Yankelovich study cited in Chapter 4, 48 percent of American youth considered college education to be a right. Such a right can be realized for the poor only if the government greatly increases scholarships for the needy. Such a policy would provide a road out of poverty for many young people born into it. Although there is rising competition for jobs among college graduates, the situation is not nearly as bad as the job competition among the uneducated for undesirable and poorly paying jobs.

Many retraining programs were tried under OEO programs; but training programs, and even education, are not panaceas. Education does not create new jobs. Bayard Rustin[39] sees correctly the limitations to the education solution when he contrasts the poor of today with the large numbers of immigrant poor that entered America in the nineteenth century. The immigrants found opportunities not because they were educated—they were not—but because they were needed. There was land to settle, and there were jobs for men with muscle, jobs for "a strong back and a weak mind," according to the old expression. We have long since grown accustomed to saying there are no longer jobs for the physically strong but uneducated, but we are also going to have to face the fact that there are not always jobs for the educated, either. This is the dilemma of education and retraining. In times of job shortages, the newly trained man can find a job only by taking the job from someone else. The situation creates a crisis that can pit man against man and race against race. To state the matter cruelly, in times of high unemployment, every man with a job has a vested interest in keeping his competitor unemployed. Education will not solve the problem; the only solution lies in more jobs.

Creating jobs   Job-training programs and education in general can help to equip people for the positions that are available, but they cannot provide jobs when unemployment rates are high. There are serious societal dilemmas to making enough jobs available. As a society, we stress the work ethic; but because of a belief in free enterprise, we seldom attempt to create the public jobs that would put people to work. Leon Keyserling[40] is one economist who has long advocated work projects as a means of relieving poverty. He is convinced that we could solve most of our poverty problems by the investment of federal money in building housing, hospitals, rest homes, parks, and playgrounds, cleaning rivers, lakes, and forests, generally beautifying the land and cities, and improving the quality of life overall. In some respects Keyserling's viewpoints are perfectly consistent with the achievement ethic and are by no means unprecedented. During the days of the New Deal, a far more burdensome problem of poverty was partly solved by work projects. Under WPA, 5,000 public buildings were constructed and 85,000 were repaired; 46,000 bridges and viaducts were built or improved; and more than 15,000 parks and playgrounds were constructed.

There are certain objections to Keyserling's proposals, however, especially in inflationary times. More money would have to be spent to create jobs than would be needed to simply pay welfare checks or to support the proposed family aid program, and the additional spending could feed inflation.

[39]Bayard Rustin, "Education?" in Robert Theobald (ed.), *Dialogue on Poverty*, The Bobbs-Merrill Company, Inc., Indianapolis, 1967, pp. 53–60.
[40]Leon Keyserling, "The Problem of Problems: Economic Growth," in Robert Theobald (ed.), *Social Problems for America in the Seventies*, Doubleday & Company, Inc., Garden City, N.Y., 1968, pp. 1–24.

Man pitted against man in the predawn rush for the dwindling supply of jobs for those with obsolete skills.

Health care   In a later chapter, considerably more will be said about the societal need for better health care. At present it should be noted that the poor start life more precariously than do the rich and live on less wholesome diets and experience more sickness. One requirement of economic independence is good health, but this is not yet guaranteed. We have provided medical aid for the aged but have established no such right for children.

Tax policies   It is generally assumed that the tax structure of the United States plays the role of Robin Hood, taking from the rich and giving to the poor. Actually, though, a proportionately greater amount is taken from the poor. Local and state governments rely heavily on sales taxes, which are generally regressive, taking a larger share of the incomes of the poor than of the rich. It is assumed that the graduated income tax more than makes up for the regressive feature of taxation, but the assumption is questionable. When it is found that hundreds of people in the $100 thousand plus income bracket pay no income taxes whatsoever, (apparently legally), one wonders about the Robin Hood nature of government. The rich have large numbers of possible tax deductions; the wage earner usually has only personal exemptions. One way to alleviate poverty would be to raise personal exemptions so that no one in the poor or near-poor category would owe an income tax. There is also considerable merit to the proposal that a negative income tax feature be used, with federal payments made to those whose incomes fall below the poverty level. Philip M. Stern[41] makes a strong case for his assertion that we subsidize the rich by writing into our tax laws a number of loopholes that save them from paying their share of taxes. For example, eight families with incomes of more

[41]Philip M. Stern, *The Rape of the Taxpayer*, Vintage Books, Random House, Inc., New York, 1974, p. 16.

than $1.5 million paid only 5 percent of their incomes in income taxes, whereas a typical laborer paid 16 percent. Under the circumstances, it would not seem too outrageous to subsidize the poor.

Protecting income   Since the poor are usually charged much higher interest rates on credit buying than are the middle class, they enjoy the benefits of less of their income. Among some employees credit unions have greatly reduced the need to pay usurious rates of interest on purchases or short-term loans. Since the poverty-stricken do not have the original capital to start a credit union, public aid to get such institutions started would probably be necessary. Such a policy, combined with better education of the poor about their rights as consumers, could do much to prevent their being robbed of what little they have. In Chapter 1 it was pointed out that FHA housing loans have done much to help the middle class. To be equitable, some arrangement should be made whereby the government could aid the poor with their credit problems.

Increasing income   A disproportionate number of poor families are headed by women. Even though the women work full time, they usually find only very low-paying jobs. If the demands of the women's liberation movement are met, more women should enter better-paying jobs; but sex inequality is only part of the problem. Usually the poor are inadequately trained and hence must take service and common-labor jobs. Although such jobs are generally covered by minimum wage laws, the minimums are so low that the head of a family of four or more, working full time, would still fall within the poverty income level. There is an escalator clause built into the present minimum wage law, but inflation is driving costs up at least as rapidly as the minimum wage increases. Either more unionization of unskilled labor or higher minimum wages is necessary to bring many of the unskilled above the poverty level.

Political and legal power   During the heyday of the war on poverty, more funds went to the urban poor than to the rural poor. The reason may well have been that there are large concentrations of voters in urban centers whose votes could swing the balance in municipal and national elections. Generally speaking, the poor are less likely to vote than the rich, and they have less means of exerting influence on their elected representatives. Legal assistance programs have done something to help the poor attain their rights and to interest them in the political process. At present, funds for legal assistance have been cut drastically. Without such funds, the poor cannot pay the court costs necessary to sue for their rights. When they are themselves sued or faced with criminal charges, the poor are assigned public defenders, who typically can spend only five or ten minutes with their clients.[42] The public defender's jobs pay very little, and each public defender is assigned such a heavy case load that not much better performance is possible.

Such measures as legal aid, better tax breaks, credit unions, and unionization can only alleviate poverty, not eliminate it; but the measures demonstrate the large number of ways in which the burdens of the poor are increased by the institutional structure of society. Small wonder that many of the poor are hostile and feel that the world is in a conspiracy against them!

[42]Barbara Babcock, cited in "Public Defenders," *Society*, vol. 10, pp. 8–9, May-June 1973.

Problems related to poverty By now we have noted that poverty is related to many aspects of the social system. It is inextricably linked to the types of industrial change that have brought automation and shifting job requirements and that have dried up the demand for rural labor. It is closely connected to education and the need for retraining programs. Although the majority of poor people are white, the proportion of poverty is greater for blacks, Chicanos, and Indians, so the study of poverty is partly a study of racial and ethnic problems. Above all, poverty flouts the moral norms of the country, especially at a time of real potential for universal abundance. Even the proposed solutions to poverty are linked to the normative order and the work ethic, with many leaders expressing a desire to provide work rather than resort completely to the present welfare system.

As the title of this chapter suggests, the problems of the poor are much more persistent than optimistic America had ever supposed they would be. These problems need constant attack on many fronts. If we merely scold the poor for being incorrigible, or deny that poverty exists, or assume that all poverty will be buried inevitably under a mountain of American productivity, the problems will remain. If the search for new solutions continues, perhaps the time will come when we will no longer have to say "the everlasting poor."

SUGGESTED READINGS

Billingsley, Andrew, and Jeanne M. Giovannoni: *Children of the Storm: Black Children and American Child Welfare*, Harcourt Brace Jovanovich, New York, 1972. History of welfare policies since the 1930s; reaches conclusion that racism has prevented fair treatment of black children compared with white. Calls for reforms that would place more decision making in the black community.

Friedland, William H., and Dorothy Nelkin: *Migrant: Agricultural Workers in America's Northeast*, Holt, Rinehart and Winston, Inc., New York, 1971. A set of anthropological case studies, this book does a very good job of showing not only poverty and exploitation but also the sociological adjustments made to poverty and a migratory life.

Kain, John F. (ed.): *Race and Poverty: The Economics of Discrimination*, Prentice-Hall, Inc., Englewood Cliffs, N.J., 1969. Discusses the close connection between being black and being poor. The last few selections are on policy alternatives and represent such varied views as those of the Kerner Commission, the late Robert F. Kennedy, and former President Nixon.

Liston, Robert A.: *The American Poor: A Report on Poverty in the United States*, Dell Publishing Company, Inc., New York, 1970. A short, hard-hitting book on poverty and hunger, defects in the welfare system, and various attempted improvements and recommendations.

The President's Commission on Income Maintenance Programs, *Poverty Amid Plenty: The American Paradox*, U.S. Government Printing Office, Washington, D.C., November 1969. Not all will agree with the proposed solutions presented, but there can be little argument with the facts disclosed by the commission—and they are grim facts—or with the need for a reexamination of our present system.

Roby, Pamela (ed.): *The Poverty Establishment*, Spectrum Books, Prentice-Hall, Inc., Englewood Cliffs, N.J., 1973. Contends that the "high government officials and corporate officer who control the poverty establishment benefit from it most." Contrasts handouts to the poor with the more generous tax allowances and subsidies for the rich.

Wilensky, Harold L.: *The Welfare State and Equality*, University of California Press, Berkeley, Calif., 1974. Explores welfare and health policies in Europe and the United States, in both areas products of social necessity, but varying greatly on the basis of ideology and political and economic systems.

QUESTIONS

1 Why has the United States negelcted poverty more than many other well-to-do countries?

2 Who are the poor in terms of age, region, rural-urban distribution, occupation, and race and ethnic group?

3 What conditions of migratory agricultural labor in parts of the Unites States tend to create a perpetual culture of poverty?

4 What are the physical and mental effects of malnutrition?

5 What are the inadequacies and inequities in the present program of welfare?

6 Why would some economists say that education and motivation will not necessarily solve the problems of poverty?

The problem of overpopulation has received so much publicity that it is hardly necessary to point out the incongruity between the needs of the times and the older ethic of maximal reproduction. Many questions remain, however. Just how severe is the problem of overpopulation in the underdeveloped world? Do underdeveloped countries have possibilities for mitigating the problem by the same rapid increase in productivity and decline in birthrate that has taken place in Europe? If overcrowding goes on indefinitely, will it have serious psychological, as well as physical, effects on the human race? Are we possibly undermining the quality of future populations by chromosome-damaging drugs, chemicals, and pollutants?

Nearly all these questions are alarming. Some could be partly answered by pointing out that the United States is not really densely populated compared with much of the rest of the world. Why, then, is overpopulation a worry to us? Another thought that might prevent too much alarmism is that trends do not always continue indefinitely. Are there any new ideas and values in the most-crowded regions of the world that might reverse the high birthrate value? If so, will such changes occur in time to prevent disaster? Finally, are there any policies that might be pursued on an international scale to head off the population disaster that so many experts see looming over the horizon?

According to the accounts of the ancient Aztecs, the earth has been destroyed four times, but each time the human race has reappeared and reproduced. Certain Brazilian Indian tribes claim the earth has been destroyed seven times. Many stories of the Near East relate only one disaster of such proportions—the Great Flood, told in the Babylonian story of Gilgamesh and the Hebrew story of Noah. In all the destruction stories the narrators have assured us that at least one male and one female survived, and they multiplied rapidly. The Biblical story is by far the best known in the Western World, and its results are unique among Bible stories. In all other cases God gave human beings commandment after commandment—not only the famous ten, but the hundreds of minor rules and regulations of Leviticus and Deuteronomy. People immediately went forth and broke all the rules and regulations but one. One rule they obeyed with vigor, enthusiasm, and glee—"Be fruitful, and multiply, and replenish the earth."

Not only were people happy to obey that commandment, they were compulsive about it. In many societies men without offspring have married wife after wife to try again for issue. Sometimes they have set up rules whereby other people's children ceremonially can become their own. There are even cases of "ghost marriages" in which a devoted widow marries to the memory of her deceased husband so as to bear him children posthumously. Everywhere the desire for offspring has been evident. For aristocracies, there has been an ambition to continue the dynasty; for the humble there has been a desire to somehow avoid the oblivion of genetic death. In most cases there has been the desire for children to love, to teach, and to put to work. Children have also helped to rekindle the fires of memory of youth in parents and grandparents and to prevent the disaster of an old age of loneliness and misery.

Once people replenished the earth, they proceeded to replenish it again and again. All the reasons for desiring children continued, even though the earth suddenly began to shrink. The earth, which once was as vast as eternity, was seen in new perspective. It became a tiny island isolated in the infinity of space, capable of being crowded, overcrowded, eroded, mined, and destroyed. This, too, human beings set out to accomplish.

THE OUTDATED NORM

The reproduction norm is obviously outdated, but it is not easily laid to rest. There are countries wherein a considerable majority of people have only from one to three children per family and population is, consequently, stabilizing, but much of the world continues to be excessively fruitful. The United States in the 1970s shows a birthrate that has declined considerably below that of the baby boom years of the 1940s and 1950s, but the population is still increasing. Before we discuss the demographic problems of the United States specifically, however, it will be good to look at certain population characteristics of the entire world. A historical study of world population will lead to an awareness of certain general principles about the reproduction habits of people and to an intimation of whether the current population explosion is only temporary or may continue far into the future.

Demographic transition A demographic transition, or population change, has occurred in the past three centuries, changing the earth from a rather sparsely populated to a somewhat crowded planet. Such changes have taken place before, but only on a minor scale. The biologist Edward S. Deevey contends that the world

Once the vast, empty earth called for human habitation; now nature is desecrated by the swarming multitudes that invade her once silent places.

has actually known three different human population explosions. The first population explosion took place in the dim beginnings of humanity when our ancestors first learned to use stone tools and make themselves better competitors for survival than most other animals. In a mere million years the population increased from only 1,000 or so to about 5 million inhabitants. The human race was growing at an unsteady pace, averaging perhaps 0.5 percent per century.

The second population explosion began about ten thousand years ago, when people began to learn how to cultivate crops and live from the agricultural produce of the land, rather than purely from hunting, gathering, and fishing. Food became more plentiful and dependable, and the world's population increased more rapidly, doubling itself in from one to two thousand years.

The third great population explosion came with the industrial-scientific age. It seemed fairly gradual at first, with the population doubling in a little over a century back in the 1600s and 1700s, but presently it is changing much more rapidly. In the 1960s the world's population seemed to be doubling about every fifty years.[1] Since then people have really knuckled down to the task and are doubling the world's population in about thirty-five years.

The most common use of the concept of demographic transition is to describe the third transitional period mentioned by Deevey. It seems important to mention the first two, however, because otherwise a question might arise about whether population explosions have been merely temporary phenomena followed by reversals in growth rates. The answer seems to be an emphatic "no," even though there have been temporary downturns caused by war, famine, or plague. There was, of course, nothing disturbing about the first two population explosions, but the third one has most of the world's demographers deeply worried.

[1] Edward S. Deevey, Jr., "The Human Population," *Scientific American*, vol. 208, pp. 194–198, September 1960.

| **Demographic transition in the Western world**   In Europe and many other areas of European settlement, such as the United States and Canada, population in the past two or three centuries has increased more rapidly than in the rest of the world. From 1600 until 1950, people of British descent increased from 3 million to 150 million, a fiftyfold increase, while the world as a whole increased about sixfold. Between 1750 and 1950 the United States broke all records by increasing from 2 million to 166 million. During the same period Europe (excluding Russia) increased in population from 125 million to 392 million, and Russia from 42 to 180 million. While most European countries were increasing population at least three or four times, China, India, and Pakistan little more than doubled their populations. In recent decades the population increase pattern has changed, with China, India, and Pakistan all expected to more than double their populations from 1950 to 2000, and Europe to increase its inhabitants by only one-fourth.[2]

The reason the population increase has slowed down in Western Europe is primarily a shift in values. Kingsley Davis believes that whenever and wherever urbanization, industrialization, education, and rising living standards take place, new values begin to replace those that are rooted primarily in family and kinship. The change is not merely a matter of availability of contraceptive devices, which are often available but not used in underdeveloped countries, but an attitude change. When standards of living and education reach a particular level, people become interested in their own careers and in the amenities of life that are finally within their reach. They do not want to jeopardize their prosperity and opportunities by too large a family.[3]

In contrast to the reduced birthrates of the industrialized countries, what is referred to here as "the outdated norm" continues in many parts of the world. There are numerous reasons besides the overall sentiment that family alone gives life meaning and value. Family also ensures a supply of children to help with the farm work and to take care of parents in their old age. Not only must there be children, but there must be many children. Until the most recent generation, large numbers of children have died young, so at least five or six children have been thought necessary to guarantee the survival of the family. The large-family norm continues even after the reasons supporting it begin to diminish under the impact of inoculations and medical care. Often religious norms insist on high reproduction rates; and sometimes large numbers of children are necessary to demonstrate a man's masculinity.

Sentiments, too, are important. Even for many ambitious, career-oriented modernists, there are moments when family and children provide the greatest psychological security in life. There is an old African folktale that is rich in wisdom about human emotions regarding children. God created a man and a woman and gave them a happy world in which to live. They asked him if they could live there forever or if they must someday die. He explained to them that there were two kinds of death between which they would have to choose. "You can die as the moon dies, or as the banana tree dies. The moon dies, but returns again the same. The banana tree dies and does not return, but it sends up the shoots that are its children." The man and woman pondered the question, and then decided to choose the death of the banana tree so that they could have children. Since then children have been more important than life itself.

[2]E. A. Wrigley, *Population and History*, McGraw-Hill Book Company, New York, 1969, pp. 205–207.
[3]Kingsley Davis, "Population," in Garrett Hardin (ed.), *Science, Conflict, and Society*, W. H. Freeman & Company, San Francisco, 1969, pp. 101–110.

We know from comparative sociology and anthropology that the urge to have children is not uniform for all people, but it is very close to being a species universal. To deny people the right to parenthood is considered cruel. In only a few societies have even slaves been denied that right. The real question, though, has to do with numbers. Can people of the underdeveloped portion of the world be persuaded to face old age with only one or two children, or will they continue to desire large families? In many parts of the world even a stable population is disastrously high. Even now China is reaching the 800 million mark and will probably pass the billion mark well before the end of the century.

Birthrate and death rate   Crude birthrate and death rate are both given in terms of numbers per thousand population. The birthrate of the United States during the baby boom after World War II reached about 25 per thousand population but dropped to 15 per thousand by 1973. Some of the world's underdeveloped countries have birthrates of between 40 and 50 per thousand, and death rates of only 15. Such vital statistics show an annual rate of natural increase that has been rare in the world's history.

If Deevey's estimates are correct, the population of the Old Stone Age increased at about 0.5 percent per century. By 1750 the world's population was growing nearly ten times as fast, 0.4 percent per year. By 1900 the annual growth rate was 0.8 percent, and by 1971 it was 2.0 percent. The United Nations projections expect a slight decline to about 1.25 percent by the year 2000. The population history of the world can be presented graphically as in the chart below.

Although birthrate eventually begins to decline, it is still far ahead of death rate, and the third population explosion goes on. There is a tragic irony in the situation: the medical advances that have lengthened human life now threaten to make that life extremely cheap.

The problem is overwhelmingly one of a lowered death rate, but there are even places where the birthrate has increased as the death rate declines. These are all in the less industrialized parts of the world. There are various reasons, one of which is that the improved medical care has prevented stillborn babies and maternal deaths at childbirth. Better medical care has also meant that far more girls live to reach the reproductive years of life and that there are fewer widows in the world. Another change has been the general abandonment of the practice of infanticide—the

Stages of population growth

We are now in the third major stage of
demographic transition, the scientific age.

killing of unwanted babies. Yet another change in the direction of greater population has been the abandonment of old taboos about sex avoidance for lactating women. When women nursed their babies for two or three years and observed rules of sex avoidance during that time, the birthrate slowed down. (The custom was generally observed only in polygamous societies in which men could continue mating relations with their other wives.) Eventually, it is hoped, the underdeveloped world will reduce its birthrate, but the immediate result of modernization is often an increase in birthrate as well as a rapid decline in death rate.[4]

> Try tracing your own family tree several generations back. How many children were born? How many survived to maturity? Compare with the present generation.

The result of changes in the birthrate and death rate is that while the industrially developed parts of the world increased by 11 percent during the decade from 1960 to 1970, the underdeveloped regions increased by 24 percent.[5] Such figures explain why population, a problem everywhere, has reached the state of crisis in the underdeveloped world. The crisis involves malnutrition and poverty, approaching starvation, and perhaps various kinds of pathologies.

BEYOND THE MALTHUSIAN NIGHTMARE

Thomas Malthus wrote an essay on population about 170 years ago that has been a subject of discussion ever since. The malthusian idea can be stated very briefly: population tends to increase more rapidly than food supply. Consequently, if a population is not checked by some kinds of controls, there will eventually be pressure against the limits of food supply, and resultant starvation. Malthus even reduced his idea to the mathematical principle that population increases at geometric progression (1, 2, 4, 8, 16, 32) and food supply at arithmetic progression (1, 2, 3, 4, 5, 6). Such a formulation is highly dubious; and even if it correctly describes a general tendency, it has many exceptions. The population of the United States increased very rapidly throughout most of its history, but the food supply increased even more rapidly. A more likely implication of Malthus's ideas is the principle of diminishing returns, although the term diminishing returns was never used by him. The law of diminishing returns holds that a time comes when increased effort and investment put into the land (or any type of production) pays less and less in dividends, until the point is reached when the payoff is not sufficient to attract further effort.

Malthus suggested gloomily that there are other natural controls on population besides famine: war, disease, and vice. None sounds like a very attractive alternative, not even vice. His contention was that people could become so debauched by vice as to undermine their strength, health, and reproductive vigor. A few periods in history suggest such a possibility—the roaring orgies of the degenerative period of Roman history, for example. Francis L. K. Hsu suggests that such was often the fate of some families of old China. After they made their way to

[4]Dudley Kirk, "World Population: Hope Ahead," in Stanford Today, pp. 10–11, Winter 1968. For a more thorough description of primitive controls on birth rates, see Burton Benedict, "Population Regulations in Primitive Societies," in Anthony Allison (ed.), Population Control, Penguin Books, Inc., Baltimore, 1970, pp. 165–179.

[5]M. A. El-Badry, "Population Projections for the World, Developed and Developing Regions," Annals of the American Academy of Political and Social Science, vol. 369, p. 11, January 1967.

Crowding in the subway, as in a scene from *The Human Zoo,* with muggings, rapes, and the types of behavior noted in experiments with crowded rats.

wealth and position, they began to decline through inactivity or vice or some type of social pathology.

If we substitute the term social pathology for Malthus's word vice, we may be looking at a result of population crowding that also acts as a brake on population increase, although not one to be recommended. Several animal studies suggest that crowding has natural limits, but some also suggest a horror that goes beyond the nightmare of Malthus. Deevey's essay "The Hare and the Haruspex: A Cautionary Tale"[6] tells, for example, of the mysterious death of overcrowded snowshoe hares in Minnesota. "Life quickly leaves them, and they die from the slightest injury." The reason is not famine or war or predators or even disease. The reason is atrophy of the liver caused by conditions of stress due to overcrowding. A haruspex was an ancient Roman soothsayer who believed he could divine the future by reading the entrails of animals. Deevey believes that we might be reading the future of the human species in a similar way. He mentions many other cases of illness caused by overcrowding and other stress, but one is particularly striking. A report from the Philadelphia zoo blames "social pressures" for a tenfold increase in deaths from arteriosclerosis among the animal population.[7]

Probably the best-known experiment on the crowding of animal populations is the one done by John B. Calhoun.[8] Calhoun conducted a number of experiments with rats, allowing them to breed to a population of very great density in his laboratory. As the population density increased, the rats would no longer eat

[6]In Eric Josephson and Mary Josephson, *Man Alone*, Dell Publishing Co., Inc., New York, 1962, p. 577.
[7]*Ibid.*, p. 584.
[8]John B. Calhoun, "Population Density and Social Pathology," *Scientific American*, vol. 206, pp. 139–146, February 1962.

alone; they seemed always to crave company, but at the same time seemed to not really *like* company. Some became detached and somnolent; others became quarrelsome. Some became "pan-sexual," attempting relations not only with estrous females but with unwilling females and also homosexual relations with males. The female rats no longer built adequate nests for their young, and many did not take care of them, but simply let them die. Male rats in some cases became cannibals, eating baby rats. By methods that could easily be subsumed under Malthus's category of vice, the population stabilized, but at a tremendously high level. Often in the final stages of crowding no sex object was sufficient to cause arousal, and the male rats showed no interest in mating.[9]

Desmond Morris, noted for his frank and brutal interpretations of human nature, wrote a book titled *The Human Zoo*. The title is drawn from a comparison between the pathological behavior of animals held captive in a zoo and what Morris considers the pathological human behavior caused by crowded, urban living. We live in a zoo, a place of unnatural crowding and stress. All species, Morris contends, have developed mechanisms for limiting their numbers, either by increased aggressiveness and fights over territory or by reduced reproductive capacity, as was noted in the rat study. He even speculates that in unconscious ways human beings tended to set brakes on their population growth by such practices as infanticide, human sacrifice, mutilation, head-hunting, cannibalism, and various sex taboos. In later societies,

> new sexual philosophies emerged that had the effect of reducing group fecundity; neuroses and psychoses proliferated, interfering with successful breeding; certain sexual practices increased, such as contraception, masturbation, homosexuality, fetishism and bestiality, which provided sexual consummation without the chance of fertilization. Slavery, imprisonment, castration, and voluntary celibacy also played their part.[10]

Whatever the explanation of the customs described by Morris, they have not succeeded in holding the world's population in check, as a daily increase of 150,000 people assures us. Not even combat, which urban civilizations changed from skirmishes to devastating wars, has been able to hold population in check. Despite pathologies, the human being remains far less restrained in his breeding habits than most of the crowded animals in the zoo. Is he in danger of decline in quality as his numbers increase in quantity?

THE QUALITY OF LIFE

We cannot be sure whether the present state of crowding will lead to pathological behavior and if such behavior will be a problem of the future, but we do know that when human population becomes too great for the food supply so that chronic malnutrition is the normal condition of existence, there is no longer any question about a decline in the quality of life. Colin Turnbull in *The Mountain People*[11] tells the bitter story of the Ik tribe of northern Uganda. Forced from hunting into agriculture by the population pressure of neighboring peoples, the Ik live in a mountainous terrain incapable of supporting their numbers. Under conditions of chronic malnutrition they have lost the cultural bonds that once linked them together as a people. Instead, each person's hand is against his neighbor. When

---

[9]John B. Calhoun, "Population," in Allison (ed.), *op. cit.*, pp. 110–124.
[10]Desmond Morris, *The Human Zoo*, McGraw-Hill Book Company, New York, 1969, pp. 150–151.
[11]Colin Turnbul, *The Mountain People*, Simon and Schuster, New York, 1974.

Turnbull attempted to give food and tea to an old man dying of starvation, younger people grabbed them from him, saying "He's going to die anyway." Parents paid little heed to their children. If any extra food was found, each person ate silently and secretly alone.

Another threat to the quality of life is caused by the declining physical and mental vigor of people who must live in a malnourished state. Brain damage can occur to children if their diet is too deficient in protein, and protein foods are hard to acquire in impoverished lands. Many children were permanently damaged in health during the Biafran war in Nigeria as well as in the better remembered Vietnamese war. It can be objected that the problem is one of war and not of overpopulation, but war and population problems are closely connected. War disrupts production and trade and destroys resources, leaving a country overpopulated relative to society's ability to sustain life. War also leaves the crippled of mind and body, who will be a further drain on the energies of a country. It is quite possible, too, that war has a long-range dysgenic effect on human populations.

Dysgenic effects For centuries, the world has been doing a very bad job of dysgenic selection—that is, eliminating many of the physically and mentally capable people from the human breeding pool. Warfare at some earlier stage in human development may have tended to eliminate the weak. Now it is much more likely to eliminate the strong. In a grim joke played against the process of natural selection, the strong and well become the "unfit," often selected to die in warfare and leave no descendants. Those with physical and mental defects are the ones who survive.

Not only do we cause disproportionate numbers of deaths among the healthiest, but we are probably adding to the burden of mutant genes that the human race must carry. Atomic fallout is a major source of mutation, although authorities disagree about how severe it is at present. Linus Pauling contends that we have already caused the births of hundreds of thousands of defective babies because of atomic fallout; Edward Teller considers the amount of damage "tolerable"; but no one denies that the rate of mutation has been increased to some degree. Even overexposure to X rays can increase mutations. As mentioned in Chapters 3 and 4, there are other known or suspected sources of genetic damage: many types of drugs, both legal and illegal, various chemicals and food additives, and possibly contaminants entering water supplies.

STARVATION: PRESENT AND FUTURE

For years the alarmists among demographers have warned of impending famines to be brought on by greater populations than the land can support. The great but little-publicized famine that cursed the Sahel region of Africa for several years may be only a portent of things to come. It is a famine that spread from Senegal and Mauritania, through Mali, Niger, Upper Volta, Chad, and even to parts of Ethiopia and Kenya to the east. The famine stemmed from a succession of dry years, an event that occurs at irregular intervals in the history of the region. Over a million people abandoned their land, moving like swarms of gaunt scarecrows toward the south, watching their cattle, and sometimes their children, fall dead on the way. Thousands died and hundreds of thousands more were expected to die before the end of the famine.

The Sahel region of Africa is the dividing line between the Sahara and the

Dysgenic effects of war:
killing the strong.

well-watered lands farther south. It is a region of roaming pastoralists living off their herds of cattle, goats, sheep, and camels. During a long, favorable weather cycle the human and animal populations increased, aided by wells and diesel pumps installed during the colonial period. In some cases wells intended for 500 cattle have had to supply 5,000. As the water supply began to shrink and the sparse grass to dry up, the cattle and sheep ate the shrubs and trees of the drier parts of the savannah. According to a German observer,

> The destruction of vegetation, overgrazing, and the mechanization of waterholes disrupted the natural ecological balance in many places. The resulting "desertification" brought about a southward shifting of the Sahara border and the spread of what is essentially a man-made desert.[12]

The picture is similar in many semiarid parts of Africa. In the Kajara district of Kenya, half the wild animals died in a few months' time in the spring of 1974 because the cattle herds of the Masai had grown too large and eaten the food supply. Next came starvation for the cattle, as well as malnutrition for the Masai children. From Wollo, Ethiopia, to the provincial capital of Dessie, people fled,

[12]Horst Menschung, "Why Did It Happen?" *Atlas World Press Review*, p. 19, June 1974.

looking for food and finding none, collapsing in the streets. More than 100,000 people died of hunger in Ethiopia between 1973 and 1975. A thousand miles to the west, in Niger, thousands of refugees who lost all their sheep and cattle and half their camels, arrived at refugee camps, hoping for a handful of grain from the meager foreign aid arriving in Africa.[13]

Starvation in the Sahel is in some ways a special case. Some of the tribes place such great prestige in owning cattle that they are tempted to expand herds beyond all practical limits. They also measure their wealth in numbers of children, so that human population also increases greatly during good years. In another sense, the situation is by no means unique. Much of the world likes to see populations grow, and all people like to display their wealth, whether in cattle or Cadillacs. The problem is that populations can expand to a point where they are maintainable only under the most favorable climatic conditions. No allowance is made for reverses in the weather cycle. In a general sense, it is the condition of a very large part of the world. Even the wheat-surplus nations now have very little by way of reserve. No allowance is made for flood, drought, or other disaster, which could easily strike in the food-surplus nations such as the United States and Canada, as well as in the poorer nations. The only hope is for a drastic downturn in births or for an equally drastic upturn in productivity—some kind of miracle harvest.

IS THERE A GREEN REVOLUTION?

"Green revolution" was a term invented to describe the possibilities of new strains of wheat, corn, and rice for feeding the hungry people of Asia and other food-deficient parts of the world. The new strains are capable of increasing productivity by growing in shorter seasons and/or by greatly increasing the yield per acre. In a few parts of India, better types of grain have increased yield by as much as 5 percent per year, but there are severe limits to where the new grains can be used. They require large amounts of fertilizer and irrigation and are most productive when heavy farm machinery is used. Most of the low-yield, underdeveloped lands do not have irrigation possibilities and the farmers cannot afford large amounts of fertilizer. Because of high rates of unemployment, such farmers require labor-intensive crops rather than machine agriculture.[14] As oil more than doubles in price, the green revolution is further jeopardized because of the price of petroleum products, not only for transportation but also for chemical fertilizers; and the fuel situation promises to be a long-term crisis.

A potential hazard of the green revolution is the trend toward standardization of varieties of farm products. If particular types of wheat and corn are developed that produce the highest yield, they often replace traditional native varieties of the same crops. If serious blights or other plant diseases develop under these circumstances, much wider areas than ever before are subject to sudden destruction. Worse yet, hundreds of local varieties from which scientists are able to develop new, resistant crop strains are dying out because of replacement by the standard varieties. The world may be buying increased yields at the price of greater vulnerability.[15] Meantime, what ground is won by the green revolution is being lost by steadily growing populations.

[13]All examples taken from "Famine: Africa's Quiet Crisis," *Atlas World Press Review*, vol. 21, pp. 13–21, June 1974.
[14]Paul Ehrlich and Anne H. Ehrlich, *Population, Resources, Environment*, W. H. Freeman and Company, San Francisco, 1970, pp. 96–101.
[15]Robert A. Jones, "Genetic Erosion of Plants Poses Threat to Crops," *Los Angeles Times*, June 4, 1974, pp. 1, 18–19.

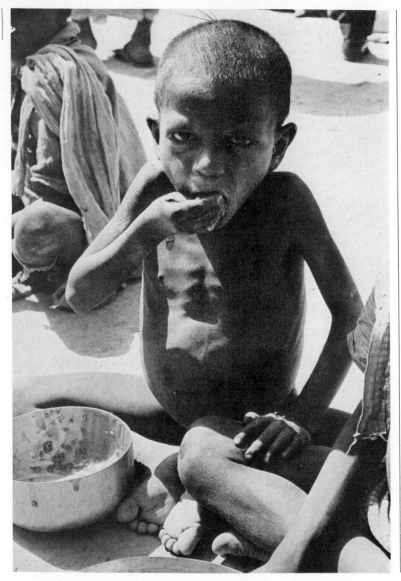

Famine becomes more frequent as the population increases and even nations with food surpluses exhaust their reserves.

POPULATION INCREASES AND POLICIES

The world's population stood at approximately 3.6 billion by 1970 and is expected to reach 6.5 billion by the end of the century. During the century from 1975 to 2075, it is expected that the population of Europe will rise approximately 50 percent and the populations of the U.S.S.R., the United States, and East Asia will nearly double. Meanwhile, South Asia (including India and Indonesia) will increase almost fourfold, Latin America fivefold, and Africa nearly sixfold.[16] World population will

[16]"A Startling Picture a Century from Today," *UNESCO Courier*, pp. 15–17, May 1974.

then stand at about 12.5 billion—nearly four people for every one now living. Such an estimate is a conservative one, assuming that birthrates will decline sharply in the next century.

With rare exceptions there are no national policies regarding birthrates, and what few there are do not work particularly well. In Africa, Kenya and Tunisia show an interest in lowering the birthrate, but with no results to date.[17] Egypt aims at lowering her birthrate to 30 per thousand—twice as high as the present rate in the United States! In Latin America, Colombia and Mexico are the only countries of any size that are considering an official policy of birth control; but so far Mexico's birthrate remains so high that her population will double in twenty-five years. A majority of Asian countries show an interest in controlling populations, but only Japan has been conspicuously successful. India has failed very badly, with a population increase of approximately one-third in the decade from 1960 to 1970, and this is in spite of government propaganda and the availability of birth control advice and pills and free vasectomies. Much of the reason for a slow decline in the birthrate in many underdeveloped countries is that of the pronatal values previously discussed. Another problem is that the majority of such countries have very young populations, with almost half still below the child-bearing age. Even acceptance of a two-child family ideal would not stabilize the population in the near future.[18]

A country conspicuously omitted from the discussion so far is China, which appears to be the one population giant that is bringing its birthrate under control. Most sources estimate China's population at 800 million as of 1970, but the Chinese government places it at about 20 million fewer. If Chinese figures can be relied upon, the population growth rate has declined in the past two decades. Early marriages are frowned upon, and so are third or fourth children. Consequently, the growth rate may be brought to zero point by the twenty-first century. It is distressing, though, to think that only a Communist nation, capable of a barrage of propaganda and thought control, can bring about drastic change in a predominantly peasant country.

In spite of its vast size, the U.S.S.R. has a population only a little greater than that of the United States. Officially, it has no policy toward births but leaving the matter up to individual decisions of its people. Nevertheless, there have been reports of articles in the Russian press urging more children.[19] Whereas the birthrate for the Soviet Union as a whole is about the same as in the United States, the rate for European Russia is only 10 or 12 per thousand population and that for Central Asia ranges from 42 to 46. David M. Heer[20] expects the government to take such steps as increasing family allotments or curbing abortions to change the situation. Besides a worry over the imbalance of Russian and Central Asian birthrates, says Heer, there is concern that the natural increase is not keeping pace with surrounding countries. Five other countries with low to moderate birthrates—France, Greece, Hungary, Romania, and Czechoslovakia—replied to a United Nations inquiry that their national policies favor population increase.[21] There is no certainty, then, that the world is reaching a zero population growth rate, either in industrialized or underdeveloped areas.

[17]"Population Policies," *UNESCO Courier*, pp. 21 and 32, May 1974.
[18]Robert Heilbroner, *An Inquiry into the Human Prospect*, W. W. Norton & Co., Inc., New York, 1974, p. 34.
[19]"Russian Birth Rates Decline: More Babies Urged," *Bakersfield California*, November 20, 1972, p. 44.
[20]Quoted in "The Population of the USSR," *Scientific American*, vol. 228, p. 46, January 1973.
[21]"Population Policies," *UNESCO Courier*, p. 32, May 1974.

| **POPULATION U.S.A.**

The crowding of the earth is part of the problem of the United States. We inhabit the same planet as the lands of greatest population explosion, and we are making our own contribution to the crowding of the earth. We must give help when famines occur. We can lose in the search for friendly relations in the world if insoluble poverty drives more underdeveloped lands into communism or into some other form of totalitarianism. If overcrowding becomes either a reason or an excuse for war, we can easily become entrapped in such conflicts. The United States is obviously involved with the rest of the world, but what about the productive land at home? Are we also in danger of overcrowding and overtaxing our land?

> **Attitude survey: ask a sample of college students how many children they would like to have. Compare with a group of noncollege people of approximately the same age.**

Population trends and policies in the United States The postwar baby boom was over by the mid-1960s, but a zero population growth rate is not yet in sight. Even as recently as 1971, federal law classified contraceptives among "obscene and pornographic materials."[22] Policies and viewpoints are changing rapidly, however. Although public opinion was almost evenly divided on the issue of legalized abortion, the Supreme Court in January 1973 ruled that states could not interfere with a decision of a woman and her doctor to have an abortion during the first three months of pregnancy. The previous year, the report of the President's Commission on Population and the American Future was issued,[23] stating no further population growth as a desired goal, calling for an end to laws against abortion, and advocating the distribution of birth control information to everyone needing it, including sexually active, unmarried girls. Neither the President nor Congress favored the dissemination of birth control information proposal, or the abortion proposal, but both have become widespread practices among public and voluntary health agencies.[24]

Whether the downturn in birthrate will be sufficient and permanent is a subject of debate. Several critics of the Commission on Population and the American Future suggest that its recommendations depend too completely on voluntary birth-control measures, and imply that much more needs to be done by way of persuasion, conversion to new values, and maybe even economic penalties for producing too many children.[25] An outspoken skeptic on the subject of declining birthrate is Judith Blake,[26] who suggests that much of the present downturn in birthrate is the result of current publicity which might not continue. Although she does not use the word, she implies that there is something faddish about family size at different times. Furthermore, although over 50 percent of respondents to a

---

[22]Frederick S. Jaffe, "Public Policy on Fertility Control," *Scientific American*, vol. 229, p. 17, July 1973.
[23]*Population and the American Future*, The Report of the Commission on Population and the American Future, U.S. Government Printing Office, Washington, D.C., 1972.
[24]Jaffe, *op. cit.*, p. 21.
[25]See H. Theodore Groat and Edward G. Stockell, "Toward an American Population Policy," *Contemporary Sociology*, vol. 2, pp. 241–244, May 1973. See also Jeanne Claire Ridley, in the same publication, pp. 244–246.
[26]Judith Blake, "Can We Believe Recent Data on Birth Expectation in the United States?" International Population and Urban Research Institute on International Studies, Reprint 445, University of California, Berkeley, Calif., February 1974.

questionnaire considered two children as an ideal family, 40 percent considered three or more children ideal, and almost no one supported a one-child family. These attitudes, Blake concludes, are inconsistent with a zero-population-growth policy. Nevertheless, our present birthrate of only about 15 per thousand is much lower than had been expected and is encouraging to those who campaign for birth control. Other encouraging signs are that declines in birthrate in recent years have been more rapid among the poor than among the middle class, and unwanted pregnancies are in sharp decline.[27]

On a comparative basis Americans are not particularly crowded; there are just over 55 per square mile, compared with approximately 200 per square mile in China, 400 in India, about 600 in West Germany, more than 950 in the Netherlands, 1,100 in Java and 2,000 in Bangladesh. What gives us the sensation of crowding is that we all choose to live in the same places. Many rural counties give the impression of having been stricken by the plague, so shrunken are their populations. Meanwhile, the vast industrial, suburban complexes of the East and the Pacific Coast spread as aggressively as the leaping roots of a mangrove forest. Like the crowded mice in one of Calhoun's experiments, we seem to have a compulsion to snuggle up to each other in vast aggregates. The obvious reason is that industrial areas provide more jobs than do scenic areas, but the crowding alarms us and makes us think that our population explosion is the worst in the world.

The real problem   In spite of these reassurances about the United States population, problems remain. The rate of increase diminishes, but the population total still grows. Even the downwardly revised estimate of the Census Bureau predicts an addition of 80 million people to our population in the last three decades of the present century. Although the large family of poverty is less common than it once was, it still exists. About 42 percent of American families with five children or more are found among the poor, whereas only 10 percent of families with one or two children are poor.[28] Regardless of the prevalence of contraception and abortion, large numbers of unwanted babies are brought into the world, some to be neglected or battered children. It is estimated that 40 percent of the unwanted children are born to the poor.[29] Little genetic counseling is done, and dysgenic traits continue in the population.

The major reason why the American birthrate is a problem is that the average American will use resources at a rate unmatched in any other part of the world. In his lifetime he will wear out from ten to twenty automobiles (assuming that he is a moderate, cautious driver) and burn up nearly 100,000 gallons of gasoline in his automobiles alone. He will probably also require such hobby items as snowmobiles, dune buggies, speedboats, motorcycles, and airplanes, all pouring out their contaminants and eating their quota of the world's limited resources. It is this tendency for the affluent American to use up the earth that causes such environmentalists as Ehrlich and Commoner to say that the birthrates of the poor are only minor problems compared with the fairly high birthrates of the affluent. Their point of view about the environment is fully understandable, but in other respects high birthrates among the poor are the larger problem, helping as they do to perpetuate poverty.

[27]Jaffe, *op. cit.*, p. 21.
[28]Ehrlich and Ehrlich, *op. cit.*, p. 246.
[29]*Ibid.*, p. 246.

Is there a Planned Parenthood Association in your community? Invite a speaker from the organization. Find out what is being done on the local level.

AVOIDING EXHAUSTION OF THE EARTH

Sometimes demographers take a grim delight in calculating how many people there will be in the world at a particular date if present trends continue, or how fast the rate of increase is at present. One film on population (*Standing Room Only*) states that every time your heart beats, three babies are born. On the cover page of Ehrlich's *The Population Bomb* is the statement "While you are reading these words four people will have died of starvation. Most of them children."[30] In the same book, Ehrlich gives the estimate that if the world's population could increase at the present rate for 900 years, there would be enough people to fill a continuous 2,000-story building covering the entire earth.

No one really expects such a fantasy to come true, but will enough of it come true to make life unlivable or to damage the earth's ecology beyond recovery? Commoner thinks that the critical mark could be as low as the 6 or 8 billion mark, which we are almost sure to attain between the years 2000 and 2050. "Any attempt to raise more food than will support 6 to 8 million people will probably strain the ecological system very severely. That is about as high as we can go."[31] Not all authorities would be quite so pessimistic in their predictions as Commoner, but none would give us more than another century or two at present rates.

The next question, then, is how to stop the world's runaway population growth. It can, of course, be stopped by the malthusian formula of war, famine, and pestilence; but the world has been through enough of the horrors of war to wish for more. We have recently seen both war and famine in Biafra, with spindly legged children with distended stomachs and glazed eyes staring blankly at approaching death. The scene is familiar to human history: Biafra actually involved far fewer people than earlier famines in India, Russia, and North China or the present Sahel region. In recent years it has usually been possible to avert famine by supplying food from regions of surplus, but there may come a day when the have countries can no longer produce the surplus needed to save the have-not lands of the earth. The products of the earth may be exhausted without feeding its billions of mouths.

Deescalation?   Until now the world's population has been growing at an ever-increasing pace. As mentioned, though, the United Nations projections call for a tapering off of growth rate by the end of the century, but by that time there will already be well over 6 billion people in the world. The question is whether the decline in birthrate will be too little and too late.

Donald Bogue is one of the very few population experts to believe the population problem may be solved before widespread famine starts (there is, of course, the slow famine of malnutrition at present). Bogue says "It is quite reasonable to assume that the world population crisis is a phenomenon of the 20th century, and will be largely if not entirely a matter of history when humanity moves into the 21st century."[32] As grounds for his optimism he cites the growing interest in birth control throughout much of the world, even including Catholic countries where church policies have been assumed to be an insurmountable barrier to birth

---

[30]Paul R. Ehrlich, *The Population Bomb*, Ballantine Books, Inc., New York, 1968.
[31]Rudy Abramson, quoting Barry Commoner, "Biologist Says World Faces Survival Crisis," *Los Angeles Times*, December 30, 1969, part I, p. 1.
[32]Donald J. Bogue, "The End of the Population Explosion," *The Public Interest*, no. 7, p. 11, Spring 1967.

control. He also mentions aroused political leadership and better research into methods of control. He takes comfort from a possible reversal of the trend toward greater death control. It looks as though the rapidly declining death rate of much of the world may be tapering off, if for no other reason than that neonatal and childhood death rates have already been reduced close to the vanishing point and there is no way to extend the old-age end of the life cycle much further.

Continued worries   In spite of all the words of cheer from Bogue, the world's population at present is increasing more rapidly than ever before, and the earth already has more people than it can possibly support on anything that Americans would consider even a minimum acceptable standard of living. One-third of the world's people are chronically hungry. The only countries to approach population stability are those with high levels of industrialization, urbanization, and education, including the United States, most of Europe, and Japan. Let it be repeated that these countries merely *approach* stability but have not actually achieved it. Such countries have been joined to some degree by Korea, Taiwan, and a few others. But despite considerable effort on the part of governments, the great population giants of India and Indonesia, together containing one quarter of the world's people, are still growing at a rate that will double their populations within thirty-five years or less. Parts of Latin America are gaining population even more rapidly. Much stronger action is needed. Ehrlich, again, has some suggestions for action on the part of the United States:

1 Refuse to send food to any country unable to demonstrate that it is doing everything in its power to lower its birth rate.

2 Refuse to help countries that are already beyond hope because of the imbalance between food supply and population.

3 Give all possible help in birth control knowledge and pills to any country willing to use the knowledge.

4 Help any country that applies for such aid with knowledge of how to increase farm yield.

5 Accept the fact that it is just as easy to use our knowledge, our wealth, our technology, and even our sacred tax money for the aid of mankind as for fighting wars.[33]

Suggestion 1 sounds harsh, and suggestion 2 sounds downright cruel. As usual, Ehrlich states his case in a dramatic manner to emphasize the gravity of the crisis, but it is hard to argue with his basic viewpoint: there is no question that more drastic steps are needed in the future than in the past if disaster is to be avoided. Human beings must increase the fruitfulness of the earth and decrease their own or the nightmare of Malthus will become reality.

SUGGESTED READINGS

Allison, Anthony: *Population Control*, Penguin Books, Inc., Baltimore, 1970. A collection of articles including animal population studies, growth of the world's human population, control attempts in several countries, and the food-supply problem. There is also a very interesting article on birth control in primitive societies.

[33]Ehrlich, "World Population: A Battle Lost?" Stanford Today, series 1, no. 22, January 1968, p. 7.

230 Ehrlich, Paul R.: *The Population Bomb*, Ballantine Books, Inc., New York, 1968. A frequently quoted book with a dramatic presentation of the problem of overpopulation and proposed solutions. The last parts are addressed to the individual with suggestions for action groups, such as Zero Population Growth.

Fleming, D. F.: *The Issues of Survival*, Anchor Books, Doubleday & Company, Inc., Garden City, N.Y., 1972. Contents include other issues of survival (war and environment) besides population, but it is very good on the issue of overpopulation.

Mandelbaum, David G.: *Human Fertility in India*, University of California Press, Berkeley, Calif., 1974. Shows the cultural roots of the problem of family planning in India in rural, familial values. Describes the efforts and shortcomings of government policies for birth control.

Morris, Desmond: *The Human Zoo*, McGraw-Hill Book Company, New York, 1969. This spicy and entertaining portrayal of the human race, now crowded and living in unnatural quarters, has its serious side. We must find small-community life, says the author, and we must not outbreed the planet's limits.

Population and the American Future: Report of the Commission on Population Growth and the American Future, The New American Library, Inc., New York, 1974. Although the commission report was turned down by the President, it has had great impact on policies both in the United States and abroad. Before the Supreme Court decision legalizing abortions, the commission had recommended the policy.

Wrigley, E. A.: *Population and History*, McGraw-Hill Book Company, New York, 1969. With many illustrations and charts the author shows the great fluctuations in population of the past and the rapid upward trend of today. Compares industrial and nonindustrial parts of the world.

QUESTIONS

1 Explain why demographic transition was not a great problem for Europe, but is much more serious for the emerging nations of the underdeveloped world.

2 If humans are similar to experimental animals, what pathological traits might result from overcrowding?

3 What policies and accidents of today could cause genetic problems for the future of the human race?

4 In what respects is the United States much less of a population problem than much of the world, and in what respect is the United States a very serious problem?

5 What is the evidence pro and con on whether the population growth of the world will slow down soon enough to avoid major disaster?

The afflicted and the possessed include many types of people, all suffering in some manner, and generally not as a consequence of their own acts. In most cases the suffering is the result of some kind of illness, but in other cases it is only the result of stigmatization by society.

There are several incongruities involved in the problem of health care: greater sympathy is shown for physical than for mental illness; the world's wealthiest nation does not provide as well for the health of all its people as do many other less wealthy countries; and certain moral dilemmas are involved in our ability to keep bodies alive long after minds fail to function, and in our increasing ability to interfere with the mind and genetic processes.

Why is adequate medical care so difficult to obtain and why are the costs out of reach of the common person? Is it really true that the poor can always receive help through county hospitals? What proposals are being made for meeting the health needs of the nation? What is the meaning of the prescientific word possessed? Is it still believed in? Are there still prejudices against the mentally ill? What are the role characteristics of mental illness that cause it to be ignored in some countries and among some segments of the population here? Is mental illness a correct designation for the phenomenon being described?

What other types of conditions can be stigmatized? How does stigmatization accompany physical as well as mental problems? What attitudinal changes are needed to alleviate the problems of the afflicted and the possessed?

An affliction is a condition of torment, whether the problem is one of disease, degenerative condition, or accidental disablement. Also afflicted are those who are seen as abnormal and are therefore stigmatized—the dwarf, the pathologically obese, the mentally defective, the ugly and disfigured, and the sexually maladjusted. For most people, the only affliction of a type to be considered here is occasional sickness, but even such an affliction can be disorganizing socially and financially. A kindly society should be expected to make all possible arrangements for the relief of any type of affliction and should seek an understanding of the possessed.

To speak of the possessed is to use an ancient and unscientific terminology for certain types of affliction. In ancient times those whom our courts might now call of unsound mind were believed to be possessed of evil spirits. Possession is referred to frequently in the Bible: in the fifth chapter of Mark, for example, Jesus commands the unclean spirits to leave a possessed man and to enter instead a herd of swine. There are reasons for using the ancient term possession in spite of our now living in a scientific age. One reason is that a belief in possession has lingered for hundreds of years, and societies have acted as though mistreatment of the victim would be a means of exorcizing the unclean spirit. Our word bedlam comes from the nickname of a London insane asylum where patients were kept on display like animals in a zoo and where passersby, to drive out the possession, were allowed to tease them until they "raised bedlam." Care of patients has improved in recent years, but there is still a stigma against the mental patient, still the feeling that he or she is possessed, and often the feeling does not go away even after the patient is pronounced well and is released from psychiatric care.

In discussing the afflicted and possessed, we shall examine first the most common type of affliction, physical illness, and discuss how well our society provides for its care. Next we shall look at the problems of those who are now usually designated as mentally ill as well as those of certain other types of people who are treated as though they had an "unclean spirit," whether or not they are regarded as ill.

WHEN ILLNESS STRIKES

For the average person, illness strikes occasionally; for some it is persistent. Whatever the case, occasional or chronic, the chances of recovery are improved if there is an assurance of good medical care and of good medical care unaccompanied by financial ruin. Such cannot be guaranteed. There is no question that over a long period of years the medical profession of the United States has improved its knowledge vastly and developed wonder drugs and wonder machines for taking care of even the most unusual complaints and also that the profession is advancing rapidly in further research. The American Medical Association has assured the public that there is no better medical care anywhere than in the United States. Such a statement is true, but only with the qualification "if you can afford it."

Medical costs The stock answer to the complaint that only a few can afford the price of good health is that the aged are now covered by Medicare and that about 75 percent of younger Americans are covered by some type of medical insurance policy. Two problems remain, however. First, what happens to the quarter of the population not covered by any type of health insurance? Second, are the policies adequate to meet the needs of medical disaster?

Long waits, dreary facilities, crowds, and perfunctory treatment in hospitals for the poor, and reduced chances for restoring health.

In answer to the first question, recall the discussion of poverty in the United States. Many rural poor live in areas that are remote from medical service. The city poor go to large public hospitals that are overcrowded and bureaucratically run. In New York, the health commissioner estimated that in a recent year 13,000 poor people died because adequate medical care was not available to them. Often the middle class considers itself worse off than the poor in some respects because the poor are eligible for free public care, whereas those with higher income are not. Admittedly, there are usually some opportunities for medical care for the poor, but "the public facilities that do exist perpetuate a grotesque circle of personal humiliation and medical lunacy."[1] There are often long, bureaucratic runarounds, referral to one clinic after another, hours of waiting, and derogatory comments. The institution begins to think the poor are unconcerned and fail to even try to take care of themselves. Perhaps some of the poor, more than the educated middle class, are inclined to ignore the need for medical aid, but much of the trouble is with the circumstances under which they must go begging for medical care—the distance they must travel—and the time they must wait. In Chicago, the medical headquarters of America and the center of the AMA, there are eighty hospitals and medical schools. Yet the west-side ghetto, with 300,000 people, has only one hospital. More than 1,000 patients per day must go to Cook County Hospital. Disease rates there are three to four times the national average. The hospital staff does its best, but it cannot cope with the situation.[2]

[1]Elinor Langer, "The Shame of American Medicine," in Jerome H. Skolnick and Elliott Curie (eds.), *Crisis in American Institutions*, Little, Brown and Company, Boston, 1970, p. 337.
[2]Daniel Schorr, *Don't Get Sick in America*, Aurora Publishing Company, Nashville, Tenn., 1970, pp. 44–45.

For the middle class, feeling protected by medical insurance policies, there are equally serious problems. Doctors, who still feel a sense of obligation to provide medical services to the poor, continue to play Robin Hood by overcharging those able to pay. It is fairly common practice to increase the rate for an operation if it is known that the patient has medical insurance. Insurance companies set guidelines on the amount to be paid for particular services, and the majority of doctors try not to exceed the suggested limits; but some *do* exceed the limits considerably. Tunley mentions a surgeon who doubled his fee for an operation because the patient had an insurance policy that paid the usual amount.[3]

However, doctors' fees are only a small part of the rising costs of medical care. Dr. John H. Knowles, former director of the Massachusetts General Hospital, tells of finding a leaflet distributed to patients at the turn of the century that listed private hospital rooms as $35 per week and the general wards as $10.50 per week. Today, he says, a similar flyer would read: "Regular charges to paying patients are $1,309 per week in a private room, $1,401 in a semiprivate room that includes intensive care units, and $1,223 in a ward."[4]

At the time of the report by Dr. Knowles, the charges listed at Massachusetts General were higher than the average throughout the United States, but they were by no means unique, and costs were rising at more than 15 percent per year.

Insurance escalation   There are certain built-in difficulties with the types of health insurance policies held in the United States. One problem is that they are generally intended as disaster insurance, not as insurance against minor illness. Although there is much to be said for such policies, they are often inadequate for the family with small children. Many times medical costs mount up for small children because of a series of sicknesses, not because of a single major disaster and with most insurance policies, usually only surgery or chronic complaints are paid for.

Another problem with present policies is that there is a tendency for insurance costs to keep escalating. If the insurance policy reads "for hospitalization of at least two days' duration," then there is a fair chance that the patient will be hospitalized for at least two days, even though he or she might have been just as well off at home. The intent of the doctor in such a case is to be considerate of the patient, but a result of such policies is that the insurance companies must pay larger claims and hence increase their rates. The doctors themselves have a very serious problem with insurance. Since malpractice suits have become more common and much more expensive, insurance companies have raised the malpractice insurance rates to doctors to as much as $40,000 per year. Doctors in turn must increase their incomes by higher fees or they cannot survive economically.

Even the Medicare program for the aged is much less than a complete solution to the problems of medical costs. All people over sixty-five are automatically covered for hospital benefits under Medicare, as part of their social security, but they must sign up three months in advance for help with doctors' bills and other medical expenses. The patient still pays a share of his medical costs, which can run to as much as one-fourth of the total bill. Medicaid, in contrast, is jointly financed by federal and state governments; it can be thought of as a welfare provision rather

[3]Roul Tunley, *The American Health Scandal*, Harper & Row, Publishers, Incorporated, New York, 1966, p. 86.
[4]John H. Knowles, "The Coming Change in Medicine," *Intellectual Digest*, pp. 15–17, February 1974 (reprinted from *Prism*, November, 1973).

than a social security program. In most states, to qualify for Medicaid, a person is generally allowed to hold almost no savings or property except a home and must turn over all but a modicum of his or her income to contribute toward costs.

The major objections to health-care arrangements for the aged are, then, that Medicare is inadequate and that Medicaid requires the recipient to be a virtual pauper. There have also been many complaints about doctors overcharging for their services. In California, for example, several doctors were reimbursed to the amount of $100,000 or more in a single year for services to the aged, and one general practitioner reaped $169,000 of the harvest.[5]

The quality of care Medicine has been able to eliminate the threat of most childhood diseases, to nearly eliminate tuberculosis and pneumonia as killers, and to stop the spread of most infections. The American Medical Association, over a period of more than a century, credited itself with eliminating the medical quacks and insisting on standards of competence in medical practice. The AMA in the period from 1900 to 1920 was the leading organization to advocate a system of national medical insurance. During the following forty-five years it reversed itself completely and fought a last-ditch action against any such insurance, thus alienating a fairly large segment of the public and quite a few doctors.

> **Attitude survey: Survey public opinion in your community regarding the quality and cost of medical services. Use such questions as (1) Have you ever postponed seeking medical help because of the costs? (2) Is your medical insurance adequate?**

In spite of all the efforts at good, honest medical practice, there remains much to be desired. Some doctors still manage to operate on a basis of old-fashioned quackery. The diet-pill specialist is a good example. Susanna McBee,[6] working for *Life*, visited ten diet doctors in various parts of the country. A few had been in trouble with the medical profession, but most seemed to be tolerated reasonably well. Although the writer was not overweight, they all took her case and charged their fees, congratulating her on stopping her problem in its early stages. Few prescribed either diet or exercise, but all prescribed pills. From the ten doctors she gathered 1,479 pills on her first visit, including amphetamines, barbiturates, sex hormones, diuretics, thyroid, and digitalis. None are drugs to be used except by a person with real need as established by careful medical examination. All are potentially dangerous. Sometimes the rewards of the unscrupulous physicians exceed those of their more conscientious colleagues.

Just as distressing as the continued presence of medical quacks is the fact that many unnecessary operations are performed. Langer tells of a common joke among medical students: "What are the symptoms calling for a hysterectomy?"—"Two children, a Blue Cross card, and a uterus."[7] A Columbia University study of medical care of a group of teamsters and their families concluded that one-fifth of the hospital admissions were unnecessary, and one-fifth of the operations were poorly performed.[8] In another case, reported by Dr. Paul A. Lembcke of the University of California, during a particular audit period of a hospital, when the

[5]Robert E. Burger, "Commercializing the Aged," *Nation*, May 11, 1972.
[6]"Diet Pills," *Life*, vol. 64, pp. 23–28, January 26, 1968.
[7]Langer, *op. cit.*, p. 338.
[8]*Ibid.*

entire staff of gynecologists was on salary, they performed twenty-six hysterecto-mies. In the same hospital at a later period, when the doctors were on a fee-for-service basis, they performed one hundred and thirty hysterectomies.[9] Tunley concluded that Bernard Shaw stated the real source of the problem years ago when he said

> That any sane nation . . . should give a surgeon a pecuniary interest in cutting off your leg is enough to make one despair of political humanity. But that is precisely what we do. And the more appalling the mutilation, the more the mutilator is paid.[10]

The implication is not that doctors are peculiarly greedy; in fact, their concern for medical ethics may make them a little more conscientious in some respects than the majority of the population. Nevertheless, the doctor has a vested interest in concluding that an operation is warranted.

A more important reason for the inadequacy of our medical care is that we do not have enough doctors. The proportion of doctors to the total population has been declining for fifty years. We need about fifty thousand more doctors than we have, but at the rate we are going we will slip even further behind existing needs in the future. Even now we have fewer doctors per population than Canada, Germany, Sweden, England, or almost any country of Western Europe,[11] and in none of those countries are people financially ruined by medical costs. Not only do we have too few doctors but also too few nurses. The United States has 700,000 practicing nurses and needs about 850,000. At the same time, we have 285,000 trained nurses who do not practice, largely because of the low status and insufficient pay given nurses[12]—a situation that is finally beginning to improve.

The United States is the only major Western country that does not produce doctors and nurses for export. The usual pattern is that the developed countries of the world produce a medical excess that is sent to the underdeveloped countries. By this criterion, the United States is one of the underdeveloped countries, importing 20 percent of its doctors from abroad.[13] The brain drain of European countries to the United States may be drawing to a close in aeronautics and many fields of science and engineering, but not yet in medicine. So great is the dearth of positions in medical schools that every opening is oversubscribed, with well-qualified students waiting for years for acceptance. Many such students resort to medical schools in other countries, the largest being the Autonomous University of Guadalajara in Mexico.

HOSPITALS: THE TRIPLE AFFLICTION

One goes to the hospital only when afflicted with sickness. In the past the affliction had to be extremely severe, even critical, before a person was sent to the hospital. Now, as we have seen, he might be sent because the hospital is the only route for collecting on his medical policy. In the more serious cases, though, the hospital is a place of great concern and anxiety. The reasons for hospitalization are such that one should expect to be reassured by every possible psychological device. Such

---

[9]Tunley, *op. cit.*, p. 128.
[10]*Ibid.*
[11]*Ibid.*, pp. 115–213.
[12]Leonard Gross, "Introducing the Supernurses," *McCall's*, vol. 98, pp. 128, 219, March 1971.
[13]Tunley, *op. cit.*, p. 92.

definitely is not the case. If the first affliction is that of the sickness itself, the second affliction is caused by the nature of the hospital, and the third by the financial worry of meeting the bills.

> Medical facilities survey: Find the number of doctors in your community (information probably available through local AMA) and the number of hospitals and hospital beds. Also survey conditions of crowding in the county hospital.

The psychological affliction   In one of Margaret Mead's[14] numerous books on primitive societies, she speaks of the problems of hospital care for primitive tribes. Much of their worry is over superstitions that do not concern us, but even more worrisome to them is the psychological problem of being placed in a building run by foreigners. They cannot be surrounded by their own kin, or by people who seem to care. Although Mead is speaking of primitives, her description sounds strangely familiar to the modern, sophisticated, twentieth-century American. The hospital tends to be a large, cold, forbidding place. It has about it an unmistakable odor of antiseptics and urine. Its cold white walls and cold white nurses and various instruments on display are unnerving. More important, the place achieves a degree of impersonality rare even in the bureaucratic world of today, with patients referred to not by name but by room and bed number or possibly as "the appendix in 107A." There are all kinds of papers to make out, proddings and probings and needles, early-morning wakings, and also long periods of relative inattention. The emphasis is heavily on science, and neglectful of human relations.[15]

Aware of the types of objections raised over the impersonality of hospital care, the American Hospital Association drew up a list of twelve rights of patients.[16] These include the right to "considerate and respectful care;" honest information about one's conditions, possible alternative treatments, and costs; and "reasonable continuity of care." Several hospitals have accepted the bill of rights; and even though a majority have not, the list may be at least an opening wedge for the idea that the relations between patient and hospital staff should be more equalitarian than in the past.

In the old days the family physician was in charge of the patient at the hospital; now he has only a casual arrangement with the hospital. Sometimes the internist fills the role of friend and confidant, and in other cases, as we shall see, the psychiatrist fills this role. For many patients, however, there is the feeling that no one except an impersonal bureaucracy is really in charge. The hospital often closely resembles the "total institution" described by Erving Goffman (see Chapter 14). One of the characteristics of the total institution is that of robbing the individual of status, dignity, and personal identity and placing him in a situation where all types of decisions are made about him without his knowledge or consultation. The needed relief from anxiety is not accomplished under such circumstances.

[14]Margaret Mead (ed.), *Cultural Patterns and Technical Change*, Mentor Books, New American Library, Inc., New York, 1955, pp. 205–208.
[15]Luke M. Smith, "The System—Barriers to Quality Nursing," in Jeanette R. Folta and Edith S. Deck (eds.), *A Sociological Framework for Patient Care*, John Wiley & Sons, Inc., New York, 1966, pp. 134–142. See also Richard M. Titmuss, "The Hospital and Its Patients," in Folta and Deck (eds.), *op. cit.*, pp. 236–238.
[16]Amitai Etzioni, "Health Care and Self-Care: The Genetic Fix," *Society*, vol. 10, pp. 28–32, September-October 1973.

Hospital costs: the reasons The third affliction, financial worry, seldom vanishes when a patient becomes hospitalized. For many people, insurance helps greatly but seldom meets the total cost of hospitalization. Congressional hearings in 1969 led to the conclusion that insurance, on the average, pays 74 percent of hospital costs, 38 percent of doctor bills, and almost nothing toward drugs and private nursing care.[17] One of the reasons for limited payment is that medical costs rise so rapidly. Another reason—the tendency to hospitalize more people—has already been mentioned. Another problem, of course, is inflation, which has driven up all costs, but medical costs more than others. Along with inflation there has been a demand for higher pay for hospital workers—an employee group that has been grossly underpaid in the past. The hospitals are also better equipped today, and the new types of equipment are extremely expensive. Another expensive policy, but one that is to a degree justifiable, is that of trying to provide more beds in case of emergency; but costs seem to rise in proportion to facilities available, whether or not they are in use.

There is still another reason for price increases that is much harder to justify: hospitals tend to be run wastefully. "Although hospitals are the third largest industry in the United States, employing about 1.7 million persons (about as many as steel and autos combined), their methods would bankrupt any other business."[18] Materials are wasted. Sometimes various departments duplicate purchases of equipment that is seldom used by any of them. There is little getting together (as in many businesses) for purchasing purposes to take advantage of reduced prices for large orders. Although there is increased specialization in the medical field, many hospitals compete with each other in generalization, each providing all possible services, even when they are close together. In Westchester County, New York, for example, four hospitals each wanted to buy a cobalt unit, which costs $100,000, for cancer therapy. In this case a planning council prevented waste by duplication, since the hospitals were within fifteen minutes of each other and could easily share the seldom-used equipment. Usually such economies are not achieved.

Whatever the reasons, some of which are unavoidable, the cost of hospital care has increased so greatly that present insurance policies are no longer adequate. New solutions to the hospital problem are needed.

Proposals The crisis in American medical care for the aged was severe enough to cause the passage of a social-security–based medical insurance, which is at least a minimal disaster insurance. The proposal, led by the late President Kennedy, was passed during the Johnson administration, in spite of the determined opposition of the AMA. There have been complaints of unfair practices arising from Medicare, but the strong opposition to it from the AMA died down almost immediately, and an attitude of living with the inevitable was adopted. Threatened strikes did not develop.

Since the passage of medical insurance for the aged, shortcomings of the program have become obvious, but the principle of government-backed health insurance was examined and found not to be the disaster its opponents had predicted.

There are also other types of suggestions for improvements in medical care. One

[17]Schorr, *op. cit.*, p. 91.
[18]Tunley, *op. cit.*, p. 130.

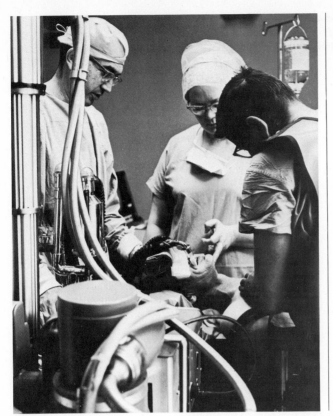

suggestion is to hire nurses with higher degrees of training who could take over part of the doctors' functions.[19] There are suggestions for improvement in home-care facilities, with the possibility of providing adequate nursing care at costs much lower than the costs of hospital care. Certainly there is room for greater efficiency on the part of hospitals and for new clauses in insurance policies that will stop the tendency of rushing more people than necessary to the hospital.

All such changes, however, would still leave the United States with a medical-care system that is in many ways years behind the other progressive countries. In 1882, Otto von Bismarck of Germany instituted the first program of universal medical insurance in the world. Since then, many governments have adopted similar schemes, and none has abandoned such policies once they were adopted. The German system is decentralized and rather complex, but it seems to guarantee good medical care without heavy costs to the ill. The British system has been greatly vilified in the United States, but it is sufficiently well liked in Britain to have passed off the stage as a political issue; neither Conservative nor Laborite wishes to tamper with the system in any major way. The national medical policies of Scandinavian countries and the Netherlands are similarly accepted and viewed with pride.[20]

[19]Gross, *op. cit.*, p. 75.
[20]Schorr, *op. cit.*, pp. 148–161.

Study proposals for more complete health insurance. Senator Kennedy has been prominent in liberal proposals for national health insurance. More conservative proposals have been made by the AMA.

The drift of thinking is in the direction of a program that will guarantee good medical care to all Americans. Public-opinion polls, such as the one by Yankelovich cited in Chapter 4, indicate increasing percentages of people in favor of the principle. Yankelovich found 54 percent of youth believing that "the best possible" medical care should be considered a right. Through the years, the federal government has steadily increased its contribution toward the nation's health care to nearly half by the early 1970s. Proposals for health care have come not only from such liberals as Senator Edward Kennedy but also from conservatives, including former President Nixon.

The features of national-health-care proposals differ in details but generally have certain common features about them. The program would be financed primarily through increases in social security contributions of employers and employees, although special provisions would have to be made for the impoverished. There would be a deductible feature, with families (except the very poor) paying the first part of the costs and the government picking up most of the bill after that. There would be an upper limit to how much an individual or family would have to pay, thus making the proposals a guarantee against medical disaster,[21] if not against persistent minor costs.

Another problem that is dealt with little, if at all, by the present health proposals is that of psychiatric care. It is noteworthy too that most insurance policies do not cover psychiatric costs, although between one-fourth and one-half of all hospital beds are occupied by the mentally ill. Even in our attitudes toward insurance, we could be accused of looking upon the mentally ill more as possessed than as sick.

THE POSSESSED

"Physical illness can play queer tricks with our thoughts and our behavior," says Dr. Richard Titmuss, "but this does not mean we are neurotics. In being querulous and ungrateful, demanding and apathetic in turn, we are in fact behaving as ill people."[22] In this description, Titmuss is clearly showing that the physically sick person can display some of the same annoying symptoms as the neurotic or psychotic, but there are marked differences. The differences are of such a nature, in fact, that at least one noted psychiatrist, Thomas S. Szasz,[23] objects to the very use of the term mental illness. Illness is one thing; mental malfunctioning is quite another, as he sees it. The mental case does not behave as a patient is expected to behave. Using Talcott Parsons' definition of how the patient should function in his role, we can see that the physically ill patient meets role expectations, but the so-called mentally ill person does not. The patient's role, says Parsons, involves four major aspects:[24]

1 Exemption from normal role responsibilities

---

[21]Eliot Marshall, "Medicaid and Its Alternatives: When Mrs. Gravely Gets Sick," *The New Republic*, pp. 14–16, April 20, 1974. See also "Insuring the National Health," *Newsweek*, pp. 73–74, June 3, 1974.
[22]Titmuss, *op. cit.*, p. 236.
[23]Thomas Szasz, *The Myth of Mental Illness*, Harper & Row, Publishers, Incorporated, New York, 1961.
[24]Talcott Parsons, *The Social System*, The Free Press of Glencoe, New York, 1964, pp. 436–443.

2 The recognition that the sick person cannot "pull himself together" and function again just on the basis of will

3 The desire to get well

4 The obligation to seek technically competent help

With few exceptions physically ill patients accept these aspects of their role; their families also accept them. If the patient fails to abide by such expectations he or she is not being a good patient. When long institutionalization destroys the desire to get well, the patient has lost status as one to be sympathized with. To quite a degree the same is true if the patient is ill but refuses to accept competent help.

The obligations of the patient role are not usually fulfilled in what is designated as mental illness. The subject is often viewed as one who ought to continue acting responsibly but will not; who should be able to pull himself together but does not. He acts as though he is not himself; he acts like a person possessed. In a more modern comparison, we might say it is as though something had shorted out a number of circuits. The result is often a personality that makes the victim a much less sympathetic type than the physically ill, and often an object of scorn.

Yet types of mental distress occur for all of us at times, sometimes reaching the level of neurosis. Neurosis is a relatively minor mental illness in which the individual is fully aware of reality but worries excessively and unproductively or develops severe headaches, indigestion, or other physical symptoms without an apparent cause. The affliction is nevertheless real to the sufferer, bringing pain, fear, and misery. Psychosis, on the other hand, is a deeper type of disturbance characterized by loss of contact with reality and frequently by both auditory and visual delusions. Hysteria, to be discussed below, is not a psychosis but a type of neurosis.

Hysteria or malingering In his criticism of the term mental illness, Szasz concentrates rather heavily on the type of mental illness referred to as hysteria. The person suffering from hysteria has the symptoms of illness—pain, indigestion, or even paralysis—without any physical causes. There are, of course, also people called malingerers, who simply pretend to be ill in order to escape obligations; and sometimes there is an argument about what is the true state of the patient claiming to be ill. Szasz shows that under such circumstances the psychiatrist tends to be the one who speaks up for the mentally ill person, showing that true affliction exists. In modern times, with many people covered by some type of medical insurance, the insurance company tends to take the side against the patient, not wanting to meet its obligations unless a physical symptom can be found.

In the Soviet Union very little attention is paid to psychiatry, and Szasz suggests that the reason is rather similar to that used by the representative of the insurance company. The Russian government tries to keep a person at work. Only the person who can prove a clear and definable physical reason for illness can be out sick. A psychiatrist does not have the power to play the role of "lawyer" for a patient, trying to prove actual affliction. In Western countries, the psychiatrist does play such a role and in some respects takes on the position of the old-fashioned family doctor.

Despite his objection to the expression mentally ill, Szasz shows that the concept of mental illness has actually done considerable good. The very term may serve to keep some psychologically disturbed people under competent care. It is also much better than seeing all such persons as malingerers or possessed of a devil. Nevertheless, Szasz argues convincingly that thinking of psychological problems as cases of mental illness produces an unfortunate result—the tendency to treat such cases as sickness, with idiosyncratic causes, and not as mental malfunctions that might have social causes.

Social class and mental illness It is generally known that tuberculosis is more likely to occur among the poor than among the rich, but once it occurs it is properly treated as the same disease. When it comes to what is called mental illness, the conclusion is not necessarily the same, even though the term mental illness makes it seem the same. A well-known study by August B. Hollingshead and Frederick C. Redlich[25] verified what would generally be expected about social-class differences in the likelihood of consulting a psychiatrist. Members of lower classes generally perceive personality problems as cases of "John's getting ornery, cantankerous, abusive, and mean lately," but they are not likely to define the problem as one of mental illness. Others have observed that among lower-class people psychiatric disorders bear far more stigma than they do among the educated. A frequent complaint among prisoners in the California prison system is against the insistence on making them admit there is something wrong with them, that they are "ill." Prisoners can stand to be told that they are bad, but they bristle at other implications. "The shrinks try to make you think you're a kook." This viewpoint is important for various reasons. In the Hollingshead and Redlich study, the lowest class accounted for 18 percent of the people sampled but for 38 percent of the mental patients. Lower-class mental patients also had a tendency to develop more severe conditions and to be hospitalized much longer.

A natural question that arises is whether the conditions are more severe simply because they are ignored in the early phase of illness, because they are given less attention, or as a result of the conditions of life among the poor. Probably all three factors have some relevance, but there are indications that the last one is most important. A very thorough study of midtown Manhattan by Srole and others[26] confirms the Hollingshead-Redlich figures about mental illness and social class. Those with moderate psychological problems were fairly evenly distributed across social-class categories. For the highest-income categories about one-sixth were designated as "impaired"; for the lowest socioeconomic group, one-third. In further refinements of their figures, the researchers found that downward mobility has a strong effect on mental impairment, both as cause and as effect.

Harry Turney-High[27] presents good evidence of an anthropological nature to show the relation between life conditions and psychological problems of various kinds. The adjustment of whole tribes of so-called Digger Indians to the American way of life could be characterized as malingering, but it is only the rejection of a culture and its status system that could explain such an adjustment for an entire people. Black Americans have higher blood pressure, on the average, than white Americans, but such is not the case with their racial relatives in Africa. Hypertension is part of the way of life imposed upon black Americans. The upward strivers in the dominant American society, especially those who strive hard but achieve little, are subject to psychosomatic disorders. In the case of downward mobility, there

---

[25]*Social Class and Mental Illness*, John Wiley & Sons, Inc., New York, 1958, pp. 171–175.
[26]Leo Srole et al., *Mental Health in the Metropolis*, McGraw-Hill Book Company, New York, 1962.
[27]Harry Holbert Turney-High, *Man and System: Foundations for the Study of Human Relations*, Appleton-Century-Crofts, New York, 1968, pp. 557–579.

are strong suggestions that alcoholism may be as frequently an effect as a cause.[28]
In general, differential stresses of life result in differential rates and types of psychiatric problems on a social-class, ethnic, and racial basis. The mental illness of the poor is a different phenomenon from that of the wealthy. As with so many of the problems of the poor, more understanding of the differential strains of life is needed, with more attempts at prevention of mental problems.

Institutional care   One-quarter to one-half of all hospital beds are occupied by people designated as mentally ill, the majority of whom are released within a few months, except for the extremely old with chronic brain syndromes or those with major psychoses entailing delusions and other serious derangements of thought processes.[29] Better medication than was available in the past helps to bring many patients to a sufficiently stable condition to make outpatient care possible. Many states have increased facilities for care outside of hospitals, but the health clinics are nearly always short on public funds. Long waiting periods are required for appointments, and large numbers of people are left untreated until their mental problems lead to disaster.

State mental hospitals have long been regarded with horror. Like public mental health clinics, they are usually understaffed and underfunded. Because they have the problem of caring for quite a few dangerous patients, some of them are prisonlike. In spite of these problems, physical conditions in most mental hospitals have improved in the past thirty or forty years. Nevertheless, they need far more public attention. In all cases where custodial care is important, it is very possible for it to become the major function of an institution, as it is with prisons, and for curing to be largely neglected.

Mental institutions have undergone a complete cycle in America in the course of a century. In the 1840s the approach was to treat the patients with the utmost consideration, hoping that kind treatment and the naturally restorative powers of the human body would return them to health.[30] Later in the century, with increasing crowds of patients and mounting costs, and especially with an attitude of contempt for some of the people of foreign origin who became hospitalized, a change in policies came about. For many years exposés of mental institutions showed up cases of malnutrition, filth, and neglect, excessive severity, and little attention to any possible improvement. The main aim was control, which was often brought about through humiliation and degradation of status, and even by creation of an atmosphere of terror.

> **Individual help: many hospitals call for volunteer aids, something very helpful and also good training. Another helpful and educational project is to visit the aged in so-called convalescent homes.**

A recent study of a Veterans' Administration hospital in Illinois[31] showed a very great change in some respects but a persistent tendency to develop an institutionalized personality. Most patients were happy with the good food, television, clean

---

[28]*Ibid.*
[29]John A. Clausen, ''Mental Disorders,'' in Robert K. Merton and Robert K. Nisbet (eds.), *Contemporary Social Problems*, Harcourt Brace Jovanovich, Inc., New York, 1966, pp. 30–39.
[30]Ailon Shiloh, ''Sanctuary of Prison—Responses to Life in a Mental Hospital,'' *Transaction*, vol. 6, pp. 28–35, December 1968.
[31]*Ibid.*

In the best hospitals, resocializing replaces tranquilizing in the rehabilitation of mental patients. In contrast, many public institutions offer only custodial care.

and comfortable beds, and generally good standards of care. They were inclined to interpret shock therapy as some kind of punishment, however, and to have no awareness of the meaning of therapy. About 40 percent of the patients were "institutionalized"; they did not want to leave; they had found a home. The institutionalized patients were a little uneasy about the man making the survey and wanted to be reassured that he wasn't involved in some kind of scheme for making them go away. Although they complained that the institution was a place of loneliness and that sometimes they might be punished by isolation, they did not want to leave. They were mentally detached from the world, hardly able to conceptualize family or friends on the outside.

The criticism that the researcher (Shiloh) makes is that despite merciful treatment in other respects, not enough is done to prepare patients for normal life. Neither the institutionalized nor the noninstitutionalized patients had any concept of what they might do to help themselves when released or where they would look for outpatient services. Not only in veterans' hospitals but wherever large masses of patients are held, it becomes impossible for the hospitals to utilize the knowledge medical science has developed for rehabilitation of mental patients.

Shiloh's conclusion can be generalized: any program of therapy that makes the patient dependent on the therapist or the institution for too long can result in chronic illness. Even welfare dependency can become a chronic illness, or a type of "addiction."

Occasionally we are horrified by a case reminding us of the inhuman treatment of the mentally ill, thinking that such treatment had disappeared long ago. In the spring of 1971, five inmates of an Ohio hospital for the criminally insane were freed. None had ever been convicted of anything; they were simply being held for observation. They had been held for twenty-two to forty years. Dr. T. J. Reshetylo, who finally released them, commented that the institution was very short of doctors and had received no replies from the courts about the cases. Dr. Reshetylo comments that there are over 100 other patients in the same category whom he hopes to release in the near future.[32]

DILEMMAS OF MEDICAL SCIENCE

So far in this chapter most of the complaints discussed have had to do with medical and psychiatric treatment, costs, hospitals, and the need for a system of national health care. But as medical science advances in knowledge and techniques, it creates new dilemmas for itself, with problems that go far beyond mere techniques and costs. The problems center on the role of the physician as arbiter of life and death, judge of the normal and abnormal, and manipulator of the genetic future. Once death was defined simply in terms of breath and heartbeat; madness was a matter of legal definition; and the unborn baby was known only to God. Now the power of medical science has cast all these phenomena in a new light, leaving a series of questions about controlling life and death, interfering with the brain, and tampering with the genetic process.

Life and death The Oath of Hippocrates called for the saving of life wherever possible, and this has generally been the position of the medical profession. Life has been extended for nearly all people. Diseases that once carried off our children have been completely conquered or rendered relatively harmless. The middle-aged are kept going with better medicines, diets, advice about their hearts, and rescue operations in case of a crisis. Lives have been saved for many years despite heart conditions or cancer. The consequence is that the majority of patients under medical treatment are no longer there for occasional but for chronic illness. Small wonder that the medical bill of the nation increases inevitably, with no possible remedy except in the field of better preventive practices! The consequence of fewer deaths in early or middle life is the increased percentage of elderly in the population. More attention is given to the avoidance of premature aging, and elderly patients are kept alive much longer than before.

The very progress is the source of a new problem—that of a very prolonged process of dying. Nearly all of us who have seen elderly people die by slow degrees in hospitals or rest homes have hoped to avoid the same fate. We might even say to a friend, "When I reach that state, be sure they let me die." The friend, however, would be powerless in such a situation. Life has been extended in quantity but not necessarily in quality. Old people cease to communicate, and frequently simply stare blankly; they must be fed and given medication; they go on breathing, alive and yet not alive. The state of Kansas has been the first to meet one of the dilemmas involved, that of defining when life ceases to exist. To the usual definition of death as the "irreversible cessation of spontaneous respiratory functions," has been added the "irreversible cessation of spontaneous brain function."[33]

The new definition of death would seem to be an easy solution to the problem of when to stop administering aid. Is there really life when there is no consciousness or possibility of consciousness? It is not easy to cut the final cord, nor is it clear

---

[32]"Forgotten by the Courts, Five Finally Freed," *Los Angeles Times*, April 24, 1971, part I, p. 6.
[33]Alexander M. Capron, "Determining Death: Do We Need a Statute?" *The Hastings Center Report*, vol. 3, pp. 6–7, February 1973. See also Robert S. Morison, "Dying," *Scientific American*, vol. 229, pp. 55–62, September 1972.

246 who should make the decision. Should it be left entirely to doctors or to the family? Or should there be a legal official whose consent is also necessary? Only a few states have adopted the new definition of death. Elsewhere the cessation of attempts to preserve life remains in at least a degree of legal doubt. The Kansas definition of death places the emphasis on the brain, where logically it seems to belong. Would altering the brain of another person, then, be a form of murder? This question poses yet another dilemma for modern medicine.

Altering the brain A later chapter will discuss drugs as a means of interfering with the functions of the brain, wherein it will be mentioned that inmates of institutions are often given drugs to keep them quiet more than to improve their condition. The subject here is that of altering the brain surgically. As long ago as the 1930s, lobotomies were used extensively to sever the fibers between the frontal lobes and the lower portions of the brain, allegedly to control violent behavior. The technique was given considerable publicity at the time and hailed as a way of correcting the dangerous psychopath. The aftermath of the operations was a high incidence of deaths, convulsive disorders, and serious loss of intelligence. Consequently, the technique has been almost completely abandoned.[34]

Brain surgery is still used, but brain surgery of a different type. Whether such operations of whatever type should be used is a subject of intense debate. Vernon H. Mark,[35] director of neurosurgery at Boston City Hospital, presents the case in favor of neurosurgery, along with the precautions that must be observed. As a first precaution, no neurosurgery should be performed on people simply because they are violent. It should be performed only when the behavior is diagnosed as the result of an abnormality of the brain. Second, inasmuch as the technique could so easily be used for political purposes, it must not be used in any instances where an individual's violence has to do with protests, riots, or any form of political disturbance. Violence of this nature is usually a result of sociological conditions and has nothing to do with a brain malady. Mark goes on to say, however, that for some people with focal brain disease, sudden outbursts of violence or attempted suicide occur that are beyond their control and are unnatural and repugnant to them. In such cases, neurosurgery would not be manipulating people but freeing them from a condition that has enslaved them. As a tragic historical example not of violence but of fatal brain tumor, the author comments on George Gershwin, who was treated psychiatrically for years while a tumor in the limbic system of the brain grew and eventually killed him. In Gershwin's case, brain surgery, and only brain surgery, could have saved his life.

Despite its necessity in some cases, surgery on the brain conjures up horrors in our minds, partly as a result of science fiction, no doubt, but also partly as a result of the experiments of the Nazi period in Germany. One case will point out the dangers dramatically. In January 1973 the *Detroit Free Press* learned of a project to perform a number of psychosurgeries at the Lafayette Clinic, a state psychiatric hospital. One of the men chosen to undergo surgery (referred to in the report simply as John Doe) had been convicted in a rape-murder case at the age of seventeen and had spent eighteen years in the mental hospital. The doctors promised him that if he would undergo psychosurgery it was very likely he would be released; otherwise his chances were poor. He consented.

[34]Paul Lowinger, "The Detroit Case: Psychosurgery," *The New Republic*, pp. 17–19, April 13, 1974.
[35]"Brain Surgery in Aggressive Epileptics," *The Hastings Center Report*, vol. 3, pp. 1–5, February 1973.

It should be explained that not all brain surgery is psychosurgery. Much neurosurgery, and the kind discussed by Mark, is performed to treat organic diseases. Psychosurgery, on the other hand, is performed to change behavior patterns, with nothing but the circumstantial evidence of bad behavior to indicate that there is anything organically wrong. In the case of John Doe, unfavorable publicity caused a delay in the surgery and finally a court order to cease and desist. In subsequent investigation, it was found that he had shown no aggressive behavior during his eighteen years in the institution and that he had had no psychotherapy in any of those years. The investigation led to his release.

The personal case of John Doe points out a danger for hundreds of people. Can it possibly be said that an inmate seeking release from prison or a mental hospital could be thought of as a free agent in consenting to such surgery? John Doe was convinced that failure to comply would go hard on him; his case is by no means unique. The same surgeons interested in operating on him had planned experimental psychotherapy on a group of aggressive psychopaths along with several mentally retarded patients for a control group. They also intended to administer a drug to sexual deviates that produces chemical castration.[36]

Genetics and the unborn   Reading the works of futurologists on the subject of tampering with our genetic structure can be quite intriguing, albeit also disconcerting. Alvin Toffler speculates on the possibilities of fertilizing human eggs in test tubes and implanting them in mothers (which reportedly has been done) as a rather common technique. He goes on to envisage a society in which embryos are produced in such a manner that with the genetic material known a mother can decide what sex, eye and hair color, and special capacities she desires in her baby. He then moves further into science fiction when discussing the idea of babies being produced completely outside the mother's body. Finally he returns to something much closer to present-day reality.

What bothers you—allergy, obesity, arthritic pain? These will be handled easily (in your children). For cancer, diabetes, phenylketonuria there will be genetic therapy. The appropriate DNA will be provided. In the appropriate dose.[37]

At present our interference with genetics can be done only in a precautionary manner: that is, we can prevent births of some types of defective children but we cannot yet interfere with a conception or pregnancy to ensure, for example, a genius. But we are confronted here with the question of how fully such knowledge should be used. For some conditions, a test of the fluid surrounding the fetus can be made to tell whether the fetus is defective or not and whether an abortion should be performed. In the case of phenylketonuria (an inherited malady that can result in severe mental retardation) tests can be made to see whether treatment is necessary to prevent the condition. In the case of the sickle-cell trait, found occasionally in black Americans, the problem is more complicated. If young people are tested and found to be carriers of the sickle cell, they would be well advised not to marry another person with the trait, since their children in that case would have a one in four chance of having sickle-cell anemia. To inherit the sickle-cell trait from only one side of the family is no health problem. Nevertheless, carriers of the trait have been branded as employment and life insurance risks. Such stigmatization can

[36]Lowinger, *op. cit.*
[37]Alvin Toffler, *Future Shock*, Bantam Books, Inc., New York, 1970, p. 203.

create serious problems for them, perhaps becoming just as bad self-fulfilling prophecies as the labels of delinquent or potentially violent.[38]

A disturbing case of the possibilities of unfavorable labeling is that presented by the XYY chromosome. About one man in every thousand is born with the double Y chromosome, which has been said to correlate with violent dispositions and deviant behavior. If genetic screening indicates a boy has the XYY chromosome, what should be done? If the parents are told about the screening, their very fear that their child might have a criminal potential could cause them to treat him differently in subtle ways that would ultimately fulfil the prediction. (Many XYY men are law-abiding citizens; and any number of violent criminals have the normal XY chromosome.) Prospective parents, by the same token, can face a problem if they are told they cannot have normal children: for some it could undermine their personal sense of worth.[39]

There are several possible roads to take with the new genetic knowledge that is emerging. Jerome Lejeune, discoverer of the chromosomal basis of one genetic defect, believes we should simply accept the defective as normal or otherwise run the risk of solving problems simply through abortion rather than learning to correct the conditions.[40] Others consider the abortion solution a satisfactory one. Senator Mondale has proposed a study of the new ethical questions by a national commission to be composed of professionals from many fields, including theology and law as well as medicine. He shows an awareness of the new moral dilemmas that come with increased knowledge. We will say more about moral dilemmas in the next chapter. Now we must turn to another topic mentioned in the title of this chapter—affliction by stigmatization.

AFFLICTION AND STIGMA

The previous pages considered physical and mental illness as the main types of affliction. Often a distinction is made between the two on the grounds that physical illness carries no implication of stigma but that mental illness does. Although the observation about a societal tendency to stigmatize mental illness can hardly be denied, there are many exceptions to the statement that physical illness is not stigmatized. Some physical illnesses certainly are not; they even attract immediate sympathy. When poliomyelitis was still a major crippler, pictures of little crippled children went right to the heart of the American public and large donations were made. On the other hand, if one were to appeal for funds to help people who have been physically impaired by the long-range effects of syphilis, the campaign would probably collapse. It has been difficult to raise funds for clinics to help people who are in physical and mental trouble with drugs, the objection being that the addicts brought the affliction on themselves. Such is not always the case with afflictions that bring stigmatization. What of cases of ugly facial disfigurement, of missing ears or noses, or of severe mental retardation? We tend to sympathize with the blind, joke about the deaf, and shun the deformed.

The ugliest man in Canada   A depressing illustration of the tendency for society to exclude completely certain stigmatized individuals was reported in the summer

---

[38]Amitai Etzioni, *loc. cit.*
[39]*Ibid.*, p. 29.
[40]Marc Lappe, "How Much Do We Want to Know about the Unborn," *The Hastings Center Report*, pp. 8–9, February 1973.

of 1970. The incident occurred in Canada, but its setting could have been anywhere. More than anything else, it points out the tendency to exclude certain of the afflicted and stigmatized to avoid thinking about them. Certain people who, in the normative definition of social problems, should be those of greatest concern, are usually excluded from the social-probelm category because they are few in number and incapable of any major protest. "Lumpy Willie" is a good example.

A few years ago, the ugliest man in Canada died. He had been spending the last year or two of his life working as a night watchman to pay off some debts. He liked to go out only at night so people wouldn't see him and stare at him. He even washed and shaved in the dark so he wouldn't see his own reflection in the mirror. He was called Lumpy Willie because he had hundreds of knobs and lumps all over his body and face, caused by a rare condition called Von Recklinghausen's neurofibromatosis. No one would give him a job; restaurants and bars refused to serve him. Children had shunned and teased him when he was a child; he had never had a date, rarely a friend. Unable to work, he stole and used credit cards fraudulently for a living and spent most of the second half of his thirty-nine-year life in prison. He drank by himself in a cheap hotel, and once while drinking he attempted suicide.

Then a good doctor, Theo Wilkie, took mercy on Lumpy Willie and worked long hours at surgery, removing many of the lumps from his face until he was nearly normal in appearance. He was over being "so ugly that I am hated by people who don't even know me." He worked, paid off his fines, made good his fraudulent checks, and very soon thereafter, on August 11, 1971, Alex Samuel Chapelski (Lumpy Willie) died.[41]

Managing stigma   The stigmatized often band together for mutual support. There are organizations of dwarfs, the obese, alcoholics, wives of prisoners, the hard of hearing, the blind, and the crippled. Misery loves company and often finds company. Not many are as alone as Lumpy Willie.

There is another side to the banding together of the stigmatized, however. Often they are segregated and have no choice. The "normals" hesitate to associate with them too much for fear of taking on something of the stigma.[42] This is particularly true at certain ages of childhood. Even the good-hearted child hardly dares champion the one who is stigmatized, whether the stigma is that of having a father in jail, of belonging to the wrong race or religion, or merely looking odd. Often the institutions of society work to set the stigmatized apart. Who else should the aged and infirm visit except the aged and infirm? So institutionalized arrangements are made. The blind must know the blind, lead the blind, and identify with the blind. A newly blind girl comments on her attempt to readjust to familiar places and routines and then how she was firmly led, instead, into the valley of the blind:

I was to spend the rest of my life making mops with other blind people, eating with other blind people, dancing with other blind people. I became nauseated with fear, as the picture grew in my mind. Never had I come upon such destructive segregation![43]

Goffman's book *Stigma: Notes on the Management of a Spoiled Identity* analyzes

[41]" 'Ugliest Man'—He Paid Debts Before He Died," *Los Angeles Times*, August 21, 1970, part I, pp. 1 and 18.
[42]Erving Goffman, *Stigma: Notes on the Management of a Spoiled Identity*, Prentice-Hall, Inc., Englewood Cliffs, N.J., 1963, p. 30.
[43]*Ibid.*, p. 37.

the ways in which people try to manage the problem of damaged identity that results from stigma. There are attempts to interrelate; to promote kinder terminology for their affliction ("hard-of-hearing," please, not "deaf"); to publish small newspapers; and to learn how to ward off intended or accidental insults, how to manipulate prestige symbols in order to compensate for stigma, how to "pass" as though there were no stigma, when to hide, when to reveal the scars of identity, when to be on guard, and when it is possible to be one's self. Always there is a psychological strain, minor for some kinds of stigma, devastating for others. Many people bear at least a slight stigma, for as Goffman says, the only completely unstigmatized person in America is "a young, married, white, urban, Northern, heterosexual, Protestant father, of college education, fully employed, of good complexion, weight, and height, and with a recent record in sports."[44]

Goffman, as always, gives a sensitive, probing picture of a problem of individual management of a difficult situation. Outside intervention is difficult because the problem is understood only by people with that particular stigma. Often there is also a sense of fear in intervening. The doctor who devotes his time to working with drug abusers, the minister who befriends the homosexuals, the leader in a drive against venereal disease—all such people take on a little of the stigma of those they befriend. Therefore, generally ignored are these and many other kinds of stigma—the ex-convict, the mental case, the attempted suicide.

The case of suicide   The person who has attempted suicide is badly stigmatized, and various explanations are guessed at: some type of insanity, drugs, or a disgraceful secret. Actually, the usual case of suicide or attempted suicide involves an individual who seems quite normal. The suicide rate among the young has risen very sharply in recent years in the Los Angeles area (from 12.2 per 100,000 in 1960 to 28.4 per 100,000 in 1969) and is one of the leading causes of death among people of college age. The Los Angeles Center for Suicide Prevention finds that the public generally believes the suicide rate to be highest among drug users and radical college students. Actually, the rate is about the same among drug users and nonusers and considerably lower among college students than among the noncollege group. Many persons who attempted suicide have complained of heavy pressures from parents or of feelings of hopelessness about society, but the most common symptom is a great feeling of loneliness. "My guess is that we have more conditions that lead to that [loneliness] today," says Michael Peck, director of the Center—"a lack of responsiveness among people and institutions."[45]

Even the brave: the veterans' hospitals   When a man fights for his country and is wounded in action, every effort is made to rush him to a military hospital, where his chances of survival despite wounds are the best they have ever been. He comes home, perhaps with his legs amputated, deserving the status of hero; he has been called upon to serve, and he has served.

Years go by. Some amputees are never completely rehabilitated, or perhaps they are unable to find jobs. Being less than whole, living restricted lives, and envying those who remained civilians does nothing for dispositions. The brave young hero changes into an old cripple, ill-tempered and ill-kept, and possibly has to spend most of his time in a veterans' hospital. Since the cost of hospitalization is very

[44]*Ibid.*, p. 128.
[45]"The Youthful Suicides," *Newsweek*, vol. 77, pp. 70–71, February 15, 1971.

great and there are always thousands of demands on the federal budget, the hospitals are only half-financed. The heroic words of old, that one can bear his afflictions proudly, cease to apply. "Heroized" becomes "stigmatized."

The Senate Subcommittee on Veterans' Affairs conducted an investigation into veterans' hospitals from November 1969 to April 1970. What they found does not reflect against the hospital personnel. Attempts were being made to handle the increasing load of patients as well as possible, but the situation was growing difficult. There seemed to be just as great a tendency to forget veterans in hospitals as there is to forget all people who get hidden away in institutions. "It's like you've been put in jail or been punished for something," Marine Marke Dumpert, an amputee, said in an interview in the Bronx VA Hospital.[46] The hospital is one of the oldest ones still used, and the picture of it in *Life* is not reassuring. Not only is it old, dirty, and crowded but it has far too few personnel to staff it adequately. An amputee, almost unable to move, woke one night to find a rat crawling across his hand. There were also complaints of inadequate equipment for training and rehabilitating the types of paralytic injuries resulting so often from the booby traps used in the Vietnam war.

It must be admitted that the *Life* article has been criticized for being excessive in its condemnations; but the cautious, conservative *U.S. News & World Report* reported a few months later along rather similar lines. No particular hopsital was taken to task, nor was the Veterans' Administration blamed, but the conclusion was that inadequate preparation was being made for the increasing numbers of wounded veterans. There has been no expansion of beds or doctors or nurses (although some growth in the number of interns) since 1965. In 1966 a payroll cut was necessitated by economy moves from the government. It has been hard to hire adequate personnel.

Senator Alan Cranston has been particularly sharp in his criticism of the treatment of our wounded.[47] The implication of the present analysis is that over a period of years the status of the wounded soldier tends to change from that of hero to that of forgotten or even stigmatized. In the opinion of Dumpert, the only thing wrong with this analysis is that it doesn't seem to take a number of years:

> I feel that the way we Vietnam veterans are being treated is abnormal. I regret having to say this, but now I have nothing but disgust for my country. I used to hate the guys who ran off to Canada to avoid the draft. Now I don't hate them. I don't like them, but I respect them for what they did. If I had known what I know now, I would never have enlisted. I don't mean just my injury, but the insensitivity and lack of care. They would have had to drag me into the service kicking. It makes me wonder about Vietnam—about whether the people I saw die, and people like me who are half dead, fought for nothing.[48]

SUGGESTED READINGS

Freeman, Howard E., Sol Levine, and Leo G. Reeder (eds.): *Handbook of Medical Sociology*, Prentice-Hall, Inc., Englewood Cliffs, N.J., 1972. Includes a discussion of the political issues involved in providing health care, of social factors in disease and chronic illness, of medical education, of the hospital as a social system, and of sociomedical research.

[46]From "Assignment to Neglect," by Charles Childs, *Life*, May 22, 1970, © 1970 Time Inc.
[47]"Growing Concern over Veterans' Hospitals," *U.S. News & World Report*, vol. 69, pp. 63–64, August 31, 1970.
[48]Childs, *op. cit.*, p. 28.

252 Goffman, Erving: *Stigma: Notes on the Management of a Spoiled Identity*, Prentice-Hall, Inc., Englewood Cliffs, N.J., 1963. Goffman writes with great sensitivity and feeling and also analyzes problems in the context of social-psychological theory. An analysis of how one manages to cope with the stigma resulting from physical defectiveness, blindness, deafness, or outcaste status.

Perrucci, Robert: *Circle of Madness: On Being Insane and Institutionalized in America*, Spectrum Books, Prentice-Hall, Inc., Englewood Cliffs, N.J., 1974. Although the theme is similar to Szasz's (1973) book, the development is based on studies of present-day institutions. Perrucci contends that treatment is much too structured in most hospitals. He also contends that many hospital patients are more the victims of social forces than of serious mental illness.

Schorr, Daniel: *Don't Get Sick in America*, Aurora Publishing Company, Nashville, Tenn., 1970. Closely parallels a TV documentary on health-care problems in America. Documents inadequacy of health insurance, lack of clinics, and shortage of doctors and medical schools. Shows how the United States, a leader in medical research, lags behind in the problem of means to pay for medical treatment.

Silverstein, Harry (ed.): *The Social Control of Mental Illness*, Thomas Y. Crowell Company, New York, 1968. A collection of excerpts from some of the best works in the field—social class and mental illness, mental health in the metropolis, the psychiatric hospital, the myth of mental illness, and the divided self.

Szasz, Thomas (ed.): *The Age of Madness: The History of Involuntary Hospitalization*, Anchor Books, Doubleday & Company, Inc., Garden City, N.Y., 1973. Ranges from early comments on the care of mental patients to articles by such modern writers as Erving Goffman. Consistent with the title, this book not only shows the errors of the past but raises questions about whether the "age of madness" is at an end.

Szasz, Thomas S.: *The Myth of Mental Illness*, Harper & Row, Publishers, Incorporated, New York, 1961. A novel point of view about mental illness is presented. Although the present designation of mental illness is meant to be a kindly definition of troubles, it lumps too many phenomena together and fails to explain age and social-class differences in type of affliction.

QUESTIONS

1 What are the special problems of the middle class and the poor in trying to get proper health care?

2 Explain what is meant by "psychological affliction" and "financial affliction" relative to the hospital.

3 Why does Szasz criticize the whole concept of mental illness?

4 What are various types of stigmata and what methods are used to try to get along in spite of them?

5 How can even the heroized turn into the stigmatized?

6 Explain some of the dilemmas of modern medical science.

In constructing a simple model of the relations between the individual
and the government in a totalitarian state and in a democratic state,
one of the most important contrasts to emphasize is that of who is
watching and who is being watched. In a totalitarian state, citizens are
constantly under the surveillance of the government, but the workings
of the government are hidden from the people. In a democratic state,
the workings of the government should, ideally, be under the constant
surveillance of the citizenry, with an absolute minimum of probing into
the lives of the people. Individual liberty is eroded if the citizens feel
that too many eyes are watching them, whether they be the eyes of the
government, the army, the police, a business, a school, an employer,
or the ubiquitous computer. The feeling of individual liberty is eroded,
too, if the government hides its activities from the people or attempts
in any way to blindfold or muzzle the press.

Is there any validity to the feeling that the power of the individual has
diminished as the power of government and economic institutions has
grown? Almost anyone would admit that we live in an age when more
information about the people is needed and that such information has
many legitimate uses; but we know, too, that there are devious means
for gathering and storing information, with wiretapping, recording, and
other eavesdropping equipment growing evermore sophisticated. Along
with the need for information and the new means of probing, data
banks have grown rapidly, storing more and more information about
the citizens. Does some of the accumulation of data exceed social
necessity? Is it carefully guarded? How far can businesses and private
investigative agencies pry into one's life? Are respondents to
questionnaires sure that their confidential answers cannot be
subpoenaed by the courts? How much certainty does the press have

that it can protect its sources of information so that they will continue
to tell reporters what they think should be made known? In short, is
our society to continue to be one in which the people vigilantly watch
the government, or is it merely to be one in which the government
watches the people?

NEW NEEDS AND NEW DEVICES

Admittedly, ours is an informational society. We need to know more and more
about job opportunities, credit ratings, shifts in population, business openings,
housing needs, health needs and costs, and the educational level of the population, as well as about crime syndicates, terrorist organizations, and spies. In both
the criminal and civil areas of investigation, amazing new devices for surveillance
constantly appear, and the temptation is to use them even when they infringe upon
the right of privacy. The American people were appalled to learn that virtually all
White House conversations during the Nixon administration had been tape-
recorded without the knowledge of the people speaking. It was also divulged that
secret taping had been used, but to a much more limited degree, by previous
administrations. Must we all learn to guard our conversations? If we must do so,
certainly we will no longer feel free.

The new means of surveillance   When the telephone first came into being, it was
hailed as a means for transmitting messages over great distances with speed and
absolute security. The speed of the message has not disappointed us, but its
security is sadly lacking. Clumsy techniques for tapping telephones have been
used for many years. With the use of induction coils, phones can now be tapped
without any wire cutting, and even at great distances. Small induction-coil devices
can be kept in a pocket to pick up conversations in waiting rooms outside
government, business, and law offices.[1] Unseen microphones can be installed in
rooms to transmit conversations, and other equipment can pick up information
from a considerable distance. Miniaturization has become so ingenious that a
microphone the size of a match head can transmit conversations for a quarter of a
mile. If access to a room is impossible, a bean-sized contact microphone can be
placed on the wall outside, sensitive enough to vibrations to translate them into
sound transmitted to listeners. Even more ingenious is the use of laser microphones:

One such device is portable and sends out an invisible infra-red beam, which may travel
for miles before reaching the target room. The returning beam having been modulated
by the sound waves in the room, a photo amplifier at the listening post makes it possible
to transform the returning light into sound.[2]

A "harmonica bug" can be installed in the base of a victim's telephone. An
eavesdropper can then dial the victim's number and play a predetermined
harmonic note whose vibrations will prevent the phone from ringing but make it
possible for the eavesdropper to listen to any conversations within earshot of the
victim's phone. There are reports that while filling a tooth, a dentist could secretly

[1]These and subsequent examples are from "Human Rights and the Threat to Privacy," *UNESCO Courier*,
pp. 7–19, July 1973.
[2]*Ibid.*, p. 8.

Is this telephone bugged? Ingenious devices make it possible to listen even if the receiver is not lifted.

insert a miniature microphone that would transmit every word a patient speaks, and all without the patient's knowing.

Watching devices are just as ingenious as are listening devices. A miniature lense for observing can be inserted into a hole drilled through the wall—a hole so small that it is unlikely to be observed. Small telescopic devices, about 8 inches in length, can photograph a typewritten page at a distance of over 300 feet.

It is not to be suggested that such devices are constantly being used by government and other official agencies, nor that such agencies alone have access to them. One of the problems that complicates the entire field of privacy is that seeing and listening devices can be purchased by all types of people, including criminals, and that their use is hard to detect. It was disturbing to read recently that an electronics magazine was offering a course in how to be a spy, including instructions in bugging. The new espionage technology moreover poses legal problems that have yet to be resolved. There may be a legitimate use for wiretapping and eavesdropping equipment in counterespionage, but the problem is to prevent illegitimate use both by individuals and the government. At present, courts disbar wiretapping evidence in most trial cases, but not necessarily in evidence presented before grand juries.

> **Try to find an example of a case in which illegal wiretapping or other illegal means of information gathering was used. If such a case is not available in the local papers, ask a defense lawyer.**

Probing the psyche   There are legitimate uses for a variety of psychological tests—although it will be recalled that too great reliance on them for the placement of students in school and the fact that they are often unfair to minority students were severely criticized in Chapter 4. Nevertheless, tests designed to fit workers to jobs for which they are qualified are often necessary and may result in greater worker satisfaction on the job.

There are other tests that go much further in looking into the minds and emotions of people, testing attitudes and emotions and, by inference, looking into political beliefs. Unless such tests are used judiciously and only by trained psychologists and psychiatrists, they can take on the aspect of an inquisition. Still other tests employ the principles of a polygraph, using such indexes as heartbeat, pupil contraction, and electrical conductivity of the skin to tell whether the answers given are truthful or not. Such tests may have their utility in criminal investigations, but for all other purposes, they can amount to an unwarranted invasion of privacy. One study conducted during a political contest was able to probe political opinions. Half the subjects of the test stated a preference for one candidate (apparently trying to keep their political opinions secret), but pupil-dilation tests ferreted out their actual preferences in the political field.[3] These kinds of uses of such tests are obviously inconsistent with political freedom.

The data banks   The final technical possibility that poses a threat to liberty is the growth of information centers and data banks, made possible by modern computers. Without modern technology, the task of handling social security, income taxes, and the multibillion-dollar credit-card industry would be virtually impossible. Despite their disturbing psychological effects on many people, data banks have a multitude of legitimate uses. But the problems the public faces regarding them lies in the nature of the accumulation of data over the years, which can be cryptically entered and wrongly interpreted, and the danger that such data will fall into unauthorized hands or include information that is no one's business.

Possible threats, then, come from new devices for secret listening and observing, from many types of tests and other means of psychological probing, and from accumulation and storage of data. Are these threats to liberty actual or mere possibilities exploited by science-fiction writers?

SURVEILLANCE BY GOVERNMENT

Senator Sam Ervin, during his days as head of the Senate committee investigating the Watergate affair, was shocked to learn of enemy lists, wiretaps, tape recordings, and burglaries carried out with the knowledge of the White House. However,

[3]*Ibid.*, p. 13.

Senator Ervin, in his long battle for the rights of privacy, had come across shocking cases of government scrutiny before. In 1970, the Senator carried on an investigation of army intelligence units that had been compiling dossiers on thousands of Americans in the course of a surveillance project known as "Consul Intel," or Continental United States Intelligence.

Consul Intel The investigations started during the period of student antiwar demonstrations and included reports on a few admittedly dangerous organizations, such as the Weathermen. Investigations did not stop, however, with dangerous or violence-prone individuals or organizations. The telephone of Senator Eugene McCarthy was tapped at the Democratic National Convention of 1968. The name of Secretary of Defense Melvin Laird's son was entered in army files for attending Moratorium Day activities at Wisconsin State. Army spies covered the meeting of a group of Catholic priests who were in opposition to the birth-control policies of their church. Philadelphia Earth Day festivities were carefully covered so as to report the names of leaders of the protests against pollution. At one peace demonstration, a female demonstrator was hauled away by the police. A man witnessing the action said it was a shame to carry away such a pretty girl. For that remark the army investigators opened a file on him. One army agent spent an entire term spying on a black studies course at New York University. The most ludicrous case was an assignment to investigate the activities of the hippie presidential candidate running in 1968. The hippies had spoofed the election process by running a pig for president—Pigasus. Pigasus is probably the only pig with a dossier in the army's secret files. Obviously, the army was diligent. One army agent explained to Senator Ervin's committee that the secret agents were asked to name the ten most dangerous groups of radicals in the area they were investigating. "If there were only four active groups, we'd have to come up with the names of six others. We didn't make any distinctions as to whether they were engaged in legal or illegal activities."[4]

Among the bits of information collected on one man suspected by the army were such comments as "A known member of the Society of Friends (Quakers); . . . Believes there should be no more wars; . . . His hair and sideburns have become progressively longer over the past two years."[5]

What bothered Senator Ervin about the individual cases of information collection and the often questionable means of spying on citizens was the feeling that such episodes could lead to intimidation of the public. What happens if we know our names might be registered on some persons-of-interest list as possible subversives? Most of the real issue behind the subversive tag was that of opposition to the Vietnam war, which eventually became a majority opinion. The then Assistant Attorney General William H. Rehnquist, (subsequently appointed to the Supreme Court) was among those who upheld the army position, saying that the government had the right to collect whatever information it wanted on anyone and that "self-discipline on the part of the executive branch will provide an answer to virtually all legitimate complaints against excesses of information gathering."[6] The Watergate investigations of 1973 and 1974 leave grave doubts about the self-discipline of the executive branch.

Eventually the argument of surveillance was halfway won by the Senate investi-

[4]"Persons of Interest," *Life*, pp. 20–27, March 26, 1971.
[5]*Ibid.*, p. 27.
[6]*Ibid.*, p. 27.

TRASH

Veterans of the Vietnamese war demonstrate against the war. Is the photographer a reporter or a government agent starting a dossier?

gating committee. The Pentagon issued orders to cease investigations of individuals or organizations unless their activities constituted a direct threat of civil disobedience and were beyond the control of local authorities.[7] However, no permanent means of controlling such army activities was written into law.

Try to find out how many people are afraid of getting their names on lists for political activities. A simple way is to circulate a completely innocent petition (for example, "We, the undersigned, support the Bill of Rights"). Judging by previous experiments of this type, some people will be afraid to sign anything.

Information files Although the Watergate affair and the army surveillance cases have attracted the greatest amount of attention to government surveillance, many less dramatic cases have occurred. Vance Packard,[8] writing in 1964, said that he found that employees in many government bureaus automatically assume that their offices are bugged. Representative John E. Moss headed a subcommittee to investigate illegal snooping and found that his phone calls had been monitored in the course of his investigations. The subcommittee reported "a dangerous drift toward a huge bureaucracy peering over the shoulder of the citizen," [9] and was highly critical of what it considered an excessive use of lie detectors. Lie detector use was usually not to protect the national security but rather to track down news leaks that might prove embarrassing to officials. Interestingly, the CIA and the

[7]Eliot Marshall, "I Spy, You Spy," *The New Republic*, p. 15, October 3, 1970.
[8]Vance Packard, *The Naked Society*, David McKay Company, Inc., New York, 1964.
[9]*Ibid.*, p. 108.

Pentagon were using lie detectors routinely, whereas the FBI, with its employees in equally sensitive positions, did not. The validity of lie detectors is open to such serious question that their results are generally not acceptable in court.

Information files are by no means limited to the Pentagon, CIA, FBI, Social Security Administration, and the Census Bureau. The Department of Housing and Urban Development has an adverse information file; the Customs Bureau has a computerized bank of suspects; the Secret Service has a dossier on undesirables; and there is even a National Migrant Workers' Children Data Bank. Arthur R. Miller sees as possible consequences of the growth in data banks not only a tendency for people to be guarded in what they say and write but the possibility that people "may increasingly base their decisions and fashion their behavior in terms of enhancing their record image in the eyes of those who may have access to it in the future."[10] He says that already some people who have knowledge of computers have been able to enter data that constructs false record-lives for themselves. Since the records for most people are never changed, opinions or activities of their youth continue to be on file. What possibilities they would open if another hysterical red scare developed, such as the one exploited by Senator Joseph McCarthy in the 1950s! In the mind of the computer there is no forgetting and no forgiveness, nor is there any recognition that opinions might change through the years. "The possibility of a fresh start is becoming increasingly difficult. The Christian notion of redemption is incomprehensible to the computer."[11]

In many agencies of government, information passes easily from one data bank to another. In contrast, the Census Bureau has long enjoyed a good reputation for guarding its files; but even in this bureau, the principle of confidentiality has been breached. In the St. Regis Paper Company case of the early 1960s, the Supreme Court ruled that files from the Census Bureau could be used by other agencies of the government, even though Congress passed a bill in 1962 making such copies of census report data immune from subpoena.

IRS, FBI, and CIA During the long investigations of the Watergate affair, more and more rumors were heard concerning alleged political operations of the Internal Revenue Service, the Federal Bureau of Investigation and the Central Intelligence Agency. IRS investigations were aimed mainly at people who had supported tax protest organizations and were thus attempts to intimidate people who were voicing perfectly legal complaints.[12] The FBI, supposedly dedicated only to preserving the public from crime and internal subversion, had kept files on large numbers of perfectly law-abiding Americans, including members of Congress. J. Edgar Hoover, for example, had a private file on the chairman of the congressional committee that handled FBI appropriations.[13] To no one's surprise, the FBI always received the appropriations it asked for. It is generally believed, too, that some of our presidents dared not take a stand against J. Edgar Hoover for fear of what might be in his files that could be damaging to them or their political allies.

The CIA, authorized by Congress to operate in the foreign field, but not in the domestic field, broke faith with Congress. Accusations against the CIA were

[10]Arthur R. Miller, *The Assault on Privacy: Computers, Data Banks, and Dossiers*, University of Michigan Press, Ann Arbor, 1971, p. 50.
[11]Vance Packard in House Hearings on Computers and Invasion of Privacy, quoted in Miller, *op. cit.*, p. 50.
[12]Robert Rawitch, "IRS Kept Spying, Documents Reveal," *Los Angeles Times*, April 7, 1975, Part I, p. 3.
[13]TRB, "House of File Cards," *New Republic*, March 15, 1975, p. 1.

printed in *Time* and other magazines late in 1974. The CIA director spent months trying to deny the accusations or explain them away. The CIA was accused of maintaining files on 10,000 or more Americans. The director said this accusation was false, but finally admitted to having 9,000 names on file. The CIA penetrated American anti-war groups with secret informants, kept files on members of congress, did wire-tapping within the United States, and inspected the mail of American citizens within the United States, in spite of its having been specifically denied any police, law-enforcement, or internal security powers.[14]

Congressional authority creating the CIA gave the agency very extensive powers for operating abroad. Its foreign activities have come under very severe criticism, but our concern here is with illegal activities within the United States itself. If members of congress are no longer free to act on legislation as they see fit for fear of being blackmailed by the very agencies they created, much of the power of representative democracy is being eroded away.

SURVEILLANCE BY BUSINESS

As we move more and more toward a cashless society, depending almost entirely on credit, business also becomes involved in checking into records. The increasing use of credit calls for credit information, the more the better. Since much information is readily available and even more can be found, old-fashioned guesswork is eliminated in hiring of employees as well as in checking on customers, and business rivals. Even though such checking can be defended on rational grounds, it seems to have led not to more honesty but only to less privacy.

Computers and credit bureaus We live in a mobile society in which the reputations of people are not known by neighbors, grocers, or bankers, but demands for credit grow exponentially. Since business concerns compete with each other to gain customers, they are continually working on methods for extending more credit to more people—especially charge accounts at 18 percent compounded interest. At such interest rates, one cannot say that the system is charitable, but it is extremely convenient and few can resist it.

Businesses cannot be blamed for wanting accurate credit information, but their methods of investigation are often reprehensible. When one credit corporation has files on 45 million Americans and another on 10 million, it is not difficult to see that some of the research could include irrelevancies and inaccuracies. If investigators for one large credit organization have reasons for suspicion about a customer, they interview neighbors, landlords, fellow workers, employers, and the like, picking up all kinds of information and misinformation. According to Miller, the research may even include biased comments from enemies, but the customer is never told what goes into the files. Worse yet is the existence of politically oriented research groups who investigate prospective employees for firms anxious to avoid hiring anyone who might be "troublesome" because of labor union or political ideas.[15] Bias of a similar type appeared when an aid of Senator Russell Long's found himself under investigation by a credit company. In this case, the company was interested not in finding out his credit rating but rather in finding out anything unsavory about the Senator's assistant. He was working to lower the price of

[14]Leslie H. Gelb, "The CIA and the Press," *New Republic*, March 22, 1975, pp. 13–16.
[15]Miller, *op. cit.*, p. 70.

prescription drugs, and the investigation was being paid for by pharmaceutical interests.[16] Insurance companies are also interested in credit ratings, but even more in the insurability of applicants. The result is considerable investigation of personal habits. What are an applicant's drinking habits or sporting activities; and is there anything worth knowing about his or her sex life?

> **You are not required to give information about neighbors and acquaintances to credit organizations. If you answer, avoid repeating petty matters that could prove an embarrassment in later years.**

If great amounts of information must be collected by or for various business concerns, it would seem that every effort should be made to keep them confidential. CBS put the question of confidentiality to the test by creating a fake corporation and writing to credit bureaus for information on a man to whom they said they wished to extend credit. The CBS-created corporation received full reports from half the credit companies, in spite of the companies' assertion that they would not give out information except in bona fide credit cases. Private investigators usually have no trouble gaining access to such information.

Circulation lists   Other files on the public perhaps have no major economic or political consequences, but they do have an extremely high nuisance value. One hardly dares contribute to a charity for fear one's name will be offered up to a host of other charitable organizations. A new subscriber to a specialized magazine is likely to be deluged with subscription offers from other magazines of the same type. A firm based in New York "offers lists of over 500,000 Democratic and Republican contributors, 93,000 doctors who attend conventions, and even 28,000 supporters of the (former) anti-Vietnam War appeals."[17] The price is $22.50. Even the federal government gets into the act. The Federal Aviation Administration sells lists of 650,000 pilots and airmen for $200.

Watching employees   Employees are not only checked upon before hiring but are secretly watched on the job. Sometimes they are listened to by electronic bugs. One company, concerned with leaks of information concerning new products, has placed miniature transmitters inside the toilet-paper rollers in washrooms.[17] Employees of another concern discovered a hidden camera in an air-conditioning duct. Private investigative agencies constantly play up to business managers the advantages of relying on their undercover agents to check upon the loyalty and honesty of employees.

Another area of continued surveillance is that of testing and the use of polygraphs. Most states do not have strict laws about the individuals who work with lie-detecting equipment; consequently much of the checking is done by people of little judgment or insight. A prominent psychiatrist has characterized the use of polygraphs under such circumstances as more of a technique of intimidation than a means for gaining information. Often the questions used by polygraph operators are insulting, frequently probing all the way back into one's childhood and sometimes dealing more with one's sex life than anything else. Packard concludes that the net result is often alienation toward the company one works for and

[16]*Ibid.*, pp. 71–72.
[17]*Ibid.*, p. 82.

Much of the surveillance by industry seems to have the effect of lowering employees' morale and loyalty.

decreasing concern for its success.[18] Along with crass attempts by companies to preserve loyalty and honesty among their employees, there is espionage and counterespionage among rival companies, with each trying to discover the latest new formula or advertising pitch of competitors. The miniature mechanical eyes and ears discussed in the first part of this chapter are used; but attempts are also made to use for industrial espionage some of the very employees whose honesty has been so scrupulously checked out in personality tests and with polygraphs.

SOCIAL RESEARCH AND PRIVACY

As is the case of the Census Bureau, the FBI, or businesses extending credit, social scientists also need large amounts of information. They need to know not only many of the characteristics of the population that are found in Census Bureau and Labor Department reports but also much more. Favorite subjects for research are social-class attitudes and motivations, delinquent subcultures, poverty areas, ethnic groups, new movements and cults, and many other fields not accessible without careful study. In making their investigations, the social scientists are open to criticisms similar to, but not the same as, those leveled against government and business. The goal of their research is different, much of it being pure science or the pursuit of knowledge for its own sake. Often there is also an altruistic motive, that is, a hope for more human understanding of the problems of minorities, the impoverished, the stigmatized, and similarly disadvantaged groups. In the proper

[18]Packard, *op. cit.*, p. 100.

spirit of science, the results of sociological research are made public, which means that the information is available for use by government or business. Consequently, the social scientist is sometimes accused of a number of abominable pursuits, such as reporting on the life-styles of minorities, delinquents, sex deviates, and the like, with the result that these groups become better understood as well as more closely watched by officialdom. Some researchers have been accused of being voyeurs, peeking into the lives of individuals.

The charges cannot be denied entirely, although the intent is a perfectly reasonable one of wanting to understand society and all its component parts, which is the essence of sociology. In the course of seeking such understanding, the typical sociological investigator more or less follows the idea of Max Weber that one must understand empathically, that is, feel one's way into the lives of the groups being researched. The consequence sometimes leads to exactly the opposite kind of criticism of sociological research, especially of those most interested in deviant subcultures—the accusation that deviants are treated kindly whereas society is vilified. Again, the answer to the charge is that the sociologist is trying to learn; and one cannot learn if one passes judgment before starting a study. In fact, most sociologists do not see it as their duty to come up with a verdict even with respect to groups that many people would not deem fit to study.

Criteria of social research If we attempt to put the question of social research into the same framework used previously in the discussion of the right of the people to know about their government as compared with the right of the government to know about the people, we can draw certain parallels. In all cases where social research is a matter of pure science, of pursuing knowledge for its own sake, it is easy to plead the right of ethical neutrality on the part of the researcher—that is, that the researcher's duty is merely to find out, and that the use to which the information is put is the responsibility of others.

Actually, most sociologists are not as neutral in their thinking as such a statement would imply. They take pleasure in the belief that sociological research has been one of several factors that have helped to promote more equality between races, to bring problems of social inequality to light, and probably to generate a more benevolent attitude toward deviates, especially those accused of "crimes without victims." The latter category includes prostitutes, skid-row drunks, gays, drug users, hobos, and vagrants. There is always the possibility that accounts written about such people will reveal their habits, hiding places, and even identities. Therefore, most published accounts use fictitious names of persons and places. Researchers are still faced with a serious problem regarding such confidentiality, however, in that their records could possibly be subpoenaed by the courts.

Attempts to control social research The Department of Health, Education, and Welfare is becoming increasingly involved in the problem of regulating certain kinds of research concerned with human subjects. The regulations insist that medical and behavioral researchers not gain government grants unless they are very careful to give full particulars to subjects about the nature of the research, the benefits to be derived from it, and the possible risks. Some kind of documentation of consent is required.[19] Sociologists are not much concerned about the problem of possible risks, since their research does not involve the hazards that medical

[19]"Protection of Human Subjects," *Federal Register*, vol. 39, no. 105, part II, sec. 46.5, May 30, 1974.

and neurological research sometimes does. There are two regulations, though, that have received less than enthusiastic reception from sociologists. One calls for a guarantee of complete confidentiality to all research subjects. All researchers would like to make such a promise, but as we shall see later, the courts have rendered it impossible. The second problem concerns a full explanation of what the research is attempting to demonstrate.

One of the difficulties this will entail in some types of sociological and psychological research is that full acquaintance of the subject with the intended results may actually influence the subject's response. Experiments sometimes seem to work merely because experimental subjects become interested in them and want them to work. It is also true that many research projects of a social-psychological type depend on a certain degree of subterfuge. Almost everyone is aware of the experiments done by Solomon Asch wherein the subjects were under the impression that they were being tested for their perception of which was the longest of a series of lines. They were permitted to listen on their earphones to the voices of four other people judging the lengths of the lines (all uniformly wrong). The actual experiment was to see whether the subjects would agree with the false statements—a test not of perception but of conformity. Had the subjects been given too much information, the whole purpose of the experiment would have been lost. There are innumerable other cases of social-psychology experiments in which a temporary deception is necessary.

When a type of deception or some kind of psychological shock is involved in an experiment, researchers try to minimize any ill effects or bad feelings. Eliot Aronson, a social psychologist strongly committed to experimental approaches, suggests several rules for such research, the most important being that all subjects should feel free to quit any time they wish. Experimenters should avoid deception whenever possible. When it is used, the reasons for the deception should be carefully explained to the subjects afterward, and they should be reassured that anyone would have been deceived under the circumstances. Otherwise they might feel they had been made to look foolish. Also, no experiment should be undertaken unless the intent is important and the importance is made clear to the subjects.

With respect to the problem of meeting the confidentiality requirements laid down by the Department of Health, Education, and Welfare, the Supreme Court does not recognize the right of complete confidentiality. It is possible that the problem could be solved if HEW were to couple its demands with a regulation protecting full confidentiality of research records under its auspices. Apparently such a policy would be possible; the Census Bureau has its confidentiality protected against the possibility of subpoena. Even such a policy on the part of HEW, however, would apply only to research projects under its sanction, not to all social science research. Some states have provided legal protection against state authorities, but there is no blanket guarantee insofar as the federal government is concerned. It is in this area of protection of sources of information that the researcher faces the same problems as the news reporter, whose duty is also that of giving the public information about what is taking place in and out of government.

THE PROBLEMS OF A FREE PRESS

The real fear for freedom is that the possibilities for surveillance of the people have increased while their access to information has decreased. Part of the problem is rooted in the nature of modern society. As all social scientists point out, the level of complexity of a modern society has grown to such a point that it is very difficult for the lay person to understand or judge public policies. Once there was a kind of equalitarianism about military matters in that one man with a rifle was almost the equal of any other, and anyone could understand the weapons available. Who understands military problems or equipment nowadays; or who has an expert opinion about whether the defense budget should be in the vicinity of $50 billion or $100 billion? The intricacies of economic, environmental, and energy problems are almost as difficult for the public to grasp as are those of defense. Nevertheless, well-informed members of Congress, and well-informed journalists and researchers, can give the public some knowledge of such problems, provided that issues can be adequately covered in the press and on the air. Otherwise the complexities of the present social, political, and industrial order are impossible for the public to grasp. What is worse still, the public cannot even tell whether the government is telling it the truth. Therefore, freedom of information is our only guarantee against both corruption and tyranny.

In light of the ever-increasing need of the public to know, and against a background of threats to that right, the Twentieth Century Fund undertook a study of freedom of the press.[20]

> Recall or try to find a recent case in which officials of the government withheld the truth from the American public but it was brought out by the press. (Try Jack Anderson's column.)

Violations of press freedoms Although the types of violations about which the Twentieth Century Fund study complains occurred before in our history, they occurred with increasing frequency during the period of the Vietnam war. The complaints fall into four major categories: (1) Representatives of the government, law, and military posed as reporters in order to gain access to political meetings, student demonstrations, and antiwar activities; (2) much of the underground press was raided and shut down; (3) there were intimidating and disruptive investigations and threats to the broadcast media; (4) a great increase came about in the use of the questionable right of courts to subpoena the notes, records, and photographs of reporters.

For officers of the law or the military to pose as reporters in order to gain information can eventually make the reporter's investigative tasks impossible. Yet the study documents dozens of cases, involving Army Intelligence, the FBI, and local police departments. So great became the infiltration into student demonstrations by army agents posing as reporters that students no longer trusted newsmen. Several reporters were attacked and some were hurt at demonstrations at Columbia, Chicago, Berkeley, and several other campuses. The duty of the reporter to present the facts to the public, along with representative views of students as well as officialdom, was being undermined.

During the same period there were many raids on small underground newspapers. The underground press was often radical, irritating, even extremist in its pronouncements; but freedom of the press must include the right to disagree, the right to be irritating and antagonizing. There is no better evidence that people are free than for them to have and actually exercise the right to criticize and condemn. In some cases there were violations of pornography laws, but the report suggests

[20]Twentieth Century Fund Task Force, *Press Freedoms under Pressure*, Twentieth Century Fund, New York, 1972.

that the pornography issue was often merely an excuse for raiding political undesirables.

The assault against the television medium will be passed over for the present in order to be covered in more detail later. The fourth complaint of the Twentieth Century Fund study—court subpoenas—links together the problems of sociological investigators and those of the reporters. Subpoenas for records have been used before, but they grew much more common in the 1960s and early 1970s. Along with an increase in the number of subpoenas was an increase in public awareness of the issue and a crescendo of complaint from the press. Typical cases involved orders for reporters to appear in court and testify regarding sources of information that had been gathered only after a promise of complete confidentiality. Often the first news of corruption in public places is based on secret leaks to the press (the Pentagon papers and the Watergate affair, for example), and such leaks could not come about unless the public believed in the integrity and power of the press to protect sources.

A number of reporters have taken upon themselves the responsibility of making their word good to people who have spoken to them in strict confidence. When ordered to appear in court, they have refused to testify. William Farr of the *Los Angeles Times* spent many days in jail and was finally released only because the court was convinced he would never reveal the source of his information regardless of how long he might be held. The most famous case of publication of information the government wished to keep secret was that of the Pentagon papers—7,000 pages of documents about American involvement and tactics in the war in Southeast Asia, leaked by Daniel Ellsberg. If government agents had not robbed the office of Ellsberg's psychiatrist, bringing about the dismissal of the case, Ellsberg would probably have been convicted. Even staunch opponents of the war who sympathized with him most strongly were usually willing to concede that Ellsberg had violated the law and was liable to prosecution. However, the right of the press to publish the documents once they were made available was upheld by a six to three decision of the Supreme Court. Later, as most people will recall, Ellsberg was released because of a mistrial, so that his case was never put to a definitive test. In the Pentagon papers case, the press seemed to be on the winning side.

The Branzburg case   A much less spectacular case, having to do only with refusal to respond to a subpoena from the courts, resulted in a decision unfavorable to the press. Paul M. Branzburg, a reporter for *The Louisville Courier-Journal*, made a confidential investigation of the manufacture of hashish by a group involved in the trade. Obviously, he could not have gained the information without having promised to keep his informants' identities and places of business secret. When county grand juries subpoenaed him, Branzburg refused to testify, appealing instead to the Supreme Court of Kentucky. When the Kentucky Court ruled against him, he turned next to the United States Court of Appeal, which upheld his right to confidentiality of sources. His case, along with two other similar cases, was carried all the way to the Supreme Court. A majority (Justice White plus the four Nixon appointees—Burger, Blackmun, Powell, and Rehnquist) ruled against Branzburg. Justice Douglas dissented, ruling in favor of the absolute right of a reporter to protect sources of information. The other three justices rendered the opinion that cases might exist in which the government would have the right to insist on the breaking of confidence, but only if the government could demonstrate "a compelling and overriding" interest in the information.[21] The majority opinion concluded that only "relevant and material" questions be answered, which protects reporters from questions only vaguely related to the case but gives no real protection to the right of confidentiality.

The previously cited Twentieth Century Fund report concedes that courts have a legitimate right to order questions to be answered if such information would prevent a heinous crime. Hardly anyone would expect a reporter to protect a source if he or she gained knowledge that a public building was about to be bombed or a murder was about to take place. The press position is generally that only such extreme cases should call for the breaking of confidences. Otherwise, the problem of finding the truth becomes much more difficult for both news personnel and researchers.

It cannot be said that all investigations by social scientists or all articles by news reporters are aimed at informing people about the government; the Branzburg case involved reporting on a deviant group. The principle holds, however, that the present court decision weakens the news media in their attempts to keep the public informed; and it also weakens the position of the social researcher engaged in more methodical, long-range studies of the society and its component parts. The decline of campus and racial disorders will probably bring about a decline in the cases of government agents impersonating reporters, but such practices could easily become a problem again in a similar crisis. Moreover, the Branzburg decision could prove crippling to the muckraking type of journalism at all times, crisis or not.

There is also another area of danger that we have so far passed over lightly: the assault against the broadcast industry.

CONTROL OF THE AIRWAVES

In turning to the problem of the airwaves, we are looking at an area of greater complexity than that of the newspapers. Theoretically, there is room for any number of newspapers in the country, representing all possible points of view; in reality, newspapers are limited in number because of the high costs of producing and gathering news. The problem is much greater with television, especially national systems, partly because the costs are even greater, and partly because the number of available channels is limited. Because of the second situation, both radio and television have long been under the supervision of the Federal Communications Commission, the members of which are appointed by the President with the consent of Congress. The Federal Communications Commission has the task of setting down rules for fairness and guidelines on pornography and slander. The Commission also licenses broadcasting and has the power to revoke licenses. Herein lies the dilemma: the existence of only a small number of national broadcasting systems makes possible a type of unfair news monopoly if no regulatory commission exists; but the existence of a federal licensing system puts the government into a position of being the judge of fairness and of potentially allowing it to interfere with freedom of the air.

This basic dilemma is discussed by Harry S. Ashmore in *Fear in the Air.*[22] In all

---

[21] Paul Nejelski and Kurt Finsterbusch, "The Prosecutor and the Researcher: Present and Prospective Variations on the Supreme Court's Branzburg Decision," *Social Problems*, vol. 21, no. 1, pp. 3–21, Summer 1973.

[22] Harry S. Ashmore, *Fear in the Air: Broadcasting and the First Amendment*, W. W. Norton & Co., Inc., New York, 1973.

268 | fairness he admits that the media—press, radio, and television—are all subject to much deserved criticism. In an attempt to maximize profits from advertising, television stations try to make sure that prime listening time goes to programs that will be listened to the most, so that many of the prime-time programs consist only of violence interrupted by advertising. Partly for this reason a Harris Poll in 1972 gave television a rating of "good" by only 17 percent of the public. In defense of the media, though, it must be admitted that special CBS and NBC reports are of much higher intellectual quality, yet such reports are more likely than the violent or fatuous programs to get the channels into trouble. The production of a report called "The Selling of the Pentagon," which was highly critical of the public-relations activities of the military, produced a storm of criticism from government circles. Furthermore, the special reports are very expensive to produce and sometimes represent a financial loss.

Another criticism of the media concerns political fairness. Back in the days of Franklin D. Roosevelt, there was considerable complaint in his administration that the press was almost solidly opposed to most of his liberal policies, and that the same was true of a majority of radio stations; but there were no open or even veiled threats made by the White House. During the Nixon administration, the claim was made that the media had moved over to the politically liberal side and were being unfair to a conservative president. Richard Salant, president of CBS news, occasionally spoke up to document the accuracy of the material presented on the air, arguing that rules of fairness were not being violated, and also that it was the duty of the media to be critical.

Another aspect of the political problem involved in broadcasting is that the national channels, in the very nature of things, give large amounts of free coverage to the President, regardless of his political party, programs, or beliefs. In fact, some people regard as too great the power of the President to broadcast so many messages to the people. The opposite party calls for, and sometimes receives, free time to reply. Thus, there are, and always have been, conflicting arguments over the issue of fairness; but the fear in the air about which Ashmore speaks is the fear that the argument might be resolved solidly on the side of the government. The fear is that the licensing power might be used to intimidate the television media. As a matter of fact, soon after former Vice President Agnew made one of his severest attacks on the *Washington Post*, a group of friends and former business associates of President Nixon attempted to get the license to run the stations in Jacksonville and Miami that belong to the *Washington Post*.

> They only dropped out after the *Post* had to spend an awful lot of money getting ready, and agreed to reimburse the contestants for their costs—which, as Joe Alsop said, is like paying a wolf's dental bill after he bites you.[23]

Harry Ashmore points out that the power of the government to intimidate consists of the threat to revoke licenses, or to take some kind of action under antitrust law. He also states that one newspaper was threatened by the Internal Revenue Service on a "spurious, politically motivated" charge.[24]

Redressing the balance Cases of attempts to intimidate the press or media are enough to convince us that the mere setting up of a federal commission with

[23]Richard Salant quoted in Harry S. Ashmore, *op. cit.*, p. 116.
[24]*Ibid.*, p. 116.

regulatory powers is not enough to guarantee First Amendment protections. Ashmore suggests for the press and television a strategy of defense that has also been suggested by social-science researchers for their field. There should be a strengthening of associations for protection against encroachments on freedom, but such associations should also formulate their own codes of ethics. For the news media, a national news council could hear complaints against the news media from the public and also protect journalists unfairly brought under fire. The effect could be that of improving the quality of reporting in all media. Neither the press, radio, television, or research are flawless; but they are in danger if governmental agencies are in a strong position to pass judgment upon them. Such an association as a national news council or a similar type of national research council would not be in a position to make legally binding decisions, but they would be able to spell out what they thought was proper conduct in their fields and would thereby be in a stronger position to defend their position.

In the light of new technology and possibilities for surveillance over the people mentioned in the first part of this chapter, there can be no feeling of absolute certainty that Big Brother will not be watching us. Possibly the future will be a period of government fairness, with little attempt by the government to infringe upon citizen rights; but it may not be. Safety lies in first putting our house in order and then preparing to defend it by all legal means.

The next time you hear a good NBC or CBS report, write to the channel that aired the program to express your support.

SUGGESTED READINGS

Harry S. Ashmore: *Fear in the Air: Broadcasting and the First Amendment*, W. W. Norton & Co., Inc., New York, 1973. Written at a time of worry over veiled threats from the Nixon administration aimed at the television networks, this book explores the basic problem of maintaining both freedom and responsibility in broadcasting. Many conversations between government and network officials are presented.

Arthur R. Miller: *The Assault on Privacy: Computers, Data Banks, and Dossiers*, University of Michigan Press, Ann Arbor, 1971. Miller is particularly concerned with the cumulative effect of data banks on individual freedom and in creating a climate of guardedness and fear. The first chapter also deals with surveillance equipment and the possible utilization of computers.

Vance Packard: *The Naked Society*, David McKay Company, Inc., New York, 1964. Packard's book, although less recent than the others, is alert to all the same problems, particularly the area of business surveillance. Much anecdotal data regarding attempts to ferret out information on prospective employees is included, especially regarding sex lives.

Twentieth Century Fund Task Force: *Press Freedoms under Pressure*, Twentieth Century Fund, New York, 1972. This work is concerned both with the rights of journalists to do honest reporting and with the freedom of the press to criticize government. Recounts the story of the assault on the press by Spiro Agnew, of fears generated by the attack, and of the dangers of discrediting the media's source of information.

UNESCO, "Human Rights and the Threat to Privacy," *UNESCO Courier*, July 1973. The entire issue is devoted to the threat to privacy. Discusses attempts by several Western nations to deal with the problems of cumulative data files and the right of the individual to examine his files, as well as the increasingly secret devices of surveillance.

| **QUESTIONS**

1 What ingenious devices of surveillance are in common use today?

2 What are the moral issues and political dangers involved in tests that attempt to probe one's mind?

3 What are the dangers inherent in permitting army intelligence to accumulate files on civilians and members of Congress?

4 What are the dangers of rapidly accumulating information files on individuals, whether the files are held by business organizations or by the government?

5 Why are social researchers and journalists so insistent on the right to keep their sources of information confidential?

6 Explain a major dilemma of television: why licensing is needed but how it gives dangerous power to the government.

III
DEVIANT
BEHAVIOR

Every society has its values and its ideas of right and wrong. It is true that in a rapidly changing society such normative values change, and that societal complexity prevents them from being the same for all segments of society. Increasingly in modern Western cultures, many types of behavior once considered sufficiently deviant to be of concern to the public and to law-enforcement authorities are looked upon as cultural alternatives—perfectly permissible variations in life-style. For this reason, sex behavior is much less subject to legal control than in the past, and laws that invade the privacy of the bedroom are looked upon as antiquated.

For a short period of time in American history, the use of alcohol was outlawed. Norms have changed, and the use of alcohol, within limits, is considered quite acceptable. When other types of drugs are mentioned, more opposition arises. Ideas vary from time to time and from group to group about what drugs are harmful and to what degree, but there is general agreement that misuse of drugs, especially the most dangerous and addictive drugs, is of concern to the total society.

Even more uniformity of opinion exists within the society regarding the types of crime listed in the Uniform Crime Reports, such as burglary and theft, murder, rape, assault, and embezzlement. Even in this area, though, there are usually deviant subcultures that give a modicum of support to their own members, finding rationalizations for their acts. On a more dangerous level are well-paying organizations of crime, living as parasites on the public, and entering and corrupting fields of legitimate business, labor, and governments. Finally, there exist areas of white-collar crime, little noted except when major scandals develop in government, finance, or industry but nevertheless taking an enormous economic toll, while also undermining morale and faith in the legitimacy of social institutions.

WHAT IS NEW

Sociological theory would lead us to expect more deviance in an urban, highly mobile society than in an older, more stable, agrarian system. Certainly, if all the behavior the older society regarded as deviant is to be included, there is no question that deviance is on the increase. However, since each age defines by its own norms what is considered deviant, we shall concentrate only on certain categories—drug abuse, crime against property, violent crimes, white-collar crimes, and organized crime. In all these areas there is something new. Narcotics addiction was mainly a problem in the slums of certain major cities for most of the period from 1914 until about 1960. Now it has spread throughout society. At the same time, the use of marijuana, a much less dangerous product but one to be looked upon with caution, has become widespread and has created a great value conflict over law and law enforcement. The product frequently overlooked in discussions of drug problems—alcohol—is being used in larger and larger amounts, posing a threat to health and well-being in millions of cases.

In the field of crime, although statistics are faulty, all indications are that the rate is increasing; and evidence will be presented to show that the underworld is better organized now than in the past. At the same time, the machinery of justice is bogged down by a greater burden of cases than it is equipped to handle. Consequently, legal delays and unpredictable treatment of cases have become sources of normative strain as well as contributory causes for the failure of our system to reform the law violators.

MEETING THE CRITERIA OF SOCIAL PROBLEMS

Not all forms of deviance are social problems, and certainly not all kinds can be discussed in a work of this length. The discussion will therefore be limited mainly to types of deviance that are considered social problems almost by definition, that is, the types of behavior defined by law as criminalistic and contrary to our legal norms. Other types of behavior will also be included, such as misuse of alcohol and drugs, because such behavior patterns have social consequences, causing accidents, economic loss, and grief for families; they are widespread and are generally looked upon as contrary to the norms.

Even more obvious as social problems are crimes of violence and crimes against property. Organized crime poses an even greater threat, taking a greater economic bite and threatening to corrupt the institutions of the society. Finally, certain types of white-collar crimes have emerged recently as the greatest threat of all. The Watergate affair, with all its ramifications, warned of a type of corruption that could destroy our system of government right at its heart.

INTERRELATIONSHIPS

Social change has made it possible to live a life of relative idleness, without clearly defined norms. The strongly competitive ethic of earlier days does not seem so relevant as it once did, and a retreat from the struggle becomes more common. Unfortunately, such an attitude seems to be one of the causes of a search for new "kicks," usually only through liquor and marijuana, but in many cases through extremely dangerous drugs.

Social change has also made the world a much more anonymous place than it once was, and the restraints of neighborhood and community are greatly reduced. The consequence is that society must depend more exclusively upon formal police power to enforce its laws and less upon primary-group controls and possible social ostracism. Like all other problems, deviant behavior is closely related to other aspects of society.

PERSPECTIVES ON DEVIANCE

Deviance is related to social change, to value conflict, and to anomie. Anomie, as the word is used by Robert Merton, refers to norms that conflict with each other and leave the individual in a normative dilemma. Merton's theory of deviant behavior, referred to briefly in the Introduction, contends that societies prescribe proper goals for individual striving and proper means for achieving such goals. In American society the proper goal is generally material success. However, people do not have equal access to success goals, partly beacuse of varying social backgrounds, abilities, financial starts in life, and encounters with discrimination. Consequently, some people resort to illegal means to attain the success goals admired by the society. Others give up and become "retreatists"—a term Merton originally used for tramps and vagrants, but which seems highly applicable to cases of drug addiction as well. Merton has one other deviant category in his theory—rebellion. By rebellion he originally referred to political rebels such as Communists and Fascists, but his term is also very applicable to mere "rebels without a cause"—including many destructive and belligerent juvenile gangs.

Another perspective on deviance involves looking at it as a type of learned behavior. It is the point of view of sociology and of the social sciences in general that human nature is causative, subject to rules of cause and effect, and that nearly all kinds of crime can be accounted for in environmental terms. For this reason the ideas of Edwin Sutherland are given considerable prominence. Sutherland shows how different types of crime are learned under different circumstances; he says that they can be best explained as learnings, not as the results of particular personality types, races, or ethnic groups. Impoverished urban areas are associated with burglary, petty theft, fighting, and drug use. Business organizations, on the other hand, often make possible the learning of an entirely different type of crime, which Sutherland calls white-collar crime. Examples of white-collar crime are tax violations, disguising records, unfair weights and measures, and false advertising. It can be seen very readily that such types of crime are learned, and they are learned under completely different circumstances from those of burglary and petty theft.

The idea of crime as learned behavior brings us to a final perspective on deviant behavior: it would seem that the worst way to deal with crime would be to put all criminals into confinement together where each could learn from the other. Yet this is what we do, and it constitutes one of the great dilemmas of punishment and one of the reasons why the problems of law enforcement and justice are included along with role failure and deviance.

The search for euphoria through the use of dangerous drugs is definitely classified as deviant behavior. But there are some agents of euphoria whose use is permitted, and societies differ in the types of drugs they prohibit and the degree of penalty imposed for violation of the norms. Under what conditions can such a very common drug as alcohol be used fairly safely, and under what conditions does it produce alcoholism? Why is heavy use of any type of drug seen as a societal threat? Why do governments not simply take the attitude that one's retreat into alcoholism or addiction is his own problem? How is the common good involved?

How has the drug problem changed over the years in America in legality, amount of use, and type of user? What situations seem to produce the highest incidence of illegal drug use? Are the various illegal drugs now in use properly classified as to their degree of danger? Is the present prohibition of marijuana almost the same thing as the prohibition of alcohol in the days of the Eighteenth Amendment? What are the pros and cons of legalizing marijuana? There is very great diversity of opinion on the issue of marijuana, but practically none on the harder drugs. Why, then, are we losing the battle against heroin? What actions are being taken now, and what new philosophies and proposals are coming about?

A state of euphoria is a feeling of unusual well being or elation that transports the individual to a realm of temporary freedom from the cares of everyday life. Evidence indicates that euphoric experience is sought much more in fast-moving, modern society than it was in previous generations. Sometimes the euphoria is mild—a mere relaxation, a heightened conviviality, or a pleasant dream. Sometimes the euphoria seems as beautiful as the passions of love or the mystic experience of religious ecstasy, but sometimes it descends to an ugly state bordering on paranoia.

Certain societies have developed ceremonies to induce strange states of consciousness in their followers or have accomplished the flight from the everyday world of reality through the heavy use of alcohol or psychoactive drugs. The ceremonies have had the function of rousing fighting blood, of releasing shamanistic powers by which the medicine man can cure disease, or of inducing spiritual visions in young men being initiated into manhood. In nearly all cases, however, the use of the agents of euphoria has been limited by social custom and ritual. Even tribes that have seen strange states of consciousness as sources of power have also seen them as sources of danger.

RITUAL CONTROL

Alcohol and other drugs have been used for ritual purposes by both primitive and advanced societies. Wine has long had a social and even a semireligious function, not only in the rites of Dionysus but even in the ritual observances of many Christians and Jews. Cannabis, from which marijuana is derived, was once considered a sacred plant, with magical and medicinal powers. Hallucinatory mushrooms of Mexico and northern South America have had sacred ritual uses for many Indian tribes.[1] Some American Indian tribes required a vision quest of their young men as part of the transition to manhood. For many the vision quest was accomplished by long periods of deprivation and even the sacrifice of a finger by the blow of a tomahawk. The South American Jívaro accomplished the vision quest by using drugs so strong that they caused convulsions and terrifying hallucinations; the drugs were used to contact the spirit world, not merely for pleasure.

Peyote and the Native American Church Peyote has been used by certain American Indian tribes for centuries. The use was very limited, however, and did not spread rapidly from tribe to tribe until the decline of old tribal ways. In the late nineteenth century the Ghost Dance developed as an expressive movement for rekindling Indian loyalty to their own culture, and later the peyote-using Native American Church served the same purpose. The rationalization for peyote use was that God had given peyote to the Indians to compensate for their heavy losses at the hands of the white man.

Paul Radin[2] relates a tale told by an Indian who joined the peyote cult. He was a Winnebago of youth, vigor, and good looks, but not happy even though he had

[1]John M. Allegro of the University of Manchester, England, equates the classical Nectar of the Gods and Indian *soma* with the psychedelic mushroom. He also contends there was a connection between early Christianity and certain mystery cults, which found both mystery and ecstasy in the sacred mushroom, John M. Allegro, *The Sacred Mushroom and the Cross*, Doubleday & Company, Inc., Garden City, N.Y., 1970.
[2]Paul Radin, *The Autobiography of a Winnebago Indian*, University of California Publications in American Anthropology and Ethnology, no. 16, University of California Press, Berkeley, 1920, pp. 48–64. Reprinted in Philip K. Boch, *Culture Shock*, Alfred A. Knopf, Inc., New York, 1970, pp. 316–326.

access to all the women he desired. He was told by some relatives who had joined the cult that a life devoted to the pursuit of women was wrong. He must learn, they said, to possess only one woman and give up his tobacco and medicine pouch and listen only to Earthmaker (God), whom he would learn about at the peyote ceremonies. Eventually he consented to listen to the strange god, as a man confused between two cultures will sometimes do. He went to the ceremonies, took the peyote, had strange feelings and visions (along with nausea), until at last:

> As I prayed I was aware of something above me and there he was; Earthmaker to whom I was praying; he it was. That which is called the soul, that is it, that is what one calls Earthmaker. Now this is what I felt and saw. The one called Earthmaker is a spirit, and that is what I felt and saw. All of us sitting there, we had all together one spirit and soul. That is what I learned.

From that day on, the young Winnebago settled down to married life and attended the Native American Church services once a week. Peyote, being less potent than the mescaline derived from it and being ritually controlled and difficult to take, did not become mentally disorganizing to any serious degree. It was easily adapted to a culture that had long emphasized a vision quest.

Alcohol and group controls Studies in the United States on the subject of alcoholism show some of the results of group controls. Among Orthodox Jews, who permit the use of wine in ceremonies, alcoholism is extremely rare. Alcohol is apparently strongly associated with religious ritual and only with religious ritual. Jewish people who defy the norms probably find some other means. Among Mormons, who decry any use of alcohol, the rate of drinking is very low. However, for those few Mormons who do drink, the possibilities of drinking to excess are considerable. Alcohol for these people is apparently a means of defying authority, and when so used, it seems to be more dangerous than when used on ritual and social occasions. In some respects the prevailing norms of America come some-where between those of the Orthodox Jews and the Mormons. Liquor is not good enough to be used as part of a religious ceremony. It is seen as bad enough to be frowned upon but not really proscribed. This is probably one of the several reasons why the rate of alcoholism in the United States is higher than in most countries.[3]

Conditions of failure of group controls When the group that defines norms about alcohol is unsure of itself, the possibility of alcoholism rises. It would be reassuring to conclude that there would be no alcohol problems for a society that trains its people in the "proper" use of alcohol. This is probably an oversimplification of the case. In Italy it is reported that a pattern of family drinking of wine seems to produce very few problem drinkers. In France, the same pattern—even more permissive—seems to result in a high rate of alcoholism. One reason for the difficulty is that in parts of rural France wine is related to manhood and virility and good health.[4] Apparently alcohol has dangers even in a society that does not create an urge to use it as a symbol of protest or liberation.

In a society with little primary-group control or strong traditional ties and with

---

[3]Seldon Bacon, "Social Settings Conducive to Alcoholism: A Sociological Approach to a Medical Problem," *Journal of the American Medical Association*, vol. 165, pp. 171–181, May 1957.
[4]Barbara Galliton Anderson, "How French Children Learn to Drink," *Transaction*, vol. 5, pp. 20–22, June 1968.

very little meaningful ritual, old patterns of behavior are vulnerable to rapid change. Modern America also has the problem of normative confusion, value conflict, discontentment and protest—all the unsettling conditions discussed so far as part of the troubled land. Many people try vigorously to work at the problems that beset their society; others follow their own pursuits in a manner as close to old cultural patterns as possible. Many others, however, find normative confusion an excuse for a certain amount of normative rejection. In a society with a fairly well defined habit of using alcohol to show independent status (and the older generation has certainly done this), it is not surprising that a new symbol of independent status—marijuana—should be taken up rather readily. Unfortunately, for many the drug experience does not stop with marijuana.

THE LAND OF THE LOTUS EATERS

In Homeric legend, Ulysses, on his way home from Troy, had to take his ships and crew through many perils, including the Land of the Lotus Eaters. In that peaceful and dreamy land the people lived on the blossoms of the lotus tree, which had a blissful narcotic effect and kept them in a state of perpetual sleep or near sleep. The lotus eaters gave some of their honey-sweet blossoms to two of Ulysses' crewmen. The allure was too strong for their willpower, and they wished to stay and dream their lives away. To stout Ulysses, determined to return to his kingdom and his wife and son, the lotus blossom was a trap to be avoided. He had his lotus-eating crewmen seized and put back on the ship.

Ulysses in the story is determined and consistent. In some respects our society resembles Ulysses in trying to keep people away from the influence of drugs, but not doing so consistently. Some drugs are approved and others are not; some uses are approved and others are not. Some people like to gormandize on the forbidden fruit, and others like only a taste. What are the appeals of the lotus blossom?

The functions of drugs   As has already been suggested by cross-cultural examples, the functions of drugs and alcohol are various. To the Native American Church the function is largely magicoreligious. For less exotic cultures, wine also often has a religious ceremonial function. Bernard Barber[5] names other functions of drugs besides the ones already listed, but several are very similar to the present use of the concept of euphoria.

Some types of drugs are believed by their users to have an esthetic function. The peyote cult discovered new ceremonial dances and new music under the influence of peyote. Rock musicians are famous for their flirtation with such drugs as LSD and marijuana. Coleridge and DeQuincy both smoked opium but complained that although it stretched the imagination it made the completion of ideas extremely difficult.

Certain types of drugs have been considered aphrodisiacs, but if they have worked for the purpose of sexual arousal, it has probably been for the same reason that placebos (pills without substance given to hypochondriacs) seem to work. People who believe in magic can make themselves think it works. The other reason some drugs might work as aphrodisiacs is that they lower inhibitions. Actually, long, heavy use of any of them eventually lowers sexual performance and even desire.

[5]Bernard Barber, *Drugs and Society*, The Russell Sage Foundation, New York, 1967.

The admittedly useful purpose of many kinds of drugs is medicinal, a fact that gives the word drug two different meanings. This discussion is concerned with medical drugs only in cases where their improper use may produce some of the same health hazards as illegal drugs—possible chromosome damage or prenatal damage, or a tendency toward addiction. The other relationship between the two meanings of drugs is that some of the present illegal products were originally considered therapeutic, for example, marijuana, opium, and LSD.

Barber uses the term "ego-disrupting" to describe another function of drugs. Their effects take one away from the usual routines, or "out of the rut." Alcohol is used often for this purpose. The idea expressed by certain popular musicians, "step outside your mind," gives an exaggerated version of the same function.

Psychological support is a similar function, but it can be extended beyond the ego-disrupting function to include tranquilizers and energizers. Under this heading could also be included the drugs used for calming the hyperactive child.

There are a few cases in which drugs have been used for political reasons. During World War II the Japanese encouraged the use of opium in China. There is shrewd reasoning behind the policy of making lotus eaters of one's enemy. There is even a suspicion in American society that some lower-class boys' gangs are not pursued too energetically if they are on drugs. The drug crowd is often more quiet than the energetic gang engaged in interneighborhood fights. The peyote cult was not deliberately started by white Americans, but it served the purpose of quieting whatever aspirations for resistance still existed in Indian America.

All these are rather obvious functions of drugs and/or alcohol. There are other functions, or other ways of looking upon the same functions: for relaxation, kicks, excitement, or the drowning of sorrows. All these are included under the idea of euphoria.

The semantics of drug use   Before asking whether or not America is a land of lotus eaters, it is time to clear up some confusion in definitions. Alcohol and drugs have not been categorically separated because it has seemed unnecessary to draw much distinction between them. Dr. Joel Fort, consultant to the World Health Organization, gives an analysis that helps to clarify definitions and to justify the grouping of agents of euphoria used in this chapter.[6] He shows that the semantics of drug use has a strong effect on popular ideas about their acceptability. For example, the advocates of LSD have wanted to call it mind expanding, implying that it does something useful; its opponents refer to it as hallucinogenic or even psychotomimetic—imitating states of psychosis. The idea of classifying alcohol with drugs is offensive to many people who use alcohol but think they would never use anything that could be called a drug. The word drug has the fault of being an omnibus term including all the functions mentioned above and probably many more.

Fort suggests that the words "mind-altering drugs" should apply to a whole range of agents, including sedatives, stimulants, tranquilizers, LSD, narcotics, marijuana, alcohol, and, to a degree even nicotine and caffein. More frequently, though, classification in the public mind is made on the basis of good and bad, or legal and illegal. Both such pairs of terms imply value judgments that not all societies agree with. During the days of the Eighteenth Amendment alcohol was

[6]"The Semantics and Logic of the Drug Scene," in Richard E. Horman and Allan M. Fox (eds.), *Drug Awareness: Key Documents on LSD, Marijuana and the Drug Culture*, Avon Books Division, The Hearst Corporation, New York, 1970, pp. 87–98.

The ego-disrupting function of drugs, a dangerous road to ecstasy, followed by oblivion and despair.

illegal and bad; now it is legal and almost elevated to the plane of goodness, in spite of the serious alcoholism problem in the United States. In countries of Moslem influence and also in India, on the other hand, alcohol is both illegal and bad. Marijuana use is generally illegal, too, but in some countries it is not condemned as strongly as alcohol.

The semantics of drug use should lead to some basis for comparing drugs in terms of types of effects. In medical terminology there are such descriptions and they are fairly precise. "Tolerance," "dependence," "addiction," and "drug abuse" are all part of the necessary vocabulary. Tolerance implies increasing use of a drug in order to produce the same degree of "highness."[7] "Addiction," or physical dependence, in addition to tolerance includes withdrawal pains and sickness when use of the drug is terminated. Psychological dependence is the feeling that a drug is necessary to "make life worthwhile" or to overcome feelings of weakness, timidity, or depression, or to bolster the self-image. Drug abuse can be defined as "excessive use of a drug or substance to the point that it interferes with the individual's social or vocational adjustment or his health."[8] "Narcotic" is generally used to apply to dangerous and illegal drugs, although in medical use it refers to pain-relieving drugs, including opium and its derivatives (morphine and heroin) and certain synthetics with a similar effect. Dangerous drugs, in federal and most state laws, also include barbiturates and amphetamines, although both have a legal medicinal use.

[7] *Ibid.*, pp. 88–90.
[8] *Ibid.*, p. 90.

Attitude survey: many studies of the use of drugs on campus have been made, but they seldom ask why. It would be interesting, although a little difficult, to probe this question. The easiest way would be an alternative choice question. What has influenced you—friends? resentments? need for kicks? a feeling of meaninglessness in life? mere curiosity? and other choices suggested by the class.

283

MEDICAL MISUSE OF DRUGS

Beginning in the 1940s with the development of sulfa and other so-called wonder drugs, and later with the development of psychoactive drugs to change mental states, there has been an increasing dependence on drug therapy for all kinds of ills, both physical and mental. Psychoactive drugs are prescribed for most mental patients, for many school children who are behavior problems, for elderly patients of nursing homes, and for prisoners. Often the use of such drugs is simply to keep people quiet so that their custodial care is easier. For others who feel considerable amounts of psychic stress and tension, barbiturates are prescribed by the millions. A philosophy seems to prevail that there are medical solutions to all problems, so that rather than face the outside world, we need only take a pill to change our inner state of mind. But as two researchers of the problem say, people who are incapable of psychic stress may become mere robots. "Many persons maintained on large doses of the antipsychotic drugs known as phenothiazines do in fact so behave, and can only be described as having been 'zombified.' "[9] They add that inadequately tested drugs are often prescribed. As in the case of many drugs being used by illegal drug abusers, no one knows what the long-range results will be. Two tranquilizers long given to elderly patients led eventually to a central nervous system disorder called tardive dyskinesia, distorting the patients' features and posture, causing spasms of hands and fingers, and rendering some of them unable to walk. The alarming part of the story is that this is just one example among many psychoactive drugs that have produced unforeseen and highly unfavorable results. Who knows what will be the long-range results of drugs administered to hyperactive children?[10]

DIMENSIONS OF THE DRUG PROBLEM

The illegal use of drugs is nothing new, but the amount of drug abuse sometimes shows dramatic increase. In the 1960s, marijuana, which had previously been used very little in the United States, suddenly took on fadlike dimensions among college students, and then among high school students and noncollege youths. LSD, when newly discovered, became the focus of a drug cult for a while. Heroin addiction, which involved perhaps 60,000 people in 1960, rose to about 700,000 by the end of the decade, largely in poverty areas of the great cities. Meantime, use of the old, legal drug, alcohol, continued to climb. How has the drug problem developed and grown?

A brief history Despite the statement that the search for euphoria seems contrary to American values, alcohol and drugs have long been around. Our ancestors in

---

[9]Arnold Bernstein and Henry L. Lennard, "Drugs, Doctors, and Junkies," *Society*, vol. 10, p. 16, May-June 1973.
[10]*Ibid.*, pp. 24–25.

colonial America included large numbers of heavy drinkers. The West was a brawling region where whisky was consumed in large quantities. There seem to have been more abstainers in earlier days than now, but those who drank were even heavier drinkers. Our ancestors thought ill of the Indians but not of their tobacco, which they chewed, snuffed, and smoked to their hearts' content (at one time both Turkey and Persia punished tobacco smoking by the death penalty).[11]

There were cases of the use of opiates in the early nineteenth century, and morphine became common during the Civil War. Many soldiers who had had morphine administered to them as a pain-killer built up a tolerance for the drug and became addicted to it so badly that morphine addiction was sometimes called the soldiers' disease. Morphine was also used in many patent medicines and soothing syrups for babies. Late in the century opium smoking became a fad in the underworld, but the use of opium and its derivatives was coming under increasing criticism from the medical profession.[12]

Opposition to narcotics led to the passing of the Harrison Act in 1914. The Harrison Act, along with court interpretations and amendments, made most drug use illegal and largely an underworld practice. A few years later the Eighteenth Amendment was passed, outlawing the use of alcohol and trying to place the United States on a road to extraordinary purity. The failure to enforce the Eighteenth Amendment, and the enormous problem of bootlegging that it created, eventually led to its repeal. During the days of Prohibition, many people of the respectable world never gave up the desire for a drink or the temptation to patronize the criminal world to get it. In contrast, the narcotics subculture sank further below the level of respectable society, and marijuana was classed as evil along with heroin. Apparently many of the old users of morphine managed to break the habit and later began to die off. Narcotics were confined increasingly to a subculture of the outcast and despised, except for a slight increase among juveniles after World War II. For many years the number of hard-narcotics addicts stabilized at about 60,000, but in the 1960s the number began to increase. The more dramatic increase in drug use, however, was in the new psychedelic drugs and in marijuana. Much less obvious was a steady increase in the use of drugs that had medical utility but could easily be abused. Amphetamines, often prescribed for weight reduction but capable of building extreme psychological dependence, are produced at a rate of 8 billion pills per year, according to some estimates.[13]

In the United States today more than 20 million people use sleeping pills, more than 10 million use amphetamines, and about 50 million use tranquilizers.[14] Of the users of amphetamines and barbiturates, about 400,000 are excessive users. In the 1960s, an estimated 20 to 40 percent of college students at least experimented with marijuana and about 5 percent with LSD.[15] Although practically all statistics are estimates, they are in fairly close agreement with respect to the extent of the drug problem. New York City reports that 8 percent of all persons sent to penal institutions from 1956 to 1965 had an admitted drug history (mainly heroin). By

[11]Stanley F. Yolles, Director of the National Institute of Mental Health, "The Problem—an Overview," *Narcotics Addiction and Drug Abuse*, U.S. Government Printing Office, Washington, D.C., 1969, p. 46. Hearings before the Special Subcommittee on Alcoholism and Narcotics of the Committee on Labor and Public Welfare, United States Senate.
[12]John A. Clausen, "Drug Addiction," in Robert K. Merton and Robert A. Nisbet (eds.), *Contemporary Social Problems*, Harcourt Brace Jovanovich, Inc., New York, 1966, pp. 199–202.
[13]"Slowdown for Pep Pills," *Newsweek*, p. 77, August 17, 1970.
[14]Kenneth L. Jones et al., *Drugs, Alcohol, and Tobacco*, Canfield Press, San Francisco, 1970, p. 16.
[15]Senator Ralph Yarborough, in *Narcotics Addiction and Drug Abuse, op. cit.*, p. 46.

A major problem finally admitted by the military, sometimes taking more lives than combat, and requiring long and uncertain rehabilitation.

1969, the comparable figure was 40 percent.[16] In Washington, D.C., where rates of drug use and crime are unusually high, the chief of police estimates that 80 to 85 percent of crimes against property are the result of a need to support addiction.[17]

Drugs in the military service Not much outcry was raised against the Civil War veterans who used morphine, but considerable outrage has been expressed over the much-less-serious problem of marijuana use. The first public incident arose when it became known that many soldiers stationed in the Panama Canal Zone in the 1920s were getting high on marijuana. Two commissions were appointed to investigate, one in 1925 and the other in 1931. Both concluded that marijuana was "not habit forming in the sense in which the term is applied to alcohol, opium, cocaine, etc." They also concluded that "delinquencies due to marijuana smoking which result in trial by military court are negligible in number when compared with delinquencies resulting from the use of alcoholic drinks. . . ."[18] The public would not believe the reports any more then than now.

Marijuana was smoked to some extent in Korea but made few headlines. In Vietnam, where the drug was readily available and extremely cheap, it was used by large numbers, probably about 35 percent, of servicemen. Soldiers reported that besides the experience of a high, lighting up helped to overcome fear at some times and boredom at others.[19] As always among military men stationed abroad, the ordinary group controls of homelife were not at work. The soldiers also resented their lot, and resentment lowers one's resistance to deviant behavior. Heroin was also readily available in Vietnam and led to addiction among some of the veterans, variously estimated at from 1 to 3 percent.

[16]Robert W. Winslow (ed.), *Crime in a Free Society: Selections from the Presidential Commission on Law Enforcement and the Administration of Justice*, Dickenson Publishing Company, Belmont, Calif., 1968, p. 234.
[17]Phillip Whitten and Ian Robertson, "A Way to Control Heroin Addiction," *Boston Globe Magazine*, May 21, 1972.
[18]Allen Geller and Maxwell Boas, *The Drug Beat*, McGraw-Hill Book Company, New York, 1971, pp. 146 and 147.
[19]*Ibid.*, p. 148.

If such an organization is available and will permit visiting, visit a chapter of Alcoholics Anonymous or Narcotics Anonymous. They make an informative study in the importance of group support.

The prevalence of alcoholism   With the national concern about drug abuse, it is easy to forget the older problem of alcoholism. People are seldom physically destroyed with such dramatic suddenness by alcohol as by some types of narcotics, but it is still true that more people suffer from alcoholism than from the results of other drugs. According to Joel Fort, some of the major long-term effects of heavy alcohol use include swelling of the brain, damage to muscle, and lowered ability of the body to resist infection. He adds that alcohol accounts for "11 million accidental injuries each year; 40% of the admissions to mental hospitals; 50% of arrests; and a suicide rate for alcoholics 58 times that of non-alcoholics."[20]

Alcohol draws less attention as a problem than would other drugs with such a record. Part of the reason, no doubt, is a reaction against the antialcohol campaign that led to the unsuccessful Eighteenth Amendment. The campaign insisted on total prohibition and depicted drinkers as mainly skid-row bums. Actually, excessive alcohol use is very common among business and professional people. Another reason alcohol receives much more kindly treatment in the press than do other drugs is that an extremely profitable industry busily promotes its use, helping to make it seem attractive and fashionable. Finally, very large numbers of people use alcohol only in moderation and with little or no harm. Nevertheless, most estimates place the number of problem drinkers in our society at about ten million. The consumption of alcohol is increasing rapidly, as shown in the graph on page 287, based on data from the Census Bureau.

One difficulty with alcohol that has not received enough attention is that it can produce unforeseen results when used in combination with other drugs. People using barbiturates should avoid alcohol. The rock singer Janis Joplin took both "downers" and alcohol, which finally depressed bodily functions to the point of causing her death. Other combinations show no immediate result but can be fatal in the long run. A study reported by HEW shows a serious multiplication effect of the combined use of alcohol and tobacco.[21] Heavy cigarette smoking was found to produce 2.43 times as high a rate of cancer of the mouth and throat as that reported for nonsmokers; moderate to heavy drinkers showed 2.3 times the rate as that of nondrinkers; but those who both smoked heavily and used moderate amounts of alcohol had 15.5 times as high a rate of cancer as those who neither smoked nor drank.

EXPLANATIONS OF DRUG USE

Until ten or fifteen years ago it was common to explain drug abuse as the consequence of an "inadequate personality,"[22] stemming from a deprived or poorly structured home background. The more the subject is studied, the less adequate such an explanation appears to be, especially if we include the milder drugs such as alcohol and marijuana. The largest number of abstainers from alcohol (62 percent) was found among the people with less than an

[20]Joel Fort, *Alcohol: Our Biggest Drug Problem*, McGraw-Hill Book Company, New York, 1973, p. vii.
[21]"Alcohol, Youth, Money, and Cancer," *Science News*, vol. 106, p. 20, July 20, 1974.
[22]D. P. Ausubel, *Drug Addiction*, Random House, Inc., New York, 1958, p. 44.

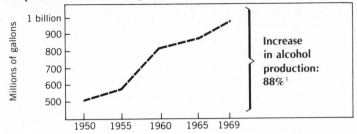

U.S. production of distilled spirits, 1950–1969

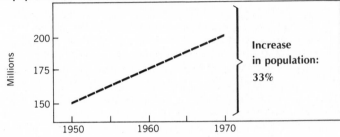

U.S. population, 1950–1970

¹Does not include beer or imported spirits figures

eighth-grade education; the largest proportion of heavy drinkers (13 percent) was among those with a postgraduate education.[23] Marijuana use in recent years has been highest among college students, a group not generally regarded as consisting of inadequate personalities.

When we turn to heroin addiction, it is true that the rate is overwhelmingly greater among people reared in the most deprived areas of our big cities. It has often been said that the addicts are "double failures," or "retreatists," turning to drugs because of failure to earn status either in the legitimate world or in the society of delinquency and crime. Harvey Feldman's[24] research over a period of years in a part of New York he calls by the fictional name of "East Highland" would lead to the questioning of this hypothesis. The street-corner boys with whom he worked all used drugs, anything from cough medicines, or benzedrine, or Seconal to heroin. Prestige in the group was highest for the more bold, daring, and aggressive, those willing to take risks. Those at the opposite end of the manhood scale were called "faggots," not because they were homosexuals but simply because they were too timid to meet the group norms. The cult of the male also extended to drugs, with the most admired being those who would try anything, including heroin. We would not argue that such a cult of manhood is reasonable or productive of success in American society, but it is a far cry from the weak type suggested by the inadequate-personality description. Furthermore, the research shows the situational components of addiction: ready availability, encouragement from compan-

[23]Harvey Feldman, Associated Press, "Heavy Smokers and Drinkers Run Big Cancer Risk, Study Says," July 11, 1974.
[24]"Street Status and Drug Users," *Society*, vol. 10, pp. 32–36, May-June 1973.

ions, and a background of defiance against societal norms, so common among people born with two strikes against them.

Among marijuana-smoking students, especially in the late 1960s, there were certain parallels. The period is often described in terms of a counterculture, that is, a culture of norm defiance. The resentment against the Vietnam war and injustices in society was turned into a rejection of other values of middle America as well, including the "square" society's abhorrence of pot. Combined with this attitude was strong encouragement from the group, ready availability of the drug, and a cult of new experience equivalent to the corner gang's cult of manhood—as well as, of course, the eternal desire to have a good time, but in a new style.

Such a description admittedly does not take in every case of drug abuse: loners have also become involved with drugs; but the large numbers involved in the phenomenon can be explained best in sociological terms. If it is true, as some of the new sources are saying, that there is a downturn in the use of marijuana in favor of alcohol, the change could well be explained by an alleviation in the felt need to defy society now that the Vietnam and civil rights crises have subsided. This does not amount to a prediction that the use of marijuana is drawing to a close. Too many people like it, and it still has a strong forbidden-fruit appeal to high school students and many others; but it may be becoming a rather stable, institutionalized phenomenon rather than a fad.

A word should be added about a pseudoreligious trait connected with the use of psychedelic drugs. Some young drug users have been off on a vision quest as surely as the Great Plains Indians pursued such a quest. In an age when old orthodoxies are no longer followed by many of the young, but there is still a feeling of religious need, a spirit quest can lead down various paths, one of which is to the perilous land of the lotus eaters.

It cannot be denied, either, that drugs have been promoted, and not just by the stereotyped pushers. The drug industry has convinced the world that there is a specific remedy for every ill; just take the right pill and it will go away. The result is a philosophy of escaping problems rather than facing them. There is also a merchandising tendency to play up the drug culture as long as it will help to increase sales; and many people push the art and fashions of a drug scene that they otherwise hold in contempt.

THE DANGERS

On philosophical grounds one might condemn any habit that turns into a pattern of escapism, even as innocuous a habit as watching TV all day. The type of escapism referred to here as the search for euphoria has further dangers. It includes the ingestion of substances that change inner feelings about life without making any real improvements in life. When one returns from the flight from reality, the old problems are still there. This problem belongs to some degree to all drugs, including alcohol, but the severity of the problem differs widely from drug to drug. A description of all the dangerous drugs is impossible in a single chapter, but the relative dangers of a few of the more commonly used should be discussed.

Barbiturates (called "sleeping pills," "goof-balls," or "reds") are sedative-type drugs, somewhat similar to alcohol. On first taking they produce relaxation and good humor; subsequent heavier use can produce gloom or quarrelsomeness. The barbiturates are much more dangerous than alcohol because large dosages can be taken without producing nausea, so they are not quickly purged from the body.

Barbiturates in combination with alcohol can cause death. Barbiturates are addictive; withdrawal for heavy users can cause convulsions. Contrary to public opinion, withdrawal from barbiturates is at least as dangerous as withdrawal from heroin.[25]

Amphetamines are nonaddictive stimulants, but they are dangerous for other reasons. They have been prescribed in some cases for weight reduction, but their use for that purpose is highly questionable. Amphetamines are commonly called "bennies" (benzedrine), "pep pills," and "speed." Speed (methedrine) is the most dangerous and can induce temporary paranoid symptoms. The amphetamines stimulate the nervous system, depress appetite, and prevent sleep for long periods of time. Truck drivers sometimes use them to stay awake on the road, and students sometimes use them when cramming for examinations. Excessive use can cause all the results of prolonged sleeplessness: mood changes, mental depression, suspiciousness, hallucinations, and even psychosis.[26] Dr. David Smith of the Haight-Ashbury Clinic in San Francisco states that there is no more connection between marijuana and heroin than there is between alcohol and heroin—but the correlation is with speed, the most dangerous amphetamine. A majority of heroin addicts known to him used speed before turning to heroin.[27]

The powerful hallucinogen LSD is declining in use. The drug is not physically addictive and has been used by various cultists looking for mind-expansion and pseudomystic-religious experiences. Usually the LSD trip produces excitement and wondrous hallucinations; sometimes it produces agonizing panic and temporary psychosis. There have been several dangerous results reported, such as a user fleeing in fright and falling out of a window.[28] Since such events were rare, they did not seem to dissuade many early LSD experimenters. In the opinion of Yolles, the decline in use came about as a result of reports of chromosomal damage, possible leukemia, and possible damage to the unborn. More research is needed before the full potential effects are known. Yolles is careful not to overstate his case, but he gives strong warning against the drug, especially for expectant mothers.[29]

Peyote, also a hallucinogen, is still permitted for the Apaches and certain other Indians in religious ceremonies. Since it nearly always causes vomiting, it is not much used by drug experimenters. Mescaline, developed from peyote, is used a little more, but it is much stronger and more dangerous. A motiveless murder of a family of five in northern California has been attributed to a mescaline-induced psychosis.[30]

The drug generally regarded as the most addictive is heroin, derived from opium. Since it is an extremely powerful drug, it is usually cut drastically for the illegal market. Sometimes it is not cut sufficiently and a user gets a much more powerful shot than he is accustomed to—one reason for many deaths from overdoses. The heroin addict typically loses ability to complete tasks or hold jobs and becomes enslaved by the drug. Family ties, recreation, nutrition, and sex interest all suffer, as well as work efficiency. In England, where addicts are treated at clinics, many

[25]Jones et al., *op. cit.*, p. 25.
[26]*Ibid.*, pp. 32–33.
[27]Berenice Chipman Fritts, "Young Doctor David Smith," *The Bakersfield Californian*, October 11, 1970, p. 19.
[28]Richard B. Allan, "LSD: The False Illusion," in Horman and Fox (eds.), *op. cit.*, pp. 259–269.
[29]Stanley F. Yolles, "Recent Research on LSD, Marijuana, and Other Dangerous Drugs," in Horman and Fox (eds.), *op. cit.*, pp. 67–86.
[30]Jerry Gillam, "Murder Suspect: A Transformation Caused by Drugs," *Los Angeles Times*, October 25, 1970, part I, pp. 1, 22.

are able to function to some degree in spite of their addiction. In the United States, where the user is an outlaw, the alienation from work and the rest of normal life is much greater. In the past, few real recoveries from heroin addiction have been recorded. At present methadone is being used as a substitute for heroin and is showing considerable promise. Although its use can be characterized as simply switching from one drug to another, people using methadone are able to function quite normally in society.[31]

Marijuana Marijuana has been left to the last because in some ways it belongs in a different category. Expert opinion is more divided on the effects of marijuana than on most of the other drugs described here. "It is estimated that nationwide it has been tried by 20 to 40 percent of college and high school students and that its use is spreading to junior high schools and grade schools."[32] It seems to be readily available in spite of all that law enforcement authorities can do.

The majority of those who try marijuana are merely experimenters, but about 35 percent continue to use it to some degree. About 10 percent become chronic users. For the mere experimenter or very occasional user, the results are in some ways comparable with alcohol: conviviality, relaxation, release of inhibitions, unsteadiness, drowsiness, impaired judgment. The chronic user may develop the habit of withdrawal from problems and from reality and also may suffer from chronic bronchitis. More study is underway by the National Institute of Mental Health to assess the long-range results of chronic use of marijuana. Meantime, Yolles[33] summarizes one of the areas of concern:

> One needs to be particularly concerned about the potential effect of a reality distorting agent on the future psychological development of the adolescent user. We know that adolescence is a time of great psychological turmoil. Patterns of coping with reality developed during the teenage period are significant in determining adult behavior. Persistent use of an agent which serves to ward off reality during this critical developmental period is likely to compromise seriously the future ability of the individual to make an adequate adjustment to a complex society.

At almost the same time that Yolles expresses deep concern about marijuana, another federal report from the National Commission on the Causes and Prevention of Violence states:[34]

> There is no reliable scientific evidence of harmful effects, nor is there evidence of marijuana's being a stepping-stone to hard narcotics. Through our harsh criminal statutes on marijuana use, and in light of evidence that alcohol abuse accounts for far more destruction than any known psychoactive substance today, the report concluded, we have caused large numbers of our youth to lose respect for our laws generally.

Public attitudes about marijuana have changed gradually but not sufficiently to give majority approval to full legalization. For the first time, in March 1973, the National Commission on Marijuana and Drug Abuse called for the legalization of the possession but not production and sale of marijuana in anything but minuscule

---

[31]John Walsh, "Methadone and Heroin Addiction: Rehabilitation without a Cure," *Science*, vol. 168, p. 168, May 8, 1970.
[32]Yolles, in *Narcotics Addiction and Drug Abuse, op. cit.*, p. 94.
[33]*Ibid.*, p. 95.
[34]Ronald J. Ostrow, "Violence Panel Staff Report Asks Legalization of Marijuana," *Los Angeles Times*, September 8, 1970, part I, pp. 1, 22. Copyright, 1970, *Los Angeles Times*. Quoted by permission.

quantities. Along with a change in attitude toward marijuana, the Commission called for an end to all advertisements of sedatives, tranquilizers, stimulants, and other mood-altering drugs. A reordering of the seriousness of drugs was taking place. The most serious drug problems in the United States today, the Commission said, are alcohol and heroin.[35]

The Commission still equivocated on the full legalization of marijuana, reasoning that such a policy would give official sanction and permanence to an "otherwise transient phenomenon." Interestingly, the Commission's statistics showed a 2 percent increase in the use of marijuana the year after the statement was first made. Although a decline in marijuana use seems possible, the idea that it will prove a transient phenomenon is highly doubtful.[36]

Although opposed to punishment for marijuana possession, the Commission by no means advocates its use. Like alcohol, marijuana is believed to lower one's resistance to disease and possibly increase the likelihood of cancer. In Chapter 3, much criticism was made of food additives and other inadequately tested chemicals in the diet, and great care with such products was called for. Certainly even greater care should be given to research into the chemical effects of all drugs, including marijuana. The question remaining, though, is whether marijuana is so much worse than alcohol that its use should be a violation of law. *Newsweek* sums up the pros and cons of the legalization argument. Proponents of legalization say that

1 Although marijuana probably does some harm, the punishment goes far beyond the crime. Alcohol is probably at least as harmful to the health as marijuana.

2 The tasks of enforcement are so great as to nearly immobilize some courts for almost anything else. The monetary cost of enforcement was estimated at $100 million for California alone in 1969.

3 The present policy increases the antagonism of the younger generation toward the law.

4 The present situation widens the gap between generations, causing constant parental worry about the law, a felt need for parental snooping and lecturing. Since parents know little about marijuana but feel compelled to give warnings, they often create a credibility gap.

5 The marijuana traffic is a major source of support for the underworld. Legalization would dry up this source of funds just as legalization of alcohol did after the repeal of Prohibition.

All such arguments have counterarguments. Opponents of legalization reply that

1 Marijuana is a stepping stone to harder drugs because it acquaints people with the drug subculture and the sources of supply.

2 Marijuana may not be addictive, but it leads to psychological dependency.

3 Marijuana users, if their use becomes heavy and chronic, become apathetic and lacking in ambition.

4 Marijuana may have long-term dangers that we do not know of as yet.

[35]"Latest U.S. Drug Study Calls for a New Approach to the Problem," *UNESCO Courier*, p. 20, May 1973.
[36]See the statistical analysis presented by Bruce D. Johnson, "Sense and Nonsense in the 'Scientific' Study of Drugs," *Society*, vol. 10, pp. 53–58, May-June 1973.

5 We cannot give in on every law just because it is hard to enforce or just because it antagonizes part of our population.

A possible compromise might be legalization, but with strict government control of its sale so that no profit could be made from marijuana and so that there would be no compulsion to advertise it. There would be merit to also stopping the advertising of alcoholic drinks, sleeping pills, and any drugs that might prove harmful.

Discuss and debate the issue of whether the use of marijuana should be legalized, and if so, at what age level.

THE SEARCH FOR SOLUTIONS

Currently there are several techniques for attempting to solve the drug-abuse problem. The first is repression by legal devices. For many years it has been wise for political candidates to promise to crack down harder on narcotics. At times the feeling has been almost equally strong against both the users and the pushers of narcotics. As more and more middle-class youth from influential homes have become involved in drug use, the clamor has been louder against the pusher and a little more moderate against the users.

The dilemmas of punishment One trouble with clamping down on narcotics peddlers but not users is that, except for the upper echelons of the narcotics racket, peddler and user are often one and the same. If one member of a marijuana crowd knows where to find a supplier, he often gets a supply and sells part of it to his friends. This makes him a pusher, as defined by law. Five boys and one girl in Boise, Idaho, ranging in age from sixteen to eighteen years, were each sentenced to five years in prison for supplying drugs to other teenagers in town, although they did not meet the stereotype of the evil underworld character sought by punitive laws.[37] Most had the misfortune of coming from families of poor reputation. They lacked good legal representation and went before a judge who felt it necessary to make an example of someone. The community felt even more strongly than the judge about the supposed good effects of long and severe punishment. One irony in the case, however, is that the judge himself is doubtful about any reformative effects of prison. Equally disconcerting to Boise is the fact that many of its youth doubt that the sentence had any deterrent effect in the long run and note that the case attracted much public sympathy from other parts of the country for the youthful convicts. A majority of similar cases get probation in other states or, at worst, short sentences to juvenile institutions—not five years in prison. Punishments tend to be grossly uneven.

Another point that must be made very clearly about the punitive approach to drug control is that although it has been the basic approach in the United States since 1914, it can certainly not be characterized as a success. Dr. John Kramer, psychiatrist and pharmacologist at the University of California at Irvine, in testifying before Senator Hughes' committee on narcotics, said "We in the United States have been on the wrong track for 40 or 50 years" in our punitive approach. He suggested that if even 10 or 20 percent of the amount of money spent on

[37]Loudon Wainwright, "A Town Deals Sternly with Its Own," *Life*, vol. 69, pp. 40–47, November 6, 1970.

apprehension, trial, and punishment of addicts had been spent on research, "there is no doubt in my mind that our drug abuse problems would this day have been handled not only more humanely, but more effectively, and, in the long run, more sparingly of both money and human life."[38] For many years the clamor has been for more and more severe laws against heroin. But along with the severe laws, the amount of heroin addiction has increased tenfold in a single decade and is still rising.

> If you need help, consult your local telephone directory for NARCOTICS INFORMATION, or HOTLINE, or DRUGS: PREVENTIVE EDUCATION. If there are no helpful local listings, write to Synanon, 1910 Ocean Front, Santa Monica, California.

Another word must be said about the difficulty with a punitive approach to addiction treatment: the place of punishment has all the problems of any other prison. John Brooks,[39] a former addict, who is founder of an organization that tries to cure addiction, states that he was in five different prisons and that in all of them every type of drug was available. His statement continues:

> In prison, everybody is clannish. All the drug addicts, all they talk about is shooting dope. A man may by physically clean while he is in prison for a while, but psychologically he is still being processed through the drug medium, so that when he comes out . . . psychologically, he is still on drugs.

The sickness approach   A second possible approach to the drug problem is to treat it as a sickness. Such has been done for years with the treatment of severe alcoholism, but even with alcoholism the policy has not been consistent. James P. Spradley tells of the endless cycle of arrests, nights in the drunk tank, "drying out," repeated drunkenness, rearrest, and escape to other cities that is a part of the meaningless round of life of the skid-row drunkard.[40] Some alcoholics do not respond to treatment or to such an organization as Alcoholics Anonymous; but whether or not they can be helped, it seems that no purpose is served by constant harassment. Those who advocate a medical approach to drug addiction believe that the same is true even for the advanced heroin addict. Permanent cure is unlikely, but with outpatient care and the use of methadone, an addict can still live a useful life.

The federal government has long maintained two centers for the treatment of addicts and is now creating more facilities, although the rate of cure is very low. There are also a number of community projects and self-help projects with group-therapy sessions for young patients. The oldest and best-known self-help clinic is Synanon in Santa Monica, California. It houses about 2,000 members and has several thousand participants who live outside. The self-help program of rehabilitation includes group-interaction and educational sessions, and business, financial, and self-support training. Founded in 1958 by Charles Dederich, Synanon has overcome vehement community opposition and is now accepted as the model of self-help organizations.

However well intended the self-help projects are, they have facilities for dealing

---

[38]Dr. John Kramer, in *Narcotics Addiction and Drug Abuse, op. cit.*, pp. 147, 152.
[39]In *ibid.*, p. 255.
[40]James P. Spradley, *You Owe Yourself a Drunk: An Ethnology of Urban Nomads*, Little, Brown and Company, Boston, 1970.

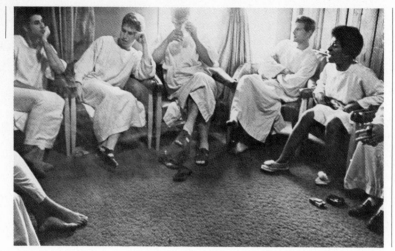

Synanon, the leader in the self-help approach to the drug problem, offers group solidarity, mutual concern, and the arts of creative expression.

with only a very small fraction of the addicts in need of help. Increasing numbers of leaders in the field of rehabilitation are convinced that society must resort much more to the present methadone maintenance system or even to heroin mainte- nance. In many cases it is possible for heroin addicts to enter state or local clinics where they are treated with methadone as a substitute for heroin. Methadone is not illegal, so addicts can take it without being considered criminals and they will not have to steal to support their habits. Furthermore, methadone users seem to be better able to regulate their lives than is the case with heroin users. Of the 2,200 methadone patients treated at Beth Israel Hospital in New York, large numbers found regular employment, and arrest rates among the group dropped to only 2 percent of what they had been.[41] Methadone is not perfect, however. It is addictive; and overdoses are even more likely to prove fatal than are overdoses of heroin. Two of its major advantages, besides legality, are that it can be taken orally and it requires no increase in dosage to avoid withdrawal symptoms.

Methadone maintenance is the method used primarily in England at present. There the addict can get a free supply of enough methadone (or in some cases heroin) to maintain his present level of tolerance. At one time the experience of the United Kingdom was discounted because many doctors had oversubscribed sufficiently to allow surpluses of heroin to reach the market. However, under more careful controls imposed from 1968 to 1971, the number of addicts in the United Kingdom declined from 5.1 per 100,000 population to 4.7. Meantime in the United States, with a mainly punitive approach, the number of addicts increased from 157.0 per 100,000 population to 335.0.[42]

There are strong arguments for using the British approach to the addiction problem. Their method has taken the profit out of the heroin trade by public dispensing of heroin to the addicts. The only threat to the addict is that if caught stealing, the drugs might be taken away. In the United States, except in a small but growing number of methadone clinics, the opposite situation exists. Unless

[41]Walter R. Cuskey and William Krasner, "The Needle and the Boot," *Society*, vol. 10, pp. 46–52, May-June 1973.
[42]Phillip Whitten and Ian Robertson, *loc. cit.*

addicts steal, they cannot get drugs, and the need for the fix is so consuming that

any crimes necessary will be committed. Some authorities argue, though, that most addicts would never go to a clinic unless they felt sure they could get their heroin fixes. Probably the ultimate solution will be to use methadone on those people who show a real desire to quit the habit and to coax the others into the program by heroin maintenance. Difficult though the system would be, it could undermine the profits from the heroin traffic and save the victims of the hundreds of thousands of robberies that take place every day for the maintenance of the habit.

The education approach As the amount of drug use increased and spread among young people from the middle-class suburbs, the demand for education on the subject also increased. The assumption was that anyone knowing the truth about drugs would avoid them. A UNESCO inquiry found that most countries with a drug problem were taking the same approach, but both Iran and France had reservations. In both cases reluctance was based on the belief that drugs would simply be given too much publicity and that the educational programs might be counterproductive.[43] After several years of drug programs in American schools, the National Commission on Marijuana and Drug Abuse had reservations about the educational program, suggesting it be suspended until better evaluation and advice were available. The Commission complained that the programs were scientifically inaccurate and ineffective.[44] Most people who try drugs have already heard enough about them to realize they are dangerous, which is probably why college campuses have generally abandoned the stronger drugs in favor of marijuana. For those who reach out for stronger and stronger drugs and heed no warnings, the search for a remedy must lie in a study of the backgrounds that have motivated them toward drugs.

A social-policy approach Although a medical approach to drug addiction is more likely to bring favorable results than the purely punitive approach, there are objections to viewing addiction too purely as a medical problem. The vast majority of addicts have turned to heroin not because they are mentally sick but because they are depressed about the situations in which they find themselves. Heroin addiction is concentrated in the poorest areas of cities among the most socially deprived populations. As we cry out against addiction, we cut back on the number of target area projects and other programs aimed at aiding the outcast. What is really needed is to offer functional alternatives to drugs—other ways in which excitement and competition for status can be expressed, along with hope for the future. It must also be noted that in the narcotics subculture, the successful underworld characters make much of their money from drugs and are admired for their success, thus setting bad models for the young. In this respect, the methadone maintenance method coincides with social policy, since it helps to remove the pusher by taking away his profit.

The other part of the social-policy approach has more to do with values than with economic and institutional change. As the national Commission suggests, there should be less advertising of legal drugs that promise relief from pain, sorrow, sleeplessness, depression, or any psychological ills we are heir to. Attitudes and values are important components of social systems, and the attitude that problems

43"To Teach or Not to Teach," *UNESCO Courier*, pp. 6–7, May 1973.
44"Latest US Drug Study Calls for a New Approach to the Problem," *UNESCO Courier*, p. 20, May 1973.

| can be solved by taking the right medicine is an unwholesome value, encouraging passivity rather than action in the face of problems.

SUGGESTED READINGS

Claridge, Gordon: *Drugs and Human Behavior*, Penguin Books, Baltimore, 1973. The author reports results of research into effects of drugs on human behavior and discusses the social use of drugs, drugs and mental illness, alcoholism, and addiction.

Fort, Joel: *Alcohol: Our Biggest Drug Problem*, McGraw-Hill Book Company, New York, 1973. Fort's position is that neither alcohol nor marijuana should be prohibited by law, but every precaution should be taken to prevent making them attractive. No advertising or fancy packaging should be permitted. He also gives a thorough analysis of the danger of heavy use of alcohol.

Geller, Allen, and Maxwell Boas: *The Drug Beat*, McGraw-Hill Book Company, New York, 1971. Advertised as a complete survey of the history, distribution, uses, and abuses of marijuana, LSD, and the amphetamines, the book does a thorough job on all three. Authoritative and interestingly presented.

Horman, Richard E., and Allan M. Fox (eds.): *Drug Awareness: Key Documents on LSD, Marijuana and the Drug Culture*, Avon Book Division, The Hearst Corporation, New York, 1970. Although the book consists mainly of official documents, many are very readable. The writers have the merit of being cautious about conclusions so that when warnings are sounded they are more likely to be heeded.

Spradley, James R.: *You Owe Yourself a Drunk: An Ethnology of Urban Nomads*, Little, Brown and Company, Boston, 1970. Although the title sounds a little farcical, the story is a pathetic one of homelessness, irresistible drinking habits, long and futile periods in jail, fleeing from city to city and from life itself. The author sees our treatment of the derelict drunkard as both fruitless and cruel.

QUESTIONS

1 What are the cultural conditions under which alcohol and certain types of drugs are most likely to be used only in moderation?

2 The story of Ulysses and the Land of the Lotus Eaters is used to symbolize the attitude of most societies toward the use of most euphoric drugs. Why do societies consider it their business to regulate such drugs?

3 Contrast the drug problem of modern America with the problem as it existed before the Harrison Act of 1914 and with the problem of the 1930s and 1940s.

4 What situations seem to cause an increase in the incidence of drug use?

5 What are the arguments pro and con on the legalization of marijuana?

6 Discuss several current proposals for what to do about the drug problem.

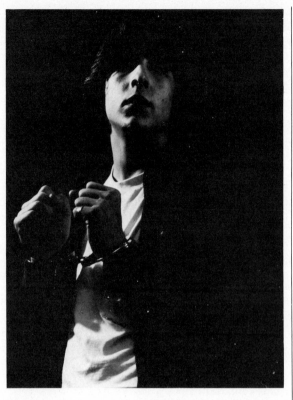

14

THE LAWBREAKERS: YOUNG AND OLD, RICH AND POOR

What are the facts with respect to the problem of crime rate? Do we really have more criminals, or do we simply report more of their crimes? What difference does it make whether a lawbreaker is young or old, rich or poor? What are the explanations of crime? Is crime a consequence of certain types of people or of certain kinds of circumstances? Is there anything about the structure of American society that helps to explain a high rate of crime? What are the variations in the type and rate of crime for different social classes, and what is the reason for such variations? Is there really an organized underworld, or are reports of the Mafia mere sensationalism? Finally, how do we fight crime? Does policy fit with theories of crime? If not, what improvements can be made?

In the following pages we shall examine crime statistics on the basis of rural and urban, young and old, and rich and poor. White-collar crime will be differentiated from other types of crime, both in type of offender and in difficulty of prosecution. We shall refer to several recent studies that deal with organized crime and see what inroads organized crime is making into legitimate business and what conditions are prevailing that allow organized crime to flourish. Finally we shall look at suggestions for fighting crime, especially the organized crime that has so far seemed to defy all efforts at control.

The problems of making laws, justifying laws, and dealing with the violators of laws become increasingly difficult in modern societies. We do not have the primary group controls that were possible for simpler societies in which people all knew each other and in which the threat of ostracism or ridicule was a major force in the maintenance of social control. Neither do we have the sacred attitudes that laws are somehow the manifestation of divine will and that the evasion of earthly justice will only make an offender more vulnerable to the fires of divine wrath. In a secular society all laws are seen as merely far-from-perfect manifestations of the will of the people and their legislators and just as fallible as all the other handiwork of man. The laws, the means of detection of crime, the courts of justice, and the means of punishment are all subjects for argument and debate. At the same time, the heterogeneity of society increases, adding normative strain and confusion; urban concentrations grow; the continuing disparity between poverty and riches becomes more repugnant to the values of the social system, and a gulf widens between the norms of older and younger generations. All such developments are to some degree "criminogenic."

Against the consequence of the forces leading to higher rates of crime, society summons its defenses, often treating symptoms rather than causes. Jails and prisons overflow. Police forces, courts, and the whole machinery of justice expand, but not as rapidly as their burden of work. Detection becomes increasingly scientific. Seldom has a society devoted more time and effort to the apprehension and processing of criminals than the United States does today. More and more lawbreakers are caught, but the amount of crime continues to increase. Apparently, for many elements of the underworld the means of evasion have become just as scientific as the means of detection. By the corruption of government, by the purchase of friends in high places, and by the manipulation of the law and its enforcement system, the lawbreakers and their henchmen continue to thrive. The public is aroused over juvenile offenders and drug abuse, and the FBI concentrates on political crimes and various forms of violence. All such problems become important political issues. Meanwhile, organized crime goes on its way, occasionally losing a battle but never losing the war.

THE PREVALENCE OF LAWBREAKING

The FBI reports that there was a 148 percent increase in the crime rate during the 1960s while the population increased only 13 percent. By the end of the decade, which had witnessed many riots and disorders as well as crimes, law and order had become a major political issue. A Law Enforcement Assistance Administration had been created in the Justice Department to give aid to local law enforcement agencies in a national war on crime. Judged by the FBI figures, the drive against crime seemed at first to be making a little progress, with crime increasing at a slower rate in 1970 and 1971 than previously, and actually showing a very slight decline in 1972. The next years, however, saw another sharp increase. Furthermore, research work done for the Justice Department by the Bureau of the Census would make it appear that official figures have greatly underestimated the rate of crime.

The new type of crime report released in 1974 was based on extensive interviews with people living in the five largest cities of the United States (New York, Chicago, Philadelphia, Los Angeles, and Detroit) to get testimony regarding victimization by criminals.[1] In all cities the number of crimes reported by citizens under these circumstances were more than twice the figures given in the Uniform Crime Reports of the FBI. Nearly 3.2 million crimes took place in the five cities during the year under study (1972).

The combined figures for burglary and household larceny indicated that about one-fifth of all households had been victimized. (Burglary refers to breaking and entry whether or not attended by theft; household larceny refers to theft in or near the home, not involving forcible entry.) For Chicago, the combined total of burglaries and household larcenies was 195 per thousand households; the figures for Los Angeles, Detroit, and Philadelphia were only slightly lower. New York's rate was considerably lower (111 per thousand) than the other cities, in spite of the unfavorable publicity New York has received. The researchers found that the burglarization rate was much higher for commercial establishments than for households. In Detroit there were 720 burglaries for every thousand retail stores during the year. Rates for the other cities averaged around 400.

In all cases of household theft, the victimization rates were higher for minority groups than for other households; and in all cities those with incomes of less than $10,000 per year were more likely to be the victims of crime than those with family incomes of $10,000 or more. The apparent reason is that the poorer residences of the city are usually closer to areas of high crime and addiction rates and are therefore easier targets for theft. The consequence is that crime can be added to many other factors that are heavier burdens for the poor to bear than for the well-to-do and that help to perpetuate poverty.

Another consequence of the fact that crime falls more heavily on the poor than on other classes may be an inconsistent public interest in the subject. At times, especially when crime is made into a political issue or is given unusual coverage by the media, the public becomes aroused about the matter. Yet a Gallup survey conducted in 1971, when crime was very much a political issue, found that crime rated tenth among public concerns (with war, jobs, family breakup, inflation, and many other problems taking precedence). People who have recently been victimized by crime, especially crime involving violence or threat, are roused about the issue. Otherwise, large numbers of people congratulate themselves on living in a safe neighborhood and worry about other matters. In fact, nearly all people feel safer in their own neighborhoods than elsewhere, regardless of what the crime rate of their neighborhood happens to be.[2]

One of the findings of the five-cities survey is that many people do not have confidence enough in the police and justice system to bother with reporting crime. Approximately one-quarter of informants thought the incidents were not important enough to report; about 9 percent said the police would not want to be bothered; and more than one-third responded in general terms that nothing could be done. Law enforcement officials see such attitudes as a serious detriment to their work.

Anonymous surveys indicate that the majority of people have committed at least an act or two defined as felonies, not mere misdemeanors. Try some anonymous polling in class or on campus. (Better stick to the campus; students are more likely than their elders to answer honestly.)

[1] *Crime in the Nation's Five Largest Cities*, Law Enforcement Assistance Administration, U.S. Department of Justice, Washington, D.C., April 1974.
[2] Kurt Weiss and Michael E. Milakovich, "Political Misuses of Crime Rates," *Society*, vol. 11, pp. 27–28, July-August 1974.

Often the FBI Uniform Crime Reports are published in the daily press as though they present a full and accurate picture of the crime rate. However, as the five-cities survey indicates, they are limited in accuracy partly because so many crimes are not reported to the police. There are other problems as well. Not all cities report. Some sections of the country are more thorough in their crime reporting than others. For example, in one recent year only 45 percent of the known crimes in Mississippi cities were reported to the FBI.[3] Moreover, only certain categories of crimes are reported. Many white-collar crimes are omitted; and most crime without victims, including such offenses as lewd conduct and pornography, are not reported, even though they occupy considerable time on the part of police forces in our more puritanical communities.

Another problem is that police forces have been known to alter their statistics. Sometimes they are tempted to show an improvement in the crime rate; at other times, they are enticed into playing up the crime rate in order to assure adequate appropriations for their police work. These problems may add up to their making crime statistics rise more rapidly than crime. However, a good reason for believing that the crime rate is actually increasing is that many cities with records of good reporting have shown fairly steady increases. Also, the characteristics of increasing urban growth, mobility, and normative conflict make an increase in crime rates seem plausible.

Crime: rural and urban Since ours is a highly urbanized population, it is important to know whether or not the traditional prejudice against the city as a center of crime is valid. As a matter of fact, the rates of most types of crimes are highest in the big cities, especially the central cities. Twenty-six such central cities, containing 18 percent of the nation's population, accounted for more than half the indexed crimes against the person and 30 percent of the crimes against property. Murder rates vary from 2 to 4 per 100,000 in rural and suburban areas to 10 per 100,000 in cities of 500,000 or more. Larceny varies from a low of 176 cases per 100,000 in rural areas to 359 in suburbs and 734 in cities of more than 1 million.[4] These figures should probably be much higher, judging by the five-cities survey.

Does your community have a Big Brother program or any other plan for helping delinquent youth? For those interested in juvenile work, trying to aid boys and girls in juvenile homes or on probation will be a very helpful experience.

CRIME: AGE, SEX, AND SOCIAL CLASS

The amount and type of crime committed is strongly influenced by age. In the FBI Uniform Crime Reports, more than half of all auto thefts (64,000 out of 121,000) were committed by persons under eighteen years of age.[5] In this case, the young can be thought of as a disadvantaged minority in terms of the greatly desired goal of access to automobiles. The under-eighteen group accounts also for slightly over

---

[3]Weiss and Milakovich, *op. cit.*, p. 29.
[4]Robert W. Winslow (ed.), *Crime in a Free Society: Selections from the President's Commission on Law Enforcement and the Administration of Justice*, Dickenson Publishing Company, Belmont, Calif., 1968, pp. 54–55.
[5]These and subsequent figures are from FBI Uniform Crime Reports for 1971, in *World Almanac 1973*, Newspaper Enterprise Association, New York, 1973.

half of all burglaries and larcenies reported. The figure is probably influenced by **301** the inexperience that causes juveniles to be caught more often than professionals. The offenses that are closer to the area of white-collar crimes are committed mainly by adults. Only one-tenth of the cases of forgery and counterfeiting and only one-twentieth of the cases of embezzlement are committed by minors. In still another category, minors are underrepresented. The largest number of arrests in any category of offenses is for drunkenness, with minors under eighteen accounting for only 40,000 cases out of 1,370,000 cases reported.

There are also social-class differences in the juvenile crime rate. Several investigations indicate that the types of crimes committed by middle-class youth are likely to be outgrown with the passing of time. An investigation by Ronald J. Chilton,[6] for example, indicates a strong economic factor in the type of delinquency most likely to become persistent. The middle-class offenses were more typically matters of drinking parties, sex affairs, and driving offenses than theft. The poorer juveniles were more likely to turn to economically remunerative crimes. Leon Fannin and Marshall Clinard[7] find other types of differences between the two classes, but, again, those which in the long run will make the middle-class delinquency less persistent. The lower-class boys studied insisted on a much tougher and more brutal definition of manhood, engaged in more fights, and had less desire to do things the clever way. Such attitudes might help account for statistics showing much higher arrest rates among the lower class. Such studies would no doubt show a higher incidence of drug problems in both classes if they had been made three or four years later; but even in this offense, as noted in the previous chapter, it is more likely that the person of better socioeconomic background will limit drug use to marijuana. For him the tensions that lead to drug use seem to be less severe.

There are very great differences in crime rates for the two sexes. If parents wish to avoid arrests among their offspring, they would be well-advised to have all girls, assuming they had the know-how for such a biological trick. The male-female arrest rate among adults differs by a ratio of about 8 to 1 (4,132,500 arrests of adult males and 582,000 arrests of adult females in one year by FBI figures). For younger people the ratio is not quite so uneven—about 3.5 to 1 (1,279,000 males arrested and 367,000 females arrested). No doubt much of the reason is due to the difference in roles assigned to the two sexes by society. The very fact that boys are expected to be aggressive and venturesome almost guarantees that many more will be arrested. Where less differentiation of role is expected, as in the impoverished ghetto, the male-female rate of involvement in delinquency becomes more even. In countries where women are sheltered much more than in the United States, the sex ratio becomes greater. A traditional Moslem woman, for example, always kept at home under a veil and watched carefully, would have little chance to commit delinquent acts. A girl of the impoverished slums, fighting for a living in a criminogenic environment, would be much more likely to get involved with the law. The majority of American girls are somewhere between these two extremes; but as the rearing patterns and expectations for boys and girls become more alike, the arrest rates for the two sexes become more even—a trend in evidence in American society in recent years.

[6]Ronald J. Chilton, "Middle-Class Delinquency and Specific Offense Analysis," in Edmund W. Vas (ed.), *Middle-Class Juvenile Delinquency*, Harper & Row, Publishers, Incorporated, 1967, pp. 91–101.
[7]Leon Fannin and Marshall Clinnard, "Differences in the Conception of Self as a Male among Lower and Middle Class Delinquents," *Social Problems*, vol. 13, pp. 205–214, Fall 1965.

| **Crime: poverty and race** Poverty is associated with crime in many cases, but not always. The poor countries do not necessarily have high crime rates. It seems more likely that the association between poverty and crime occurs in situations where poverty is so close to riches as to cause a strong feeling of relative deprivation. Another possible explanation of why crime is often associated with poverty in an affluent society but not in impoverished countries is accounted for by a special use of the sociologist's concept of anomie—a strain within the norms. Merton has characterized American society as one that sets a universal achievement goal for all people and judges people by their success or, more bluntly, by how much money they make. If ours were a society that gave high honors to the honest poor or that looked askance at all people who have made wealth in a crafty manner, then there would be no compulsion to get ahead by fair or foul means. We *do* expect success of everyone, however, so the temptation to dishonest means is usually great, especially since people do not have equal access to honest means for success. Poor family background, racial discrimination, and various other factors guarantee inequality in respect to achievement by honest means. It must not be forgotten, too, that the offenses of the poor are more likely to lead to arrest and conviction than are the types of fraud and graft sometimes practiced by the well-to-do.

> **Make a survey of juvenile crime in your community (usually the police will give you the needed information). Chart high delinquency areas on a map, then travel through them and study their physical characteristics.**

Whatever the reason, poverty, especially urban poverty, is closely associated with high crime rates in the United States. Urban poverty areas are usually areas of high unemployment rates, few opportunities, ready access to drugs, petty theft patterns to imitate, family disorganization, and hostility toward police and authorities.

Race has been included along with crime and poverty because racial differences in crime rate are mainly a reflection of greater poverty and emotional tensions for the black and brown than for the white. There are probably secondary causes as well. Black people, for example, are strongly overrepresented in arrests for "suspicion." Since suspicion is defined in the Uniform Crime Reports as arrest for no particular offense, the charge could be a coverup for an error by the police.[8] It is evidence, at any rate, that more blacks than whites are arrested for trivial causes, which in turn makes their crime rate look higher than it really is. Even for solid causes, though, the arrest rate is higher, as is inevitable for a people highly concentrated in urban poverty areas and suffering the hostile feelings that often go with minority status.

Crime and criminal types Years ago there were many efforts to describe a criminal type as a human type somehow physically or mentally or emotionally inferior by birth. Such early attempts have been discredited, but there have been more creditable attempts to describe psychological types—particular types created by their environments. Sociologists do not deny the possibility of character types with far more hostility than others, nor can they deny that individuals adjust differently to the same circumstances. However, the sociological approach is

[8]Leonard Savitz, *Dilemmas in Criminology*, McGraw-Hill Book Company, New York, 1967, p. 27.

usually one of analyzing environments rather than isolating personality types. In sociological theory, the right set of social circumstances will call forth a considerable percentage of people who will be lawbreakers. Over a period of years, similar city areas have produced similar amounts of juvenile delinquency, even though the ethnic groups inhabiting them and the particular personalities have changed.

The future may cause us to take new looks at physical causes. There have been a few isolated cases of brain tumors or concussions associated with berserk behavior. Recently courts have listened to arguments about the XYY chromosome pattern but have generally ruled against it as being an actual cause of crime. We may eventually prove that some types of crime are associated with brain damage from accidents, drugs, or faulty chromosomes. Even if such cases should acquire plausibility, however, they could not be assumed to account for any but a tiny part of crime. In sociology, we are more impressed with the degree to which crime rates relate to deteriorated city cores, poverty, faulty types of success drives, value conflicts, and inability to succeed by legitimate means. It is much easier to show that such factors are associated with rising crime rates than it would be to prove that some strange type of physical or mental deterioration has afflicted vast numbers of people in modern America. Furthermore, there are types of crimes closely associated with the more reputable elements of society—people of high intelligence, good education, and enviable position.

WHITE-COLLAR CRIME

A large amount of crime is committed by respectable, well-placed members of society. This is the type of crime referred to as white-collar crime. The analysis of white-collar crime was first started by Edwin H. Sutherland, who defined it as "crime committed by a person of respectability and high social status in the course of his occupation."[9] Bribery and graft are types of white-collar crimes, and so are most of the means of beating the consumer discussed in Chapter 4. Sutherland used many examples from the days of the nineteenth-century robber barons, who were generally willing to admit that they could not carry on business if they had to stay strictly within the law. Since Sutherland's book was written many years ago, more timely examples will be used here, but his analysis of the distinction between white-collar crime and common crime is still completely valid.

First of all, Sutherland finds considerable fault with the type of analysis that shows a concentration of crime mainly in areas of poverty. Certainly there is such a concentration, but it is of particular types of crime: burglary, petty larceny, auto theft, and aggravated assault. Violating labor laws, cheating the government out of income tax money, milking insurance companies, conspiring to restrain trade, contributing illegally to political parties and candidates, fixing weights and measures, and disguising true interest rates are all examples of crimes that have no connection with poverty areas, deprived home backgrounds, or personal pathologies. Furthermore, although they are all defined as crimes, they are treated differently. One reason for different treatment is that such crimes are perpetrated by people in a position of influence who can usually escape arrest and publicity. Second, even if the wrongdoers are arrested, their crimes are often treated as civil offenses. Furthermore, as Sutherland shows, the public has little awareness of such crime, usually does not understand it, and does not get excited about it. The

[9]Edwin H. Sutherland, *White Collar Crime*, Holt, Rinehart and Winston, Inc., New York, 1961, p. 9. (The book was written in 1948 and republished with slight revisions in 1961.)

small-time thief or narcotics agent excites public fury. Probably the loss to the public through white-collar crime is many times greater than that through common larceny. Sutherland mentions, for example, the dramatic case of the suicide of Ivar Kreuger, who had finally trapped himself in financial manipulations that resulted in losses of more than $550 million for stockholders.

With the passing of time, new differences in the types of crime have become apparent. The dividing line between crime and noncrime in the white-collar world is often indistinct. If a man robs a service station, there is no question that he has committed a crime. But what are we to say when we learn that four corporations earning net profits totaling over $350 million paid no federal income tax whatever, or that 394 families with incomes of over $100,000 per year paid no income tax, even after passage of the Tax Reform Act of 1969 that provides for a minimum tax for all people regardless of deductions?[10] The irony is that these people are not even considered lawbreakers. They have committed no crime. They have found legal loopholes—no doubt they helped to persuade Congress to leave legal loopholes—so that they could evade taxes legally.

We also read in the daily press that firms providing supplies, consultations, and technical assistance to the OEO are growing rich on the war on poverty. Contracts worth over 11\frac{1}{2}$ million were awarded to companies that have thirty-five former OEO officials working for them.[11] Somehow the whole idea of profits out of the war on poverty sounds a little immoral. But is it illegal? No. Tie-ins between all kinds of businesses and agencies of the government are inevitable; we even have to admit they are necessary. At what point does the tie-in become too close and make the profiteer or the influence peddler a lawbreaker? It has happened frequently, even at high levels of government, and we do not have to go back to such graft-ridden administrations as those of Grant and Harding to find examples. Bobby Baker, a friend of former President Johnson and one-time Senate secretary, was convicted of fraud through income tax evasion, pocketing campaign contributions, and illegal influence peddling. The Eisenhower administration was embarrassed by improper dealings by the White House Secretary Sherman Adams. In 1968 Senator Thomas Dodd, a man of solid accomplishment and believed to be of unimpeachable reputation, was censured by the United States Senate for diverting $203,000 of campaign contributions to his own personal use and also evading income tax on the amount.[12] In a previous chapter it was mentioned that the former mayor of Newark, New Jersey, and several of his friends were sentenced to prison for embezzlement. In 1963, Billie Sol Estes, a young multimillionaire friend of President Johnson and many Texas politicians and a man who seemed to have the King Midas touch, was found guilty of various counts of fraud, totaling about $22 million.[13]

During the Nixon administration, the white-collar crimes of the immediately previous administrations began to pale to insignificance as the facts surrounding the Watergate break-in and large numbers of other scandals became known, and as the trail of suspicion was seen to lead directly to the White House. Former Vice President Agnew had already been forced to resign his office for offenses committed during his governorship of Maryland. He admitted to a charge of

[10]Philip M. Stearn, *The Rape of the Taxpayer*, Vintage Books, Random House, Inc., New York, 1974, pp. 16–17.
[11]"Firms Get Rich in War on Poverty," *Los Angeles Times*, November 30, 1970, part I, page 2.
[12]Fred C. Cook, "Large Questions about Our Times," *Saturday Review*, vol. 51, pp. 31–32, March 16, 1968.
[13]"Silent Partners of Billie Sol Estes," *The Nation*, vol. 196, pp. 485–495, June 1, 1963.

Crimes can be committed by people of high status, power, and arrogance. John Ehrlichman, a top-ranking advisor to Nixon, was convicted and sentenced in one of the cases arising from the Watergate scandal.

income tax evasion in return for having a series of other indictments dropped. After the Agnew case, increasing amounts of evidence began to accumulate about the activities of immediate advisors of former President Nixon, including not only the famous break-in and bugging of the Democratic headquarters at the Watergate Hotel but also the burglary of the office of Daniel Ellsberg's psychiatrist. More and more cases of political foul play began to emerge, including illegal campaign contributions, hiding of donations, possible misappropriation of campaign funds, invasions of privacy by taping and bugging of conversations, suspicion of bribery by the milk interests, and campaign dirty tricks that amounted to slander. Very important in the final charges brought by the House Impeachment Committee against Nixon was the misuse of agencies of the government, including attempts to interfere with the workings of the FBI, the CIA, and the Justice Department and attempts to use the Internal Revenue Service to frighten political opponents. Violations of campaign laws were certainly nothing new, but the magnitude of the offenses exceeded anything that had gone before. Eventually most of the top Nixon advisors were indicted and many were sent to prison, although generally for very short terms. Nixon, finally realizing that an impeachment trial was inevitable, was persuaded to resign. The hand of the law fell much more gently on the malefactors of high office than on the lowly narcotics users discussed in the previous chapter.

The Watergate scandals are not typical cases of white-collar crime and may therefore seem a little out of place in this discussion. However, they take on a singularly threatening aspect, producing questions about how completely the will of the people can be subverted by government, how secretly the government can operate, how easily government can spy on its political enemies. A collective sigh of relief was raised as the more seemingly open and communicative Ford administration took office. People generally felt that the constitutional processes had been vindicated and that the system works. However, the problems of campaign financing remain, giving too much political power to big contributors. A certain amount of presidential secrecy involving foreign and military affairs is necessary, but no policy has yet been formulated to guarantee that such privileges will not be abused.

The more usual types of white-collar crime involve business moreso than government and include such practices as false advertising, price-fixing, and robbing the consumer by the various means mentioned in Chapter 3. However, some of the same policies are at work in business as in government, with companies spying on each other and books and transactions kept carefully hidden from the government, the people, and the shareholders.

Embezzlement Many types of white-collar crime are cases of lawbreaking that are encouraged by company policy. Such is not the case with embezzlement. In either case, however, the crimes are committed by supposedly respectable individuals in positions of trust; and in both cases the violators find rationalizations to preserve their self-image as good, honest citizens. With respect to crimes stemming from company policy, one's self-image can be preserved in terms of one's having faithfully and loyally complied with the policies of a respectable corporation and associates. In the case of embezzlement the rationalization is more difficult, but it is accomplished.

Donald Cressey[14] summarized the process of becoming an embezzler after studying a number of cases. The most typical case of appropriating funds occurs when a man in a position of trust finds himself in serious need of money. The need is usually occasioned by an incident that would be embarrassing to have to admit—gambling debt, extramarital affair, or other situations of possible blackmail. In practically all cases, the violator of financial trust takes the money, telling himself that it is really a loan, a loan that he will eventually pay back. Serious need, plus opportunity, plus a means of rationalization makes this type of white-collar crime possible.

Other types of white-collar crime are numerous: public officeholders receiving kickbacks from public employees, business executives padding expense accounts, politicians accepting bribes, business heads giving bribes, doctors overcharging patients or health insurance companies, labor leaders beating fair labor laws, black marketeering, false advertising, and adulterating foods. All these practices are carried on by the respectable world. As is the case with commonly indexed crime, the acts are committed when the need is considerable, when restraints are not too

---

[14]Donald R. Cressey, "The Criminal Violation of Financial Trust," *American Sociological Review*, pp. 738–743, December 1950.

violation is already established by which others can learn.

Below the level of white-collar crime, but operating in fields that tie the respectable world to the underworld—the lawmakers with the lawbreakers and the victims with their exploiters—is the world of organized crime. Like white-collar crime, much organized crime has been overlooked in the crime statistics and in the outcry against criminality. The organization is nevertheless there, growing, spreading, and corrupting—the "syndicate," the "family," the Mafia, Cosa Nostra, or whatever its name, the organization is a pervasive part of the troubled land.

ORGANIZED CRIME: COSA NOSTRA

Organized crime differs from other types of crime not only in its level of organization but also in its relationship to the legitimate world. The white-collar criminal is typically a legitimate businessman, politician, or professional. The blue-collar criminal is outside the law and not connected with the legitimate world except in the relationship of predator to its prey. Although a creature of the underworld, organized crime, on the other hand, is closely connected to the legitimate world. It provides gambling and night life for ordinary citizens, it caters to their vices by providing houses of prostitution and various kinds of pornographic entertainment, and for a usurious sum, it will lend them money to get them out of a tight spot. Organized crime also supplies the vast and growing narcotics market, which is by no means legitimate, but has the same characteristic as so much of the business of organized crime—meeting a need not met by legitimate business by catering to the desires of people who are otherwise not criminalistic.

For many years there has been the feeling that there is tight organization within the world of crime. Even in the writings of such late nineteenth-century muckrakers as Lincoln Steffens there was reference to the growing degree of underworld organization. References to the Mafia and the Black Hand have been made for generations, but the period of a virtual monopoly in the world of organized crime is fairly recent in America's history.

From godfather to chairman of the board   There has long been the feeling that reference to an American Mafia partakes more of melodrama than of reality. Even J. Edgar Hoover avoided the word Mafia, although after about 1961 he used the name Cosa Nostra, the modern name of the organization.[15]

The Mafia as it existed in Sicily was an underground organization whose members were considered one big family, linked together by close kinship loyalty. Just as in Mario Puzo's novel *The Godfather*, important members were often referred to as godparents and the institution of godparenthood (*compradazo*) made it possible to extend a kinship organization past the ties of actual blood relationship. There were also initiation rites for joining Mafia families and becoming fictive kinsmen. The American underworld character Joseph Valachi underwent such an initiation into Mafia kinship in New York in 1930.[16] Just as fictive

[15]Donald R. Cressey, *The Theft of the Nation*, Harper & Row, Publishers, Incorporated, New York, 1969, pp. 22–23.
[16]Robert T. Anderson, "From Mafia to Cosa Nostra," *American Journal of Sociology*, vol. 71, pp. 302–310, November 1965.

kinsmen could be adopted into the organization by initiation, actual kinsmen could be excluded if they were not good at criminal activities.

Apologists for the Mafia say that in Sicily it sometimes had the function of supplying measures of government where government was nonexistent or of supplying opposition to tyrannical government. However, such secret organizations, whatever their function, are easily given to terrorism, and many common Sicilian peasants and shopkeepers were victimized by the Mafia.

The organization was headed by a *capomafia* (Mafia head), and subdivided into *setta* (cells). All members of the organization were treated as kinsmen unless they failed in their loyalty to the group, in which case they were likely to be murdered. There was little formality or structure within the organization in the nineteenth century; in recent years the formality has increased somewhat, but the old familial characteristics are still preserved.[17]

Small groups of Mafialike gangs have existed in American cities since the late nineteenth century, but they were not organized into one great syndicate. In fact, strong rivalries for leadership existed, resulting in a war between Italian and Sicilian groups in 1930. Giuseppi Masseria, leader of one gang, passed a death sentence on prominent members of the opposition. In a period of two or three days, forty leaders of the older organization of the Mafia were killed, and later Masseria, who had started the war, was also killed. Eventually Charles "Lucky" Luciano became the head of the organization and expanded the leadership to a commission of nine to twelve men. Sometimes the organization is still called the Mafia; sometimes it is called Cosa Nostra (Our Thing), or the Outfit, or the Syndicate, or simply the Organization. Whatever it is called, it now combines the old close-kinship ideal of brothers-in-crime with many of the characteristics of modern, bureaucratic organization.[18] It has all the loyalty and secrecy of the former and the efficiency of the latter.

Cosa Nostra today   The syndicate has flourished. According to the President's Commission on Law Enforcement and Administration of Justice, the core of organized crime consists of twenty-four families operating in all the biggest cities of the United States.[19] Five families are located in New York City. The term Cosa Nostra is a little misleading because it is such a purely Sicilian name. Many people can therefore deal with non-Sicilian associates of Cosa Nostra and have no idea they are part of the Syndicate. However, the inner core of the families remains Italian- and Sicilian-American. So great are the rewards of their well-organized business that they have another trait in common: they are all rich; most are millionaires.[20] Outside the inner circle there are thousands of poorer people of all ethnic stocks working for Cosa Nostra. Crime knows no class or ethnic barriers as long as it pays.

The fact of the Sicilian- and Italian-American leadership and organization of Cosa Nostra is a source of embarrassment to the millions of honest Italian-Americans in the United States, who outnumber the Cosa Nostra members 1,000 to 1. A very good statement of the attitude of the honest Italian-American was made by Ralph Salerno of the New York City police and author of *The Crime Confederation*. A member of the mob accused him of being against "his own people":

[17]*Ibid.*
[18]Ralph Salerno and John S. Tompkins, *The Crime Federation*, Doubleday & Company, Inc., Garden City, N.Y., 1969, pp. 85–88.
[19]Winslow, *op. cit.*, pp. 191–209.
[20]Cressey, *op. cit.*, p. 84.

Gambling is a lucrative field for organized crime; the victim is often led to bankruptcy and to the loansharks of the underworld.

309

I'm not your kind, and you're not my kind. My manners, morals, and mores are not yours. The only thing we have in common is that we both spring from a common Italian heritage and culture—and you are the traitor to that heritage and culture of which I am proud. . . . [21]

The commission that heads the syndicate continues as it was founded by Lucky Luciano, still consisting of nine to twelve members. The twenty-four families range in membership from twenty to as many as seven hundred, with several specialized positions. Most sinister of the specialities is that of "enforcer," whose duty is to maim or kill those members who fail to cooperate.

The fields of operations   Organized crime once made most of its profits from bootlegging liquor. After the repeal of the Eighteenth Amendment, other lucrative activities had to be found. The most profitable field of operations of the underworld today is gambling. Very few gambling houses are independent of the organization, although the network leading from the bottom to the top of the organization is so complex that many people have no knowledge of who makes the final profit. A conservative estimate is that the net profit per year to the Syndicate from the gambling interests is about $7 billion.[22]

Because of its tragic consequences, the narcotics trade is more in the public mind than gambling. It is estimated that heroin alone nets $350 million annually for the Syndicate. There is no area in which the chain or organization is more apparent to the person with even the most casual knowledge. Users become dealers in order to earn money for their addiction, and they buy from an agent closer to the organization, who knows a wholesale supplier yet nearer to the top of the pyramid. Those who sit at the top are isolated by such a long chain of command as to be invulnerable to arrest unless they make a mistake. The best legal advisors available are hired to make sure there are no mistakes.

Prostitution, which was once important in the profits of organized crime, is much

---

[21]Winslow, *op. cit.*, p. 205.
[22]*Ibid.*, p. 196.

more difficult to organize than many other enterprises. It has declined to relatively little importance.

Various forms of labor racketeering have become a major source of profits to organized crime. Infiltration into unions has resulted in the raiding of union retirement funds. Sometimes Syndicate members accept pay from companies to prevent unions from striking or otherwise pressing for more benefits. Sometimes they extract funds from management by threatening to stir up labor sentiments and force a strike.

Usury and the penetration of legitimate business   There are no reliable figures on the total profit of the loan-shark business, but it is one of the most profitable rackets of the Syndicate. Cressey tells of one man who increased his fortune from $500,000 to $7,500,000 in four years in the usury business. Interest rates vary, but a common charge on short-term loans is "six-for-five." The loan shark lends $500 and demands repayment of $600 at the end of the week. If the debtor is as much as one hour late, he owes another $100. Longer-term loans range from about 10 to 250 percent per year. The loan shark closest to gambling joints usually charges 10 percent per day.

People are most frequently driven to such loans when financial reverses destroy their credit ratings or when a possible blackmail situation prevents their going to legitimate sources of loans.

The loan sharks working for the Syndicate seem unusually generous about making loans, but their leniency ends on payday. One man who borrowed from a California loan shark to buy some jewelry introduced two friends to the money lender. They also took out loans. When they were unable to repay, the original borrower was held responsible for their debts. When he refused to pay, he was met by four goons who beat him with a blackjack, knocked out two of his teeth, and tied him to an overhead pipe and took turns punching him in the stomach. They also stole his car and phoned a threatening message to his girlfriend. After his release from the hospital he was given a brief "stop-the-clock" period for raising the money.[23]

It is unusual for the Syndicate to kill a debtor, although they occasionally do so to set an example. More likely, a stop-the-clock period will be called, meaning a brief halt in the interest rate while a person tries to work all his friends and relatives for the money to pay his debts. To kill him would be too much like killing the goose that laid the golden egg. He is kept alive and bled as long as possible. A favorite device is to bring him into the organization, if his only possible way of paying off the debt is to commit a crime for the Syndicate. After that he can easily be blackmailed into committing more crimes. He is hooked.

Another serious result of the loan-shark business is the invasion of legitimate business. Often, if a person in business has borrowed and cannot repay, the person is forced into accepting "partners" in the business. Sometimes the Syndicate becomes the complete owner. If the business does not pay well, the Syndicate is as clever at disposing of it as at acquiring it. The procedure is to sell all the inventory and then declare bankruptcy, always through an individual who fronts for the organization, often the original owner himself.

The tie-in   As we have seen, organized crime bilks the public of billions of dollars. It adds immeasurably to the other costs of crime. It furnishes the narcotics that

[23]Cressey, *op. cit.*, p. 83.

destory so many lives; it wrecks legitimate business and corrupts labor unions.
Even more sinister, organized crime corrupts our court system and gains control
over many of the political and economic institutions of our metropolitan areas. In
Donald Cressey's words,

> The danger of organized crime arises because the vast profits acquired from the sale of
> illicit goods and services are being invested in licit enterprises, in both the economic
> sphere and the political sphere. It is when criminal syndicates start to undermine basic
> economic and political traditions and institutions that the real trouble begins. And the
> real trouble has begun in the United States.[24]

CRIME THEORY AND PRACTICE

There are many theories of crime that stress different aspects of the phenomenon
without being contradictory. Some are interested primarily in explaining juvenile
gangs, others in more remunerative crime, and yet others in crimes of violence.
Two well-known theories of crime that are particularly apt for explaining the types
of crimes just discussed are those of Merton and Sutherland. Merton's is the more
comprehensive theory, aiming first at explaining why America has a high crime rate
and second at explaining different types of crime.

Merton's[25] theory is basically one that stresses a strain between societal goals
and access to those goals. Our cultural norms, says Merton, are unusually strong in
expecting a good measure of material success from everyone, and they stress the
success goal more strongly than the honest means to the goal. Moreover,
insufficient attention is given to making sure that all people have access to the
goal. Four possibilities result from the situation:

1 One can conform to both success goals and honest means, winning the highest
applause of the society.

2 The second-best adjustment is to win the success goals by deviant means,
especially if the means are clever and one gets by with them. Society's tendency
to admire the clever scoundrel helps to cause less-clever people to also try
deviant means. People with unequal access to the goals (those born poor and
culturally deprived) are almost forced into deviance or to give up pursuit of the
goal.

3 The third possibility is to remain poor but honest. If goals were stressed less, and
means more, this adjustment would be greatly admired; but, says Merton, it
receives little praise.

4 The fourth possibility is to reject both means and goals and become a vagrant or
an addict.

5 There is even a fifth possibility—accept some of the social norms and reject
others, in the name of a new order. This is the rebellion adjustment.

For our purposes, Merton's second adjustment will be stressed, although his
fourth point has a bearing on the previous chapter. Merton attempts to explain why
there is so much crime in society, and his explanation certainly covers many cases.
It would have to be stretched a little, however, to account for all the types of
white-collar crime discussed by Sutherland, especially cases of crime committed

[24]Cressey, *op. cit.*, p. 1.
[25]Robert K. Merton, *Social Theory and Social Structure*, The Free Press, New York, 1959, chap. 5.

by people who are already quite successful but desire more or who were born into wealthy Mafia families. In one respect, though, there is perfect harmony between the two theories: they both point out the desire to succeed by fair or foul means.

Sutherland sees deviant behavior as the result of an interplay of forces, with both legally supportive norms and deviant ways being learned by all people. Those for whom illicit learning is stronger than legal learning would be most likely to commit crimes. For the person reared in a Mafia family there is little ambivalence about entering a life of crime. For the perpetrator of most kinds of white-collar crime, on the other hand, there must usually be a gradual process of unlearning many of the normative attitudes already acquired and a means of rationalizing the change in attitudes.

The internalizing of deviant means usually depends upon group influences. Albert Cohen and James Short have sought to demonstrate that the delinquent gang is able to accept antisocial ways by creating a subculture of its own that defines rights and wrongs for its own members in opposition to the rights and wrongs of the larger society. Such a redefinition is easiest in a subculture that is hostile toward authorities. Sutherland showed, though, that a similar type of redefinition of norms was at work for a young businessman learning the used car business or learning the arts of disguising accounts. He learned such practices as standard operating procedure, supported by the actions and rationalizations of the rest of the crowd. The Cosa Nostra members, similarly, hold deviant-group norms, supported by the family, who are able to make them feel right about themselves as long as they remain loyal to the organization. Cressey found that for the embezzler there was no similar group support; therefore, the task of rationalization tended to be more protracted and more ingenious.

The rewards of crime The rewards of crime differ from the mere chance to show hostility and blow off steam, as in the case of certain types of juvenile gangs, to the millions of dollars made by white-collar crime and organized crime. Sometimes the rewards of crime could be best described in terms of Merton's theory, discussed earlier in this chapter, of trying to reach success goals by illegal means. For a few, especially for the organized-crime world, the goals are reached and it is impossible to preach in such cases that crime does not pay. For most ordinary thieves, however, crime is an unrewarding way of life, interrupted by years in prison and strewn with broken resolutions to go straight. Why, then, is there so little success in dealing with crime?

If we believed, as people once did, that crime occurs mainly because bad blood flows in the veins of certain families, the obvious solution to the crime problem would be a eugenics program to stop such families from breeding. We now know that such an explanation is nonsense. If we believe that crime is essentially learned behavior, tempered by normative conflict, group support, inducement, and a failure of access to more legitimate opportunities, we at least have a basis for judging the methods of control that are now applied and for attempting new methods of control. Obviously, the desirable attack would be to remove opportunities for learning crime, make its inducements unattractive by catching a much larger proportion of offenders, and widen opportunitites for legitimate roads to success for the culturally deprived. We would also have to try to resolve some of the cultural conflict within our society in order to arrive at laws that would be more uniformly accepted.

Judging by the annual statistics on crime, and knowing as we do that a majority of all crime is hidden, we cannot be very optimistic about present methods. None of the objectives discussed above is being achieved to any great degree. What is even more troublesome is that although our theoretical knowledge suggests many improvements for dealing with the crime problem among the poor, the problem of control of white-collar crime and of the great crime syndicates is much more baffling. It is in these areas that crime pays best. Are there any ways of removing the profit?

The framing of law   Part of the problem of white-collar crime is a matter of clearer definition. Although the man who presents false claims to an insurance company might gather more in ill-gotten gains than the man who robs a service station, neither the public nor the authorities consider the crime as serious. False advertising is even less clearly defined, although it can have serious consequences. Cressey's conclusion in his study on embezzlement is that any law that forces people to conceptualize their acts as crime rather than as clever tricks has a beneficial effect. What is true for the embezzler is probably true for many people who commit white-collar crimes. How the public looks upon their acts is important. In war years, black marketeering can be rampant or virtually nonexistent, depending upon whether the public sees it as a necessary act or as something akin to treason. In the case of much white-collar crime, where the difference between legal and illegal is a very thin line, it would not seem wise to impose heavy criminal penalties. Fortunately, though, the white-collar-crime area is one in which even small penalties have a strong deterrent effect. The person of respectable reputation is seriously injured by being involved in crime, and even a short jail sentence can be devastating. In addition to careful framing of the law, then, a problem with white-collar crime is to arrive at legal sanctions that are more than a mere slap on the wrist but not severe enough to ruin one's career for doing almost exactly what a more clever competitor has done without quite transgressing the law.

Dilemmas of deterrence   The whole problem of deterrence needs more investigation. It is a rather fundamental principle of learning theory that desired behavior should be rewarded and undesirable behavior punished, but the kind and degree of reward or punishment are questionable. Most people are familiar with contradictory statistics about the effect of capital punishment. In a few cases the removal of capital punishment has been followed by a slight increase in homicide rates; in other cases it has actually been followed by a decrease. The conclusion seems to be that the murder rate is influenced more by such factors as urbanization and geographical mobility than by capital punishment.[26] One reason is that murder is usually a crime of desperation rather than cool calculation.

Dr. David G. Hubbard, a psychiatrist, has arrived at an amazing conclusion about the failure of deterrence in another type of crime of desperation, hijacking airplanes.[27] His conclusion is that the typical hijacker is neither a confirmed criminal nor a Communist. He is usually a man of serious psychological problems, with feelings of inadequacy and fantasies of suicide. He identifies with the astronauts and dreams of achieving a manly glory that will wash away his pitiful inadequacy. The desperate venture of hijacking a plane excites his imagination. The more publicity such ventures receive, and the more frightening the promised

[26]Thorsten Sellin, "Experiments with Abolition," in Thorsten Sellin (ed.), *Capital Punishment*, Harper & Row, Publishers, Incorporated, New York, 1967, pp. 122–125.
[27]Fletcher Knebel, "The Skyjacker," *Look*, vol. 35, pp. 23–26, February 9, 1971.

New York State undermines a major source of profit for the Syndicate by means of off-track betting—legalized, state-controlled gambling.

punishment becomes, the more it appeals to his sense of adventure. The fear of capital punishment seems to be no deterrent, since the man's fevered dream is to die anyway. If Hubbard is right, the skyjacker is a better-than-average case of the misfit between reasons for crime and common assumptions about deterrence.

In turning to organized crime, however, we are returning to a case of calculation for profit, not mental illness or desperation. Is there any possible deterrence to the Syndicate?

Fighting the Syndicate   Nothing in the field of crime is more discouraging than the struggle against Cosa Nostra. If laws become more severe, the organization becomes more cautious and devotes more of its funds to the search for loopholes. In the field of narcotics, few top men are ever caught. As suggested in the chapter on drugs, a system of medical dispensing of methadone or even heroin to drug addicts would be a means of undermining the profits of the narcotics trade.

In the case of illegal gambling, the Syndicate receives little opposition from public opinion, for the public does not regard gambling as a major evil. Most evils of gambling are secondary evils, not of the act itself but of its corrupting influence under our present legal system. Judge John Murtagh[28] shows how gambling has

[28]John M. Murtagh, *Atlantic Monthly*, vol. 206, pp. 49–53, November 1960.

been able to corrupt police forces more easily than any other kind of crime. Probably part of the reason is that police, like the general public, do not think of gambling as a very serious crime. If a police force allowed a payoff for murder, the whole nation would be outraged, but little interest would probably be shown for gambling. Members of the gambling underworld are let off easily; records are falsified so that they all seem to be first offenders. Such covering up of gambling, Murtagh says, has been going on in New York for over a century. In our time, the profit is generally made by Cosa Nostra.

Murtagh suggests cutting out the gambling profit by legalizing gambling, believing that it could dry up the money source for the underworld almost as effectively as the repeal of the Prohibition Amendment did years ago. Although not much opposed in principle to legalized gambling, Cressey is a little dubious about its possible success. He contends that the present operators make gambling more glamorous and attractive than do state lotteries and other public gambling enterprises. Nevertheless, he sees the solution to the problem of enriching the Syndicate in much the same way as Murtagh. Perhaps reputable business concerns could run gambling for the government. He also suggests that the states institute loan agencies to help people in desperate straits. Such an enterprise would probably lose money, but the cost would be far less than the present cost of enriching organized crime. Cutting the profits of crime would cut its power, which is now spreading over both legitimate business and government.

| Discuss and debate the case for and against legalized gambling.

SUGGESTED READINGS

Cressey, Donald R: *The Theft of the Nation*, Harper & Row, Publishers, Incorporated, New York, 1969. A treatment of organized crime by a well-known criminologist and member of the President's Commission on Law Enforcement and the Administration of Justice. The author, deeply concerned over the growth of organized crime, conveys a sense of urgency throughout.

Hills, Stuart L.: *Crime, Power, and Morality: The Criminal-Law Process in the United States*, Chandler Publishing Company, San Francisco, 1971. Hills presents the problem of crime in a new perspective: why society defines criminal law as it does and why it stigmatizes some types of criminals more than others. In this perspective he examines marijuana and the law, Cosa Nostra and organized crime, and white-collar occupational crime.

Jackson, Bruce: *On the Inside Looking Out*, Mentor Books, New American Library, Inc., New York, 1975. Based largely on narratives told by prison inmates and by criminals still on the street. "We share the worlds of those who turn tricks, deal dope, heist banks, swindle and peddle hot merchandise."

Kassenbaum, Gene: *Delinquency and Social Policy*, Prentice-Hall, Inc., Englewood Cliffs, N.J., 1972. Analyzes juvenile delinquency and the laws and agencies that deal with the problem. Views much of juvenile delinquency in the light of conflicts within the society of age, race, sex, and social class.

Winslow, Robert W.: *Crime in a Free Society: Selections from the President's Commission on Law Enforcement and the Administration of Justice*, Dickenson Publishing Company, Belmont, Calif., 1968. An authoritative study of many aspects of crime, well edited. Covers also police, courts, and corrections.

Yablonsky, Lewis: *The Violent Gang*, Penguin Books, Inc., Baltimore, 1967. Based on firsthand study of violent juvenile gangs, Yablonsky's book attempts to explain their rise and to look into possibilities for control. Much of the account is told in the words of gang members.

QUESTIONS

1 What are some of the social-class differences in types of juvenile crime and their likelihood of persistence?

2 Explain the meaning of white-collar crime and give some examples.

3 What are the major sources of profit for Cosa Nostra? Would there be any way to cut out their profits?

4 Show how the occurrence of crime tends to fit the Sutherland theory of crime as learned behavior.

5 Under what conditions does punishment seem to be a real deterrent to crime, and when is it uncertain or of little value?

What is the theory behind systems of justice—revenge, deterrence, or rehabilitation? The process of criminal justice must start, obviously, with catching the criminal, a task assigned usually to the policeman. Why is the policeman's role so difficult and such a subject of bitter debate? Do age, race, and social-class differences influence the handling of justice? Why do we hear complaints about delay in justice, about the unevenness of bail systems, and about detention without trial? What is military justice like? Are modern jails and prisons organized so as to be centers of reform and rehabilitation, or are they still schools for crime? Is the whole subject of justice keeping pace with psychological and sociological knowledge and changing norms, or does it reflect earlier views and attitudes? What new ideas are being tried?

In attempting to answer these questions, we shall have to admit there are great difficulties in the way of improvement. Although there is considerable upgrading of police training and selection in many communities, police power is still easily subject to abuse and corruption. Efforts are needed to speed up the court system; but it must also be remembered that part of the reason for a slow process of justice is protection of the innocent. Prisons are regarded as necessary evils, and the public likes to think about them as little as possible, yet there must be more public interest in all aspects of justice if significant changes are to be made. We shall see that there are reasons for increased public interest at present and, therefore, hope for a better system of justice.

The concept of justice is so important to social systems that the magistrate has occupied a position close to the throne since ancient times. In fact, in many archaic systems magistrate and king were one and the same. The givers of law have been lauded in history and tradition—Moses, Hammurabi, Solomon, Solon—and often their laws have been attributed to God. The time-honored philosopher Plato made the concept of justice the central accomplishment of his visionary Republic, and Immanuel Kant saw the craving for justice as one evidence of a divine order. However, in spite of the great intellectual effort that has gone into defining justice, justice systems have a tendency to revert to the harsh and futile principle of *lex talionis*, the law of revenge, found in Hammurabi's code and in Deuteronomy 19:21: "And thine eye shall not pity, but life shall go for life, eye for eye, tooth for tooth, hand for hand, foot for foot."

Even in a modern society in which the principle of an eye for an eye is outmoded and systems for processing criminals are called agencies of reform, the ancient attitudes continue to appear. A court system overburdened with a backlog of cases that grows more staggering every year finds it impossible to ponder the meaning of justice; it strives only to get cases off the books. Arrests are made by a much vilified and underpaid police force, recruited from very ordinary men and expected to exemplify a judgment, moderation, and detachment rare in the human species.

The system of punishment is a system repellent to most people, so they think about it as little as possible. The federal prisons and a few state prisons attempt to bring humane treatment into institutions that make no provisions for most of the psychological needs of the human being. Many other prisons do not make such attempts at modern enlightenment and are understaffed, overcrowded, and essentially brutal. Whatever the ills of federal and state prisons, however, they are often summer camps compared with the thousands of county and city jails—the pestholes most frequently encountered by the first-time offender.

All three major links in the system of justice are being subjected to increasing criticism by a society that claims to believe more in reform than in revenge. The first link, the most criticized but not necessarily the weakest, is the police force.

THE POLICE

An organized police force is newer to American experience than the courts or the jails and prisons, but an encounter with the police is usually the first step in the modern process of justice. The first metropolitan police force was established in New York City in 1841. Previously, arrests had been made by ordinary citizens, hired guards, or deputized agents of the sheriff's office.[1] New, official police forces were looked upon as possible concentrations of power that would threaten the citizen and lead to a diminution of his rights to due process of law. After well over a

---

[1]Gresham M. Sykes, *Crime and Society*, Random House, Inc., New York, 1967, pp. 144–145.

Role expectation for the police: the friendly protector, guardian of the innocent.

century of institutionalized police forces, and the general feeling that such forces are indispensable, there is still the same concern. There is even greater feeling about the growth of an all-seeing federal force, so that the exercise of police power in the majority of cases remains in the hands of the county, city, and state governments. However police power is exercised, it is an inevitable center of controversy, part of which stems from the contradictory roles of the police officer.

Conflicting demands Many of the routine assignments of policemen and police-women are of a community-service type, such as answering emergency calls, looking for lost children, giving escort for emergency trips to the hospital, and helping in cases of natural disaster. In such cases there is little ambiguity about their position; they are the friends of the public.

  When police activities are involved in the pursuit of crime, however, the police image often changes. Their job is that of catching the guilty, but it is just as important to protect the innocent. The police are in a position where they must exert strong force occasionally and react to situations of danger but must be expected to use restraint even in such cases and must not develop hostility and suspicion toward the very citizens they are hired to protect. Ideally, their position calls for a rare combination of courage, judiciousness, and self-control, and a moral resistance to all corrupting temptations to which police departments are subject. Obviously, not all police officers can live up to all these requirements, nor is the public willing to pay the price that would be necessary for recruiting and training such a model force.

  The nature of a police officer's job results in certain characteristics and attitudes of personality that Jerome Skolnick[2] analyzed in a study of two large city police forces. The position of the police officer combines authority with considerable threat of danger. Judging by the number of police officers who prefer criminal

[2]Jerome H. Skolnick, *Justice without Trial*, John Wiley & Sons, Inc., New York, 1966, pp. 42–70.

The policeman's other role: the forceful agent of the state, reacting (and sometimes overreacting) to danger.

investigation to other types of work, it could be said that they tend to welcome the more dangerous role. Their work trains them to search for all suspicious characters and situations—to take a second glance at loiterers, at occupied cars parked near children's playgrounds, at eccentric people, at the oddly dressed, the unusual, the person with poor motor control, and leather-jacketed juvenile crowds. Suspiciousness becomes part of their personality. At the same time, they find that other people are a little uncomfortable around them; they therefore make friends in their own circles and their world becomes isolated. Sometimes there is even a slight antagonism toward the general public, who, in police experience, will simply stand by in an emergency, expecting the police to do everything. As noted in the previous chapter, the public often fails to cooperate even to the extent of reporting crime. The police are also charged with upholding the morality laws of a puritanical society, although such puritanism is not necessarily associated with the person willing to risk danger and assert authority. In the course of their work, the police are often assigned to ghetto areas which they sometimes find threatening. They are therefore accused of racial bias by a society that itself displays just as much racial bias—otherwise, why would blacks be segregated into ghettos? They are more pragmatic than philosophical in their attitudes toward the law and see little reason for court decisions that restrict their right to search and interrogate and that insist they follow constitutional procedures.

Interview or invite a well-informed police official to explain the problems of the job of policeman and also to answer questions from the class.

Police personnel and the public image American police officers have been predominantly Caucasians, although changes have occurred in many cities as a result of riots and subsequent attempts to improve relationships within the ghettos and barrios. In 1960, city police forces were 96.5 percent white; and only 0.2

percent of state police officers were black. In the years since then, improvement in racial and ethnic balance has progressed fairly rapidly in some of the cities, but very slowly in state police forces. A *New York Times* survey of New York and several other Eastern cities found that recruitment policies mirrored racial and ethnic distributions. Where there were high concentrations of black and Puerto Rican people in the area, these groups were recruited for the police forces.[3] On the other hand, another *Times* survey indicated that state police systems were making little racial progress. Only five states had as many as ten black policemen on their forces, and many had none at all. A federal court ordered recruitment of blacks for the Alabama state police force in a decision that should affect other states as well.[4]

Applications for police-force jobs have come most frequently from low-paid, white-collar, manufacturing, or service workers and former servicemen. The National Commission on Justice Standards and Goals recommends at least one year of college for all members of police forces. One goal of the Commission is that police work will require four years of college education by 1982.

Police forces have had their difficulties with public image. Especially during the period of frequent demonstrations and riots in the late 1960s, they received much hostility from young militants and minority groups. A survey showed that 70 percent of police officers considered their prestige to be only fair to poor. Actually, opinion surveys cited by the President's Commission on Law Enforcement indicated higher respect for the police than police officers believed to exist. Only 9 percent of the public said that police do a poor job; 75 percent rated them as good or excellent.

When cases of corruption come to light, however, the negative effect on public support for the police is greater than it was during riots and demonstrations. Ever since the days of the muckrakers of the late nineteenth century, frequent disclosures of police corruption have occurred, usually accompanied by general corruption at city hall. In 1961 it became apparent that members of the Denver police force had been operating a criminal ring for more than fifteen years and had stolen over $250,000 in cash and much more in merchandise.[5] Several years later, it was reported that 400 pounds of narcotics, taken by the New York police, were missing, with the suspicion it had been sold.[6] A lengthy investigation of the New York police revealed that many plainclothesmen were accepting payoffs from gamblers, with each man in the ring receiving a monthly share from $300 to $400. In a number of cases, narcotics agents were shaking down peddlers rather than arresting them. The largest amount taken by a narcotics agent was $80,000. Patrolmen were less tainted than plainclothesmen or narcotics agents, but many of them also accepted money.[7] In Chicago, 60 policemen were indicted and 40 convicted for bribery. A shakedown of nightclubs had been going on for six years, netting thousands of dollars for corrupt members of the force.[8] In Indianapolis, the *Star* launched an investigation into police corruption, accusing the local force of bribery, theft, extortion, and protection of prostitutes.[9]

In some cases the standard explanation that "there are a few bad apples in every barrel" is fairly adequate; but in other cases the barrel may prove rotten through-

---

[3]*New York Times*, October 21, 1973, part IV, p. 8, col. 1.
[4]*New York Times*, April 17, 1972, p. 1, col. 2.
[5]Sykes, *op. cit.*, p. 149.
[6]W. P. Brown, "Police Corruption: The System is the Problem," *Nation*, vol. 216, pp. 456–459, April 9, 1973.
[7]"We Found Corruption to be Widespread," *U.S. News & World Report*, vol. 74, pp. 76–79, January 29, 1973.
[8]"Chicago Rogue Cops," *Newsweek*, vol. 82, p. 85, December 3, 1973.
[9]"The Indianapolis Two," *Time*, vol. 104, p. 76, September 30, 1974.

out. One investigator with years of experience on police forces concludes that the rotten-apple theory is hardly adequate. In his opinion, those police forces are least corrupt that have the best training, the strongest feeling about professionalism in police work, and that work for city governments that are themselves honest.[10]

Following the civil rights and antiwar demonstrations there were more complaints about police brutality than about corruption, and such charges came more from the poor, the young, the black, and the Chicano than from other elements of the population.

Race and the police   In answer to the question "Are police often conscienceless and brutal in performing their duties?" in Los Angeles 11 percent of the whites said yes; 38 percent of the blacks said yes; and 44 percent of the Mexicans said yes.[11] Such a statement is a matter of opinion, obviously, but it is probably opinion based either on personal experience or on known or rumored experiences of others in the social group to which the respondent belongs. The term police brutality lacks a consistent definition. The Wickersham Commission of the 1930s described many conditions of unquestionable brutality used in trying to extort confessions from suspects. Partly because of Supreme Court rulings, such offenses are much less common today. Often in the ghetto area the complaint referred to as brutality is more correctly called harassment. People are stopped for questioning more frequently in the ghetto than elsewhere, there are more insults, and there is greater feeling of mutual hostility between citizen and police. A Presidential commission, reporting in 1968,[12] found far less brutality than in earlier days but still enough unjustified interrogation and enough abusive language to explain part of the negative feelings. Interracial couples as well as youths were particularly subject to being stopped and interrogated. Although the commission was extremely critical of racism in American life, it felt that the main reason for so much singling out of the police forces is that they are the front line of contact between the ghetto and the outside world. The evil was seen as essentially societal racism, not just police racism.

For the Mexican-Americans, mistreatment at the hands of local sheriff's officers was found in case after case of the testimony before the Senate committee investigating migrant labor (see Chapter 10). In Los Angeles, which has made great efforts in recent years to achieve a well-trained, well-paid, professionalized police force, there are still strong complaints within the Mexican neighborhoods, especially about the great shortage of Mexican-Americans on the police force.

It was also in Los Angeles in 1971 that an experiment was tried to determine what effect Black Panther stickers on cars would have on arrest rates. Fifteen California State College students—five Mexican, five white, and five black, and all with perfect driving records—agreed to test the results of such signs. Within seventeen days they received a total of thirty-three traffic citations.[13] The feelings of police were stronger than usual on the subject of Black Panthers, as there had been some recent deaths in encounters with them. Nevertheless, the experiment indicates that feelings have a strong influence on perception of law violations.

[10]W. P. Brown, *op. cit.*

[11]Robert W. Winslow (ed.), *Crime in a Free Society: Selections from the President's Commission on Law Enforcement and the Administration of Justice*, Dickenson Publishing Company, Belmont, Calif., 1968, p. 273.

[12]*Report of the National Advisory Commission on Civil Disorders*, Bantam Books, Inc., New York, 1968, pp. 203–204.

[13]F. K. Heussenstamm, "Bumper Stickers and the Cops," *Transaction*, vol. 8, pp. 32–33, February 1971.

Police and poverty Part of the ground for complaint against police is not so much a matter of racism as of social-class discrimination. A Michigan study conducted by Edward Green found that arrest rates bore a close relation to social class, unemployment, migration from rural to urban areas, and attitudes associated with lower-class position, regardless of race.[14] In fact, it was found that the black arrest rate was declining slightly but that of the unemployed was showing considerable increase, regardless of race.

Albert J. Reiss, Jr.,[15] in a study aimed more directly at the problem of police brutality, found quite a number of cases of the use of excessive force in connection with arrest and interrogation. Because the study of police actions was done under the known observation of sociological investigators, one cannot help but wonder if the situation is not worse when unobserved. On the subject of race and poverty, however, it is interesting to note that 67 percent of the cases of excessive force were of white officers against white suspects. Those who were obviously poor were much more subject to abusive language and to being hit or shoved than the others. The defiant and the deviants were especially subject to excessive force. The worst aspect of excessive force, according to Reiss, is that much of it took place in police stations after the suspect was already under control. There were also thirty-seven cases of excessive force used on the streets in the process of arrest, but only one witness complained.

Reiss draws two other important conclusions. Sometimes the poor white is even more vulnerable to abuse than members of minority groups, which are now developing organizations to protest cases of mistreatment. He says that such organizations once existed among white ethnic groups—and sometimes still do—but for the rootless and unknown white there is little recourse. His other conclusion is that investigations into complaints carried on by police forces themselves have all the faults of an army self-investigation. Whatever wrong practices are discovered are not made known to the public so that the organization can appear clean. The New Orleans police force, for example, received 268 complaints in a recent year, investigated 106, dismissed 14 officers, and took other disciplinary action against 72 others, but no details were given about what violations had been committed.

Whatever other conclusion is valid, it is obvious that one should not be poor and isolated.

Juveniles and the police Although the stigma against wearing long hair is probably wearing off with the passing of time, most long-haired male juveniles have felt themselves subject to social discrimination and negative appraisal by much of the adult world, including the police. Do such antagonistic appearances really matter in actual arrest rate? A study by Irving Piliavin and Scott Briar,[16] although done before long hair was much of an issue, would indicate that such matters as appearance are very important. Their study was conducted in an American city of about 500,000 population. The policy of the police department allowed considerable choice about the kind of work the officer might do, so that juvenile work generally attracted a rather select group of those interested especial-

[14]Edward Green, "Race, Social Class, and Criminal Arrest," *American Sociological Review*, vol. 35, pp. 478–489, June 1970.
[15]Albert J. Reiss, Jr, "How Common Is Police Brutality," *Transaction*, vol. 5, pp. 10–17, July-August 1968.
[16]Irving Piliavin and Scott Briar, "Police Encounters with Juveniles," *American Journal of Sociology*, vol. 70, pp. 206–212, September 1970.

To what extent are such traits as color, age, dress, and far-out appearance accepted by the police as clues to character?

ly in the young. The juvenile workers on the force were given considerable discrimination in handling cases, and they tried to use their discretion in ways that would help young people they considered to be basically good and perhaps in trouble for the first time. None had any confidence in the correctional process—of which more will be said later—and they were reluctant to stigmatize individuals by giving them a police record. In their intent, they could certainly not be characterized as ill-willed, brutal, or even indifferent.

In using their discretion about who to bring into court, the police admitted using many cues to character—age (the younger ones were more likely to be perceived as innocent), race (blacks and foreigners were perceived as more incorrigible than native whites), grooming and dress, and demeanor. Apparently, then, a young, white, good-looking, well-dressed, polite boy or girl was almost sure to receive only a good talking to. The same could happen to a person failing in one of the other criteria—color, age, or even appearance; but any individual failing in demeanor or a combination of the other traits was in serious trouble.

The police attitude toward demeanor, however, is understandable. In an interaction situation, rudeness on one side provokes hostility from the other side. Teachers and others working with the young also find it easy to be antagonized—even infuriated—by rude or surly manners, even though there may be plausible psychological and sociological explanations for such behavior.

The police attitude regarding cues to character has its equivalent in jury attitudes. In the 1970s, with larger representation of minority groups on juries, the credibility of the police in court cases in the big cities has declined. However, especially in smaller towns, the police are nearly always believed in cases brought against groups that antagonize the juries—motorcycle clubs, homosexuals, and radicals, for example.[17]

[17]"Cops' Credibility," *Time*, vol. 103, p. 79, February 4, 1974.

The case of college militants   In demonstrations that have taken place in the past
several years, there is no question that the police have often been provoked in ways
that it is hard for people in authority to tolerate. There are cases in which the
feeling of danger or the anger of the moment has led to overreaction, which is at
least understandable. What is impossible to condone is the violence that has
sometimes taken place with people who are already subdued. An example from
Berkeley will illustrate the point. The violence of the guards at Santa Rita Prison
was much worse than that of the police, but in both cases the action was excessive
and of the type that further radicalizes the students.[18]

There had been a series of demonstrations in Berkeley over the demand to use
some University of California land for a people's park, and demonstrations and ill
will had been mounting. Finally, on May 22, 1969, the police decided to make an
example. They arrested people indiscriminantly on the streets of Berkeley, catching a large number of nonstudents as well as students. No rowdy demonstration
was in progress, but it was suspected that something was about to start. One of the
men arrested, and the one who wrote the story for *Life* magazine, was a professor
from San Francisco State College who happened to be in Berkeley in connection
with an environmental project. He and his friends were arrested and put in a paddy
wagon. They could not explain their business in Berkeley because they were
threatened with beatings if they opened their mouths. The treatment was rough
and terrifying. They were hauled off to Santa Rita Rehabilitation Center and Prison
Farm, where they, along with more than 400 others, were made to lie face down on
the concrete and remain silent. They were cursed, prodded, clubbed, and kicked.
One diabetic who complained of his condition was unmercifully beaten. Those with
long hair were particularly subject to beating and abuse and were called addicts,
perverts, and reds. For hours no one was allowed to contact a lawyer. They were
told that the other prisoners hated them and wanted to get at them and that they
were going to be turned over to hardened criminals and sex perverts.

Finally, after a long night of intermittent torture, all the prisoners were released.
For all 480, charges were dropped; there had been no evidence against them in the
first place. The sheriff explained that maybe his guards had been "a little
improper." Several, he said, were just back from the war and felt that any prisoners
could be treated as Viet Cong. Twelve guards were dismissed. The incident was an
unusually bad case, but it is the type of experience that proves the need for
constant vigilance over the strong arm of police power.

Justice without trial   The power of the police to decide, within certain limits, how
to dispose of a case is the main theme of Skolnick's book, *Justice without Trial*.[19]
He shows that too much authority beyond the arrest level devolves upon the police.
Part of the reason is that the courts are already so badly overcrowded that they
require a certain amount of police disposal of cases. As in the case of the juveniles
previously cited, the police have the power to decide whether to bring an individual
in and make the case one of record or a dismissal with a scolding and warning.

Other cases of justice without trial are more serious. In criminal cases having to
do with narcotics, the police often find it expedient to bargain with suspects in
return for information that might net several suspects or someone higher up the
narcotics ladder. When possible penalties are high, the police's bargaining power

[18]Jesse P. Ritter, Jr., "Nightmare for the Innocent in a California Jail," *Life*, vol. 76, pp. 51–54, August 15,
1969.
[19]Skolnick, *op. cit.*

is greatly increased, and they can decide whether to report a person caught in the act or to use the person as an informer. The city police are usually placed under great pressure to clear cases, which sometimes results in a further police decision of a judicial nature. Sometimes an arrest is made of a person who readily confesses to a number of previous offenses, so they all get cleared from the books at once. Skolnick tells of one case in which a burglar, James, confessed to over 400 previous cases that had not yet been cleared by arrest. James was so cooperative in confessing to so many baffling cases and in helping to implicate several other people that he got off almost completely free. Other minor offenders, whose thefts had been uncovered by James' testimony, received stiff sentences.[20]

The police are assigned very difficult roles in society, roles often performed by people of minimal training. Although there have been improvements in the quality of police work in recent years, there are still numerous complaints. One complaint—that of police judgment being substituted for court judgment—is also a complaint against the next stage of the justice system, the courts.

BREAKDOWN IN THE JUSTICE MACHINE

We like to look upon such instruments of American justice as judges, juries, attorneys, and constitutional guarantees as an achievement of modern enlightenment. American children, while still too young to really understand, start to study some of the basic principles of justice. They learn of the right to a speedy trial by a jury of their peers, of the presumption of innocence until guilt is proved, of the need for warrants for search and seizure, and of the right to a writ of habeas corpus, which their teachers tell them guarantees that Americans cannot be held in jail for long periods of time without trial.

Partly because of the crowded conditions of our courts, and occasionally because of corruption, there are innumerable exceptions to all the rules just given. The situation of overcrowding has reached such a state that the Chief Justice of the United States Supreme Court has been moved to speak of the crisis of our courts. Justice Burger delivered the first "State of the Judiciary" address in August 1970. He referred to a famous statement by Roscoe Pound sixty-four years before, in which the eminent professor of jurisprudence stated that surely the twentieth-century courts of justice would not be run by the methods and machinery of the nineteenth century. Roscoe Pound was wrong, Burger continued, "We are still trying to operate the courts with fundamentally the same basic methods, procedures, and machinery he said were not good enough in 1906."[21] Burger expressed fear that the sense of confidence in the courts, so necessary for a system combining liberty and order, could be destroyed if people come to believe that inefficiency and delay are rendering justice ineffective, or if the law cannot protect the safety of the people or save them from exploitation and fraud.

The inefficient machine Sykes[22] has likened our total handling of law violations to an inefficient machine or a conveyer belt that keeps dropping part of its load at various places along the way. The original load on the conveyer belt could be thought of as the total number of crimes committed and known to the police. The second stage is the number of crimes cleared by arrest, a very much smaller

---

[20]Skolnick, *op. cit.*, pp. 176–179.
[21]Chief Justice Warren E. Burger, "Burger on the Courts, Improvements Long Overdue," *Los Angeles Times*, August 16, 1970, section G, pp. 2 and 3.
[22]Sykes, *op. cit.*, pp. 143–164.

number in nearly all cases. The load is further diminished by the number of people found innocent, whose cases are dismissed for lack of evidence, or who are paroled and never actually punished. Finally, there is a small minority left who are actually sentenced to pay their "debt to society."

Sykes says, quite correctly, that a justice machine in a democratic society with strong feelings against punishment of the innocent has to be somewhat inefficient. A justice system that always caught every offense and always punished everyone to the limit of the law would be impossible and can be dreamed of only in a nightmare of totalitarianism. Although Sykes' reasoning is perfectly correct, the present situation is beginning to overload the machine with a burden it was never meant to carry and is forcing its inefficiency so far as to render it almost totally ineffective.

Other disturbing pictures come to mind as one tries to conceptualize a justice conveyer belt. Conveyer belts in mineral processing always carry the essential load to the refinery, dropping out only what is irrelevant to the process. The justice belt, on the other hand, tends to drop all the big, well-connected criminals and convey to prison mainly the minor cases. Furthermore, there is frequent slippage in the gears, so that parts of the process are omitted, or even reversed. In *Alice in Wonderland*, the Queen cries "First the verdict, then the trial." In some of our cases the cry becomes "First the punishment, then the verdict." Suspects have been known to wait in jail for months (in a few cases even years) before trial, then, after having received their punishment, been dismissed for lack of evidence.

There is yet another breakdown in the machine. The old saying "The mills of the gods grind slow, but they grind exceeding fine" implies great thoroughness and accuracy about a slowness of process. In the case of the courts, the slower they grind, the less likely they are to grind at all. "Delay is my best weapon. Time will beat any case if you have enough of it," says a defense attorney from Dallas.[23]

> Visit a local courtroom, preferably hearing a criminal case. Is the suspect well represented by an attorney? Was the defendant released on bail while awaiting trial? Was the court so overloaded with cases that it had to postpone the trial?

The law's delay   In most big cities both population and crime rates increase much faster than do court facilities, and simultaneously the length of time required for a major case lengthens—partly for the commendable purpose of giving the accused every legal protection that is afforded defendants, especially if they can hire a good lawyer.

The result of the vast increase in numbers of people and numbers of crimes is an overtaxing of the big city courts. The biggest city of all is New York, and its dilemma illustrates the court problem extremely well, although it is by no means unique. Of the 14,000 inmates of New York jails in 1969, 8,000 had been convicted of nothing; they were simply awaiting trial. In an attempt to speed up the legal process, Judge Stanley H. Fuld ruled that as of April 1972 all people who had been awaiting trial for over six months should have their cases dismissed. When the deadline arrived, the New York State Legislature ruled it was necessary only that the district attorneys have the cases *prepared* within six months. Otherwise the courts were given four more years to catch up, with no guarantee that they could do so.[24]

[23]Dale Wittner, "Logjam in Our Courts," *Life*, vol. 69, p. 19, August 7, 1970.
[24]"Slow Speedup," *Time*, vol. 99, p. 61, May 8, 1972.

Two years after Judge Fuld's ruling, the *New York Times* conducted a survey of the city's criminal justice system, finding that "no appreciable dent had been made into the backlog of 10,000 cases [note the increase!] awaiting disposition." Large numbers of defendants had been in jail awaiting trial for more than a year—one for thirty-five months. It was expected that the arrest rate would increase because 2,340 police had been added to the force; but no comparable additions to the courts had been made.[25]

One result of the overcrowding of the courts is that many jobs are lost while people wait in jail for the time of their trials. Family breakups also occur. Although the legal system speaks of a belief in innocence until proof of guilt, treatment of suspects is not what should be given presumably innocent citizens. The accompanying fact that bail is usually provided for members of Cosa Nostra so that they can await trial in freedom (freedom to commit more crimes) is a hard reality that embitters the incarcerated suspects.

Another disillusioning practice for those who retain a mental picture of the dignity of the law is plea bargaining. In plea bargaining, suspects are given promises of light sentences if they plead guilty so their case can clear the courts; even more likely they will be given a sentence for a lesser offense than the one committed. The practice saves many hours of time, but it ensures that justice will be only approximated. The alternative is likely to be one of waiting for months for the case to be tried—months during which witnesses' memories grow dim and a "reasonable doubt" begins to arise. To condemn such a system is not to accuse courts of deliberate dishonor; they have no alternative. The real problem is that it reduces justice to a joke, to a process of making a deal. Occasionally even the innocent are caught up in the system, feeling it is better to plead guilty to a small offense than to antagonize the court.

Los Angeles "Authorities sometimes remark that the only thing worse than not catching a criminal is catching him."[26] The present situation in Los Angeles County is also one of delayed justice and of a county jail system that is overloaded, but the overloading is only starting. Using a computer fed with crime rates and court and jail capacity, a University of Southern California team concludes that in six or seven years Los Angeles authorities will have to have a telephone answering service programmed to say, "Sorry, we cannot accept any more crime or civil complaints. We are full to capacity."

In California, even more than in other states, a vast amount of court crime is taken up with cases involving auto accidents and damages. There are proposals for either doing away with jury trials in such cases or reducing the size of the jury in order to save time.

The machinery of military justice The military justice machine is much more efficient than the civilian machine, if conviction rate is taken as a measurement of efficiency. Again it must be stated, though, that total efficiency sounds suspiciously totalitarian. The military conviction rate is 94 percent, compared with only 81 percent in civilian courts.[27] Military justice, admittedly, can have problems not faced by civilian justice. Especially under combat conditions, military forces must

[25]*New York Times*, August 13, 1974, p. 71, col. 4.
[26]William J. Drummond, "L.A. Crime Rate Could Collapse Justice System," *Los Angeles Times*, September 13, 1970, sec. B, pp. 1, 7.
[27]Editors of *Newsweek*, "U.S. Military Justice on Trial," *Newsweek*, pp. 18–23, April 31, 1970.

submit to a discipline not encountered in ordinary civilian life, and some of the amenities of freedom are difficult to maintain. A democracy has for its servant a regimented, disciplined, authoritarian organization, which includes between 3 and 4 million men and women who have been brought up to believe in the principles of civilian justice. Consequently, the military justice system comes under increasing attack, as it did at the end of World War II.

Military justice in the early days of our republic had none of the amenities of civilian justice—no bail, no defense lawyers, no indictments, no impartial judges or due process—and both branding and flogging were permitted until 1861. In 1950 more reforms were made, creating a Court of Military Appeals and providing a lawyer representation in both special and general courts-martial. Legal representation is not provided in the simple summary court martial, which can only impose a penalty of thirty days or less. In spite of reforms, there are remaining grounds for criticism. The commanding officer selects members of the court martial—his junior officers, who have a stake in staying on good terms with him. Although there are cases in which an enlisted man on trial can call for an enlisted member of the court martial, such an enlisted representative is selected by the officers and is likely to be the first sergeant, a man very close to the commanding officer. One has to have served in a low-ranking position in the Armed Forces to understand the feeling of insurmountable social distance that separates the enlisted man from a group of officers sitting as the trial board. Fortunately, a Court of Military Appeals has been created so that unreasonable decisions can be overruled and progress made in the direction of uniformity of sentencing. The progress, however, remains very slow. Twenty-two defendants who protested conditions at the Presidio guard house in San Francisco were prosecuted for mutiny—a tremendous overstatement of their offense. They were sentenced to many years in prison, but the sentences were drastically reduced by the appeals court. Sentences still remain grossly inconsistent. Refusal to obey orders has in recent years brought punishment ranging from a mere reprimand to sixteen years in prison.[28] In August 1974, CBS news reported on the case of a young American army officer in Germany on trial for refusing to cut his hair. For that heinous crime, he could conceivably receive five years' imprisonment and a dishonorable discharge for refusing to obey an order—although such a sentence is extremely unlikely.

THE PRISON

The principle of an eye for an eye sounds savage in the twentieth century, and yet it is hardly as savage as some of the punishment prescribed. In the American system of justice persons are frequently sentenced to prisons for terms of 100 to 200 years or more, and the prisons are by no means places of merciful treatment. Louis Wolfson charges that in a Florida prison one inmate was stomped to death by three guards; two asthmatics were denied treatment and died; a convicted forger with a wounded hand was denied treatment until gangrene set in and his hand had to be cut off.[29]

To another federal prison was sentenced a feeble-minded, impoverished black girl, not for causing loss of life or even property but for having pasted a canceled stamp on a letter she had mailed.[30] Elsewhere a man sentenced for a $70 robbery of

[28]Ibid., p. 22.
[29]Jack Anderson, "What It's Like to Be in Prison," Bell McClure syndicated dispatch of June 24, 1970.
[30]James V. Bennett, "A Cool Look at the Crime Crisis," Harper's, vol. 228, pp. 123–127, April 1964.

a gasoline station served eleven years, over seven in solitary. His hostile behavior caused a constant lengthening of his sentence. Finally he murdered a guard and was sentenced to give life for life.[31] No less an authority than James V. Bennett, longtime director of the U.S. Bureau of Prisons, says of our prison system:

> Except possibly for "enemies of the state" in countries where people are sent to prison for political reasons, the American criminal on the average serves several times as long a sentence as his counterpart anywhere else in the world.[32]

In the popular mind the reason for long and severe punishment is deterrence, although there is little evidence that prisons work to this purpose. As Durkheim analyzed punishment, it serves largely as a societal ritual for preserving the sense of righteousness of the law-abiding (or those who manage not to get caught). As Karl Menninger sees it in *The Crime of Punishment*, we secretly identify with the lawbreakers but expiate our sense of guilt by punishing them. Whatever the case, there is constant public clamor for longer sentences, and it seems to be good politics to cry for blood—eye for eye, tooth for tooth, and life for life.

Have a member or two of the class visit the local jail or a state prison if one is nearby. If you visit a prison, try to find out what sort of rehabilitation program is in progress, if any. Are modern improvements being tried? Is the institution overcrowded?

The place of forgetting One reason that well-run prisons are rare, in spite of frequent agitation for reform, is that they house a forgotten segment of the population. The stocks and the pillory were brutal, but at least people saw them and knew what took place. Cruelty was always present, but it was limited to what public opinion could countenance. In the prison, public opinion is generally inoperative because the life of the prisoner is not known. In the prisons of medieval France was a deep dungeon known as *l'oublière*, or "the place of forgetting." Men in the dungeons were shut out of the minds and memories of the rest of society, there to live in dampness and filth, and there eventually to sicken and die. Although many state and federal prisons have made wholesome reforms, there are still in twentieth-century America places of confinement that can be called nothing but *les oublières*. They are places of double tragedy, not only bringing misery but failing in their purpose of curing crime as well.

Occasionally stories of outrage are brought to light, as in the case of Tucker Prison Farm, Arkansas, which was run by the more brutal prisoners until 1967. Fear was instilled by beatings, insertion of needles under the fingernails, starvation, stompings, and "an electric device whose terminals were attached to the genitals of an inmate while a trusty or 'warden' gleefully turned the crank." It was in this prison that three mutilated bodies were found, bodies of men apparently killed and buried secretly by the prisoner guards.[33] This is an extreme and unusual case, but it points out the fact that in many prisons hostility between inmates and guards mounts dangerously, resulting in violent acts by prisoners and severe punitive measures from guards.

Theories of crime versus the prison In the previous chapter, two theories of crime were emphasized: crime as the latent function of too strong a success

---

[31]"The State of the Prisons," *Time*, vol. 97, p. 54, January 18, 1971.
[32]Bennett, *op. cit.*
[33]Tom Murton, "Too Good for Arkansas: One Year of Prison Reform," *The Nation*, January 12, 1970.

requirement, and crime as learned behavior. Hostility resulting from deprived conditions, of course, plays its part, and so does a disorganized family background. A prison system temporarily protects the public from some types of criminals and has at least some deterrent effect. At the same time, especially as seen from the point of view of crime theory, the prison has certain latent functions that promote crime. If crime is a consequence of too strong a desire for success even by deviant means, then the prison serves the latent function of being a place for discussing such means and planning how to succeed better next time. If crime is thought of as mainly learned behavior, then the prison can be seen as an excellent teacher. If crime is a result of hostilities, there is little doubt that hostilities are increased in the majority of prisons. If crime is partly a consequence of family disorganization, certainly imprisonment adds to the problem, for it drives family relationships further apart.

If we add to these characteristics of the prison the tendency for the most hardened, old-line criminals to become kingpins in an informal organization that helps the system to function, then we will have added almost the finishing touch to a description of the perfect school for crime. The informal social system that grows up within the prison even permits crime within prison walls—blackmail, loansharking, beatings, homosexual attacks, and smuggling of narcotics.

In short, there is little about the analysis of causes of crime that seems to mesh with the manner of running prisons. If one did not know better, one would assume that the purpose of imprisonment is to ensure the continuance of crime.

The inmate world of the total institution The "total institution," as described by Goffman, is any institution that takes complete control of the individual, leaving no free will and no direction of one's own life. Most prisons closely approach the following description, based largely on Goffman's work,[34] although some are making real improvements.

In the inmate world there is no such thing as a separation between time on the job and time devoted to one's own purposes; one has no purposes of one's own. The total life is part of the inmate world. Antagonisms are developed between the inmate world and the guards, and also between the total institution and the outside world. For the inmate, one of the most important processes, described with great feeling by Goffman, is the process of mortification. Previous roles are eliminated, obedience tests are forced upon the inmate, and a will-breaking contest takes place. One not only dares not speak back but also dares not defend a sense of pride even with facial expressions or gestures; prisoners must be abject, total slaves, or face further punishment. They must be dispossessed of any property that sets them off from others or gives them special personality or dignity. They must be stripped of any personal characteristics of appearance; they must be personally disfigured through inmate clothing and haircut, and this very disfigurement marks them for inmate status and makes them subject to disciplinary methods. No face-saving is possible to help them retain a sense of self; no privacy is possible, either in one's letters to the outside world, one's body, one's idiosyncrasies, one's natural functions, or one's sex nature. If prisoners submit to the system for enough years, they become institutionalized types who can no longer stand life on the outside.

Within the inmate world a privilege system develops, but there are no rights.

[34]Erving Goffman, "On the Characteristics of Total Institutions: The Inmate World," in Donald R. Cressey (ed.), *The Prison*, Holt, Rinehart and Winston, Inc., New York, 1961, pp. 15–45.

What effect does the "steel-
bound coffin of a cell" have on
the prison inmate?

Privileges can be obtained only in terms of the rules of the system. Such simple
matters as how prisoners want their coffee, when they can talk, when they can take
a moment's rest, whether they can smoke a cigarette or a cigar—all the little details
that seem a part of a person's vital self become special privileges to be won in the
inmate system. Even the privilege of "release-binge fantasy," of talking to someone about what one will do on the outside, is a revokable privilege. Punishment by
a silent system or by solitary confinement is always possible.

There is also the problem of learning the informal rules within the inmate system,
of knowing who can be trusted and who is a stoolie. There are various possible
adaptations to the situation, mentioned by Goffman, sometimes that of withdrawing or being uncooperative and intransigent. Sometimes "colonization" takes
place—the acquiring of what privileges and amenities are possible within the
system and forgetting the outside world. This is the type of adjustment made by a
prisoner who after many years "finds a home" and usually returns to prison,
almost willingly, soon after release. One might adopt a "conversion" attitude,
taking on the ways of the guards, identifying with authority. Most frequently,
though, the idea is to "play it cool," meeting all the rules well enough and relating
to one's fellow inmates well enough to speed the process of getting out physi-

cally undamaged, for the prisoner is in danger from fellow inmates as well as from
the authorities.

The case of the conscientious objectors   Of all groups of prisoners, one would expect that the Vietnam draft resisters of the war period would be the least likely to take on prisonized traits of the type described by Goffman. A study of 545 men sentenced for violations of the Selective Service Act indicates that they did not change their minds about the Vietnam war, but their personalities were strongly affected by the experience of imprisonment. One change was that they learned to hate, and another was that they learned a prisoner's indifference to suffering. According to the reporter Robert Rawitch,

> The prison code, which dictates that each man "does his own time and does not see anything that happens around him," is strictly adhered to by most resisters, regardless of their earlier moral convictions.
>
> An inmate told of seeing a man lying on the floor with blood streaming from his head and another man running away. He just walked on as though he had not seen a thing.[35]

The transformation that takes place in the personality of the prisoners apparently has its equivalent effect on the guards. Dr. Zimbardo conducted an experiment at Stanford University in which he hired a number of young college men to simulate the roles of prisoner and guard in a block of cells he had equipped on the university campus. The game was played so realistically that it was terminated after a little over a week because Zimbardo could not stand the brutalizing effect it was having upon the guards.[36]

Sex and the prison   Not only does prison deprive inmates of freedom, the ability to make decisions, a feeling of purpose in life, and most of what makes human existence tolerable, but it deprives them of any normal outlet for their sexual nature. In earlier times entire families were sometimes kept in English gaols or workhouses (the distinction was not too great), and, bad as the system was, it allowed for a degree of normality. Many Mexican jails allow wives to visit for periods other than short, observed daylight hours. Mexico's jails are generally dreaded like the plague, and yet La Mesa Prison in Tijuana is an interesting experimental institution making a certain amount of family life possible and also encouraging gainful employment.[37] In Sweden, where the average prison sentence is for only five months and the repeater rate is only 15 percent, inmates are allowed regular furloughs for visiting their families. North Carolina has recently started experiments with such a system, and so have several California prisons.[38] In the majority of state and federal penitentiaries, however, normal relations are impossible.

For years there has been an awareness of homosexuality in prisons, but it was

---

[35]Robert Rawitch, "Resisters: Problems in Prison," *Los Angeles Times*, August 16, 1970, sec. G., pp. 1 and 2. Copyright, 1970, *Los Angeles Times*. Quoted by permission.
[36]Philip G. Zimbardo, "Pathology of Imprisonment," *Society*, vol. 9, pp. 4–8, April 1972.
[37]Charles Hillinger, "Tijuana Prison: There's No Place Like It," *Los Angeles Times*, December 27, 1970, part I, pp. 1, 24.
[38]*Time, op. cit.*, pp. 53–54.

little talked about. Hayner and Ash stated the matter rather delicately years ago: "Love your fellow man gets a new definition in the prisoner community . . . for perversions are regarded as inevitable."[39] Hayner and Ash give the impression that homosexual relationships within the prison are a matter of mutual consent. Such was not the case in the Philadelphia prison system, according to a thorough investigation by the Philadelphia District Attorney's office and the police department, completed in September 1968.[40] The report is a horror story in which the young man new to the prison system is the victim of gang rapes and of severe beatings if he resists. Sometimes his complaints are ignored by guards, who wish not to be bothered or have such contempt for prisoners as not to care. Sometimes those who complain are placed in solitary "for their own protection," until they finally realize that the only way out is a homosexual relationship with a hardened criminal. The cases of homosexual assault are by no means unusual. The District Attorney's office estimated that 2,000 such cases occurred during the twenty-six months of the study.

The problem of public awareness   There are several reasons why reports of homosexual attacks and other types of irregularities within prisons are seldom published. For one thing, people are little interested in prisoners who are "only getting what they deserve." Another problem is that credibility is low and reports are often not believed until such an official investigation as that of the Philadelphia system is conducted. It was surprising in the late summer of 1970 to read newspaper accounts of a group of judges visiting a prison in Nevada—in fact, spending a night there. They were shocked at the conditions. What could easily be more shocking to the public was the implication that a group of men who had spent their lives sentencing suspects apparently had little knowledge of what the typical prison is like.

In recent years there has been one note of encouragement. There are more protests than ever before about the condition of America's prisons, and several states are working in the direction of reform. It is to be hoped that the protests will not die. In 1917, John Lafflin, a British subject imprisoned for his pacifist activities, wrote his protest of the "burial alive" that has been so typical of prisons:

Mourn not the dead that in the cool earth lie—
Dust unto dust—
The calm, sweet earth that mothers all who die
As all men must;

Mourn not your captive comrades who must dwell—
too strong to strive—
Each in his steel-bound coffin of a cell,
Buried alive;

But rather mourn the apathetic throng—
The cowed and the meek—
Who see the world's great anguish and its wrong
And dare not speak.

[39]Norman S. Hayner and Ellis Ash, "The Prisoner Community as a Social Group," *American Sociological Review*, vol. 4, pp. 362–369, June 1939.
[40]Alan J. Davis, "Sexual Assaults in the Philadelphia Prison System and Sheriff's Vans," *Transaction*, vol. 6, pp. 8–16, December 1968.

Obviously, some serious rethinking about our system of justice is needed. Such thinking might start with Shakespeare's observation

That in the course of justice, none of us
Should see salvation

In Piliavin's study, the police officers who were concerned with saving the delinquents they perceived as essentially worthwhile were acting in the interests of mercy. An evenhanded justice would not have permitted such leniency. The difficulty is, though, that for the officers the quality of mercy extended only to certain types of people. This, we noted in the previous chapter, is also true of certain categories of lawbreakers. Those in the white-collar category are more apt to know the blessings of mercy than those in the Uniform Crime Reports. Since mercy is a concept more common to religion and poetry than to jurisprudence, it can only be approximated in the great legal systems of the gigantic society, but it is approached. In some of the best systems of juvenile courts the interest of the young offender is primary, rather than the interest of retributory justice. In police work, much of the same quality has been present at times in the history of American cities.

In the old days of Tammany Hall, in spite of the notorious corruption of the organization, little acts of kindness were extended by the ward boss and the police. The police were part of the neighborhood, knew the people, and related to them. If we could have similar types of community relations without having the graft of the old-time political machine, there would be considerable restoration of respect for the law.

Community and police   Arthur Waskow[41] suggests that there are three possible ways of improving community relations with the police and preventing frequent charges of police harassment. The first approach would be to restructure metropolitan police forces into neighborhood police forces, with local elections of commissioners. The second possibility would be to create countervailing power by organizations able to hear grievances and to protest injustices. Actually, some minority-group organizations are approximating this solution at present. The third possibility is implied fairly well within the second: break down the barriers that separate the police from the citizens to avoid the social isolation of the police. For several years the thinking about police forces has been of a development of greater professionalization, the creation of elite forces with more sophisticated knowledge of all the detection devices of today. Certainly such knowledge is needed, but perhaps it belongs only to special units of the police forces. Otherwise the separation of citizen and police is intensified.

In spite of the need for local control and local involvement with the police, at the time of the Presidential commission's report on law enforcement, only about 10 percent of the cities had participating citizens' groups. Where they have been instituted they have been helpful in closing the gap that has increasingly isolated the police from the communities they serve.

The other major recommendation of nearly every commission that has investigat-

[41]Arthur Waskow, "Community Control of the Police," *Transaction*, vol. 7, pp. 4–7, December 1969.

**Police and the sense
of community.**

ed ghetto problems is to encourage a larger participation of nonwhites on police forces. Sometimes the very antagonism of the ghetto toward the police makes it difficult to recruit many black police officers, but there are cities where the policy is succeeding.

Improving the court system   As noted, there are inevitable incongruities between efficiency and justice. A police system completely unrestrained by any of the niceties of constitutional rights could be much more efficient than at present, but at a cost a democracy could not afford to pay. What is true of the police system is equally true of the courts. Burger notes that criminal cases now take twice as long to prosecute as they did ten years ago, and part of the reason is our commitment to "values higher than pure efficiency." There are other areas, however, in which Burger sees possibilities for improving the pace of justice. He strongly believes that long periods of delay and uncertainty do much to keep the crime rate high, and that some administrative details of the court could be rendered more efficient so that the process of justice could be speeded. Several suggestions by Burger are:

Increase the number of courts, and also establish a judiciary council that would advise Congress of the probable impact of new legislation upon the court system.

Create more administrative efficiency within the courts. The Institute for Court Management, opened in Aspen, Colorado, is viewed by Burger as the most encouraging recent development.

Set up administrative rather than court handling of several minor categories of crime, including vagrancy, drunkenness, and prostitution, as well as traffic violations.

Strive for a great reduction in our adversary system of justice. American court trials are prolonged partly because of our desire for courtroom showmanship of conflicting attorneys playing before a jury, a system that has sometimes been called "trial by combat."[42]

Burger elaborates on the final point because at first glance it might seem to run counter to constitutional guarantees. His contention is that many countries of Western Europe are able to dispense justice in a manner every bit as sure as ours and much more swiftly, without being abusive to people's rights. The swift handling of justice, however, is followed by careful and humane treatment of the offender, with a far better record of rehabilitation than we have.

Burger sees little possibility of a reduction in plea bargaining; he considers such procedures indispensable. On this point the President's Commission on Law Enforcement is much more critical, noting cases of "excessive leniency for habitual criminals who generally have expert legal advice and are best able to take full advantage of the bargaining opportunity."[43] Both Burger and the Commission agree that some uniformity of standards in plea bargaining is needed.

There are, unfortunately, certain barriers in the way of court reform. One problem is that the public is not particularly interested, not knowing the danger of the fire until burned. Another problem is that many lawyers have a vested interest in the present system. The following set of statistics illustrates their vested interest: the Department of Transportation estimated that in accident suits settled in 1968, victims collected a total of $700 million and lawyers collected $600 million. The California State Legislature in 1971 and again in 1974 defeated a bill for no-fault insurance. To no one's surprise, much of the opposition came from lawyers.

Yet another problem in the way of judicial reform is that of correlation between police work, court systems, and systems for dealing with those convicted. Clark,[44] among others, makes suggestions for a system in which detection, conviction, and disposition of cases are correlated. Too often the right hand doesn't know what the left hand is doing.

The treatment of offenders Certainly there is need for the courts to know more about the disposition of cases, and there is need for the public to know more about this as well. The Scandinavian countries can show their prisons with pride; we can show most of ours only with profound embarrassment. To quote Burger again:

[42]The Views of the Chief Justice," *Life*, vol. 69, p. 26, August 7, 1970. Also, Justice Burger in *Los Angeles Times, op. cit.*
[43]Winslow, *op. cit.*, p. 295.
[44]Ramsay Clark, "Criminal Justice in Times of Turbulence," *Saturday Review*, vol. 53, pp. 21–24, 51, September 19, 1970.

In part the terrible price we pay in crime is because we tend, once the drama of the trial is over, to regard all criminals as human rubbish. It would make more sense, from a coldly logical viewpoint, to put all this "rubbish" into a vast incinerator instead of storing it in warehouses for a time only to have most of the subjects come out of prison and return to their old ways.[45]

Actually, many of our juvenile courts try to treat the offender rather than merely punish him. The juvenile court system is subject to criticism, however, because since it attempts to deal with the individual case rather than with general legalistic principles, it is only as good as the authorities handling the case. A majority of juveniles in custody are being held for offenses that would not be crimes if committed by adults—running away, having premarital sex, drinking alcohol, or getting "out of control." Many are placed in juvenile halls because they have been abandoned by their parents and have nowhere else to go. Often juvenile homes are poorly run, receiving little tax support and thus unable to pay for an adequate staff. There is, consequently, a need for a great improvement in the personnel placed in charge of offenders, whether juvenile or adult.

The adult treatment, in spite of all that has been written about rehabilitation, still tends to be only custodial care. And it should be noted that correctional facilities are so crowded that by no means are all minors sent to special institutions. More than 100,000 minors are now housed in our state prisons, learning the attitudes and the techniques of the world of crime. Obviously, a first step toward reform would be to spend a little more money to create the needed facilities for separating minors from adults.

New directions in rehabilitation   There are some observable areas of progress in the American prison systems. California has at least tried new techniques, although they are not always successful. The California prisons are considered the nation's best and are oriented toward a philosophy of correction. The courts give indeterminate sentences, with the understanding that the offender can remain imprisoned or not, depending on his own behavior. Very recently, a policy of allowing overnight visits for wives has been instituted in some California prisons. Two-thirds of convicted offenders are given probation, and a small number work in forestry crews under minimum security. Only 13.5 percent actually go to prison.[46] Nevertheless, the situation is far from satisfactory. The recidivist rate is high, and the much-lauded training program serves only a small percentage of the inmates. Jessica Mitford calls the whole subject of reform of the California prisons a vast hoax.[47] She does not give enough mention to the large numbers of individuals placed on probation, but she does have some disturbing statistics for those actually serving time. Under the California indeterminate sentence system, allegedly merciful, the average first sentence is longer than in any other state in the union. There are the same complaints over filth, overcrowding, bad food, and homosexual problems as elsewhere, but the greatest hatred of the inmate is leveled against the indeterminate sentence. The system gives vast judicial power to prison officials; they can decide whether a sentence of one to fifteen years will actually be one year or the maximum of fifteen. Since Governor Brown took office in 1975, the indeterminate sentence has been used much less than previously.

[45]Burger, in *Life, op. cit.*
[46]*Time, op. cit.*, p. 50.
[47]Jessica Mitford, "Kind and Usual Punishment in California," *Atlantic*, vol. 227, pp. 45–52, March 1971.

Despite an emphasis in recent decades on prisons as rehabilitation centers, they seldom serve such a purpose. Robert Martinson[48] speaks of rehabilitation as a dangerous myth. It is a dangerous myth partly because it leads the public to assume that new methods are maximizing public protection while minimizing the harm done to people by the prisonization process. The myth is dangerous, too, because it seems to absolve the public from tackling the problems of social causes of crime. Martinson admits that prisons cannot yet be entirely avoided, but he feels that a number of methods could be used to reduce the harm they do. To a degree, some of the methods are already being used.

Kansas, following the advice of Menninger, has set up a diagnostic clinic similar to those found in Swedish prisons. The result has been probation for far more offenders than in the past and a reduction in the percentage of individuals who break probation. North Carolina has pioneered a work-release program that allows prisoners on good behavior to go to regular jobs during the day or to take courses in school. Senator Mansfield has introduced a bill to try to handle cases of criminal negligence by providing for working off debts to the victims or their families rather than spending idle years in prison.

Probation is a reform measure that is being used more and more, and further study is underway to achieve a degree of predictability about who will or will not break the terms of probation. The problems of city jails can be solved partly by releasing more people on their own recognizance, if they are unable to put up bail. Experiments in this direction in Los Angeles indicate that no more people fail to appear for trial if released on their own recognizance than if they have posted bail.[49] Such a system does not discriminate against the poor as a bond system does.

One of the problems that is slowing down progress on rehabilitation is that most prisoners cannot find a place in the outside world once they are released. Employers are oftentimes leery of hiring ex-convicts and state laws place additional barriers in the former convicts' way. New York prohibits an ex-convict from becoming an auctioneer, junk dealer, pharmacist, undertaker, embalmer, or poolroom operator. Kentucky will not allow ex-convicts even the lowly job of cleaning septic tanks. In forty-six states, they are prohibited from becoming barbers. In Texas, a convict who had done an impressive job of education among his fellow convicts was not allowed to teach within the prison after his release because of a law against ex-convicts having any contact with prisoners. Such laws undoubtedly help to account for an approximate 70 percent recidivist rate.[50]

The problems of the prisons continue with only very slow change, if any at all. Although the federal system is run by professionals of good conscience, the Bureau of Prisons nearly always has its budget cut drastically. Consequently, many old prison facilities, built as much as 50, 100, or even 150 years ago, are still in use. The pay scale of prison attendants is generally too low to attract well-trained, capable personnel. The 200,000 convicts in federal prisons are served by a total of about fifty psychiatrists and psychologists, in contrast to Denmark where there is one psychiatrist for every 100 prisoners.[51] The ball and chain, the flogging, and

[48]Robert Martinson, "The Paradox of Prison Reform," a series of four articles in *The New Republic*, April 1, 8, 15, and 29, 1972.
[49]Robert Rawitch, "Jail Releases without Bond," *Los Angeles Times*, January 4, 1971, part I, p. 1.
[50]"The Ex-Con's Unhappy Lot," *Newsweek*, pp. 84–85, February 25, 1974.
[51]Chief Justice Warren E. Burger, "A Typical American Prison," address to the American Bar Foundation, February, 1970, reprinted in Gary E. McCuen (ed.), *America's Prisons*, Greenhaven Press, Anokar, Minn., 1971.

bread-and-water diet are almost things of the past, but other types of reform move very slowly for a system that the public likes to think about as little as possible.

SUGGESTED READINGS

Cressey, Donald R. (ed.): *Crime and Criminal Justice*, Quadrangle Books, Inc., Chicago, 1971. In his introductory essay Cressey points out that the enforcement of law and administration of justice are more complex than merely following rules. Discretion must be used to maintain the consent of the governed. Particularly authoritative in the field of organized crime.

Finn, James (ed.): *Conscience and Command: Justice and Discipline in the Military*, Vintage Books, Random House, Inc., New York, 1971. The essays in this book deal with the differences between civilian rights and military justice and also with the dangers of a blind following of orders. Contains essays by experts and testimony by military men.

Menninger, Karl: *The Crime of Punishment*, The Viking Press, Inc., New York, 1969. Although Menninger gives credit to men of goodwill who have worked hard to improve the treatment of offenders, he sees most of our penitentiaries as pestholes, lagging far behind our knowledge of reform possibilities. He is strongly condemnatory in his attitude toward the concept of revenge, which he contends still permeates the prison system.

Sellin, Thorsten (ed.): *Capital Punishment*, Harper & Row, Publishers, Incorporated, New York, 1967. A well-structured book of readings on one of the punishment problems constantly debated in American society. Especially good on the question of deterrence, with several articles written by Sellin himself.

Shecter, Leonard, and William Phillips: *On the Pad*, G. P. Putnam's Sons, New York, 1973. "On the pad" means being under protection from arrest for a fee. As the title suggests, the subject is mainly a narration of corruption within the police force, based partly on the Knapp Commission of New York, appointed by former Mayor Lindsay to investigate police corruption in New York City. The authors also have ideas for remedies of corruption.

Silver, Isador (ed.): *The Crime Control Establishment*, Spectrum Books, Prentice-Hall, Inc., Englewood Cliffs, N.J., 1973. A collection of articles having to do with the FBI, the Justice Department, and agencies that make the decisions about how anticrime funds will be allocated, what types of crimes will be pursued most vigorously, and how to legitimize the agencies' authority by "manipulating public fears."

QUESTIONS

1 Why is the role of police officer difficult and subject to conflicting demands?

2 What types of people are often treated with undue severity by the police?

3 Give some examples of and explanations for the long delays in the justice system.

4 How does military justice—in spite of recent reforms—still fall short of constitutional guarantees for the person accused of a crime?

5 What are some of the abuses found in the worst of our jails and prisons? What problems remain even in the best of our prisons?

6 What attempted reforms and further suggestions are being made for improving police forces, courts, and the prison system?

EPILOGUE: CONTEM- PLATING A FUTURE WORLD

In troubled times particularly, we seem to stand on the edge of tomorrow, trying to divine the future, sometimes with hope, sometimes with fear, but never with certainty. In earlier times our ancestors consulted the oracle or the haruspex to find meanings in mysterious sounds and signs. We now consult economists and sociologists to extrapolate from the trends they find, but always with the same unease about the fallibility of prediction. In the old days we would have explained the uncertainties by saying "Man proposes; God disposes." Now, in our scientific age, we speak instead of the many variables we cannot manipulate or, in some cases, even discern.

We can only speculate about the problems presented in the previous chapters, realizing that possibilities range all the way from triumph to disaster. Earlier America was usually radiantly optimistic. The experience of two world wars, of Korea and Vietnam, of sadistic acts by so-called civilized people, of depressions, and of food and energy shortages have dulled the luster of that optimism. We have grown too sophisticated to believe some kind of millenium will come and that the City of God will descend upon us. Nevertheless, the pessimism of our age may prove premature. We cannot continue the world's present rate of population growth and its ruthless exploitation of resources, but there is no reason why a controlled world population cannot live a life more satisfying to the majority of people than we have known in the past. Cities need not be ugly and decayed. The air need not fill our nostrils with a chemical stench, nor need the land be eroded and poisoned. Prices can be honest and products dependable. Workers can be guaranteed much greater safety and security in their work, and no social class or minority need be underpaid, exploited, or scorned. Schooling can become a happier and more rewarding experience. Although we cannot continue to increase our abundance of cars, campers, motorcycles, and other fuel-hungry equipment, no one need know the pangs of hunger. Crime can be attacked at its sources and justice made more fair and equitable. All these things can be done, and the nightmare of the all-seeing state can be avoided too. But most of these desired changes can come about only if peace is prevalent throughout the world and if the nations cooperate in trade, finance, and resource conservation.

Since progress against poverty and ill health depend upon a prosperous economy, progress is linked to the outside world. Air and water pollution are also world problems, as is the ever-increasing population of the earth. Since world trade, population, the environment, resources, and food supply depend upon the maintenance of peaceful cooperation, we must ask what the prospects for such cooperation are. What are the possibilities for maintaining peace or, at least, for avoiding another major war? What are the possibilities for a growing amount of economic and social cooperation in the world?

IS PEACE POSSIBLE?

The historical period of human history has been so bloody that it is easy to come to the conclusion that warfare is simply written into human nature. But in view of the fact that many nations have not gone to war for generations, such a conclusion would be overly simplistic. There is, however, a widely accepted theory that comes fairly close to the assertion that we fight because *Homo sapiens* was born to fight—a theory that equates human nature very closely with our subhuman ancestors and is sometimes referred to as the "killer-ape theory."

The theory of the killer ape   Raymond Dart was the first scientist to take a strong interest in an apelike skull found in one of the mines of South Africa in the 1920s.[1] It was many years before more specimens were unearthed, but eventually they appeared in abundance. Dart had been correct in recognizing the first skull as something advanced beyond that of any living ape and in analyzing it as of a species that bridged the gap between ape and human. Dart is universally praised for his early discernment of the importance of the skull, but he has roused a controversy over interpretation. In his opinion, the South African beings (*Australopithecus africanus*) were the direct ancestors of modern human beings and unlike most apes were primarily hunting, meat-eating animals. Since they were rather small, Dart reasoned that the Australopithecines could have lived only by inventiveness, using stone and bone weapons; and only the strong and aggressive could have survived. Therefore, the argument goes, aggression and ferocity were components of the human species from the beginning, helping to account for our wars and our generally bloody history.
   One popularizer of Dart's idea about human aggressiveness is Robert Ardrey, whose book *The Territorial Imperative*[2] contends that we hold, along with many other species, a type of instinct to defend territory. Threats to one's territory rouse a fighting response that accounts for the defensive side of the human-being's fighting behavior. The much more authoritative animal ethologist Konrad Lorenz holds much the same view. "In every individual," he says, "the readiness to fight is greatest in the most familiar place, that is, in the middle of the territory."[3] Such a trait would predispose us to fight in self-defense, but Lorenz thinks there is an instinctive basis for fighting in other cases as well. In most mammalian species, the males fight occasionally when competing for territory or food supply or when cornered; but most of their fighting is done in competition for mates, the consequence of which is elimination of the weaker males from the breeding pool and in turn the strengthening of the species. Part of the competition for females is also a competition for prestige and dominance. The ambition to reach for positions of prestige has been helpful to a degree in organizing and controlling animal groups, but it may have been carried too far in a species that can devise deadly weapons. Aggression can thus be turned from the primary biological purpose of strengthening the species to that of destroying the species. It

[1]Raymond A. Dart, *Adventures with the Missing Link*, Harper & Row, Publishers, Incorporated, New York, 1959.
[2]Atheneum Publishers, New York, 1966.
[3]Konrad Lorenz, *On Aggression*, Bantam Books, Inc., New York, 1967, p. 32.

It is true that people sometimes resemble the killer ape of which Dart speaks, but is such savagery really a matter of instinct?

might be objected that people have enough mental capacity to save themselves from such a tendency, since they are governed so much by reason. But all the inconsistencies between our reasoning capacity and propensity to act irrationally in groups, says Lorenz, begin to make sense when it is realized that man is still "subject to all the laws prevailing in all phylogenetically adapted instinctive behavior."[4] Lorenz even goes on to say that the social organization of humans is similar to that of rats, who are generally peaceful within their clans, "but are veritable devils toward all members of their species not belonging to their own community."[5]

A refutation Lorenz does not quite go so far as to say that war is inevitable because of the aggressive nature we have derived from our prehuman ancestors, but he accepts our genetic history as an adequate explanation for the wars we fight. According to his view, aggression might be channeled into less harmful competitive sports, but it must always be reckoned with. Since he sees aggressive nature as instinctive, no type of socialization process can weed it out.

A strong criticism of the Lorenz point of view is that it assumes that no major change has come about in human nature, regardless of childhood conditioning, society, or period of time. He reminds us of lines from Omar Khayyam:

Of earth's first clay they did the last man kneed
And there of earth's last harvest sowed the seed.

The Lorenz philosophy would even go further and say "Of earth's first ape they did the last man kneed." The point is that tremendous gulfs of time and evolutionary change separate the modern human being from his remote Australopithecine ancestors. True, people often show terrible ferocity, but the ferocious nature must be

[4]*Ibid.*, p. 229.
[5]*Ibid.*, p. 230.

triggered by something other than instinct, since it is far from uniform among people.

Prominent among the opponents of Konrad Lorenz is Ashley Montagu, an anthropologist with a background in biology and medicine. Primate instinctive drives have been suppressed, he says, and replaced by the much more adaptive mechanism of human intelligence. "If there are any residues of instincts, they amount only to such insignificant matters as a natural fear reaction to loud noises or to falling. For the rest, man has no instincts."[6]

As Montagu sees aggression, it must be accounted for in other ways. Fighting can, of course, be an intelligent force of adjustment for driving away potential foes. It is also possible that aggression is instilled in people by particular socialization patterns and values of the cultures in which they live. Geoffrey Gorer,[7] an anthropologist with views similar to those of Montagu, feels that the idea of basic human aggression is refuted by the presence of a few tribes of people who display no aggression whatsoever. (The Arapesh of New Guinea, the Lychas of the Himalayas, and the Pygmies of the Ituri Forest are the people he names.) Gorer concludes that all the pacifist tribes have one trait in common: a cultural pattern that lacks any cult of manhood based on fighting and dominance. In all the tribes he mentions, boys and girls grow up with similar character-trait expectations.

Before very much anthropological knowledge had developed, it was a common belief that tribes of people who were most primitive in their means of hunting, housing, and toolmaking would also be the most brutal. Anthropological studies have shown almost the opposite to be the case, with a handful of hunting-gathering bands being about the only peoples who never fight wars. In some cases there are violent quarrels, but no organized warfare or even sporadic raids. The discovery of the Tasaday people of the Philippines seemed almost enough to win the argument for those that maintain that human nature, when uncorrupted by civilizations, is peaceful. The Tasaday, a small band of people living in isolation in the forests of Mindanao and not discovered by the outside world until 1969, are kind, considerate people, full of love for one another, without jealousies or rivalries, and completely without violence.

Robert K. Dentan[8] describes a similarly peaceful people, the Semai of the bamboo jungles of Malaya. They are a small tribe, but much more numerous than the Tasaday. They rear their children in a pattern of total nonaggression, teaching that anger will result in a kind of evil spiritual pollution. They frequently ask themselves, "What would you do if you hit a child and he died?" Although quarrels occur, they are quarrels of words not of physical violence. Yet, surprisingly, when the Semai were drafted by the British to fight against Malayan communists, they fought with an almost berserk fury when they saw some of their own people being killed.

It seems logical to conclude, then, that all people will fight under some circumstances but not others, and that they can be reared in socialization patterns that will prevent them from physical violence except when they are severely threatened. Response to threat can certainly be interpreted more simply as a natural consequence of human intelligence than as an irresistible instinct. No attempt is being made to contend that human nature is always mild and kindly or to deny that sadistic cruelties occur. The important conclusion is simply that explanations other than instinct can be found to account for human behavior. Wars in which violence is done on each side and many people are killed help to rouse emotions to a dangerous height. Socialization patterns that extol violence, war, and vigilantism undoubtedly help produce violence-prone individuals. Conversely, mild rearing methods and

[6]Ashley Montagu, *Culture and the Evolution of Man*, Oxford University Press, New York, 1962, Introduction.

[7]Geoffrey Gorer, "Man Has No Killer Instinct," in Herman M. Bleibtreu and James F. Downs (eds.), *Human Variation*, Glencoe Press, The Macmillan Company, New York, 1971, pp. 119–126.

[8]Robert Dentan, *The Semai: A Non-Violent People of Malaya*, Holt, Rinehart and Winston, Inc., New York, 1962, pp. 55–64.

prolonged absence of war have the reverse effect of "making mild a savage race." Think of the contrast between the modern Scandinavians and their Viking ancestors.

One explanation of human violence is that children are generally reared in patterns of violence. Does this apply to our society? (Discuss movies, TV, traditional and modern children's stories, military toys, etc.)

It would be possible to make a case for the killer-ape theory of humanity based on the Vietnam war. Villages were bombed, women and children were killed by both sides, and prisoners were tortured. Some men were brutalized by the war; rumors of mass slayings were widespread and were definitely established in trials resulting from the atrocities at My Lai. This certainly proves that many men can behave in a killer-ape manner; but does it prove that their behavior is instinctive, unavoidable, and rooted in our ape-like ancestry? One reply is that most apes are not nearly that vicious. An even more important observation is that the United States had an extremely difficult task recruiting an army to fight in the war. Such reluctance to go to war does not fit well with a theory of aggressive instincts.

The roots of war   If people do not fight wars because of aggressive instincts, then why do they fight? Economic motives of nations are very important, including the desire for land and resources. Religions and ideologies have also played an important role. Occasionally wars have started between two peoples and have continued as actions of vengeful reciprocity—the type of behavior observed in family feuds, or in feuds between primitive tribes. Once tensions are created, fear can lead to war, with one side convinced it must strike before the enemy strikes first. The background of World War I was characterized by mounting fear on the part of two opposed alliances, each not daring to wait until the other became stronger. Many wars have started partly by blunder; some have been planned.

Another explanation for wars is what modern social critics have called the military-industrial complex, a situation in which industrial and military leaders gain such a vested interest in heavy military spending that they become blinded to any possibilities for peace. John Kenneth Galbraith[9] stops short of calling the military-industrial complex a conspiracy to gain funds for the military service. He labels it rather a case of "group-think" that includes the entire military bureaucracy. Part of the thinking that supports staggering military spending is that (1) we can trust the Russians only if an agreement could be made with airtight guarantees, (2) there is no way of making airtight guarantees, so (3) we must continue the arms race forever. There are undoubtedly members of the Russian military-industrial complex who look upon us in exactly the same way. Occasionally, though, there are thaws in the relations between the two countries and leaders of both sides can see great advantages in slowing down the arms race.

By using neither the military-industrial complex nor any other theory as an explanation of war, however, can we prove that wars start solely from an unreasoned urge for whole nations of people to fight. Usually the recruitment of armies has been accomplished only with a large amount of propaganda, deception, and coercion.

Conduct an opinion survey regarding willingness to fight. Suggested question: "Under what circumstances should a person be willing to fight?" Multiple choices: (*a*) In any war for his country, right or wrong; (*b*) if drafted, accept service with no attempts at evasion; (*c*) only in a thoroughly justified war; (*d*) only if the country is invaded; (*e*) never under any circumstances.

[9]John Kenneth Galbraith, *How To Control the Military*, New American Library, Inc., New York, 1969, pp. 20–21.

An attempt has been made so far to prove that there is nothing in human nature that makes wars inevitable. It is much more difficult, though, to say just how human intelligence is to be applied to prevent further major wars. Many attempts have been made in the past to ensure peace in the world. Some have worked quite well for a long period of time, but the majority have eventually failed. A glance at history will show some of the reasons for past failures that can be a partial guide to future efforts.

APPROACHES TO PEACE

Wars launched by such marauding adventurers as the Mongol Hordes under Genghis Khan no doubt paid dividends in loot and plunder. Some of the minor skirmishes of the colonial powers in the conquest of empires paid dividends in the short run, but most wars of history have been devastating to both sides, even in the time before such ultimate weapons as nuclear missiles. Consequently, many attempts have been made to bring about world peace, or at least peace in the part of the world known at a particular time in history.

The Pax Romana approach   Historically, periods of peace have sometimes been maintained by the triumph of one empire over a large section of the world, as in the days of the Roman Empire in the period known as Pax Romana, or the Roman Peace. The Chinese Empire at times in history became strong enough to prevent wars in its part of the world. To a limited degree, the power of Great Britain in the nineteenth century seemed sufficient to prevent major world wars, although fights over the expansion of colonial empires continued. It was believed for a time after World War II that there would be a long-lasting Pax Americana. Because of the American monopoly on atomic weapons and the great financial power and prestige of the United States, no major conflict contrary to her interests was deemed possible. As in the case of all other seeming triumphs of one nation, however, the dominant position faded. Nuclear power is now held by many hands, and the United States, along with the rest of the world, faces military counterthreat. No country can reign supreme indefinitely, either militarily or economically.

From balance of power to balance of terror   If there is no Pax Americana to assure us of freedom from mass slaughter, then the next approach is that of more traditional diplomacy. Throughout the nineteenth century, Great Britain depended not only on a navy but also on a diplomacy called "balance of power." Balance-of-power tactics consist of keeping each of two or more opposing nations or alliances equally strong. The weakness of either side might tempt the other to aggression. Conversely, if the power of one side appears to be growing too rapidly, the other side might strike while there is yet time.

The post World War II period assumed a balance-of-power situation for years, with the United States and its allies on one side and Russia and the other Communist states on the opposite side. But with both sides equipped with nuclear bombs, the phrase of Sir Winston Churchill—"a balance of terror"—described the world situation perfectly and grimly. The new balance was not perceived in terms of a juggling of existing systems of alliance but rather of simple addition and subtraction. Each side could count steel production, nuclear weapons, and allies. There were many uncommitted countries in the world that were the remaining stakes to be gambled for. The United States felt hurt that the Republic of India decided to walk a neutral course and remain unaligned. Some elements in America tended to regard all neutrals as secret supporters of the U.S.S.R.

In the counting of bombs, steel, and allies, the United States came in far ahead of Russia for a number of years, and it seemed the terror balance was strongly on

The possible outcome of the balance of terror is reflected in the staring eyes of a manikin used in a bomb test.

our side. Yet there was always fear in the balance-of-terror situation, fear that communism could not be contained within its existing territorial limits. The fear became greater when China fell to the Communists, for in those days there was a certainty about the idea of monolithic unity—the idea that all Communist countries would work together in close accord, and all would be directed from the Kremlin. There was even a myth that every untoward event in the world was the consequence of a "Lenin time plan," which had to be blocked at all costs.

A multinational world   A number of world events have dimmed the picture of a two-sided world—the breakup of Communist unity, American disillusionment with such anticommunist wars as those in Korea and Vietnam, the increasing willingness of the Chinese and Russian leaders to negotiate, and the increasing impact of the Third World. The Third World can be defined roughly as the developing countries that remain unaligned with either Russia or the United States and are committed to their own interests as opposed to those of the major industrial powers. The result of fewer firm alignments is a more complex, multinational world that cannot be dealt with in any simple balance-of-terror situation. At worst, the multinational world could lead to larger numbers of local tensions and threats of localized wars. At best, multinationalism could prevent localized conflicts from breaking into major wars, since the partisans to local quarrels would not be backed by one or the other of the major power blocs.

   In the present world situation it cannot be denied that the balance of terror continues to a degree, but there are strong indications that both Russia and the

United States are less mutually suspicious than formerly. They may be achieving what Paul Kecskemeti calls a "convergent reorientation"[10]—a new view of the world on the part of both antagonists. In the case of Russia and the United States, the convergent reorientation consists of a change in the previous Communist view that the capitalist world will not long allow Communist regimes to live at peace, and the view of the capitalist world that the Communist powers are determined on a course of world conquest. If this much of a convergent reorientation has taken place, then each country can think of the others as attempting to pursue their national goals in traditional ways, and not as threats to one another's existence. The Third World consists of countries also trying to pursue their own interests, sometimes in contradistinction to those of the major industrial powers. In the present world situation, it is possible that international organization will be a more important approach to world peace than either some kind of modern Pax Romana or a balance of power. Several attempts have been made to build an international organization for the maintenance of peace.

Universal systems A third approach to the problem of maintaining world peace is to set up a large or even universal international system, such as was tried at the Congress of Vienna following the collapse of Napoleon's forces. The alliance formed was a reactionary one, dedicated both to peace and to the preservation of monarchies. Herein lies one of the dilemmas of such international organizations: they may easily be just as dedicated to maintaining the status quo as to preserving peace.

The League of Nations, formed after World War I, was brought about at the insistence of Woodrow Wilson, who was as devoted to democracy and liberalism as to world peace; but unfortunately for his cause, the League was tied in to the Treaty of Versailles. The result was that from the beginning the League was looked upon with disfavor by Germany and the Central Powers as an instrument for maintaining an unfavorable status quo. To Wilson's great disappointment, the United States failed to join. Communist Russia was excluded from the League until it had already become a moribund organization. When Italy, Germany, and Japan took aggressive actions in the 1930s, the League proved incapable of action. However, the idea of such an organization did not die, and after World War II another attempt was made to create an effective international organization.

THE UNITED NATIONS

When the United Nations was formed, great care was taken to learn from history and not duplicate previous mistakes; but historical predicaments are never precisely the same, and what might have worked in the 1920s was only a qualified success in the post World War II period. The great lesson learned was not to exclude the vanquished enemy or other potential antagonists. The defeated powers were all eligible for membership in the United Nations without signing a document admitting their guilt. Russia was included from the first, with the eminently reasonable explanation that it was better to meet a rival across the conference table than across the battlefield.

Do you have a local chapter of the United Nations Associates? If so, attend a meeting and make a study of its work. If not, write to the United Nations for informative pamphlets about its work.

To many knowledgeable diplomats there was never a real expectation that the United Nations would serve the purpose of stopping potential wars between the great

[10]Paul Kecskemeti, "Political Rationality in Ending War," *Annals of the American Academy of Political and Social Science*, vol. 392, pp. 105–115, November 1970.

powers;[11] but to many idealists and to many common people this was the expectation. The UN has been a success or a failure depending on what one expects of such an organization. Like the League of Nations before it, the UN has provided a forum for discussion and has promoted many helpful international projects: aid of refugees, prevention of famine, improvement of world agriculture and health, care of war orphans, and cooperation in air-sea rescue. It should not be forgotten, either, that the UN has helped settle disputes between minor powers, such as Greece and Turkey and, at times, India and Pakistan. International forces under the United Nations have been called upon repeatedly to maintain cease-fire lines between Israelis and Arabs. For the first time, the Soviet Union contributed funds for the UN forces patrolling the Golan Heights and Sinai in 1974–1975. A similar UN force patrolled Cyprus during the last battle between Greek and Turkish Cypriots, undoubtedly preventing much bloodshed. In 1974 the United Nations started performing what may become an even more significant role: calling international conferences on modern world problems. The first world conference on population was held in Bucharest, the first food conference was held in Rome, and the first conference on the law of the seas was held in Caracas. Such conferences are, of course, mere forums for discussion, not legislative bodies; but they point to a growing world interest in some of the major problems with which we must cope if the world as we know it is to survive.

One or two weaknesses of the United Nations are matters of structure and organization. Like the League before it, the UN has given priority to certain "great powers," making them permanent members of the Security Council. By a fluke of history, China was overthrown by the Communists soon after being accepted into the Big Five, but the new regime was not recognized for over twenty years. The result was that for many years, the official government of China was actually the government of the tiny island of Taiwan, ruled over by the aged General Chiang Kai-shek. Insufficient allowance is made for the fact that the great powers of one period of history may not be the great powers of another period. The China issue was debated for almost twenty-five years before Red China received official recognition and was accepted into the United Nations.

Although there is gross inequality in the Security Council, there is a strange type of democracy in the General Assembly. Each nation has one vote, whether that one vote represents the estimated 800 million people of China or the 125,000 people of the Maldive Islands. More important, the General Assembly vote has little weight, since no nation can be compelled to comply with decisions of the United Nations. It is the general reasoning behind the creation of an international organization without teeth that is the crux of the problem. Neither the United States nor Russia wanted to join an international organization that could actually have the authority to tell national governments what to do. Consequently, both countries, along with the other permanent members of the Security Council, were given the veto power. Russia has used the veto power on many occasions, and the other countries only rarely; but the important point is that none of the major powers is willing to surrender any important measure of national sovereignty. In fact, among conservative elements in the United States, there has been vehement opposition to the United Nations mainly for fear that it might someday acquire a measure of decision-making power superior to that of the nation. The doctrine of total national sovereignty is incompatible with a strong, effective international organization. The only world union that could ensure world peace would be one with the power and the means to make and enforce decisions. At present the great powers of the world are not willing to take a step toward that degree of internationalism.

The closest approach to decision enforcement on the part of the United Nations

[11]Eugene Rostow, *Law, Power, and the Pursuit of Peace*, University of Nebraska Press, Lincoln, 1965, p. 4.

came about when the Russian delegate walked out of the Security Council during the period of the Korean war. Russia's absence gave the United States the opportunity to refer the Korean war to the General Assembly, where a resolution was passed calling on members to unite (the Uniting for Peace Resolution) in opposition to the invasion of South Korea by North Korea. Only a few countries complied but enough to give United Nations sanction to the Korean war. Since then, no country has walked out on the Security Council.

The General Assembly and the Third World   In the General Assembly, the many developing nations that are allied with neither Russia nor the United States have very great influence. For years they have used the Assembly as a forum for protesting racism and colonialism in the world. One of the countries to come under fire constantly has been South Africa because of its apartheid (official racial segregation policies). In 1974 the General Assembly voted to expel South Africa from United Nations membership, but the matter had to be referred to the Security Council, where it was vetoed by the United States, France, and Britain. Nevertheless, the Assembly succeeded in denying the South African delegate an Assembly seat on procedural grounds.

The same year, the Assembly broke precedent by recognizing Yasir Arafat, leader of the Palestine Liberation Organization: it allowed him to speak and gave him all the prerogatives of a member, even though he represents no recognized government. In a similar vein, the majority membership of UNESCO, supposedly a nonpolitical organization, refused to allow Israel to participate on grounds that Israel was making too many changes in Jerusalem, that is, was altering its cultural character. In keeping with American policy, John Scali, our delegate to the General Assembly, denounced the decision. Public opinion in the United States was becoming less favorable to the United Nations than in the past, and there were even murmurs about abandoning it.

Use a United Nations General Assembly procedure in class in which each member acts as a delegate from a different nation, presenting that nation's opinion on an important current issue.

The disappointment of the United States with some of the General Assembly decisions is mitigated by the fact that the decisions do not have the force of law. The major impact of such decisions is a blow to our prestige and the unhappy realization that the majority of the member nations do not agree with our point of view. We must realize, of course, that no one country can be on the winning side on all decisions. Unreasonable though the pro-Palestine actions may seem to us, it is worth our while to be aware of the thinking of the rest of the world. Adlai Stevenson once expressed this attitude by saying that what the United States needs most is a hearing aid.[12]

The decision of the Third World in regard to South Africa is actually fairly close to previous United States positions. We have voted in favor of resolutions calling for South Africa to abandon its segregationist policies; we differ from the Assembly majority only in not going so far as to call for South Africa's expulsion. The vote in favor of the Palestine Liberation Organization was obviously unfavorable to Israel, but it might also be interpreted partly as a reaction of the Third World against the major powers over other issues not directly concerned with the PLO. Charles Yost[13] reminds us that for years the Third World has been passing resolutions calling on the richer nations to assist in their development. They have also called for better trade terms and for international supervision of multinational corporations, which they charge

---

[12]Charles W. Yost, "Whose United Nations," *New Republic*, vol. 171, p. 18, December 28, 1974.
[13]*Ibid.*, pp. 19–20.

The United Nations, whatever its weaknesses, represents another attempt to substitute the conference table for the battleground.

have exploited the underdeveloped nations. Little reply has been given to such requests. A course of action in which one side votes against the interests of the other partly out of spite is obviously not a good solution to international problems. It should be realized, however, that means must be found to prevent the division of the world into rich and poor nations, with the gulf between the two ever widening.

A forum for conflicting views   This brief comment on the disputes within the United Nations during a recent eventful year gives some idea of the problems as well as possibilities facing such an organization. Because of conflicting ideas and interests in the world, the General Assembly will inevitably be a place of heated dispute. It is important, though, in that it gives each part of the world an idea of how problems look from another viewpoint. To the industrialized nations, the developing countries seem to be impossible to satisfy and unreasonable in their demands. To the hungrier parts of the world, the wealthy, industrialized nations appear blind and heartless, as well as wasteful of the goods so much of the world so desperately needs. Perhaps for this reason, the grasping nature of the petroleum-rich regimes of the Near East is overlooked, because they remain part of the underindustrialized world despite their sudden wealth.

If they do nothing else, the debates in the General Assembly prove to us how deeply interdependent the world has become and how the interrelationships between major segments of the world are being seen more and more as moral issues, not merely as political and economic issues. For this reason, many of the smaller and less industrialized countries have always taken a greater interest in the United Nations than have the major Western powers.

Particularly for the industrialized world, there are other means to international cooperation besides the United Nations. International conferences were held long before either the UN or the League of Nations was formed. Regional trade blocs, the major example of which is the European Common Market, promote international agreements and cooperation. Multinational corporations, although matters of grave concern because of their economic and political power, can in some cases promote international cooperation. All kinds of approaches are useful, although each has its drawbacks. Regional organizations have the drawback of promoting one part of the world at the possible expense of the rest. Special international conferences usually involve only the major powers; in the nineteenth century they were usually called for the purpose of dividing the colonial world among the European powers. Multinational corporations (with the very notable exception of the Organization of Petroleum Exporting Countries) have their power bases in the major industrialized nations. The United Nations has very great difficulty in reaching decisions and has the serious organizational weaknesses already cited. Nevertheless, it has the dual advantage of being nearly all-inclusive as an international forum and of being well established.

THE INTERNATIONAL ENTERPRISE

Much more important than the organizational means by which new policies are made is the shape of the policies themselves. There can be no certainty that the world has a future unless there is a great international enterprise aimed at solving its most pressing problems—war, environmental decline, depletion and monopolization of raw materials, starvation, and overpopulation.

World peace   It is impossible to predict peace for the future. Local war clouds gather in the Near East and elsewhere. The major grounds for hope are that the Communist forces, which the United States fear so greatly, are split among themselves; and that the major Communist powers appear much more anxious to develop internally than to export revolution. Meantime, the United States has found its policies of intervention in distant wars on the Asian continent to be militarily futile and politically disasterous. Without changing attitudes, the UN machinery for the settlement of disputes may yet be used as it was intended.

The world environment   The second chapter of this book contained a long description of environmental pollution and its causes. The facts presented were quite discouraging, but at the same time it was noted that environmental improvement is well within the realm of scientific possibility. All that can be added at this point is that an awareness of environmental problems has spread to all industrial states. International conferences on the environment have been held and the problems have been widely discussed among the experts. In other countries as well as our own, though, there are temptations to ignore the environment in favor of profits or short-term gains. The result could be increased burning of coal with high sulfur content, rapid offshore drilling and more oil spills, and even careless use of atomic reactors. Possibly the first international conventions on the environment will take the form of regulations regarding the safety of atomic reactors, the means of cleaning up coal-burning furnaces, and the drilling and transport of oil.

Raw materials   For many years the world had seen progress in the direction of open trade so that raw materials were available to all nations. In 1973 a shocking reversal of the free flow of goods came about when the Organization of Petroleum Exporting Countries (OPEC) nations quadrupled the price of oil and demonstrated their ability to cut off the oil supply to countries too sympathetic to Israel. The situation has concentrated the attention of the world on resources in a way that might eventually bring beneficial results. We have long needed to take stock of available resources, with the aim of conserving, of finding new sources, or of finding alternatives. A new problem regarding resources now faces the world: the problem of making sure they are available, and at a price that will not prove ruinous. If oil can be used as a political weapon, will the same problem occur with other resources? The high price of oil is actually even more ruinous to many underdeveloped countries than to some of the industrialized nations. Perhaps their economic distress will eventually cause them to make common cause with the Western powers on the oil issue and to add to the pressure being placed on the OPEC. The cartel may eventually be broken by internal rivalries or diplomatic maneuvering, but there is no chance that oil will ever return to the prices of earlier years. The petroleum crisis points out the need for some means of regulating multinational corporations—one of the demands the Third World has been making for many years. Unless some means can be found to prevent the monopolization of vital resources, we may witness the "wars of redistribution" or "preemptive seizures" of which Robert Heilbroner warns in *An Inquiry into the Human Prospect*.[14]

Feeding a hungry world   Very closely linked to the energy crisis is the food crisis. As was noted in Chapter 10, the green revolution, consisting of new high-yield crops for the underdeveloped world, has proved disappointing. The high price of nitrogen fertilizers, derived from petroleum, has prevented the expected expansion of agriculture. The consequence is that dependence on the United States, Canada, and Australia is increasing rather than diminishing. Although crop yields are higher in the United States than anywhere else, no other country is as dependent on petroleum products for agriculture. The amount of energy required for running tractors in the United States is as great as the amount of energy contained in all the food produced. If all energy costs are added, including the fossil fuels used for making fertilizer, each calorie of food is produced at a cost of 10 to 20 calories of fossil energy.[15]

Not only do we produce food at a very high energy cost, but we turn much of our grain into feed for cattle, which yield only one-fifth as much food as the amount of grain they consume. When there were vast surpluses of wheat in all our granaries, production of beef was given hardly a second thought. Now our high meat intake can become a subject for resentment from a world that is starving for the grain we feed our cattle. We can hardly be expected to become vegetarians, but our meat consumption could be reduced to a level considered optimum for our health. At present most dietitians think we eat considerably more than is good for us.

Invite a member of the agriculture or biology department to speak on the problems of agricultural improvements in the developing nations.

While the industrialized world overeats and is plagued with the problems of overuse of chemical fertilizers, much of the underdeveloped world desperately needs more food and more fertilizer for growing yet more food. There appear to be only three alternatives to the world food situation: distribute modern agricultural technology to a limited degree; let the food-surplus nations feed the hungry world indefinitely; or accept widespread starvation. Not even the first alternative is a happy one, since it will call for the use of far more nitrogen fertilizers developed from fossil fuels; but the two other alternatives are much worse. As Heilbroner states the case, "Paradoxically perhaps, the priorities of the present lie in the temporary encouragement of the very process of industrial advance that is ultimately the mortal enemy."[16] In the

[14]W. W. Norton & Co., Inc., New York, 1974, p. 135.
[15]Wilson Clark, "U.S. Agriculture is Growing Trouble as Well as Crops," *Smithsonian*, pp. 59–64, January 1975.
[16]Heilbroner, *op. cit.*, p. 134.

While affluent countries overeat, much of the under-developed world looks desperately for food and the agricultural technology for producing food.

meantime, says Heilbroner, we will have a short period in which to develop new
sources of energy and new techniques that will prevent the collapse that could come
about if petroleum resources were completely exhausted. It may be necessary in time
for some kind of allocation system to be developed on a world scale, so that the
poorer countries of the world can have access to the fertilizers and equipment they
need to save themselves from starvation.

Population control   No amount of food, of course, can supply the world if its
population continues to grow. The population-explosion countries, mainly of the
underdeveloped world, must be made to bend every effort toward population control.
The industrialized countries, for their part, must cut drastically their waste of materials
and rapid depletion of resources. World conferences on food, population, pollution,
energy, and raw materials must become frequent and effective.

Tomorrow's world, then, must be one in which resources are treasured. The
compulsion toward growth of cities, automobiles, supersonic aircraft, and more power
machinery to replace labor must all be curtailed. Growth can still continue in areas
that are economical of the use of resources, including better health facilities,
improvements in education, more permanent and better insulated housing, and all the
human-centered improvements discussed in the foregoing chapters.

The quality of life cannot be measured in terms of tons of steel, the level of the
stockmarket, the size of the latest products of engineering, or the military power and
magnificence of nation-states. Again quoting from Robert Heilbroner,

[We can place hope in] our knowledge that some human societies have existed for
millenia, and that others can probably exist for future millenia, in a continuous
rhythm of birth and coming of age and death, without pressing toward those
dangerous ecological limits, or endangering those dangerous ecological tensions,
that threaten present "advanced" societies.

There is no inevitability to the future. The future will call for much greater
concentration on social problems of nation and world than we have ever given before,
but such a concentration of effort is well within the range of human potentialities.
Whatever human nature may be, it contains the potentialities for cooperation,
intelligent concentration of effort, and the ability to foreswear some of the pleasures
of the moment in order to ensure a future.

SUGGESTED READINGS

Annals of the American Academy of Political and Social Science, Vol. 392, November
   1970. The entire issue is devoted to a discussion of conflict resolution—historical,
   experimental, and theoretical.

Douglas, William O.: International Dissent: Six Steps toward World Peace, Vintage
   Books, Random House, Inc., New York, 1971. Justice Douglas worries over our
   attempts to establish a Pax Americana and our frequent support of entrenched
   upper classes in emergent nations. Then he turns to his six steps toward world
   peace. Controversial and thought-provoking.

Deutsch, Karl W., and Stanley Hoffman, (eds.): The Relevance of International Law,
   Anchor Books, Doubleday & Company, Inc., Garden City, N.Y., 1971. Contains essays
   by such distinguished international relations experts as Hans J. Morganthau and
   Quincy Wright. Examines the meaning of international law, problems of colonialism
   and of equality among nation-states, and the possible fields for application of law
   among nations.

Heilbroner, Robert L.: An Inquiry into the Human Prospect, W. W. Norton & Co., Inc.,
   New York, 1974. The distinguished economist Heilbroner raises many doubts and

358　　fears about the future world—the problems of food, energy, resources, and environment. He looks especially into the question of how the necessary regulation and planning can come about without authoritarian governments and beehive societes.

Kissinger, Henry A.: *American Foreign Policy: Three Essays*, W. W. Norton & Co., Inc., New York, 1969. Gives a good insight into the thinking of a man who has been so influential in the shaping of American foreign policy. Especially good on the dilemmas of deterrence and the fallacy of strictly bipolar conceptualization of international problems.

Lorenz, Konrad: *On Aggression*, Bantam Books, Inc., New York, 1970. The best-known and most authoritative book presenting human beings as a clearly recognizable part of the animal kingdom with many of the same mechanisms of aggression found in other species.

Munves, James: *A Day in the Life of the UN: The Hundred Faces of Peace*, Washington Square Press, a division of Simon & Schuster, Inc., New York, 1970. A brief glance at the activities of a score of agencies working for international cooperation: Food and Agriculture Organization, International Labor Organization, UNESCO, International Bank for Reconstruction and Development, United Postal Union, and World Health Organization, among others. Also describes the work of the Security Council and General Assembly.

QUESTIONS

1 What is the evidence pro and con for looking upon the human species as instinctively aggressive?

2 What is meant by Pax Romana? What similar attempts at world order have been attempted?

3 What historical lessons were learned from the Congress of Vienna and the League of Nations that the United Nations tried to take into consideration?

4 What are the fallacies in thinking of the world in purely bipolar terms, i.e., as though its only major division is between Communist and noncommunist forces?

5 What does the Third World expect of the major industrial powers?

6 What are the major areas in which there must be greater international cooperation in the future if the world is to avoid a serious breakdown in the quality of human life?

DATE DUE